Cisco Secure Internet Security Solutions

Andrew G. Mason, CCIE #7144
Mark J. Newcomb

Cisco Press

Cisco Press
201 W 103rd Street
Indianapolis, IN 46290 USA

Cisco Secure Internet Security Solutions

Andrew G. Mason
Mark J. Newcomb

Copyright© 2001 Cisco Press

Cisco Press logo is a trademark of Cisco Systems, Inc.

Published by:
Cisco Press
201 West 103rd Street
Indianapolis, IN 46290 USA

Printed in the United States of America 1 2 3 4 5 6 7 8 9 0

Library of Congress Cataloging-in-Publication Number: 00-105222

ISBN: 1-58705-016-1

Warning and Disclaimer

This book is designed to provide information about Cisco Secure. Every effort has been made to make this book as complete and as accurate as possible, but no warranty or fitness is implied.

The information is provided on an "as is" basis. The authors, Cisco Press, and Cisco Systems, Inc. shall have neither liability nor responsibility to any person or entity with respect to any loss or damages arising from the information contained in this book or from the use of the discs or programs that may accompany it.

The opinions expressed in this book belong to the authors and are not necessarily those of Cisco Systems, Inc.

Trademark Acknowledgments

All terms mentioned in this book that are known to be trademarks or service marks have been appropriately capitalized. Cisco Press or Cisco Systems, Inc. cannot attest to the accuracy of this information. Use of a term in this book should not be regarded as affecting the validity of any trademark or service mark.

Feedback Information

At Cisco Press, our goal is to create in-depth technical books of the highest quality and value. Each book is crafted with care and precision, undergoing rigorous development that involves the unique expertise of members from the professional technical community.

Readers' feedback is a natural continuation of this process. If you have any comments regarding how we could improve the quality of this book, or otherwise alter it to better suit your needs, you can contact us through e-mail at feedback@ciscopress.com. Please make sure to include the book title and ISBN in your message.

We greatly appreciate your assistance.

Publisher	John Wait	
Editor-in-Chief	John Kane	
Cisco Systems Program Manager	Bob Anstey	
Managing Editor	Patrick Kanouse	
Development Editor	Andrew Cupp	
Project Editor	Marc Fowler	
Copy Editor	Ginny Kaczmarek	
Technical Editors	Sean Convery	Masamichi Kaneko
	Duane Dicapite	Joel McFarland
	Steve Gifkins	Brian Melzer
	Per Hagen	Ruben Rios
	Jeff Hillendahl	Joe Sirrianni
	Tom Hua	John Tiso
Team Coordinator	Tammi Ross	
Book Designer	Gina Rexrode	
Cover Designer	Louisa Klucznik	
Production Team	Argosy	
Indexer	Larry D. Sweazy	

CISCO SYSTEMS

Corporate Headquarters
Cisco Systems, Inc.
170 West Tasman Drive
San Jose, CA 95134-1706
USA
http://www.cisco.com
Tel: 408 526-4000
     800 553-NETS (6387)
Fax: 408 526-4100

European Headquarters
Cisco Systems Europe
11 Rue Camille Desmoulins
92782 Issy-les-Moulineaux
Cedex 9
France
http://www-europe.cisco.com
Tel: 33 1 58 04 60 00
Fax: 33 1 58 04 61 00

Americas Headquarters
Cisco Systems, Inc.
170 West Tasman Drive
San Jose, CA 95134-1706
USA
http://www.cisco.com
Tel: 408 526-7660
Fax: 408 527-0883

Asia Pacific Headquarters
Cisco Systems Australia,
Pty., Ltd
Level 17, 99 Walker Street
North Sydney
NSW 2059 Australia
http://www.cisco.com
Tel: +61 2 8448 7100
Fax: +61 2 9957 4350

Cisco Systems has more than 200 offices in the following countries. Addresses, phone numbers, and fax numbers are listed on the Cisco Web site at www.cisco.com/go/offices

Argentina • Australia • Austria • Belgium • Brazil • Bulgaria • Canada • Chile • China • Colombia • Costa Rica • Croatia • Czech Republic • Denmark • Dubai, UAE • Finland • France • Germany • Greece • Hong Kong • Hungary • India • Indonesia • Ireland • Israel • Italy • Japan • Korea • Luxembourg • Malaysia • Mexico • The Netherlands • New Zealand • Norway • Peru • Philippines Poland • Portugal • Puerto Rico • Romania • Russia • Saudi Arabia • Scotland • Singapore • Slovakia • Slovenia • South Africa • Spain • Sweden • Switzerland • Taiwan • Thailand • Turkey • Ukraine • United Kingdom • United States • Venezuela • Vietnam • Zimbabwe

About the Authors

Andrew G. Mason, CCIE #7144, CCNP Security, and CCDP, is the CEO of CCStudy.com Limited (www.ccstudy.com), a United Kingdom-based Cisco Premier Partner specializing in Cisco consulting for numerous United Kingdom-based companies. The CCStudy.com web site is a fast-growing online Cisco community for all of the Cisco Career Certifications.

Andrew has 10 years of experience in the network industry and currently is consulting for Energis-Squared, the largest ISP in the United Kingdom. He is involved daily in the design and implementation of complex secure hosted solutions, using products from the Cisco Secure product range.

Mark J. Newcomb, CCNP Security and CCDP, is a senior consulting network engineer for Aurora Consulting Group (www.auroracg.com), a Cisco Premier Partner located in Spokane, Washington, USA. Mark provides network design, security, and implementation services for clients throughout the Pacific Northwest.

Mark has more than 20 years of experience in the microcomputer industry. His current projects include designing secure communication systems for wireless devices and providing comprehensive security services to the banking industry.

About the Technical Reviewers

Sean Convery is a network architect in Cisco's VPN and Security business unit. He has been at Cisco for three years. Prior to that he held positions in both IT and security consulting during his six years in the network security industry.

Steve Gifkins is a CCIE and CCSI of four and five years, respectively. He is based in the United Kingdom, where he runs his own independent Cisco-only consulting and training business. He is married with no children, and his hobbies include anything to do with outdoor life. Having retired with a knee injury from playing active sports such as squash, rugby, and soccer, he has taken up new hobbies in horse eventing and show jumping. In addition, he enjoys skiing and hill scrambling.

Brian Melzer, CCIE #3981, is an Internetwork Solutions Engineer for ThruPoint, Inc., out of their Raleigh, North Carolina, USA office. He has worked as a consultant for ThruPoint since September of 2000. ThruPoint is a global networking services firm and one of the few companies selected as a Cisco Systems Strategic Partner. Before working for ThruPoint, he spent five years working for AT&T Solutions on design and management of outsourcing deals involving Fortune 500 clients. As a member of the Wolfpack, Brian received his undergraduate degree in electrical engineering and his master's degree in management at North Carolina State University.

John Tiso, CCIE #5162, is one of the chief technologists of NIS, a Cisco Systems Silver Partner. He has a bachelor's degree from Adelphi University, Garden City, New York. John also holds the CCDP certification, the Cisco Security specialization, the Cisco Voice Access specialization, and Sun Microsystems, Microsoft, and Novell certifications. John can be reached by e-mail at johnt@jtiso.com.

Dedications

I would like to dedicate this book to my beautiful wife, Helen. Once again she had to put up with me coming home from work during the summer months and disappearing straight into my study to research and write this book. I thank her for being so patient and understanding, and giving me the space to write this book. I would also like to thank my wonderful daughter, Rosie, as she keeps me smiling throughout the day.

—Andrew Mason

This work is dedicated to my lovely wife, Jacqueline, without whose help I could never have accomplished as much as I have.

—Mark Newcomb

Acknowledgments

I would like to thank Mark Newcomb for working on this book with me. We live at different ends of the world and have only met once, but still have built a long-lasting friendship. My thanks also go out to John Kane, Andrew Cupp, and the rest of the Cisco Press team for pulling all of this together and providing an editorial service that is second to none. The technical reviewers, John Tiso, Brian Melzer, and Steve Gifkins, helped us both a lot with the technical direction of the text, thanks to you all. I would like to thank Sean Convery and Bernie Trudel for allowing us to include their excellent white paper as an invaluable reference in this book.

Finally, I would like to thank Sean Convery, Duane Dicapite, Per Hagen, Jeff Hillendahl, Tom Hua, Masamichi Kaneko, Joel McFarland, Ruben Rios, and Joe Sirrianni. This group of Cisco employees provided helpful feedback that immensely improved the quality of this book.

—Andrew Mason

As with all works of any consequence, this book was not simply the work of two authors. There were a great number of individuals behind the scenes that made this work a reality. I would like to list a few.

I want to acknowledge the technical reviewers, Steve Gifkins, Brian Melzer, and John Tiso, all superior engineers. These three individuals showed us where we did not cover enough material, showed us where we were unclear, and provided a large number of suggestions that added to the quality of this work. Their efforts are truly appreciated.

I thank Andrew Cupp and John Kane at Cisco Press for their ceaseless pursuit of the best possible work. They, along with many others at Cisco Press, have provided us with everything necessary to successfully complete this book.

I would also like to express my gratitude to Sean Convery and Bernie Trudel for letting us use their Cisco SAFE white paper as a reference in this book.

I want to thank Sean Convery, Duane Dicapite, Per Hagen, Jeff Hillendahl, Tom Hua, Masamichi Kaneko, Joel McFarland, Ruben Rios, and Joe Sirrianni, all from Cisco, for their time and very helpful suggestions.

Finally, I want to thank Andrew Mason for all of his work on this book. Even though we live on opposite sides of the world, I consider him one of my best friends.

—Mark Newcomb

Contents at a Glance

Contents

Introduction

The Internet is a core business driver for many large corporations. Along with the expanded business, however, come security issues. Recent news headlines often feature articles about large e-commerce sites getting hacked, with potentially disastrous results.

Cisco Systems strives to help customers build secure internetworks through network design that features its Cisco Secure product family. At present, no available publication deals with Internet security from a Cisco perspective, using the Cisco Secure product family. This book covers the basics of Internet security and then concentrates on each member of the Cisco Secure product family, providing a rich explanation with examples of the preferred configurations required for securing Internet connections.

The book starts by explaining the threats posed by the Internet and progresses to a complete working explanation of the Cisco Secure product family. The individual components of the Cisco Secure product family are discussed in detail, with advice given about how to configure each individual component to meet the requirements of the situation. The Cisco Secure PIX Firewall is covered in-depth, from presenting an architectural point of view to providing a reference of the common PIX commands and their use in the real world. Although the book is concerned with Internet security, it is also viable for use in general network security scenarios.

Audience

Cisco Secure Internet Security Solutions is for network engineers and network designers. The primary audience is network engineers and network designers responsible for the corporate Internet connection or the installation of Cisco Secure products. The secondary audience is other networking staff members that have an interest in security or Cisco Secure products in relation to their specific corporate environment.

Also, CCIE and CCDP/CCNP candidates will take interest in the title to improve their Internet security skills.

The book should be read and used by an intermediate to advanced reader. Because of the unique content, industry experts could reference this book.

Audience Prerequisites

The content in this book assumes that the reader is familiar with general networking concepts and terminology. This includes a thorough understanding of the network protocol TCP/IP, and a familiarity of the topics covered in the Cisco Press books *Internetworking Technologies Handbook* and *IP Routing Fundamentals*.

What Is Covered

The book is organized into 11 chapters and one appendix:

- **Chapter 1 "Internet Security"**—This chapter provides a historical overview of the Internet and the growing number of risks that are associated with it.

- **Chapter 2 "Basic Cisco Router Security"**—This chapter looks at Cisco routers and the related security threats and vulnerabilities from an Internet point of view. Sample configurations and tips are provided for implementation on your corporate Internet routers.

- **Chapter 3 "Overview of the Cisco Security Solution and the Cisco Secure Product Family"**—This chapter provides an overview of the Cisco Security Solution and the Cisco Secure product range. The following six chapters look at each device in more detail.

- **Chapter 4 "Cisco Secure PIX Firewall"**—This chapter covers the Cisco Secure PIX Firewall. A technical overview of the PIX is provided, along with a configuration guide and sample configurations based against a case study.

- **Chapter 5 "Cisco IOS Firewall"**—This chapter looks at the Cisco IOS Firewall. Sample configurations are provided, and the major technologies are explained.

- **Chapter 6 "Intrusion Detection Systems"**—This chapter looks at one of the latest and most emergent security technologies, intrusion detection. It gives a brief explanation of the various types of intrusion detection systems, and then provides configurations for both a Cisco router and a Cisco Secure PIX Firewall based on perimeter intrusion detection.

- **Chapter 7 "Cisco Secure Scanner"**—This chapter covers the Cisco Secure Scanner. A brief explanation of network scanning and its uses, good and bad, is provided before looking in-depth at the offering from Cisco, the Cisco Secure Scanner.

- **Chapter 8 "Cisco Secure Policy Manager (CSPM)"**—This chapter covers the Cisco Secure Policy Manager. The CSPM provides a centralized management platform for an enterprise network that incorporates Cisco routers running the Cisco IOS Firewall and Cisco Secure PIX Firewalls. This chapter provides a sample installation and configuration of CSPM.

- **Chapter 9 "Cisco Secure Access Control Server (ACS)"**—This chapter looks at the Cisco Secure Access Control Server and its uses within an internetwork. Configuration guidelines are provided for both the network access server (NAS) and the Cisco Secure ACS server component.

- **Chapter 10 "Securing the Corporate Network"**—This chapter looks at a common corporate network and identifies the risks associated with external connections. Numerous tips and configuration solutions are provided to overcome the associated risks.

- **Chapter 11 "Providing Secure Access to Internet Services"**—This chapter focuses on Internet services and the protection that can be offered to them. The chapter is written with servers hosted either at an ISP or on the corporate DMZ in mind. Each Internet service is looked at individually, and potential vulnerabilities and remedies are proposed.

- **Appendix A "Cisco SAFE: A Security Blueprint for Enterprise Networks"**—The principle goal of SAFE, Cisco's secure blueprint for enterprise networks, is to provide best practice information to interested parties on designing and implementing secure networks. SAFE serves as a guide to network designers considering the security requirements of their networks. SAFE takes a defense-in-depth approach to network security design. This type of design focuses on the expected threats and their methods of mitigation, rather than on "put the firewall here, put the intrusion detection system there" instructions. This strategy results in a layered approach to security, where the failure of one security system is not likely to lead to the compromise of network resources. SAFE is based on Cisco products and those of its partners.

Command Syntax Conventions

Command syntax in this book conforms to the following conventions:

- Commands, keywords, and actual values for arguments are **bold.**
- Arguments (which need to be supplied with an actual value) are *italic.*
- Optional keywords or arguments (or a choice of optional keywords or arguments) are in brackets, [ ].
- Choice of mandatory keywords or arguments is in braces, { }.

NOTE   Note that these conventions are for syntax only. Actual configurations and examples do not follow these conventions.

Device Icons Used in the Figures

Figure I-1 contains a key of the most important device icons used in the figures in this book.

Figure I-1 *Device Icon Key*

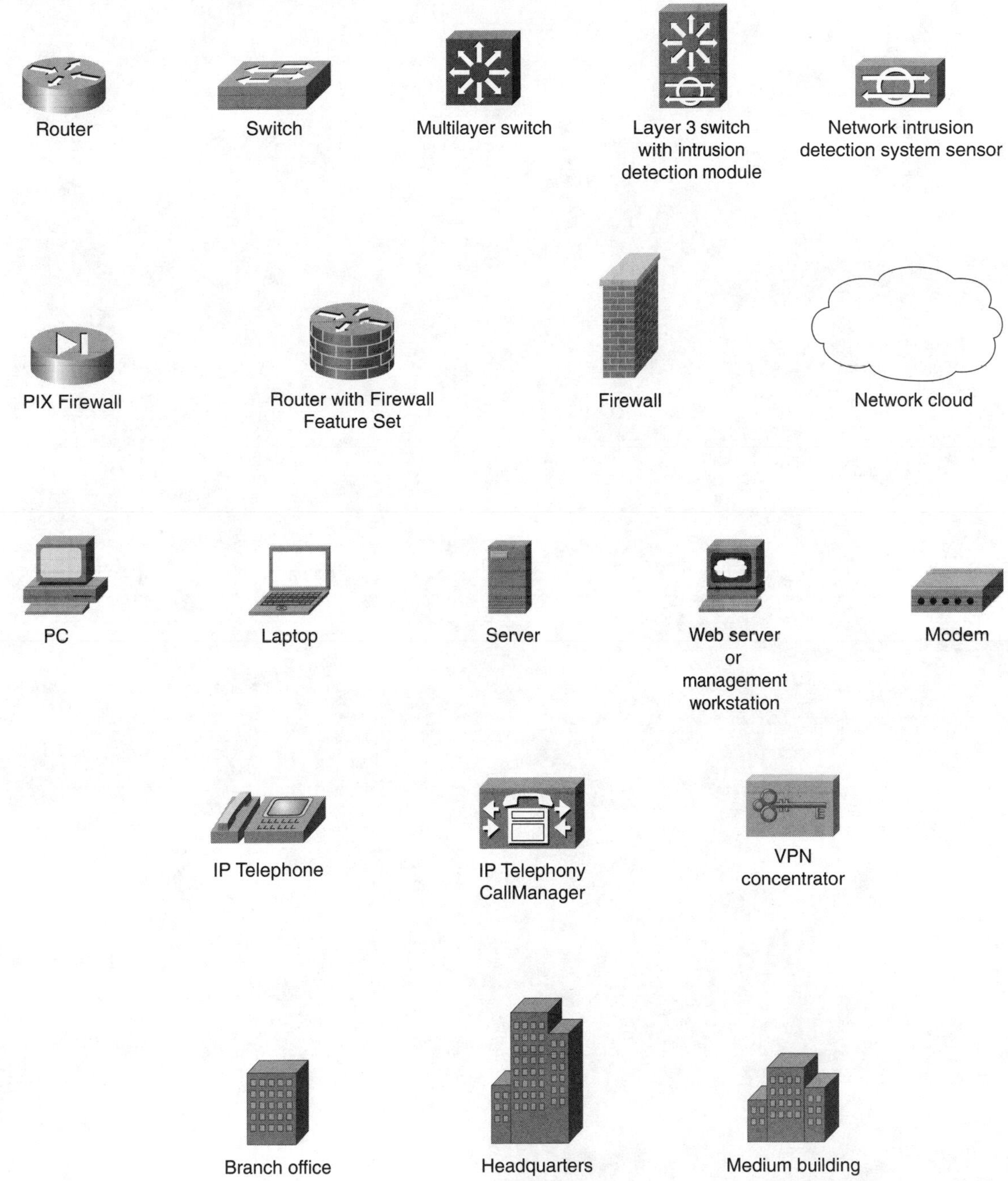

Router

Switch

Multilayer switch

Layer 3 switch
with intrusion
detection module

Network intrusion
detection system sensor

PIX Firewall

Router with Firewall
Feature Set

Firewall

Network cloud

PC

Laptop

Server

Web server
or
management
workstation

Modem

IP Telephone

IP Telephony
CallManager

VPN
concentrator

Branch office

Headquarters

Medium building

PART I

Internet Security Fundamentals

Chapter 1   Internet Security

Chapter 2   Basic Cisco Router Security

This chapter contains the following sections:

- Internet Threats
- Network Services
- Security in the TCP/IP Suite
- Denial of Service (DoS) Attacks
- Creating a Corporate Security Policy
- Summary
- Frequently Asked Questions
- Glossary

Internet Security

This chapter introduces some of the basics of network security. It starts with a brief description of some of the most common forms of attacks. Next, the chapter describes the characteristics of several types of network devices.

The Cisco Secure IOS software is specifically designed to prevent attacks from affecting your network. Cisco Secure provides the highest levels of protection from unauthorized access, denial of service (DoS) attacks, man-in-the-middle attacks, and many other common methods used either to deny service or to obtain unauthorized information. The Cisco Secure IOS relies on a number of configuration techniques, hardware solutions, and technologies, including the Adaptive Security Algorithm (ASA). These provide the best security available to the network administrator today.

As technologies evolve, Cisco continuously refines its hardware and software solutions to remain on the cutting edge of network security. This book explores the methods of protecting the network that are available through use of the Cisco Secure solutions.

To set the foundations necessary for preventing attacks, the first chapter covers the format of several protocols, including Transmission Control Protocol (TCP), Internet Protocol (IP), Address Resolution Protocol (ARP), and User Datagram Protocol (UDP). The more common forms of DoS attacks are then examined. Specific techniques for dealing with DoS attacks are provided in later chapters.

This chapter concludes by examining the need for and use of a corporate security policy.

Internet Threats

The Internet is a collection of privately and publicly owned hosts. Virtually anyone owning a computer is able to get onto the Internet. There are hundreds of thousands of individuals on the Internet at any given time. Although most of these individuals have no ill intentions, there are a number who, for one reason or another, choose to try and penetrate or disrupt services on corporate networks. Sometimes networks are attacked by a technique where an innocent third party is used to launch the attack. For example, an individual whose system has been infected by a worm inadvertently passes along this worm to all known e-mail contacts. This book is designed to show the administrator how to design networks that are resistant to attack.

There are a number of ways that the data on a corporate network can be compromised. Among them are the following:

- **Packet sniffing**—In this method, the attacker uses a packet sniffer to analyze the data for sensitive information traveling between two sites. One example is to use a packet sniffer to discover username and password combinations.

- **IP address spoofing**—In this method, an attacker changes the source IP address of packets to pretend to be a trusted user or trusted computer.

- **Port scans**—This method determines the ports on a network device where a firewall listens. After the attacker discovers the weaknesses, attacks are concentrated on applications that use those ports. Port scans can be launched against firewalls, routers, or individual computers.

- **DoS attack**—The attacker attempts to block valid users from accessing a resource or gateway. This blockage is achieved by sending traffic that causes an exhaustion of resources.

- **Application layer attack**—This method attempts to exploit weaknesses in server software to obtain the permission of the account that runs an application or to limit use of the system through a DoS attack.

- **Trojan horse**—In this method, the user is made to run a malicious piece of software. The Trojan horse attack uses an apparently safe application or data packet to transport destructive data to the recipient. After the destructive data has reached its destination, the program or script launches, causing damage. Trojan horse attacks can exploit technologies such as HTML, Web browser functionality, and the Hypertext Transfer Protocol (HTTP). These attacks include Java applets and ActiveX controls to transport programs across a network or load them on user Web browsers.

Network Services

At this point, it is important for you to understand some security services available on networks. Each of these services is fully discussed later in this book. The following services are discussed within this chapter in a general manner. There is overlap among these services; for example, basic authentication services are included on all Cisco routers. Therefore, this section should be referred to only for general guidelines.

Router Services

Routers have two general ways of providing security services on a network. The first is through routing. If, for example, the administrator does not want any user to be able to send or receive from a given network, the administrator can simply set a static route for that network to go to the *null interface*. The administrator can also set up route mappings to dump certain protocols or individual ports to the null interface or to a nonexistent network.

Although this is a rudimentary way to protect a network, it is still effective in limited circumstances. The problem with relying on this technique is that it does not scale well in large installations; it is static and can be overcome by a persistent attacker. Most network administrators need more granularity in their security settings than simply to allow or disallow traffic to a network.

When more flexibility is needed, administrators rely on the second way that routers can provide security services on a network: access lists. Four main types of access lists are used on Cisco equipment:

- Standard
- Extended
- Reflexive
- Context-based Access Control (CBAC)

Standard access lists allow or deny packets based only on the source address of the packet. Extended access lists are more extensible, allowing filtering based on source or destination address, in addition to protocol, ports used, and whether the connection is already established.

Reflexive access lists dynamically change in response to outgoing requests for data. As a local host establishes a connection by requesting data, the access list attached to the inbound interface changes to allow returning packets through. Once the session is closed, returning packets are again denied access. Context-based Access Control (CBAC) is used with a limited number of programs to allow ports to open and close dynamically based on the needs of that particular application. Figure 1-1 gives an example of basic router services. Each of these types of access lists will be thoroughly explored throughout this book.

Figure 1-1   *Basic Router Services*

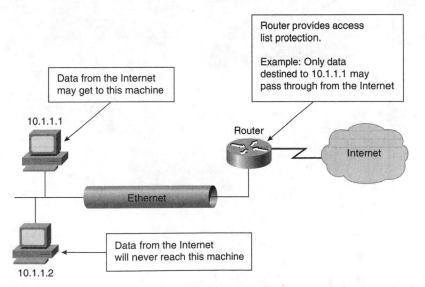
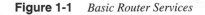

Firewall Services

Firewall services tend to be more sophisticated than routing services. One example of this is the granularity of packet filtering on a firewall compared with a router without the firewall operating system.

On a router, it is not unusual to use the keyword **established** in extended access lists; this keyword is only useful while working with connection-oriented protocols. The keyword **established** does not allow for protocols such as UDP where there is no connection.

Additionally, the keyword **established** merely checks to ensure that the data packet is formatted to look like there has been a connection established. The Cisco Private Internet Exchange (PIX) Firewall, on the other hand, actually checks to make sure that data from a host has gone outbound before allowing data inbound.

The Cisco PIX Firewall that will be discussed in Chapter 4, "Cisco Secure PIX Firewall," filters both connection-oriented and connectionless protocols based on whether a host inside has requested data. This is only one example of many where the granularity of a firewall exceeds that available on a router. Figure 1-2 gives an example of firewall services.

Figure 1-2 *Firewall Services*

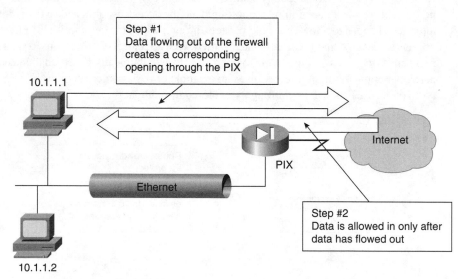

Authentication and Authorization Services

Authentication refers to the process of ensuring that a claimed identity of a device or end user is valid. Authorization refers to the act of allowing or disallowing access to certain areas of the network based on the user, system, or program. Both services can be provided through either a Remote Access Dial-In User Service (RADIUS) or a Terminal Access Controller Access Control System (TACACS) server. Encryption is also available for authentication and can run on a firewall or a router. Figure 1-3 shows an example of authorization services implemented on a network.

Figure 1-3 *Authorization Services*

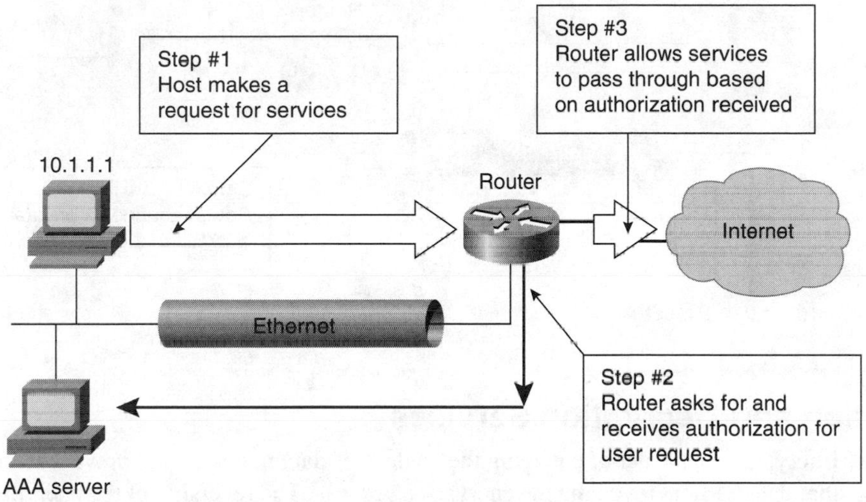

Network Address Translation (NAT) Services

Many corporate networks choose to hide their local-area network addresses from all outside users. Network Address Translation (NAT) changes the local Layer 3 IP network addresses, generally called *private addresses*, to what are generally called *global* or *public addresses*. This translation can occur at a router or on a firewall. There are both security and practical advantages to using NAT. The security advantage is that attacks cannot be made directly to the end device, because the NAT device must translate each packet before forwarding that packet to or from the end device. The practical advantage is that NAT is easily done at both firewalls and routers, allowing the corporation to use a large number of public IP addresses without being forced to purchase more than a handful of private IP addresses. NAT is defined by RFC 1631. Figure 1-4 shows an example of a network employing NAT.

Figure 1-4   *NAT Services*

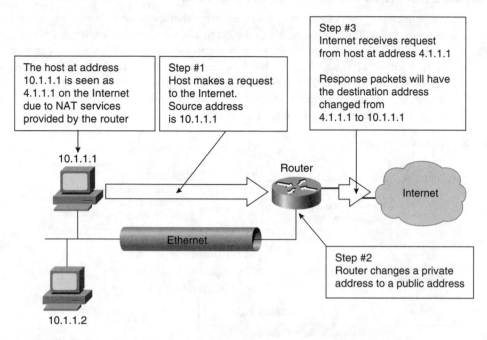

Encryption and Decryption Services

Encryption is the act of changing the content of data in a way that prevents recognition of that data without reversing the encryption process. The reversing of the encryption process is called decryption. Encryption and decryption services can be accomplished on end devices, routers, and firewalls.

A Virtual Private Network (VPN) is created when an encrypted connection is established through a public packet network. A VPN can be established between two hosts at different locations, between two networks of the same company, or between the networks of two different companies. Figure 1-5 shows how encryption services can secure data through the Internet.

Figure 1-5   *Encryption Services*

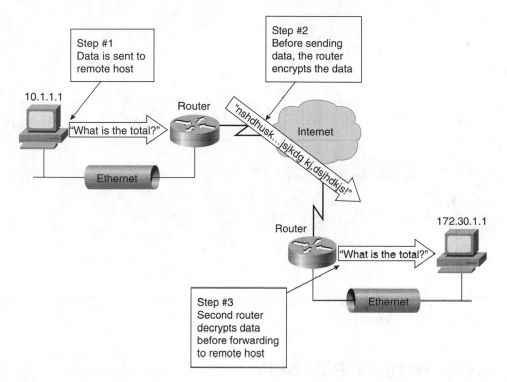

Proxy Services

A *proxy* is an intermediary. In networking, it is a device that sits between a local host and remote hosts. Acting as an intercept device, the proxy server accepts requests from the remote site as if the proxy server were in fact the local host. The proxy then sends its own request to the local host. The local host answers the proxy server, which then responds to the remote site's request. A proxy server isolates the local host from all requests made from remote sites. Unless the remote site is able to bypass the proxy server, the local hosts will never be subject to direct attack. Figure 1-6 shows proxy services in use on a network.

Figure 1-6   *Proxy Services*

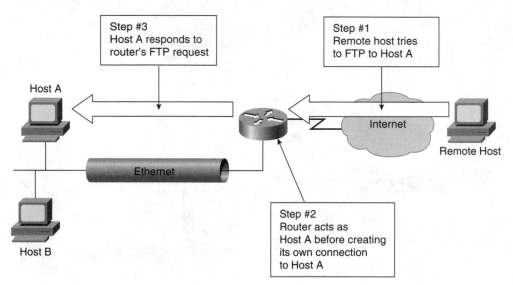

Now that you have looked at some of the basic security services available on networks, you can move on to the next section to see how TCP/IP pertains to security issues.

Security in the TCP/IP Suite

To understand security issues regarding the TCP/IP protocol suite, you first need to understand how TCP/IP works. This section will explore how TCP/IP works before going on to explore how the protocol suite can be used in attacks against a network.

Overview of TCP/IP

TCP/IP was originally developed by the U.S. Defense Advanced Research Projects Agency (DARPA) to interconnect Department of Defense (DoD) computers. The objective of the DARPA project was to build a robust communications protocol able to recover automatically from any node or communications failure. This reliability and recovery from node failure, which was necessitated by the fact that communications needed to be maintained under battlefield conditions, spawned the creation of the Internet.

TCP/IP is the predominant routed protocol suite used within the Internet. Virtually all of the major software and hardware manufacturers offer support for the full TCP/IP protocol suite.

TCP and IP in the Open System Interconnection (OSI) Model

The Open System Interconnection (OSI) model consists of seven layers. Each of these seven layers interacts and communicates with the layers directly above and directly below it.

In contrast, TCP/IP was built around a four-layer model, well before the advent of the OSI reference model. This four-layer model is referred to as the DoD or DARPA model. The functionality of the DoD model can be mapped closely to the functionality of the OSI reference model, as shown in Figure 1-7.

Figure 1-7   *The Seven-Layer OSI Model and the Four-Layer DoD Model*

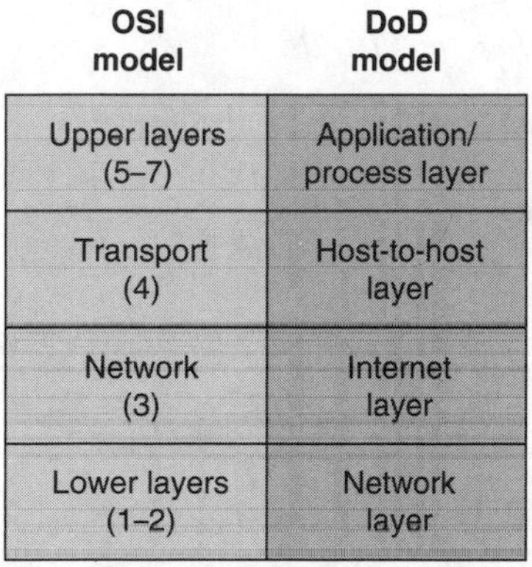

OSI model	DoD model
Upper layers (5–7)	Application/ process layer
Transport (4)	Host-to-host layer
Network (3)	Internet layer
Lower layers (1–2)	Network layer

The following list of the DoD layers further explains their mapping to the OSI model:

- **Application/process layer**—The DoD application/process layer defines the upper layer functionality included within the application, presentation, and session layers of the OSI model. Support is provided for application communications, code formatting, session establishment, and maintenance functions between applications.

- **Host to host layer**—The DoD host-to-host layer maps directly to the transport layer of the OSI model. The transport layer defines connectionless and connection-oriented transport functionality. Host-to-host is the DoD layer where TCP resides. The transport layer is the OSI layer where TCP resides.

- **Internet layer**—The DoD Internet layer maps directly to the network layer of the OSI model. The network layer defines internetworking functionality for routing protocols. This layer is responsible for the routing of packets between hosts and networks. The Internet layer is where IP resides in the DoD model. The network layer is the OSI layer where IP resides.

- **Network layer**—The DoD network interface layer maps to the data link and physical layers of the OSI model. Data link properties, media access methods, and physical connections are defined at this layer. Please note the very different functions of the DoD network layer (listed in this bullet) and the OSI network layer (called the Internet layer in the DoD model).

The authors will refer to the TCP/IP in relation to the OSI model for the remainder of this book because this is the industry standard.

Within the TCP/IP suite, there are several different protocols in addition to IP and TCP. Figure 1-8 shows where each of these protocols sits in relation to the OSI model.

Figure 1-8 *The Seven-Layer OSI Model and TCP/IP*

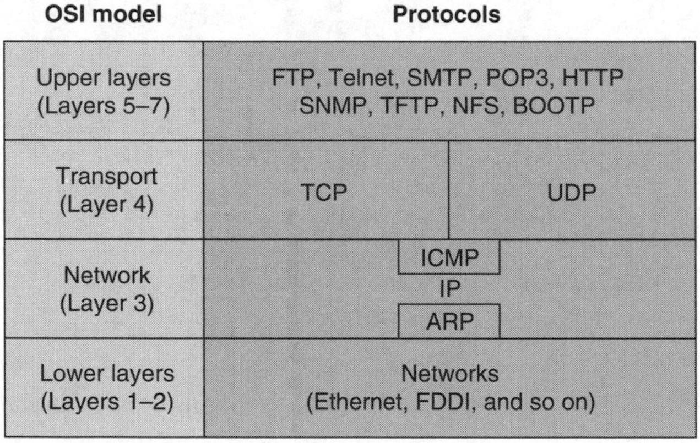

OSI model	Protocols	
Upper layers (Layers 5–7)	FTP, Telnet, SMTP, POP3, HTTP SNMP, TFTP, NFS, BOOTP	
Transport (Layer 4)	TCP	UDP
Network (Layer 3)	ICMP IP ARP	
Lower layers (Layers 1–2)	Networks (Ethernet, FDDI, and so on)	

Internet Protocol (IP)

IP, the network layer datagram service of the TCP/IP suite, is used by all other protocols in the TCP/IP suite except the address resolution protocol (ARP) and the reverse address resolution protocol (RARP) to transfer packets from host to host over an internetwork. This function isn't supported by any other protocols contained within the TCP/IP suite. The other main feature of IP, congestion control, is found on nearly every layer of the OSI model. IP performs basic congestion control that is very primitive in comparison with that offered by the TCP.

Routing is described as the delivery of packets or datagrams from the source node to the destination node across multiple intermediate networks. When hosts reside on the same physical network, they can be delivered using the routing services provided within their own IP modules. When hosts are located on separate connected networks, the delivery is made through routers that connect the networks.

IP is controlled by RFC 791, which defines the set of rules for communicating across the internetwork. Addressing and control information that allows the IP packets to be routed to their intended destination over the internetwork is included.

The two primary rules defined by RFC 791 relate to

- A connectionless, best-effort packet delivery service routing across an internetwork.

- Provisioning for fragmentation and reassembly of packets to support data links with differing maximum transmission unit (MTU) sizes. This is basic congestion control.

IP provides a connectionless, best-effort packet delivery system. From a logical point of view, this service has three characteristics that are important for understanding the behavior of IP routing. These three characteristics are as follows:

- **Connectionless protocol**—IP is classified as a connectionless protocol. Each packet is delivered independently of all other packets. The packets might be sent along different routes and might arrive at their destination out of sequence. No acknowledgements are sent or received to indicate that the IP packets were received by the intended destination.

- **Unreliable delivery**—Because IP is a connectionless protocol, it is also classified as an unreliable protocol. IP cannot guarantee that any packet transmitted will be received by the host intact or in the original sequence in which it was sent. IP has no provision for notification that a packet is dropped en route to the destination.

- **Best-effort delivery**—IP uses its best effort to deliver the packets to their intended destination. IP only discards a packet when it is forced to do so because of hardware issues, such as resource allocation problems, or errors caused at the physical layer. If an error occurs while a packet is being sent, IP attempts to retransmit the packet.

IP packets or datagrams consist of the IP header and the data. The data is received from the upper layer protocols such as TCP or UDP, and encapsulated into the IP packet. The IP header is created by IP and is used by IP on intermediary systems to route the packet to its final destination. The IP header contains information to enable IP to route the packet independent of any other process.

IP Header Datagram Format

Figure 1-9 shows the format of an IP datagram header. The IP datagram header contains a number of items that are interesting to the administrator who is concerned with security issues. Throughout this book, you'll see references to datagrams with various attributes, such as a fragmented IP datagram. This section explains how these packets are formed and the relevance of a field's settings.

Figure 1-9 *IP Header Datagram Format*

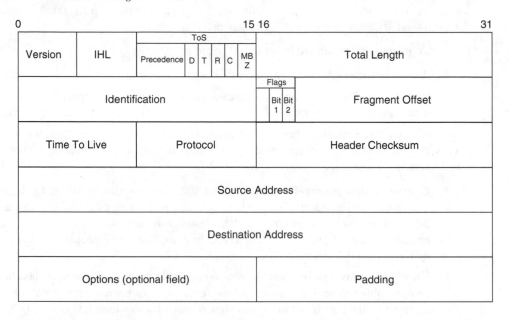

A list of the fields in Figure 1-9 and their functions follows:

- **Version**—The version field is 4 bits and represents the IP version for this packet. Most systems use IP version 4. In the future, most systems will use IP version 6 (IPv6) or IP: The Next Generation (IPng).

- **IP Header Length (IHL)**—The IHL field defines the length of the IP header. The options field that is discussed later in this list is optional and can affect the length of the header. The IHL field occupies 4 bits of the IP header.

- **Type of service (ToS)**—The ToS field occupies 8 bits of the IP header. This field specifies how both hosts and intermediate devices should handle the packet. This field can also be broken down further into subfields. These subfields contain information on precedence, delay, throughput, reliability, cost, and MBz.

- **Total length**—The total length field occupies 16 bits in the IP header. This field contains 16 bits specifying the total length of the IP packet up to 65,535 bytes.

- **Identification**—The identification field occupies 16 bits in the IP header. This field, used in conjunction with the flag and offset fields, is used in the packet fragmentation and reassembly process.

    A packet needs to be *fragmented*, or broken down, when the original packet size is larger than the MTU at the receiving node or any router along the route. IP breaks the original packet into smaller packets that are within the MTU limitations. Each fragmented packet is a true IP packet and contains both an IP header and IP data.

A unique number is entered into the 16-bit identification field. If the packet is fragmented, the original IP header is copied into each of the new fragmented packets. The receiving host uses the identification field when reassembling the packet into its original form.

- **Flags**—The flags field occupies 3 bits of the IP header. Its only purpose is in fragmentation. Each bit is interpreted independently as follows:

  — *Bit 0*—Bit 0 is reserved and not used.

  — *Bit 1*—Bit 1 is the Don't Fragment or DF bit. When this bit is cleared (value of 0), it is an indicator that the packet can be fragmented. When the bit is set (value of 1), it indicates that the packet cannot be fragmented.

  — *Bit 2*—Bit 2 is the More Fragments or MF bit. When this bit is cleared (value of 0), it indicates that this is the last fragment of the packet. When the bit is set (value of 1), it indicates that more fragments are to follow.

- **Fragment offset**—The fragment offset field occupies 13 bits of the IP header. This field identifies the offset of this portion of the original packet before it was fragmented.

- **Time To Live (TTL)**—The TTL field occupies 8 bits of the IP header. This field specifies how long the packet can exist before being dropped or copied to the bit bucket by an intermediate router. When a router receives a packet it decrements the TTL value by 1. If this value is 0, the router discards the packet by copying it to the bit bucket; otherwise it forwards the packet to the next hop router or to the destination network if the destination network is directly connected. This method ensures that an IP packet will eventually be dropped if there is a routing loop somewhere in the network.

- **Protocol**—The protocol field occupies 8 bits of the IP header. This field is used to identify the upper layer protocol that should receive the data contained in the packet. The 8-bit field facilitates 255 different protocols that are represented as numeric values.

Table 1-1 lists the protocol assignments for IP.

Table 1-1 *IP Protocol Numbers*

Value	Keyword	Protocol
0	HOPOPT	Hop-by-hop option (IP version 6)
1	ICMP	Internet Control Message Protocol
2	IGMP	Internet Group Management Protocol
3	GGP	Gateway-to-Gateway Protocol
4	IP	IP in IP Encapsulation
5	ST	Stream
6	TCP	Transmission Control Protocol

Table 1-1   *IP Protocol Numbers (Continued)*

Value	Keyword	Protocol
7	CBT	CBT
8	EGP	Exterior Gateway Protocol
9	IGP	Interior Gateway Protocol
10	BBN-RCC-MON	BBN RCC Monitoring Protocol
11	NVP-II	Network Voice Protocol version II
12	PUP	PUP
13	ARGUS	ARGUS
14	EMCON	EMCON
15	XNET	Cross Net Debugger
16	CHAOS	CHAOS
17	UDP	User Datagram Protocol
18	MUX	Multiplexing
19	DCN-MEAS	DCN Measuring Subsystems Protocol
20	HMP	Host Monitoring Protocol
21	PRM	Packet Radio Measurement
22	XNS-IDP	Xerox NS IDP
23	TRUNK-1	Trunk-1
24	TRUNK-2	Trunk-2
25	LEAF-1	Leaf-1
26	LEAF-2	Leaf-2
27	RDP	Reliable Data Protocol
28	IRTP	Internet Reliable Transaction Protocol
29	ISO-TP4	ISO Transport Protocol (Class 4)
30	NETBLT	Bulk Data Transfer Protocol
31	MFE-NSP	MFE Network Services Protocol
32	MERIT-INP	Merit Inter-Nodal Protocol
33	SEP	Sequential Exchange Protocol
34	3PC	Third Party Connection Protocol
35	IDRP	Inter-Domain Routing Protocol
36	XTP	XTP
37	DDP	Datagram Delivery Protocol

Table 1-1   *IP Protocol Numbers (Continued)*

Value	Keyword	Protocol
38	IDPR-CMTP	Inter-Domain Routing Protocol Control Message Transport Protocol
39	TP++	TP++ Transport Protocol
40	IL	IL Transport Protocol
41	IPv6	Internet Protocol version 6
42	SDRP	Source Demand Routing Protocol
43	IPv6-ROUTE	Routing Header (IP version 6)
44	IPv6-FRAG	Fragment Header (IP version 6)
45	IDRP	Inter-Domain Routing Protocol
46	RSVP	Reservation Protocol
47	GRE	General Routing Encapsulation Protocol
48	MHRP	Mobile Host Routing Protocol
49	BNA	BNA
50	ESP	Encapsulation Security Payload
51	AH	Authentication Header (IP version 6)
52	I-NLSP	Integrated Net Layer Security Protocol
53	SWIPE	Encrypted IP
54	NARP	NBMA Address Resolution Protocol
55	MOBILE	IPO Mobility
56	TLSP	Transport Layer Security Protocol (Kryptonet Key Management)
57	SKIP	Skip
58	IPv6-ICMP	Internet Control Message Protocol (IP version 6)
59	IPv6-NoNxt	No Next Header (IP version 6)
60	IPv6-Opts	Destination Options (IP version 6)
61	HOST	Local Host
62	CFTP	CFTP
63	NETWORK	Local Network
64	SAT-EXPACK	SATNET and Backroom EXPACK
65	KRYPTOLAN	Kryptolan
66	RVD	MIT Remote Virtual Disk Protocol
67	IPPC	Internet Pluribus Packet Core
68	FILE	Distribute File System

Table 1-1 *IP Protocol Numbers (Continued)*

Value	Keyword	Protocol
69	SAT-MON	SATNET Monitoring
70	VISA	VISA
71	IPCU	Internet Packet Core Utility
72	CPNX	Computer Protocol Network Executive
73	CPHB	Computer Protocol Heart-Beat
74	WSN	Wang Span Network
75	PVP	Packet Video Protocol
76	BR-SAT-MON	Backroom SATNET Monitor
77	SUN-ND	SUN-ND Protocol
78	WB-MON	Wideband Monitor
79	WB-EXPAK	Wideband EXPAK
80	ISO-IP	ISO Internet Protocol
81	VMTP	VMTP
82	SECURE-VMTP	Secure VMTP
83	VINES	Banyan Vines
84	TTP	TTP
85	NSFNET-IGP	NSFNET Interior Gateway Protocol
86	DGP	Dissimilar Gateway Protocol
87	TCF	TCF
88	EIGRP	Enhanced Interior Gateway Routing Protocol
89	OSPFIGP	OSPF Interior Gateway Protocol
90	SPRITE-RPC	Sprite Remote Procedure Call
91	LARP	Locus Address Resolution Protocol
92	MTP	Multicast Transport Protocol
93	AX.25	AX.25 Frames
94	IPIP	IP in IP Encapsulation
95	MICP	Mobile Internetworking Control Protocol
96	SCC-SP	Semaphore Communications Security Protocol
97	ETHER-IP	Ethernet in IP Encapsulation
98	ENCAP	Encapsulation Header
99	ENCRYPT	Private Encryption Schemes

Table 1-1 *IP Protocol Numbers (Continued)*

Value	Keyword	Protocol
100	GMTP	GMTP
101	IFMP	Ipsilon Flow Management Protocol
102	PNNI	PNNI over IP
103	PIM	Protocol Independent Multicast
104	ARIS	ARIS
105	SCPS	SCPS
106	QNX	QNX
107	AN	Active Networks
108	IPPCP	IP Payload Compression Protocol
109	SNP	Sitara Network Protocol
110	COMPAQ-PEER	Compaq Peer-to-Peer Protocol
111	IPXIP	IPX in IP Encapsulation
112	VRRP	Virtual Router Redundancy Protocol
113	PGM	PGM Reliable Transport Protocol
114	NOHOP	Zero Hop Protocols
115	L2TP	Layer 2 Transport Protocol
116	DDX	D-II Data Exchange
117–254	UNASSIGNED	Unassigned
255	RESERVED	Reserved

- **Header checksum**—The header checksum field occupies 16 bits of the IP header. This field is calculated as a checksum for the IP header only.

- **Source address**—The source address occupies 32 bits of the IP header. Under normal circumstances, this is the actual 32-bit IP address of the source node.

- **Destination address**—The destination address occupies 32 bits of the IP header. Under normal circumstances, this is the actual 32-bit IP address of the destination node.

- **Options**—The options field is an optional field following the destination address. If present, it contains the security, timestamp, and special routing subfields:
  - *Security*—The security subfield specifies the security level and distribution restrictions.
  - *Timestamps*—The timestamps subfield contains a 32-bit value. This value is normally set to the number of milliseconds since midnight universal time.
  - *Special routing*—The special routing subfield specifies either host-discovered paths or the specific path that the datagram should travel.
- **Padding**—The padding field always contains zeros. This field is used to round the length of the IP header until it contains an exact multiple of 32 bits.

Address Resolution Protocol (ARP)

The Address Resolution Protocol (ARP) is defined by RFC 1122. ARP creates an interface between the data link layer and the network layer of the OSI model. The primary function of ARP is to resolve IP addresses to network layer addresses, such as a Media Access Control (MAC) address.

Routers and hosts both use ARP to resolve IP addresses to MAC addresses. All network communications eventually take place over the network layer of the OSI model, and a network layer address such as a MAC address is required for this to take place. The MAC address corresponding to the IP address can be either statically entered prior to communications by entering a static ARP entry, or dynamically learned by ARP.

To learn a MAC address dynamically, ARP sends out a broadcast frame requesting the MAC address of a host with a specified IP address. All hosts on the segment receive the broadcast, but only the host with the specified IP address responds with its MAC address. At this point, Layer 3 communication can begin. Reverse ARP (RARP), which is used to translate a MAC address to an IP address, uses the same header format as ARP.

The header of an ARP packet differs depending on the underlying networking technology in use. The header fields of an ARP packet contain values specifying the lengths of the successive fields. A list of fields follows:

- **Hardware type**—Indicates the type of hardware in use.
- **Protocol type**—Indicates the network level protocol.
- **Hardware address length**—Indicates the length of the hardware address in bytes.
- **Protocol address space**—Indicates the length of the protocol address in bytes.
- **Operation code**—Indicates the operation for this packet: ARP request, ARP response, RARP request, or RARP response.
- **Sender's hardware address**—Indicates the hardware address of the sender.

- **Sender's protocol address**—Indicates the network layer address of the sender.

- **Target hardware address**—With a RARP request, this contains the destination hardware address. With a RARP response, this carries both the destination's hardware and network layer addresses.

- **Target protocol address**—With an ARP request, this carries the destination's network layer address. With an ARP response, this carries both the destination's hardware and network layer addresses.

Internet Control Message Protocol (ICMP)

ICMP messages are encapsulated within IP packets. Using a connectionless, unreliable transfer mechanism, ICMP is used to report errors within a network. Usually, only higher-level protocols are encapsulated within another protocol. However, ICMP is an integral part of the IP protocol suite that still is encapsulated within the data portion of an IP packet. RFCs 792 and 1700 define ICMP.

Even though ICMP message formats vary based on which service is requested, all ICMP messages have the first three fields in common. These fields are type, code, and checksum. Code is a single byte field whose purpose is to explain the type field further. The ICMP checksum is a 2-byte field that uses the same algorithm as the IP checksum field. However, the ICMP checksum only pertains to the ICMP portion of the IP message, not to the whole IP packet. All ICMP messages that report errors also carry the header and the first 8 bytes of the datagram that caused the error. Because the most critical information of a higher-level protocol using IP is carried within these first 8 bytes, this helps with detecting what caused the error.

The formats of echo request, echo reply, and destination unreachable messages are shown in Figure 1-10. Remember that this ICMP message is imbedded within the data portion of an IP packet, which is in turn encapsulated within another protocol, such as Ethernet.

Figure 1-10 *ICMP Message Formats*

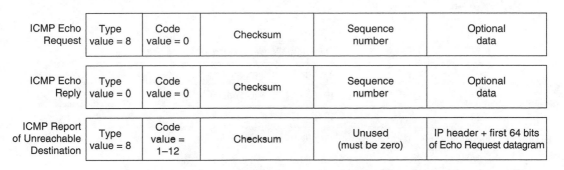

ICMP Echo Request	Type value = 8	Code value = 0	Checksum	Sequence number	Optional data
ICMP Echo Reply	Type value = 0	Code value = 0	Checksum	Sequence number	Optional data
ICMP Report of Unreachable Destination	Type value = 8	Code value = 1–12	Checksum	Unused (must be zero)	IP header + first 64 bits of Echo Request datagram

The main use of ICMP is to provide a reporting function that identifies error conditions on network devices. Routers usually generate ICMP messages as they receive and route the IP packet. These ICMP messages contain three fields at the beginning of the packet:

- **Type field**—The type field is an 8-bit field that identifies the message. These type field values are displayed in Table 1-2.

Table 1-2   *ICMP Type Field Values*

Type Value	Message Type
0	Echo Reply
1	Unassigned
2	Unassigned
3	Destination Unreachable
4	Source Quench
5	Redirect
6	Alternate Host Address
7	Unassigned
8	Echo Request
9	Router Advertisement
10	Router Selection
11	Time Exceeded
12	Parameter Problem
13	Timestamp Request
14	Timestamp Reply
15	Obsolete (Information Request)
16	Obsolete (Information Reply)
17	Address Mask Request
18	Address Mask Reply
19–29	Reserved
30	Traceroute
31	Datagram Conversion Error
32	Mobile Host Redirect
33	IPv6—Where Are You?
34	IPv6—Here I am.
35	Mobile Registration Request
36	Mobile Registration Reply
37–255	Reserved

- **Code field**—The code field is an 8-bit field that provides further information about the ICMP message.

- **Checksum field**—The checksum field is a 16-bit field that is used to verify the integrity of the whole ICMP message.

Transmission Control Protocol (TCP)

TCP, defined in RFC 761, operates at the transport layer of the OSI model. TCP encapsulates IP and provides a connection-oriented and reliable transport protocol. Services using TCP include Hypertext Transfer Protocol (HTTP), Simple Mail Transport Protocol (SMTP), Post Office Protocol 3 (POP3), and File Transfer Protocol (FTP).

The fields in the TCP header are shown in Figure 1-11.

Figure 1-11 *TCP Header Format*

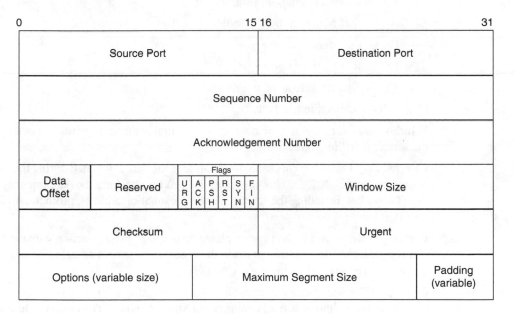

An explanation of each of the fields in the TCP header follows:

- **Source port**—The source port is 16 bits and contains the value of the source port where data originates. Because both UDP and TCP use ports, a list of valid source ports is included within the UDP section.

- **Destination port**—The destination port is 16 bits and contains a value of the source port to which data is sent.

- **Sequence number**—The sequence number is 32 bits. The value of this field is the sequence number of the first data octet within this segment when the SYN bit is not set. When the SYN bit is set, the value of this field is the Initial Sequence Number (ISN), and the first data offset is set to ISN + 1.

- **Acknowledgement number**—The acknowledgement number is 32 bits long. Once a connection is established, this field always contains a value equal to the next sequence number expected by the receiver. A connection is assumed to be established if the ACK bit is set.

- **Data offset**—The data offset field is 4 bits in length and specifies the number of 32-bit words within the TCP header, thereby specifying where the data begins.

- **Reserved**—This unused field is 6 bits in length and is set to 0.

- **Flags (control bits)**—The flags field is also known as the control bits field. This field is 6 bits in length and contains the following subfields, each a length of 1 bit:
  — URG—Urgent pointer field significant
  — ACK—Acknowledge field significant
  — PSH—Push function
  — RST—Reset connection request
  — SYN—Synchronize sequence numbers
  — FIN—Connection finished

- **Window size**—The 16-bit window size field contains the number of data octets that the sender is willing to receive.

- **Checksum**—The 16-bit checksum field contains the data calculated during the cyclic redundancy check (CRC). This checksum is used for checking the data integrity for the TCP packet, including the source address, destination address, protocol, options, and TCP length.

- **Urgent pointer**—The 16-bit urgent pointer field is used in conjunction with the URG control bit. If the URG control bit is set, the urgent pointer field contains the sequence number of the octet following the urgent data.

- **Options**—The options field is variable in length aligning to an equal multiple of 8 bits. An option within this field begins on an 8-bit boundary. The option field can be formatted as a single octet. An alternative format is the combination of an option followed by an octet describing the option length and the option data octets.

- **Maximum segment size**—The optional 16-bit maximum segment size field is only used on packets with the SYN control bit set. This field contains the maximum receive segment size of the sender.

- **Padding**—The variable length padding field is used to ensure that the TCP header ends on a 32-bit boundary. This field always contains zeros.

User Datagram Protocol (UDP)

UDP is defined in RFC 768 and operates at the transport layer of the OSI model. UDP is a simple packet-oriented transport layer protocol that is connectionless and therefore unreliable. The UDP datagram resides within the data portion of an IP packet.

UDP packets are sent with no sequencing or flow control, so there is no guarantee that they will reach their intended destination. The receiving host compares the UDP header checksum, and if a problem is detected, the packet is dropped without reporting the error back to the sending host.

This is a very fast transport protocol because no acknowledgements or advanced sequencing are carried out at the transport layer. Upper layer protocols can enforce their own error detection and recovery to utilize the speed of UDP. UDP is typically used when the data is not essential, such as in video or voice streaming live content over the Internet. The Trivial File Transfer Protocol (TFTP) that is used to upgrade software images on Cisco routers and switches is also based on UDP. A breakdown of the UDP header fields is shown in Figure 1-12.

Figure 1-12 *UDP Header Format*

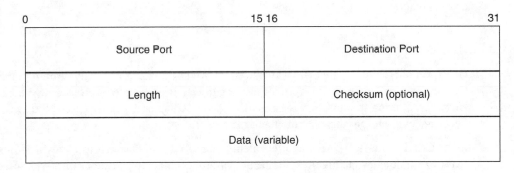

Denial of Service (DoS) Attacks

A DoS attack is designed to overwhelm the victim's network to the point that the victim cannot use the network for legitimate business purposes. A Distributed DoS (DDoS) is simply a DoS that is launched simultaneously from more than one source. Sometimes these attacks are used in an attempt to confuse the equipment to a point where unauthorized access is able to penetrate inside the network. At other times, the attacks are launched merely because the perpetrator wishes to bring down the victim's network connections. In either case, there are some common methods used in DoS attacks that are explored in this chapter, in addition to ways to avoid becoming a victim of these attacks.

SYN Flood Attacks

To understand how a SYN flood attack can occur, you must first understand how a connection is established. When a host wishes to establish a connection, a TCP packet with the SYN bit set is sent to the remote host. The remote host looks at the port within this TCP packet. If the port corresponds to a service that is running, the remote host replies with another SYN packet. The initiating host then sends an ACK packet that starts the data transfer stage of the communications.

Because there is no guarantee of how quickly the ACK packet will be received by the remote host, a partially opened connection, also called a *half-open connection*, is maintained by the remote host. Maintaining half-open connections uses CPU cycles and memory and exposes the remote host to an inherent vulnerability from SYN flood attacks.

In a SYN flood attack, the perpetrator repeatedly causes the remote host to maintain half-open connections. As the number of half-open connections increases, more memory and CPU cycles are used in an attempt to maintain these connections. Unless measures are taken to limit the time that each half-open connection is maintained or the total number of half-open connections permitted, eventually the remote host will spend all of its resources trying to maintain these connections. SYN flood attacks can be further understood through an explanation of the LAND.c attack.

LAND.c Attacks

One form of SYN flood attack is known as the LAND.c attack. Originally written in the C programming language, this form of attack can be devastating to unprotected systems. However, filtering spoofed addresses as discussed in Chapter 2, "Basic Cisco Router Security," will prevent this type of attack from being successful.

In the LAND.c attack, a perpetrator repeatedly sends TCP SYN packets to a known address. In the example shown in Figure 1-13, the perpetrator is launching an attack on a Web server. In this example, the SYN packets would have both the source and destination address set to 10.1.1.30, which is the address of the machine under attack.

Figure 1-13 *LAND.c Attack*

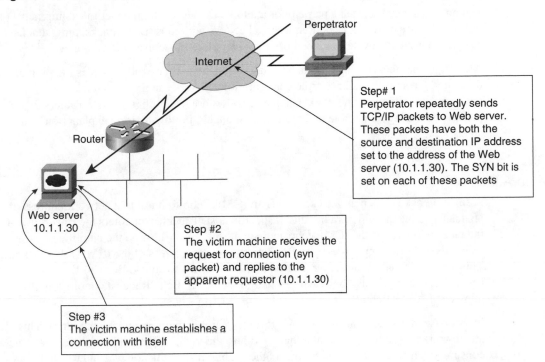

Perpetrator

Internet

Step# 1
Perpetrator repeatedly sends
TCP/IP packets to Web server.
These packets have both the
source and destination IP address
set to the address of the Web
server (10.1.1.30). The SYN bit is
set on each of these packets

Router

Web server
10.1.1.30

Step #2
The victim machine receives the
request for connection (syn
packet) and replies to the
apparent requestor (10.1.1.30)

Step #3
The victim machine establishes a
connection with itself

Within the TCP packet, the perpetrator sets a port number. Any port number associated with a running service could be used. Because the attacked machine's main function is to service Web pages, the perpetrator is likely to set the port number to 80, which is used for Web services.

The attacked machine receives the SYN packet and checks the port requested. If the port requested is currently running a service, the attacked machine replies with another SYN packet to the "requesting host," attempting to complete the connection. In this case, the requesting host, as defined by the source address of the IP packet, is the same as the destination host. Therefore, the attacked host tries to establish a connection with itself. While waiting for a response that will never come, the attacked host holds open a connection until a timeout period has passed. This timeout period varies, depending on the operating system of the attacked host.

The host soon becomes overwhelmed by the repeated opening of connections to itself and ceases to function because of exhaustion of resources.

Ping Attacks

A ping attack occurs when a perpetrator attempts to overwhelm the victim's equipment through the use of ICMP Echo Request packets. As with most DoS attacks, ping attacks attempt to use CPU cycles and memory to prevent legitimate use of equipment.

Although a number of ping attacks have been launched successfully, such as the ping of death and the smurf attacks, simple configuration changes can prevent attacks from adversely affecting your network. Chapter 2 shows how to configure Cisco routers to prevent becoming vulnerable to these forms of attack. Following is an explanation of a smurf attack.

Smurf Attack

A smurf attack is when an attacker sends an ICMP Echo Request to a network address of an unsuspecting amplifier, rather than a specific host. The attacker enters the IP address of the targeted server as the ICMP echo source address. Every host on the amplifier network responds and sends an ICMP Echo Reply to the source address of the ICMP echo packet. This address is that of the server that the attacker wanted to attack. Because the amplifier network has many hosts, they each respond to the ICMP Echo Request, amplifying the number of ICMP Echo Replies received by the victim's host.

In this case, the attacker uses another's resources and network to attack the victim. This attack works by simply consuming bandwidth to the victim. Once this bandwidth is consumed, all access to the server from other public hosts will slowly grind to a halt.

Creating a Corporate Security Policy

A corporate security policy is a necessary piece of any network design effort. Security is as important to a network design as bandwidth requirements and choosing the network protocol. Failing to consider security during the design stage leads to situations where extra efforts must be taken to ensure safety. Security measures incorporated within the design are much easier to implement, generally less expensive, and usually more robust. The corporate security policy is a formal statement that specifies a set of rules that users must follow when gaining access to corporate assets.

You need to differentiate the security policy from the technical design of the security features. For example, a proper security policy does not state that a PIX 515 Firewall will be used on Internet connections. Instead, a well-formed security policy states that a firewall will be used on Internet connections and that this firewall will have certain minimum capabilities. The network security administrator chooses the best equipment and configurations to accomplish the goals, using the policy as a guide.

For a security policy to succeed, some general guidelines must be followed:

- Management must support the policy.
- The policy must be technically feasible.
- The policy must be implemented globally throughout the company.
- The policy must clearly define responsibilities for users, administrators, and management.
- The policy must be flexible enough to adapt to changing technologies and company goals.
- The policy must be understandable.
- The policy must be widely distributed.
- The policy must be enforceable.
- The policy must provide sanctions for users violating the policies.
- The policy must contain a response plan for when security breaches are exposed.

Once a security policy is implemented, the company will see a number of benefits. Some of these benefits include:

- A framework from which all security efforts are built.
- Lessened uncertainty about whether an action is permissible.
- A basis for punitive action to be taken in cases of unacceptable network usage.
- A comprehensive system for auditing security efforts.

As defined in "The Site Security Handbook" (RFC 2196), a security policy does not dictate how a business runs. Rather, the business needs dictate the security policy. The policy does not dictate the exact equipment or configuration to be used; instead, it gives guidance to the administrator.

Summary

This chapter introduced some of the basics of network security. Starting with a brief description of some of the most common forms of attacks, it quickly moved on to a description of common network devices.

Security provided by the TCP/IP protocol set was discussed, delving into the format of the more common protocols. Understanding the format and use of each of the fields within a protocol is necessary for the administrator to thwart attacks successfully. The chapter examined a few of the more common forms of DoS attacks. Specific examples of how to deal with each of these types of attacks will be shown in later chapters.

In this book, the focus of how to deal with and prevent attacks is on solutions provided by Cisco Secure.

Finally, the chapter covered the need for and requirements of a corporate security policy. The remaining chapters of this book will build on the foundations within this chapter.

Frequently Asked Questions

Question: Why do I really need a written security policy? Why can't I just secure my network?

Answer: Although this may seem reasonable for a smaller network, failing to implement a written security policy has many ramifications. First, the policy defines the goals and parameters around which the configurations are designed. Failing to write down the policy is similar to implementing a network before designing the network.

Second, as networks and technologies grow in complexity, you need a base reference to look back on in order to compare where you are to where you wish to be. The written security policy provides you with this information.

Finally, as network administrators are replaced or added to the workforce, the written policy gives new administrators guidance about how equipment should be configured. Having a single document to rely on allows new administrators to avoid guessing about what should be allowed and what should be denied.

Question: How secure should I make my network? Isn't there a point at which the network becomes unusable?

Answer: The security on a network must fit the corporation. A suit that is too tight is not comfortable; neither is one that is too loose. If the security is too tight, users will constantly complain. If the security is too loose, the network runs the danger of being hacked or exposed to a DoS attack. The task of the administrator is to find the middle ground that follows the policy, protects the network, and does not cause the users to complain. Again, this is where a well-defined written security policy comes in.

Question: My office network doesn't have any critical data. Do I still need to protect it?

Answer: Yes. Even if your own network does not have critical data, which is doubtful, there is another reason to protect the network. Failing to protect your own network might leave you in a position where your network is used to launch attacks on other networks. Protecting your own network prevents attackers from using it to launch attacks against others. Also, even if your data is not critical, your operation probably is, and a DoS attack will still be devastating.

Glossary

ASA (Adaptive Security Algorithm)—A Cisco proprietary methodology of ensuring security.

CBAC (Context-based Access Control)—A Cisco proprietary method of allowing returning traffic through a router only after packets requesting that session have traveled out the same interface.

DoS (denial of service)—A form of attack that attempts to deny the availability of a network or host, usually by overwhelming that network or host with requests.

NAT (Network Address Translation)—NAT is the process where the source or destination address of IP packets is changed as these packets traverse a router or firewall. NAT allows a network using private IP addresses to connect to the Internet using public IP addresses.

RADIUS (Remote Access Dial-In User Service)—A protocol used to authenticate users on a network.

TACACS (Terminal Access Controller Access Control System)—A protocol used to authenticate users on a network. Also provides authorization and accounting facilities.

This chapter contains the following sections:

- Basic Management Security
- Access Lists
- Password Management
- Physical Security
- Out-of-Band Management Security
- Cisco Discovery Protocol (CDP)
- HTTP Configuration Services
- Simple Network Management Protocol (SNMP)
- Network Time Protocol (NTP)
- Banners
- Recommended Minimum IOS Security Settings
- TCP Intercept
- Summary

CHAPTER 2

Basic Cisco Router Security

The first question any administrator should ask about a service is whether it is necessary to run that service in the present environment. If a service is not required, it should be disabled. Running a service that provides no functionality only burns up CPU cycles and exposes the network to potential attacks. If a service is required on the interior of the network, the administrator should make efforts to prevent that service from being seen from the exterior. Likewise, if a service is required on the exterior of the network, the administrator should attempt to limit the scope of the service to only the exterior portions.

Throughout this chapter, you will find several examples of services that pose potential risks of security breaches. Some of these services might be disabled by default, depending on the version of IOS being used. In these cases, the administrator is still urged to turn off the service specifically. The reason for this is to ensure that the administrator does not rely on his or her memory regarding which services are off by default on which versions of the IOS. Taking the time to turn off questionable services specifically will also make certain that the service is off even if the default changes.

As hackers, crackers, and script kiddies try new and inventive ways to break into your network, new threats will continue to emerge. One of the best ways to stay ahead of security threats is to keep current on the IOS version used on routers. Major security threats are consistently eliminated through new IOS versions. However, this does not relieve the administrator of the responsibility of using common sense and basic configurations that are sound. This chapter provides the basic configuration changes necessary to prevent your network from becoming susceptible to common attacks.

Throughout this chapter, you will be reminded that you should never intentionally divulge information regarding your network. The reason for this warning is that any information received by someone trying to breach security can and will be used against you. You should never intentionally divulge any information that does not need to be shared. Remember that the topic is security; in the realm of security, there is no such concept as being too careful.

This chapter is designed to teach the basic configurations necessary to begin securing your network. Advanced topics such as Terminal Access Controller Access Control System (TACACS), TACACS+, and Remote Access Dial-In User Service (RADIUS) authentication are explored in Chapter 10, "Securing the Corporate Network." This chapter is limited in scope to the rudimentary commands.

Basic Management Security

Before delving into specifics regarding how routers should be configured to help avoid attacks, the differences between internal and external devices must be explored. For purposes of this chapter, the authors use the word *external* as in *external interface*, meaning that the interface is directly connected to an untrusted entity. This can be the Internet, another company, or even a subsidiary of your own company. An internal interface is one that connects directly to a fully trusted network.

Many factors determine whether an entity is trusted. If there is doubt that the connected entity can be trusted, the authors recommend that the administrator not trust that entity. The initial reaction of many administrators will be to question why a wholly owned subsidiary should not be trusted. Consider the following example: Company A has a connection to the Internet. The administrator has done everything reasonable to ensure that the network is safe. Company B is a wholly owned subsidiary that has its own connection to the Internet. The administrators of these companies have sent a few e-mails to each other and talked on the phone a number of times to establish connection procedures and procedures for maintaining connections. However, Company A's administrator has no authority, either explicit or implied, over Company B's administrator. Upper management has decided that all subsidiaries will be entirely responsible for their own networks. If Company B's administrator is not careful, Company A may become a target of attack through Company B's network. Figure 2-1 illustrates this scenario.

This situation becomes more complicated when a company acquires several hundred subsidiaries. In a multinational company, one cannot possibly assume that each of the subsidiaries will always observe good security practices. Therefore, administrators should assume that any subsidiary of which they do not directly have control is easily breached. Likewise, the subsidiaries should assume that the main office is easily breached. Unless the administrator at the subsidiary personally knows all of the security steps taken within the main office, security should be implemented. Additionally, even if all offices provide adequate security, the only drawback to increased security will be a slight increase in latency and additional CPU requirements on the interface routers—both of which are very reasonable trade-offs for increased security.

In any case, a connection to another company that is not owned by your own company should be treated as a possible threat and considered an external interface. The reasoning behind this is the same as that for a subsidiary. Unless the administrator is able to constantly verify the security on any connection, it must be assumed to be a threat.

Now that the basic differences between internal and external connections have been explored, the chapter will move on to cover some specific settings on routers to discourage the most common forms of attack.

Figure 2-1   *Company A Is Exposed Through Company B*

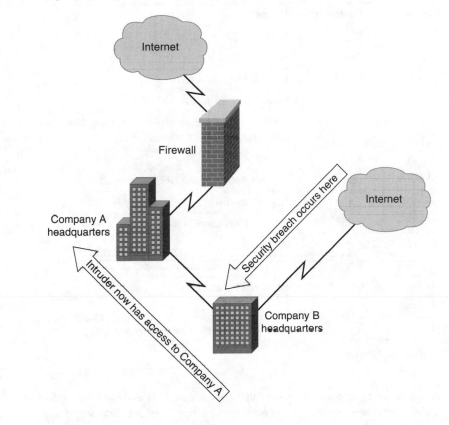

Access Lists

Access lists are created to deny certain packets the ability to traverse a router interface. By default, a router will allow all packets to travel through an interface. The router may not know where to forward a particular packet but will still allow that packet to cross the interface. An access list is a list of packets that is consulted before allowing or disallowing a packet to travel forward toward its ultimate destination.

Although this text assumes that you have at least an understanding of access lists, this section contains a brief review of the basic forms of IP access lists before moving onto the more complex reflexive and context-based access lists. The examples within this chapter will focus on IP access lists. A wide variety of protocols are available, all of which might have access lists applied to restrict access. A listing of the available access list numbers and their associated protocols can be found in Table 2-1.

Table 2-1 *Access List Numbers and Associated Protocols*

List Range	Protocol	Notes
1–99	IP	Standard IP access list
1–100	Vines	Standard Vines access list
100–199	IP	Extended IP access list
101–200	Vines	Extended Vines access list
200–299	Type Code	Ethernet Type Code, transparent bridging Type Code, or source–route bridging Type Code access list
201–300	Vines	Simple Vines access list
300–399	DECnet	DECnet and Extended DECnet access list
400–499	XNS	XNS access list
500–599	XNS	Extended XNS access list
600–699	AppleTalk	AppleTalk access list
700–799	Vendor Code	Source-route bridging Vendor Code access list
800–899	IPX	Standard IPX access list
900–999	IPX	Extended IPX access list
1000–1099	IPX	IPX Service Access Protocol[1] access list

[1]SAP=Service Access Protocol

Any interface on a router may have up to two access lists assigned: one will control inbound traffic, and the other will control outbound traffic. All access lists, regardless of protocol or interface, operate based on six principles:

- Access lists usually deny that which is not specifically permitted, because traffic is generally allowed by default.
- Access lists control traffic in one direction (inbound or outbound) on an interface.
- Every packet traversing the interface is examined against an applied access list in the direction of that packet.
- Packets are compared to the access list starting at the top of the access list and continuing until a match is found. The implied deny statement at the end of an access list is considered a match.
- Outbound packets are routed to the appropriate interface before the access list is applied.
- Inbound packets are compared to the access list and, if permitted, are routed to the appropriate interface.
- Any interface may have a maximum of one access list applied to the inbound traffic and a maximum of one access list applied to the outbound traffic.

Access lists are made in one of several forms; the most common are standard and extended. Because standard access lists are simpler by nature, they will be examined first.

Standard Access Lists

Standard access lists deny or permit packets traversing a router interface based solely on the source address of the packet. Numbered 1 through 99 for IP, standard access lists must be defined before they can be used. Figure 2-2 shows that a router, by default, allows all traffic through to the intended destination.

Figure 2-2   *By Default, a Router Allows All Traffic Through*

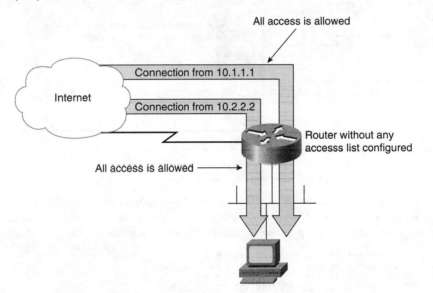

Applying an access list, however, will change this behavior. When an access list is applied, a router acts as a firewall. The function of a firewall is to restrict traffic traveling through itself. As shown in Figure 2-3, adding an access list changes the behavior of the router. When an access list is applied, only traffic that has specifically been allowed will be able to travel through the router. In the example shown in Figure 2-3, traffic from the 10.2.2.0/24 network is allowed to traverse the router. Because no other traffic has been allowed, traffic originating from the host 10.1.1.1 will not be allowed through.

The syntax for creating a standard IP access list is as follows:

```
access-list access-list-number {deny | permit} source [source-wildcard]
```

With this syntax, *access-list-number* is any number from 1 through 99 that defines the access list number. The parameter **permit** or **deny** specifies whether to allow or disallow the packets. The parameter *source* is the IP address of the host sending the packets to be denied, and *source-wildcard* is the wildcard mask for the host or hosts sending the packets.

The logical flow for a standard access list is shown in Figure 2-4. Notice that if the source address is either not found or found but not permitted, the packet is denied.

Figure 2-3 *Access List Limits Which Packets Travel Through a Router*

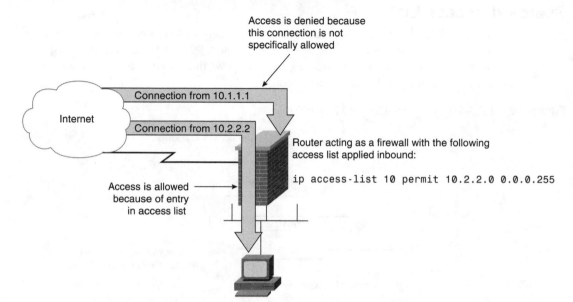

An example of a standard access list follows. Although this access list will reveal some inconsistencies, it is useful for the purposes of discussion. Each line of this access list will be discussed. For the purposes of this discussion, each line is labeled with a line number:

```
1) access-list 3 permit 172.30.1.0 0.0.0.255
2) access-list 3 permit 10.1.1.0 0.0.15.255
3) access-list 3 deny 10.1.1.2 0.0.0.0
4) access-list 3 permit 192.168.10.0 0.0.0.7
5) access-list 3 deny 172.31.1.0 0.0.0.255
6) access-list 3 deny any
```

Line 1 accomplishes a number of objectives. The keyword **access-list** is used to define that this line is used to specify an access list. The number **3** assigns the following permit or deny statement to access list number 3. The word **permit** tells the router to allow the following combination of IP address and mask through the interface. Using the keyword **deny** would tell the router to deny the packets.

Notice that all of the lines have an IP network address and what looks like a reversed subnet mask. The reversed subnet mask is called a wildcard mask and works very much like a subnet mask, only in reverse. In line 1, **172.30.1.0 0.0.0.255** describes the source address of packets to permit through the interface. This means that all packets with the source address of 172.30.1.0 through 172.30.1.255 will be permitted through an interface with this access list applied.

Line 2 looks similar to line 1 and allows all packets between 10.1.0.0 and 10.1.15.255 through an interface to which this access list is applied. At this point, you might be questioning exactly how that conclusion was reached. This is explained in the following sidebar, "Wildcard Masks."

Figure 2-4   *Logical Flow of Standard Access List*

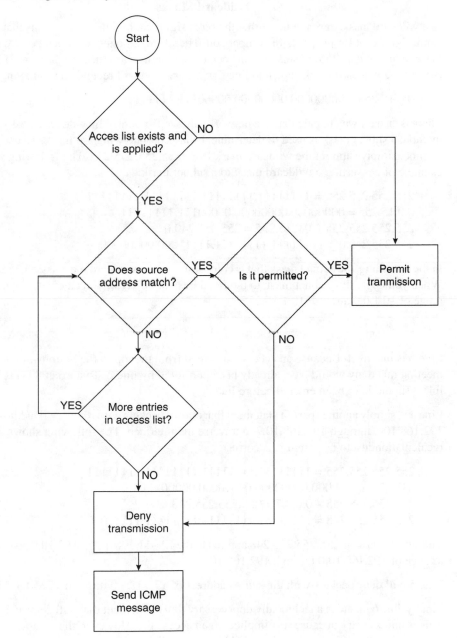

Wildcard Masks

In a wildcard mask, zeros indicate that the bit is significant while a one means that the bit is not significant for purposes of comparison. Therefore, all ones in an octet of a wildcard mask, expressed as 255, means that this octet is not significant for comparisons. If you convert the wildcard mask shown in line 2 to binary, you will receive the following:

0.0.15.255 = 00000000.00000000.00000111.11111111

There is an easy way to calculate the networks allowed or denied by wildcard masks. In this method, a subnet mask is used to determine the appropriate wildcard mask. To use this method, simply subtract the wildcard mask from 255.255.255.255. The following is an example of converting a wildcard mask to a subnet mask:

255.255.255.255 = 11111111.11111111.11111111.11111111
0.0.15.255 = 00000000.00000000.00000111.11111111
255.255.255.255 – 0.0.15.255 = 255.255.240.0
255.255.240.0 = 11111111.11111111.11111000.00000000

In the preceding, the subnet mask that is comparable to the wildcard mask is 255.255.240.0. When you apply this subnet mask to the IP address of 10.1.1.0, you calculate the network range of 10.1.0.0 through 10.1.15.255.

Line 3 is incorrect. Because an access list is read from the top to the bottom, any packet meeting this **deny** would have already been permitted by line 2. To correct this problem, line 3 should have been entered before line 2.

Line 4 is simply another permit statement that allows packets with a source IP address from 192.168.10.0 through 192.168.10.7 to traverse the interface. The following shows a recalculation just to be sure this is correct:

255.255.255.255 = 11111111.11111111.11111111.11111111
0.0.0.7 = 00000000.00000000.00000000.00000111
255.255.255.255 – 0.0.0.7 = 255.255.255.248
255.255.255.248 = 11111111.11111111.11111111.11111000

The subnet mask of 255.255.255.248 applied to the IP address of 192.168.10.0 provides for a range of 192.168.10.0 through 192.168.10.7.

Line 5 will deny packets with the source address of 172.31.1.0 through 172.31.1.255.

Finally, line 6 includes a technically unnecessary **deny** statement that will deny all sources. This is unnecessary because it is implied on an access list. However, the author recommends that it is specifically stated for clarity. Since consistency promotes understanding, the author usually adds a specific **deny any** to every access list. This is also an important point when working with reflexive access lists. Additionally, when using extended access lists, it is possible to log matches. Logging of access lists will be explored in the later section, "Extended Access Lists."

Applying Access Lists

Once an access list is created, it must be applied to an interface. To apply an access list to an interface, use the **ip access-group** or **ip access-class** command. The **ip access-class** command is used on virtual terminal interfaces, while the **ip access-group** command is used on all other interfaces. The access list is applied to either the inbound or outbound packets of the interface. The keywords **in** and **out** determine whether the access list is to be applied on the interface to deny inbound or outbound packets. The following is the command for applying access list number 3 to an interface to deny inbound packets. Note that you must first be in configuration mode and within the interface configuration to apply an access list.

```
ip access-group 3 in
```

The access list could alternatively be applied to the interface to deny outbound packets with the following:

```
ip access-group 3 out
```

To apply an inbound access list to a virtual terminal, the following command is used. The only difference in applying an access list between a virtual terminal and any other terminal is that the virtual terminal uses **access-class** instead of **access-group**. Again, the user must first be in configuration mode on that particular interface before applying an access list.

```
ip access-class 3 in
```

Any interface can have a single access list inbound and another single access list outbound. Only one access list should be applied in any given direction. In other words, one and only one access list should be applied inbound on an interface, and one and only one access list should be applied outbound on an interface. If an interface is using subinterfaces, such as on a serial interface connecting in a point-to-point method to remote sites, each subinterface is considered a separate interface. Each subinterface can have separate access lists. In this case, however, the root interface cannot have a separate access list. Figure 2-5 shows acceptable settings for access lists on interfaces with and without subinterfaces.

Extended Access Lists

Standard access lists are limited because they make no distinctions between the ports being used. A standard access list will allow or deny packets based solely on the source IP address and are able to log only those packets that have not passed through the access list. Extended access lists overcome these limitations and form the basis for context-based and reflexive access lists, which are discussed in Chapter 5, "Cisco IOS Firewall."

Figure 2-5   *Access Lists Applied to Interfaces*

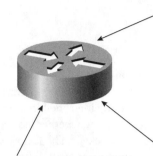

Interface with subinterfaces and multiple access lists:

```
INT S2
...
INT S2.1
access-group 105 in
access-group 106 out

INT S2.2
access-group 107 in
access-group 108 out
```

Interface with subinterfaces
and a single access list:

```
INT S1
access-group 103 in
access-group 104 out

INT S1.1
...
INT S1.2
...
```

Interface with no subinterfaces:

```
INT S0
access-group 101 in
access-group 102 out
```

As with a standard access list, that which is not specifically permitted is denied. Because extended access lists can look at the source address, the destination address, and ports, any one item might cause a packet to be refused traversing the router. Extreme care should be taken when working on extended access lists to ensure that exactly those packets that should be traversing the router, and only those, do, in fact, traverse the router.

The following example is an extended access list with one of the simple forms available. In the example, a number of differing services are allowed to travel through the interface. A number of protocols are also prevented. Study the following list before moving on to the detailed discussion:

```
1) ip access-list 101 permit tcp any host 10.1.1.2 established log
2) ip access-list 101 permit tcp any host 172.30.1.3 eq www log
3) ip access-list 101 deny tcp any host 172.30.1.4 eq ftp log
4) ip access-list 101 permit tcp any host 172.30.1.4 log
5) ip access-list 101 deny any any
```

In the preceding example, line 1 allows access through the TCP protocol to host 10.1.1.2, if a connection has already been established from 10.1.1.2 to that remote host. This line will not permit any packets to traverse the interface unless the session was initiated from the inside of the corporate network.

Line 2 allows any host to connect to 172.30.1.3 for WWW services (HTTP). All other types of connection to this host will be denied because of the implied (and in this case specified) **deny any any** at the end of the access list.

Line 3 denies access to host 172.30.1.4 if the remote host is trying to connect using FTP services. Line 4 allows all other types of connections to 172.30.1.4.

Notice that each of these lines has the word *log* added at the end of the line. This causes the router to log all attempts at connection. A standard access list using the **log** option will only log those packets that have been denied.

Named Access Lists

Named access lists, first introduced in IOS Version 11.0, allow the administrator to use a character string instead of an access list number. One benefit is that the limitations of 99 standard access lists (1–99) and 100 extended access lists (100–199) no longer apply. The administrator can also name an access list something meaningful. For example, an access list named "from-internet" could be created to limit access into the corporate network from the Internet. Naming access lists in a meaningful way tends to make troubleshooting easier.

Another advantage to named access lists is that entries can be removed. However, new entries are still added to the bottom of the access list, which is usually not what is intended.

Reflexive access lists, discussed in Chapter 5, require a named access list, and access lists dealing with packet filters and route filters cannot use named access lists. A standard and an extended access list cannot both have the same name.

Password Management

Passwords are the primary defense against unauthorized access to networking equipment. The best way to prevent unauthorized access is to use either a TACACS+ or a RADIUS authentication server. Even if you are unable to use these services, some basic configuration issues should be addressed concerning password management.

The first issue to be addressed is choosing passwords. No matter what type of encryption is used, some general rules should be followed. When a password is being chosen, the following list will help the administrator in determining the appropriateness and the treatment of passwords:

- Passwords should not reflect the company name.
- Passwords should not reflect the business of the company.
- Passwords should not reflect the equipment where they are used.
- Passwords should not be decipherable based on any other configuration parameter. This includes model number and network address.
- Passwords should not be any word that appears in a standard dictionary.
- Passwords should be unique.
- Passwords should not be sequential.

- Passwords should include both uppercase and lowercase characters and nonalphabetic characters if possible.

- Passwords should be as long as reasonably possible.

- Passwords should be changed on an irregular basis.

- Any list containing passwords should be closely guarded.

- Critical passwords should be changed whenever any person with that level of access leaves the company. This holds especially true if a contractor is involved or if a person was terminated involuntarily.

- As few people as possible should have access to passwords, but critical passwords should always be known by more than one person. This is an exception to the generally accepted rule that passwords should not be shared.

- Nontechnical managers generally do not and should not know system passwords. Knowing a password without knowing how to effectively configure equipment serves no legitimate purpose.

- Passwords should not be distributed over the Internet.

Although some of the preceding guidelines might seem overly restrictive, they are designed to reduce the severity of a security breach, as well as to prevent breaches from happening. For example, the author has seen companies that set router passwords based on the serial IP address. If a single router was penetrated, the password scheme would quickly become apparent. When you don't use a common password scheme, someone trying to break into your network will need to start over with every device.

The next sections examine how passwords are set with the **enable password** and **enable secret** commands. Then the chapter moves on to console passwords and AAA (authentication, authorization, and accounting) password management.

The enable password Command

The **enable password** command is an old command that is not considered secure and therefore should not be used. When **enable password** is combined with the **service password-encryption** command, the IOS encrypts the entered password using the Vigenere algorithms. These were never intended to prevent any but the most casual observer from gaining access. Any dedicated or fairly knowledgeable person can easily break this algorithm. A number of programs are also available on the Internet that allow you to break a password that is entered using the **enable password** command. The **enable password** command can be disabled with the use of the following global configuration command:

```
no enable password
```

The enable secret Command

Using the **enable secret** command in conjunction with the **service password-encryption** command provides a decent level of decryption resistance. In this case, MD5 hashing is used to encrypt the password. Although there have been no known cases of MD5 hashing being decrypted as of the time of this writing, there are other ways in which an **enable secret** password can be broken. The easiest way to break an **enable secret** password is by using a brute-strength *dictionary attack,* where a list of words is compiled (the dictionary) and then each word is used as the password sequentially. Dictionary attacks are the reason for the guideline against using any word that appears in a dictionary.

The **enable secret** command allows the administrator to specify up to 16 privilege levels through the use of numbers 0 through 15. If no level is specified, level 15 is assumed. This command, combined with the **privilege level** command, allows the administrator to give some administrators access to specified commands while denying access to others. The full syntax of the enable secret command is

```
enable secret [level level] {password | encryption-type encrypted-password}
```

The following example shows how to enable a secret password at level 7 using "9%ad100gbellisnon" for the password. The second line starts service password-encryption.

```
RouterA(config-if)#enable secret level 7 9%ad100gbellisnon
RouterA(config-if)#service router-encryption
```

The optional *encryption-type* and *encrypted-password* are used when copying previously encrypted passwords from other router configurations. Currently, the only encryption type available is MD5, which is specified with the number 5. This allows the administrator to copy configurations with an **enable secret** password across multiple routers. Although having the same password on multiple routers should usually be avoided, there are some circumstances, such as during initial deployment, where it is acceptable.

The command **service router-encryption** is used in the preceding example to ensure that all passwords in the configuration are shown encrypted. Before this command is entered, all passwords other than the **enable secret** password are shown exactly as they are entered. When the **service router-encryption** command is used, all passwords within the configuration are encrypted. This prevents revealing the password when distributing printed copies of the configuration.

Physical Security

Physical security should always come first in the mind of the security administrator. If you cannot guarantee physical security, you cannot guarantee any security. This is especially true where the console and auxiliary ports of a router are concerned. Anyone with physical access to a Cisco router and who possessed a PC, the proper cable, and the required knowledge can break into your router. Using the password recovery techniques that are widely published by Cisco will allow someone to gain total control of the router. If you set all of your router passwords to be the same or used a logically based scheme for router passwords, your entire network is now open to the will of the intruder.

Physical security deals with restricting physical access to equipment. Locking equipment-room doors, requiring employee badges, and moving routers to their own secure room is the basis for physical security.

Although you cannot prevent people who are authorized to enter the room with the router from rebooting and changing the password, you can limit what they are able to accomplish by merely connecting into the console port or by using Telnet to access the router.

One good method of preventing casual hackers from gaining access to the console port is to physically disconnect the console port from the router's motherboard. This requires the router case to be opened. This is really the equivalent of hiding a door key under the doormat; it will not stop any but the most casual hacker. Anyone opening the case to the router will quickly see that the console port is disconnected. However, this method is better than not securing the console port in any way. Chapter 9, "Cisco Secure Access Control Server (ACS)," deals with how to use AAA to ensure that console port access is truly secure.

Another method is to change the connection properties to an unusual value. This will require someone who is casually trying to connect to the console port to set something other than the defaults. At this point, it becomes a guessing game for the hacker.

Although neither of these methods is foolproof, they do provide some additional security. The only true method of preventing someone from accessing the router through the console port is to physically lock the router in a room where no unauthorized personnel have access.

Controlling Line Access

Line access can easily be controlled on a Cisco router. Lines—consisting of console ports, auxiliary ports, and Telnet ports—all have the ability to limit the users who can gain access.

Adding an access list to the vty (Telnet) ports is relatively easy. First, a standard access list (numbered 1–99) is defined as follows:

```
access-list 8 permit 172.30.1.45
access-list 8 permit 10.1.1.53
access-list 8 deny any
```

This access list allows only hosts with one of two IP addresses to Telnet into the router. After creating the access list above, you still need to apply that access list to an interface. Applying an access list to a line uses the **access-class** command instead of the **access-group** command that is commonly used at the interface level. When applying the access list to the Telnet ports, use the following commands:

```
line vty 0 4
access-class 8 in
```

An access list can also be applied to one of the lines to limit where a connected user can Telnet. Using a standard access list and applying it to the outbound interface will limit Telnet sessions. An example follows:

```
access-list 9 permit 172.30.1.45
access-list 9 permit 10.1.1.53
access-list 9 deny any

line vty 0 4
access-class 9 out
```

In this case, the user can Telnet to only one of the two listed IP addresses. This might seem like a useless command set at first, because an administrator can simply remove this access list. However, depending on which level of authentication the administrator logged on with, he or she might not have the ability to configure the router. In the earlier section regarding the **enable secret** command, you learned that a privilege level could have an associated password. Every secret level can have its own password, and the administrator has the ability to limit functionality of each level. The **privilege exec** command is used to do this. Assume that you want to limit a new junior administrator to be able to use only the **show** commands. This can be accomplished with the following lines:

```
enable secret level 6 110%gdfsfej
privilege exec 6 show
```

In the preceding example, logging on with the level 6 password allows the user to access only the **show** commands. Limiting which administrators know passwords allows you to control how much access the administrators have.

Unfortunately, because the console and auxiliary ports are directly connected to the router, it is impossible to add an access list to these interfaces. Other configuration options are available, such as TACACS+ and RADIUS authentication. Both of these techniques are covered in Chapter 9. However, limiting the ability to administer the router through the use of enable levels, as shown in this section, helps to control the amount of damage an inexperienced administrator can cause.

On all of the line interfaces, you should specifically set a timeout parameter. If there is no activity on the line for a period of time, which is specified in minutes and seconds, the connection will automatically disconnect. This makes it harder for a terminal that has been left unlocked to become a security breach. You can set a timeout parameter for 5 minutes and 0 seconds with the following command:

```
exec-timeout 5 0
```

Out-of-Band Management Security

Out-of-band security can pose unique problems for the administrator. By definition, out-of-band access bypasses all of the security measures that are put into place throughout the network. Out-of-band management is the ability to configure a piece of equipment by a means other than the transmission media used for transferring data. For example, if a remote site used Frame Relay for connectivity, using an ISDN dial-up or modem connection for management purposes is considered out-of-band. The easiest way to avoid all out-of-band security issues is simply not to allow any out-of-band access. In most cases, however, there are legitimate reasons to allow such access. The primary reason is to enable troubleshooting and repairs from a remote location when the primary link fails.

When using out-of-band connections, be especially aware that there is usually only a single line of defense between the outside world and the interior of your network. Because out-of-band management usually bypasses firewalls, perimeter routers, and other security measures, extra precautions must be employed to ensure that the out-of-band management connections do not present a new opportunity for security breaches.

If at all possible, combine all available methods of access limitation, logging, and authentication on out-of-band access points. Out-of-band telephone numbers should be guarded in a similar fashion as passwords. If it is possible to limit access to predefined telephone numbers and to use a callback method of authentication, you should do so.

One possible way of remotely managing equipment combines out-of-band management with existing equipment. For instance, assume that administrators need to access equipment on the local network from their homes. In this case, using an existing access server to connect to the local network and then using Telnet to connect to the equipment in question combines both in-band and out-of-band management. The advantage of this method is that the entry points to the network are concentrated, presenting a smaller opportunity for security breaches, and that the strongest security methods including call back and AAA services may be applied at this entry point. When feasible, using a combination of services as described in this paragraph increases security and lessens the routine maintenance required.

See the section "Physical Security" earlier in this chapter for specifics on configuring access lists and other security methods so that interfaces can be set in the most secure manner.

Cisco Discovery Protocol (CDP)

Cisco Discovery Protocol (CDP) uses Layer 2 inquiries to find information about neighboring devices. CDP, enabled by default on IOS versions 11 and later, is extremely useful for both managing and troubleshooting devices. However, CDP has an inherent flaw: it will answer any device that sends the proper request. Because CDP information contains such items as the IOS version number, the name of the device, the network address of the device, and how that device is connected, the administrator should limit on which interfaces CDP packets are answered and sent.

If CDP is not being used internally on the network, it can be disabled with the following global command:

```
no cdp run
```

If CDP is required on the interior of the network, the administrator should still disable CDP on all external interfaces. To disable CDP on any given interface, enter the following interface command:

```
no cdp enable
```

Hypertext Transfer Protocol (HTTP) Configuration Services

Many Cisco devices allow the use of a Web browser for configuration and monitoring. Although this method of configuration might be convenient, especially for the new administrator, special considerations are required to ensure security. HTTP services are also used on the Cisco 1003, 1004, and 1005 routers for use with the Cisco IOS ClickStart software.

Access lists must be used on perimeter routers to limit who can access a router from outside of the local network. If HTTP services are used, you need to adjust access lists to allow only specific IP addresses access to routers through WWW services.

HTTP services are turned on with the **ip http server** command. Use the **no** form of the command to disable this service. HTTP services run by default on TCP port 80; this can be changed to virtually any port required. It is recommended that you change the default port. Changing from the default port of 80 requires a hacker to know which port is in use before being able to exploit any possible security holes.

Control over who accesses the HTTP services is managed by a standard access list, as well as by the **ip http access-class** command. Note that unlike other **access-class** commands, the **ip http access-class** command is entered in the global configuration mode. Additional security can be achieved through AAA authentication, which is covered in Chapter 10. If AAA authentication is not used, the **enable password** is used for logging onto the router.

The following is an example of setting HTTP services on a router, creating and applying an access list, and adding AAA authentication. Note that all commands are entered in the global configuration mode. Also note that the use of an exclamation mark (!) at the beginning of a line indicates that the line is a comment.

```
ip http server
!Starts HTTP services on the router.
!Services can be stopped with the no ip http services command.

ip http port 10120
!This changes the port used for management from port 80 to port 10120.
!Port 10120 was an arbitrary number chosen because it is not commonly used.
!To change the port back to 80, use the no ip http port command.

access-list 91 permit host 10.1.1.50
!Allow host 10.1.1.50 access.
access-list 91 permit host 10.1.1.52
!Allow host 10.1.1.52 access.
access-list 91 deny any any
!Deny all others. This line is included for clarity.
!All access lists have an implied deny all at the end.

ip http access-class 91
!Apply access list 91 to HTTP services.

ip http authentication aaa tacacs
!Use TACACS for authentication.
```

Simple Network Management Protocol (SNMP)

Simple Network Management Protocol (SNMP) is used by a variety of programs involved with network management. The beauty of SNMP is intertwined with its dangers. Because SNMP is designed to allow an administrator to monitor and configure devices remotely, SNMP can also be used in attempts to penetrate the corporate network. This section explores how to minimize vulnerability while using SNMP.

A few simple configuration changes, as well as a few logical choices that should be made by the administrator, can greatly reduce the risks involved with SNMP. Both logical choices and configuration considerations are covered in this section.

The first consideration an administrator should make regarding SNMP is to turn it off. If SNMP is not being used, running it only takes away from available bandwidth, needlessly burns CPU cycles, and exposes the network to unnecessary vulnerabilities.

Before using SNMP in read/write mode, rethink the requirement to do so. Running SNMP in read/write mode with just a few minor configuration errors can leave the whole of your network susceptible to attacks. A great number of tools can scan any network over SNMP. These can map out your entire network if SNMP has a hole left open.

In late February of 2001, Cisco released information that there are also security issues with SNMP even when using only the read mode. Due to a defect within the Cisco IOS versions 11.0 and 12.0, SNMP is vulnerable to certain denial of service attacks designed to confuse products such as CiscoWorks. In order to fix these potential security problems, an IOS upgrade must be accomplished. If you have not upgraded your IOS since this time, it is strongly recommended that you read the information at the following two URLs to see if your specific equipment is affected:

```
www.cisco.com/warp/public/707/ios-snmp-ilmi-vuln-pub.shtml
```

```
www.cisco.com/warp/public/707/ios-snmp-community-vulns-pub.shtml
```

SNMP is available in versions 1, 2, and 3. There are some major differences between versions. First, version 1 sends passwords in clear-text format, and version 2 allows password encryption using the MD5 encryption algorithms. Second, although virtually all management programs can use SNMP version 1, the choice is limited when using SNMP version 2. One of the original goals of version 2 was to provide commercial-grade security through authentication, privacy, and authorization. Version 2 failed to accomplish these goals because version 2c, while having the endorsement of the Internet Engineering Task Force (IETF), failed to implement these security measures. Versions 2u and 2* implemented security but failed to gain acceptance from the IETF.

Version 3, available on the standard Cisco IOS since release 12.0(3)T, uses MD5, Secure Hash Algorithm (SHA), and keyed algorithms to protect against data modification and masquerade attacks. Version 3 can optionally use Data Encryption Standard (DES) in the cipher block chaining mode when security is required.

From a security viewpoint, the passing of clear-text passwords should become a primary concern, especially because most SNMP applications send passwords repeatedly during normal operations. If your management software and equipment is compatible with version 2, there is no reason to run version 1. Assuming that the network in question is using only SNMP version 2, the administrator can ensure encryption by using the following command:

```
snmp-server enable traps snmp authentication md5
```

This command replaces the older and no longer valid command:

```
snmp-server trap-authentication
```

Unless you are purposely using SNMP version 1, the following command must be avoided at all costs:

```
snmp-server communityname
```

This command not only sets the community name, but also enables SNMP version 1 instead of version 2.

If version 1 is running, pay close attention to the name of the community. Because the community name is passed in clear text, this name should give no indication of either the company name or the type of company associated with the name. For example, assume that the company in question is Cisco Systems. Using the word "*cisco*" in any part of the community name might alert hackers that they have gained access to Cisco Systems. Using a community name "*routers*" might also give hackers unnecessary information. When using SNMP version 1, Cisco suggests that all equipment use differing community names. Although this might seem like an unreasonable restriction in a large network, using multiple community names will reduce the number of routers that are vulnerable because of the revealing of a single community name. If it is not possible to assign a different community name for all devices, find a balance between using a single community name and using a differing name on each piece of equipment. Finally, avoid using the names "*public*" or "*private*," because they are so commonly used.

Most networks have a few select management stations from which SNMP messages can legitimately originate. When using version 1 and the community name command, it is recommended that the optional access list number be included. This allows the administrator to control which stations have access, through a standard access list (numbered 1–99) applied to the SNMP services as if SNMP were an inbound router port.

Access control lists (ACLs) should be placed close to the edge of your network, preventing outside parties from probing your network over SNMP. Additionally, if the CPU cycles are available on interior routers, it might be worth the effort to add ACLs on certain routers in the interior of the network. This allows for the limitation of breaches, if they do occur.

If you are using SNMP in read-only mode, you need to ensure that it is set up with appropriate access controls. An example of proper protection follows:

```
access-list 7 permit 172.30.1.45
access-list 7 permit 10.1.1.53

snmp-server community 85tres76n RO 7
snmp-server trap-source Loopback0
snmp-server trap-authentication
snmp-server enable traps config
snmp-server enable traps envmon

snmp-server contact Joe Admin [jadmin@hotmail.com]
snmp-server location main server room router 8
snmp-server enable traps bgp
snmp-server enable traps frame-relay
snmp-server host 172.30.1.45 85tres76n
snmp-server host 10.1.1.53 85tres76n
snmp-server tftp-server-list 7
```

The preceding example uses ACL 7 and allows SNMP messages from only two IP addresses to be accepted. Because there are only two possible SNMP servers (172.30.1.45 and 10.1.1.53), these are the only IP addresses where SNMP is allowed to respond. SNMP messages from all other IP addresses would be implicitly denied.

Because the community string is not encrypted, care is taken to use "85tres76n," which has no known relation to the company or the services that the company offers. Once a community string is known outside of the organization, a point of possible attack is created. Unless SNMP is set up to pass community-name authentication failure traps, and the SNMP management device is configured to react to the authentication failure trap, the community name is easily discovered.

Keep in mind that accepting SNMP from only known good IP addresses does not necessarily guarantee security because of IP address spoofing. Unless serious antispoofing measures are in place, you cannot rely on IP addresses as the primary means of security on any system. With all security configurations, the objective of the administrator should be to build many obstacles to unauthorized personnel while providing seamless operation to authorized users.

Notice that even the e-mail address of the administrator is not a company e-mail address. This is done in case the SNMP does become violated. If the SNMP system is violated, this information could give clues about the company name to the violator.

The **snmp-server host** configuration shown in the preceding example lists the hosts to which SNMP information can be sent. If a means of collecting SNMP traps is not available, don't configure **snmp-server hosts**. When using an SNMP server host, make sure that this host is configured to receive and respond to SNMP traps. Read/write community strings should not be used on networks in order to limit the risk of SNMP sets being used by unauthorized parties.

Network Time Protocol (NTP)

The Network Time Protocol (NTP) allows for time synchronization of equipment on the network. As commonly used, one router is set as the master to which other devices look for the current time. If the current time is different than the time received from the master time device, the time is adjusted accordingly. The master device also looks at a known time source. This time source may be a local device, a radio device connected locally, or a publicly available device on the Internet. Cisco's implementation of NTP allows for the delay that the packet carrying the current time experiences while crossing the Internet. By having all the devices synchronized to one clock, understanding an outage on a network is easier. By examining logs that have been time-stamped by one common time, the order in which events occurred can be determined, and the outage thus isolated to the proper culprit.

A device that uses radio to get the current time is the safest from a network security perspective. This is illustrated in Figure 2-6. Using this method, no NTP services are expected or accepted over the Internet.

Figure 2-6 *Using NTP Through a Radio Device*

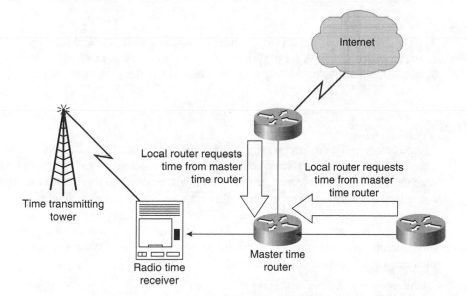

If the router gets NTP times from an Internet source, as shown in Figure 2-7, you need to open up your network to the Internet for this protocol. This is an accepted method because NTP does not usually pose a large threat to most networks. However, some precautions should be taken. When you are using NTP services, use MD5 hashing to authenticate the issuer of the NTP packets. When you are not using NTP, specifically turn NTP off with the following interface command:

```
no ntp enable
```

Figure 2-7 *Using NTP Through a Network Device*

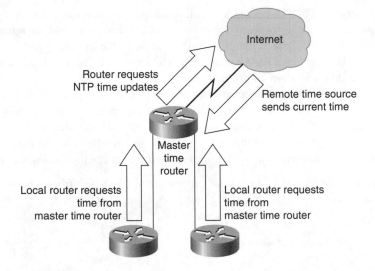

You should recommend that a single router be used to gain the current time and that internal routers look to this master for the time. This not only is the way in which NTP was designed to be used, but also exposes only a single router to any threat through NTP.

Banners

Cisco routers have two different types of banners: login and EXEC. Both of these banners should be enabled with a stern warning that all access attempts are logged, and unauthorized attempts to penetrate the system will be prosecuted to the fullest extent of the law. Placing a warning about logging all attempts at access is the equivalent of placing a home security system placard on your front lawn. Even if you do not log access, it might discourage some attempts. The name of the company, the IP address, or any other information that unnecessarily reveals information about your system should not be included on the banner. A sample banner is as follows:

```
This equipment is privately owned.
All access to this equipment is logged.
Disconnect immediately if you are not an authorized user.
Violators will be prosecuted to the fullest extent of the law.
Contact jadmin@hotmail.com
```

As with most other security settings, this banner has purposefully avoided giving any information, including using an e-mail address that will disclose no more information than absolutely necessary.

Recommended Minimum IOS Security Settings

This section deals with the basic minimum configurations that all enterprises should employ on their routers. Although some of the commands explained in this section are disabled by default, the administrator is urged to deny specifically those services and routes that are not needed. The following topics are covered:

- Denying RFC 1918 routes
- UDP and TCP servers
- Finger service
- IP unreachables
- ICMP Redirect messages
- Directed broadcasts
- Proxy Address Resolution Protocol (ARP)
- IP Unicast
- IP source routing

Denying RFC 1918 Routes

All border routers within a company that is concerned with security should have some specific routes denied. RFC 1918 defines the ranges of IP addresses available for use on the Internet, as well as those considered private. A private IP address should not be used on the Internet. The source or destination addresses of all packets on the Internet should not be within these private ranges. Common attack methods rely on private addresses to hide the true source of the attack. This section shows a typical method of blocking access from these forms of attack. With the exception of Network Address Translation (NAT), no one from the Internet or from within your own network should be sending packets from any of the addresses in the following list. The following is a sample ACL that will be applied to routing updates to prohibit the private address spaces as defined by RFC 1918:

```
access-list 191 deny ip host 0.0.0.0 any
!This prevents packets with a source address of 0.0.0.0
!from traversing the network
access-list 191 deny ip any host 0.0.0.0
access-list 191 deny ip 10.0.0.0 0.255.255.255 any
!10.0.0.0 through 10.255.255.255 is a non-routable address range
!and should not traverse the network from the Internet.
access-list 191 deny ip 127.0.0.0 0.255.255.255 any
!127.0.0.0 through 127.255.255.255 addresses are used for loopback testing
!and should never traverse the Internet.
access-list 191 deny ip 169.254.0.0 0.0.255.255 any
!169.254.0.0 is reserved by Microsoft as the address given to a host
!unsuccessfully attempting to use DHCP services.
access-list 191 deny ip 172.16.0.0 0.15.255.255 any
!172.16.0.0 through 172.31.255.255 are non-routable addresses.
```

```
access-list 191 deny ip 192.168.0.0 0.0.255.255 any
!192.168.0.0 through 192.168.255.255 are non-routable addresses
!and should never be traveling over the Internet.
access-list 191 deny ip 224.0.0.0 31.255.255.255 224.0.0.0 31.255.255.255
!224.0.0.0 through 255.255.255.255 as a source address is invalid
!because these are reserved for multicast broadcasts.
!Here, you are stopping these packets from traversing the network if the
!destination is a multicast and the source is a multicast.
!A correctly formed multicast packet will have a valid source address
!with a multicast destination address between 224.0.0.0 and 255.255.255.255.
access-list 191 deny ip any 255.255.255.0 0.0.0.255
!Packets should not be sent to the 255.255.255.0 network,
!because this is a reserved network.
access-list 191 permit ip any any
!You need to allow traffic that is not specifically blocked
!through the router.
deny any any
!The deny any any line is shown for clarity.
!This line is implied by all access lists.
!Any packets that are not specifically allowed are denied.
```

This access list should be applied to both the inbound and outbound interfaces of border routers. If you are running NAT services, some of these interfaces will not necessarily apply. For example, if you are using the 10.0.0.0 network inside your organization, you will need to allow this network to travel to the device providing NAT services. Additionally, on the inbound interface of all border routers, the internal network addresses should be specifically denied. The preceding list is a minimum list that is designed to prevent commonly spoofed IP addresses from being allowed to traverse your network. If other routes are known to be invalid, they should also be prohibited. Besides specifically preventing packets with a source address matching your internal network from entering through the Internet, administrators should consider ways in which they can prohibit unauthorized external network addresses from traversing to the outside of the network. This will help prevent someone from using the network to launch an attack on a third party.

As with all access lists, these might cause excessive CPU usage on routers. However, the additional CPU usage is usually justified by the added security provided by the access lists. If your router is unable to effectively function with the preceding access lists, chances are that the router is already overworked and should be upgraded.

User Datagram Protocol (UDP) and Transmission Control Protocol (TCP) Servers

The User Datagram Protocol (UDP) and Transmission Control Protocol (TCP) servers are generally those with port numbers below 10. These typically include echo ports and discard ports. Echo ports replay the packet (echo) out of the port received. Discard throws away the packet. Because either throwing away or echoing packets consumes CPU cycles, they are commonly used in denial of service (DoS) attacks. When too many packets requesting echoes overload a router, for example, the router must delay other processes. This delay can cause problems, such as an inability to process routing updates. Therefore, both of these should be disabled unless there is a specific reason to run them. This is especially important on the router directly connected to the Internet. These can be disabled as follows:

```
no service-udp-small-servers
no service-tcp-small-servers
```

Finger Service

The finger service can be used to resolve usernames on remote systems. Specifically, finger was designed to show active users on a system. Although the prevalence of finger has been reduced in the last few years, several administrators still allow finger requests to traverse their networks. Because of the many known ways that finger can be abused, no router should ever run finger unless there is a very specific reason to do so. An administrator can (and should) stop finger services with the following command:

```
no service finger
```

IP Unreachables

By default, when a router receives a nonbroadcast packet with an unrecognized protocol whose destination address belongs to that router, it will send an Internet Control Message Protocol (ICMP) Protocol Unreachable message back toward the source. A router will also send back an ICMP Host Unreachable message if it receives a packet whose destination address is not known. This is illustrated in Figure 2-8.

Figure 2-8   *ICMP Host Unreachable*

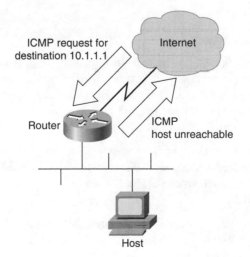

Although this behavior might seem reasonable, it also opens the router to vulnerability from ICMP DoS attacks. If a router spends all of its time responding to ICMP messages, something else is not being processed. Additionally, disabling ICMP unreachables might help out the innocent victim of a DoS attack.

A DoS attack can occur in many ways. Here is just one scenario: When sending an ICMP echo request, the perpetrator changes the originating IP address on the packet to a legitimate IP address of the victim. The perpetrator sends numerous ICMP requests to the network broadcast address of the bystander. The bystander, who is unaware of what is occurring, responds to these ICMP requests. The response is sent to the IP address within the original request. If the source address is valid, some router will start receiving these responses. Take a moment to look at Figure 2-9.

In this case, the ICMP requests were sent to the broadcast network address on the bystander's network. Each host on the network received the request and responded. This means that the bystander amplified the power of the effectiveness of the requests by the number of hosts responding. Very quickly, the bystander's available bandwidth will be used by ICMP messages. The victim's bandwidth will also be used by these ICMP messages. In effect, both the victim and the bystander lose all effective communication capabilities. It becomes very hard to tell exactly who the intended victim is in this case. If the perpetrator sends out requests to more than one bystander at a time, the effect can be devastating to the victim.

It is recommended that all external interfaces be configured not to respond in this manner. Preventing a router from sending out ICMP Host and Protocol Unreachable messages is easily accomplished with the following interface command:

```
no ip unreachable
```

ICMP Redirect Messages

Under certain circumstances, routes might not be optimal. Although most of these cases can be prevented by proper configuration, it is usually prudent for the administrator to ensure that routers do not send packets out the same interface over which they have been received. When a packet is sent back out the interface on which it was received, an ICMP Redirect message is also sent. This is illustrated in Figure 2-10.

The ICMP Redirect message tells the sender of the original packet to remove the route and substitute a specified device that has a more direct route. This feature is enabled by default, but it becomes disabled when the Hot Standby Router Protocol (HSRP) is in use on the particular interface.

Because you should be concerned about any ICMP messages leaving your network, you should manually disable this feature. Instead of using your bandwidth to inform other, usually unknown routers where a network exists, you should reserve your bandwidth for your own purposes. This is especially important on external interfaces where large amounts of these ICMP messages might be a form of DoS attack. Figure 2-10 gives an example of how ICMP Redirect works. To manually disable this behavior, use the following interface command:

```
no ip redirects
```

Figure 2-9   *ICMP Redirect Affects Both Bystander and Victim*

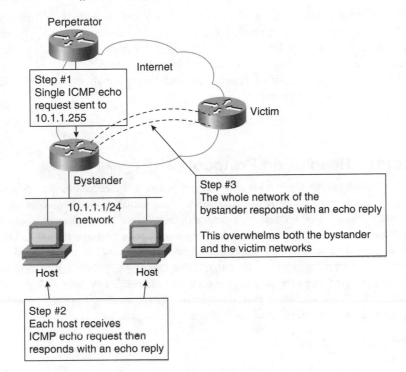

Figure 2-10   *ICMP Redirect DoS Attack*

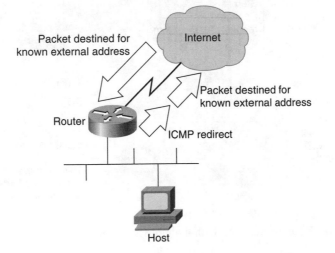

Directed Broadcasts

It is possible within the IP protocols to send a *directed broadcast,* which is when a packet that is received contains a request to translate the broadcast packet to another interface on the device, usually the LAN interface. If this is left enabled, the LAN might experience excessive broadcasts from a DoS attack. The default on IOS 12.0 and later is to have directed broadcasts disabled. However, the administrator should still specifically disable it with the following command:

```
no ip directed-broadcast
```

Proxy Address Resolution Protocol (ARP)

Proxy Address Resolution Protocol (ARP) is a system where one device answers an ARP request destined for another device if that MAC address is known. When a proxy ARP device sees an ARP request for a device on a different known Layer 3 network, the proxy ARP device will reply to the ARP and forward the request to the remote LAN segment. This is usually done so that ARP requests will not have to travel over a relatively slow link. The problem with using proxy ARP is that it can expose the network to potential security problems. One way of exploiting the security hole caused by proxy ARP is to launch a DoS attack that uses bandwidth and router resources responding to repeated ARP requests. Figure 2-11 illustrates this attack.

Figure 2-11 *Proxy ARP DoS Attack*

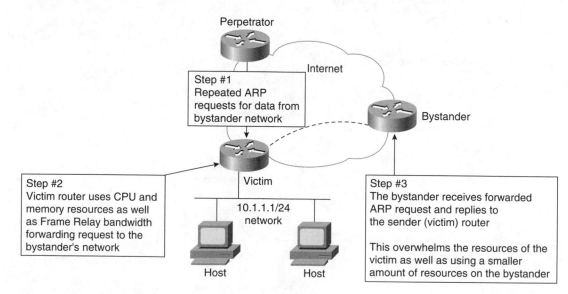

Proxy ARP can be disabled with the global command:

```
no ip proxy-arp
```

IP Verify

The **ip verify unicast reverse-path** command is useful in preventing address-spoofing attacks on systems running Cisco Express Forwarding (CEF) and IOS version 12.0 and higher. While running CEF with this interface level command, all packets are evaluated for the source address. If the source IP address does not have a CEF route in the table corresponding to the interface on which the packet was received, that packet is dropped. The result of this configuration is that attacks depending on address spoofing and received on an interface other than the expected interface are automatically dropped. Because most IP spoofing packets do not come over the expected interface (or subinterface), another layer of protection is added.

CEF must be turned on for the router. However, there is no requirement that CEF must be turned on for the specific interface or subinterface where the filtering is used. The following will start packet filtering on an interface:

```
ip verify unicast reverse-path
```

IP Source Routing

The Cisco IOS is designed to examine the options within the header of every IP packet. According to RFC 791, these options can include Loose Source Route, Record Route, or Time Stamp. When the IOS receives a packet with one of these options enabled, it responds appropriately. If the packet contains an invalid option, the router sends an ICMP parameter problem message to the source and discards the packet. If the packet contains the source route option, it is interpreted to mean that the packet is requesting a specific route through the network. Although the default is to use source routing, ISPs usually do not want the customer deciding how to route through the network. Also, IP source routing has a number of known security problems. The main security problem is that a remote entity controls where data travels, meaning that it is possible for data to travel through a hacker's network before going on to its ultimate destination. The hacker is able to record all data intended for another network. Figure 2-12 shows an example.

IP source routing can be disabled with the following command:

```
no ip source-route
```

Figure 2-12 *IP Source Routing Vulnerability*

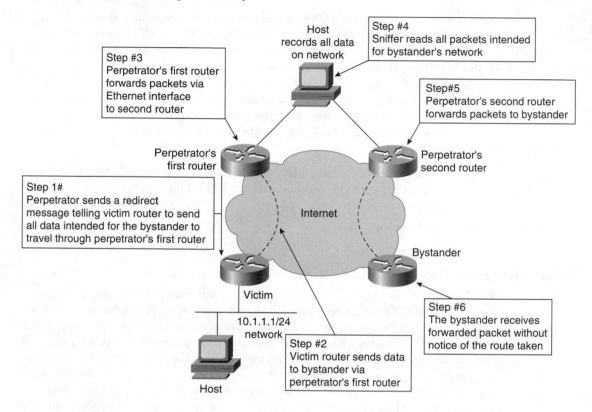

TCP Intercept

TCP Intercept tracks, intercepts, and validates TCP connection requests. This shields the local host from being contacted directly by a nontrusted network or host. Therefore, any DoS attacks attempted on the host are actually carried out against the router, which will be prepared to survive such attacks. TCP Intercept uses fast switching, except on the RS/RP/SSP-based Cisco 7000 series, which only uses process switching.

TCP Intercept operates in one of two modes, monitor mode and intercept mode. Monitor mode allows connections directly to the local host while monitoring the status of these connections. The router, because of the number of open connections or timeout limitations, drops existing and partially opened connections as needed to protect the local host. Intercept mode is used to protect the local host from all direct contact with the remote host. The router, acting in a manner similar to that of a proxy server, responds to requests from the remote host. The router then establishes its own connection with the local host and merges the connections between the two hosts. Figure 2-13 shows a router acting in intercept mode.

Figure 2-13 *IP TCP Intercept*

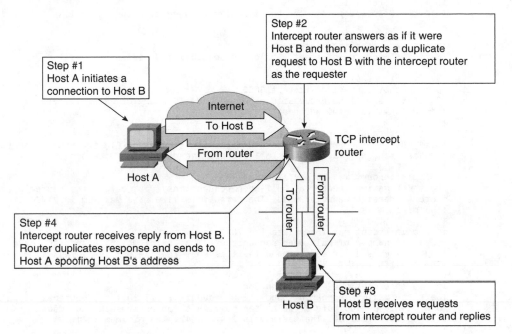

Exceeding preset thresholds in either mode causes aggressive behavior mode to start. Dropping back below another set of thresholds causes the router to move back to normal. During aggressive behavior mode, new connection attempts force a drop of an existing partial connection. Additionally, the retransmission and watch timeouts are cut in half.

TCP Intercept is relatively easy to configure by a five-step process:

Step 1 Create an intercept access list.

Step 2 Enable TCP Intercept.

Step 3 Set intercept mode.

Step 4 Set thresholds.

Step 5 Set drop mode.

The following example configuration shows how to accomplish all of these tasks and gives comments on parameters available:

```
!Create an extended access list.
!TCP Intercept access lists must be extended access lists (101-199).
access-list 101 permit 172.30.1.15 255.255.255.255 host 10.1.1.1
!Allow access from the single host at 172.30.1.15 to the single host at 10.1.1.1.
access-list 101 permit 172.30.2.0 255.255.255.0 host 10.1.1.2
!Allow any host on the 172.30.2.0 network to get to host 10.1.1.2.
!
```

```
!Enable TCP Intercept.
ip tcp intercept list 101
!Starts IP Intercept for the hosts listed as permitted in access list 101.
!
!Set the intercept mode.
ip tcp intercept mode intercept
!Sets the mode to intercept. The other possible mode is watch.
!
!Set the thresholds.
ip intercept connection-timeout 3600
!Connections will be reset after 3600 seconds (1 hour) of no activity.
!The default is 86400 seconds (24 hours).
!
ip tcp intercept finrst-timeout 3
!Sets the time in seconds (3) after receiving a reset or FIN that the connection
!remains managed. The minimum is 1 second. The default is 5 seconds.
!
ip tcp intercept max-incomplete high 900
!Sets the maximum number of half-open connections (900) before the router goes
!into aggressive behavior mode. The default is 1100. The maximum is 2147483647.
!The minimum is 1.
!
ip tcp intercept max-incomplete low 700
!Sets the number of half-open connections (700) below which the router leaves
!aggressive behavior mode. The default is 900. The maximum is 2147483647.
!The minimum is 1.
!
ip tcp intercept one-minute high 800
!Sets the maximum number of connection requests (800) that may be received in a
!one-minute period before the router goes into aggressive behavior mode.
!The default is 1100. The maximum is 2147483647. The minimum is 1.
!
ip tcp intercept one-minute low 600
!Sets the number of connection requests (600) that may be received in a
!one-minute period below which the router leaves aggressive behavior mode.
!The default is 900. The maximum is 2147483647. The minimum is 1.
!
ip tcp intercept watch-timeout 20
!Sets the time in seconds (20) for a partially opened connection to complete
!the connection sequence before sending a reset command to the local host.
!
!Set the drop mode.
ip tcp intercept drop-mode random
!Sets the drop mode (random) to randomly choose which half-open connection
!while in aggressive behavior mode. The default (oldest) will drop the oldest
!partial connection first.
```

Summary

This chapter explores the basic configurations and practices that will help prevent the most obvious forms of attack from affecting your network. There are some very specific commands that most, if not all, administrators should employ, at least on their external routers.

No book can possibly tell you exactly how your routers should be configured. If there were, we would all be out of jobs. Every network is different and requires configurations that reflect the organization's unique goals and needs. Use this chapter as a guideline for the options available while setting up your routers. Some of the items discussed should be set on every router, no matter what the circumstances of your particular network. The configuration on other items will depend on the individual variations within networks and what you are trying to accomplish. Knowing the options that are available and how they operate can help administrators protect their networks from most intrusions.

A recurring theme is presented in this chapter that should be carefully considered while configuring routers: If a service is not needed, it should not be run. If a service is needed only on the internal network, do not run it on the external network. This is especially true of ICMP services. Restricting how ICMP messages are handled might protect not only your own network, but also some other administrator's network.

To give a concise overview of the salient configurations explored in this chapter, the following sections show sample configurations that incorporate all of the suggested settings. Remember that some of these commands might not be viable on your routers because of internally used IP addresses and special circumstances within your network. However, they will still serve as a guideline for your configurations. Review the following configurations before moving on to Chapter 3, "Overview of the Cisco Security Solution and the Cisco Secure Product Family."

Global Commands

```
no enable password
!prevents the older non-secure enable password from being used

enable secret level 7 9%ad100gbellisnon
!uses a secret password that follows the rules for passwords

service router-encryption
!encrypts the passwords

no cdp enable
!prevents CDP from sending information

access-list 7 permit 172.30.1.45
access-list 7 permit 10.1.1.53
!sets up access list 7 for use with SNMP

access-list 8 permit 172.30.1.45
access-list 8 permit 10.1.1.53
access-list 8 deny any
!sets up access list 8 for use with telnet on vty 0 through 4

snmp-server community 85tres76n RO 7
!sets the version 1 community name (use version 2 if possible)

snmp-server trap-source Loopback0
snmp-server trap-authentication
snmp-server enable traps config
snmp-server enable traps envmon
snmp-server enable traps bgp
snmp-server enable traps frame-relay
!sets the SNMP traps

snmp-server contact Joe Admin [jadmin@hotmail.com]
snmp-server location main server room router 8
!sets the contact information following the password rules
```

```
snmp-server host 172.30.1.45 85tres76n
snmp-server host 10.1.1.53 85tres76n
!sets what servers may request SNMP information

snmp-server tftp-server-list 7
!sets a valid SNMP TFTP server

no ntp enable
!stops unneeded NTP services

no service finger
!stops finger service

no service pad
!old command dealing with x.25

no service udp-small-servers
no service tcp-small-servers
!stops the small server services

no ip directed-broadcast
!stops directed broadcasts

no ip proxy-arp
!prevents answering ARP requests in proxy mode for another device

no ip source-route
!prevents outside entities from directing the routes a packet takes
```

Interface Commands

```
!apply to both inside and outside interfaces

no ip redirects
!do not send packets out the same interface they came in on

no ip unreachable
!do not respond with host unreachable messages

access-list 191 deny ip host 0.0.0.0 any
access-list 191 deny ip 10.0.0.0 0.255.255.255 255.0.0.0 0.255.255.255
access-list 191 deny ip 127.0.0.0 0.255.255.255 255.0.0.0 0.255.255.255
access-list 191 deny ip 169.254.0.0 0.0.255.255 255.255.0.0 0.0.255.255
access-list 191 deny ip 172.16.0.0 0.15.255.255 255.240.0.0 0.15.255.255
access-list 191 deny ip 192.0.2.0 0.0.0.255 255.255.255.0 0.0.0.255
access-list 191 deny ip 192.168.0.0 0.0.255.255 255.255.0.0 0.0.255.255
access-list 191 deny ip 224.0.0.0 31.255.255.255 224.0.0.0 31.255.255.255
access-list 191 deny ip any 255.255.255.128 0.0.0.127
access-list 191 permit ip any any
!do not route to any of the private networks
```

vty Commands

```
line vty 0 4
access-class 8 in
!sets access list 8 to limit Telnet access

exec-timeout 5 0
!automatically times out the Telnet connection after 5 minutes of no activity
```

PART II

Cisco Secure Product Family

732This chapter contains the following sections:

- Cisco Security Solution
- Cisco Secure Product Family
- Summary
- Frequently Asked Questions
- Glossary
- Bibliography
- URLs

CHAPTER 3

Overview of the Cisco Security Solution and the Cisco Secure Product Family

> The only system that is truly secure is one that is switched off and unplugged, locked in a titanium-lined safe, buried in a concrete bunker, and is surrounded by nerve gas and very highly paid armed guards. Even then, I wouldn't stake my life on it....
>
> —Gene Spafford, Purdue University

This statement is true. No matter what system you implement, you will never have a truly secure system. The best that network professionals can do is to implement a solution that is as secure as current technologies allow and then redesign when hackers find a new vulnerability. This method of prevention has been around since the first misuse of the Internet.

This chapter provides an explanation of the Cisco Security Solution and an overview of the Cisco Secure product range. The Security Solution is designed to ease the implementation of your security policy and introduce you to the idea of security as an ever-evolving requirement that needs constant monitoring and redesign.

Contained within this chapter is a brief overview of the functionality and role of each product in the Cisco Secure family. This overview can be used as a quick reference when designing the security approach for a Cisco network. As with any tool, a complete understanding of the tool's full capabilities, as well as any implementation issues, is of supreme importance in order to help you make a qualified design recommendation. Internet security is a very complicated field of study that requires constantly keeping one step ahead of prospective attackers. New security threats and loopholes appear all the time, and unscrupulous people capitalize on them. The Internet security designer faces a very tough task: to design the security around ever-changing criteria.

The Cisco Secure product range is covered in great detail in Chapters 4 through 9.

Cisco Security Solution

The Cisco Security Solution comprises five key elements. These elements enable a consistent approach to be administered that prevents unauthorized entry and protects valuable data and network resources from corruption and intrusion.

The key elements of the Cisco Security Solution are

- Identity
- Perimeter security
- Secure connectivity
- Security monitoring
- Security management

For more information on the Cisco Security Solution, see www.cisco.com/warp/public/cc/so/neso/sqso/index.shtml.

Identity

The first element of the Cisco Security Solution is identity. This element is concerned with the unique and positive identification of network users, application services, and resources. You want to ensure that any entity accessing your network, whether it is a remote user or software agent, is authorized to do so. Standard technologies that enable identification include authentication protocols such as Remote Access Dial-In User Service (RADIUS), Terminal Access Controller Access Control System Plus (TACACS+), and Kerberos. New identification technologies include digital certificates, smart cards, and directory services.

Identity through authentication has to take place at the network boundary before the user or service has access to the secured network. This protects the inside network from unauthenticated users or services.

The Cisco Secure product that provides the security function at the identity level is Cisco Secure Access Control Server (ACS). This product provides authentication, authorization, and accounting (AAA) of all users trying to access the secured network.

Perimeter Security

Perimeter security provides the means to secure access to critical network applications, data, and services so that only authenticated and authorized users and information can pass through the network. As the name indicates, this level of security is applied at the perimeter of the network, which can be thought of as the point of entry that untrustworthy connections would take. This could be the point between the corporate network and the ISP network or the point between the corporate network and the Public Switched Telephone Network (PSTN). An example of a perimeter is displayed in Figure 3-1. It can also be a point between two organizations within the corporation (such as the marketing and engineering departments.)

Security control is provided at the perimeter by access-limiting devices, commonly classified as *firewalls*. These devices can be Cisco routers with traffic-limiting access lists and basic firewall features or dedicated firewall solutions such as a Cisco Secure PIX (Private Internet Exchange) Firewall.

Figure 3-1 *Network Perimeter*

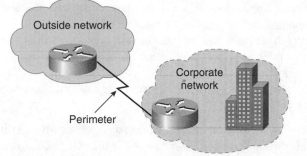

Other tools that assist at the perimeter security level are virus scanners and content filters.

Security at the network perimeter is discussed in detail in Chapter 10, "Securing the Corporate Network."

Secure Connectivity

When highly sensitive information is traversing your corporate network, it is very important to protect it from potential eavesdropping or sniffing of the network. You can achieve secure connectivity in three ways:

- The traffic can be isolated from the rest of the network by employing a tunneling protocol, such as generic route encapsulation (GRE) or Layer 2 Tunneling Protocol (L2TP).

- A simple way to increase data privacy is to implement Layer 2 switches to every client and server on the network. By design, a switch will only forward unicasts to the port on which the destination resides. Only broadcast traffic is flooded out on every port. Therefore, a network sniffer plugged into a switch would not automatically receive traffic that was not destined for the sniffer itself.

- If a more secure method is required, a VPN technology, such as Internet Protocol Security (IPSec), can be used to encrypt the data against a 128-bit digital signature.

Secure connectivity is discussed in detail in Chapter 10.

Security Monitoring

Security management, like network management, is a dynamic, ever-changing process. Once you have designed and implemented a security solution, it has to be measured. One way of measuring the integrity of your solution is with a network scanner, which will scan every live IP address on your network and check the results against well-known vulnerabilities. A full report is then created, and actions can be taken to remedy any shortcomings in the design or implementation. It's important to make the changes and then scan the network again to ensure that the changes have been effective and their implementation hasn't caused any further security vulnerabilities. The security vulnerability database for all leading network scanners is upgradable on a periodic basis, ensuring that most new vulnerability that is discovered is added to the database. When you run a network scan, you can be sure that you are scanning for the latest vulnerabilities. Cisco Secure Scanner is a full, network-scanning utility that can be used for regular security monitoring purposes.

In addition to network scanning, the other aspect of security monitoring is intrusion detection. Intrusion detection systems monitor the network and respond to potential threats in real time. *Shunning* is a term widely used in intrusion detection and describes the capability of the intrusion detection system to actively reject all packets from a specific source if the system suspects sinister activity. As with the security scanner, an intrusion detection system operates by checking internal network traffic against a database of known vulnerabilities. Both the IP header and the payload are checked against these known threats.

Cisco Secure Intrusion Detection System (IDS) is an intrusion detection system that can be used for real-time network security.

Security Management

Today's networks are constantly growing in size; with this growth comes the need for centralized security management. There are various security management tools available, one of which is the Cisco Secure Policy Manager. This tool enables the administrator to centrally administer the security policy and distribute policy changes to a number of Cisco PIX and Cisco IOS Firewall devices by automated command-line configurations without detailed command-line interface (CLI) knowledge.

Cisco Secure Policy Manager is explained in great depth in Chapter 8, "Cisco Secure Policy Manager."

Cisco Secure Product Family

To complement Cisco's leading presence in the internetworking device market, Cisco's range of security products has been built and recently amalgamated under the Cisco Secure product family title.

These products provide various security functions and features to enhance the service provided by the current range of routers and switches. Every product in the Cisco Secure product family has its place in the Cisco Security Solution as outlined previously and in Appendix A, "Cisco SAFE: A Security Blueprint for Enterprise Networks," confirming Cisco's stance and commitment to the preservation of network security.

This section provides a brief overview of the product range and explains the main features of each product.

The following products make up the Cisco Secure product family:

- Cisco Secure PIX Firewall
- Cisco IOS Firewall
- Cisco Secure Intrusion Detection System
- Cisco Secure Scanner
- Cisco Secure Policy Manager
- Cisco Secure Access Control System

Cisco Secure PIX Firewall

The Cisco Secure PIX Firewall is the dedicated hardware firewall in the Cisco Secure product family. The PIX Firewall is the industry leader in both market share and performance within the firewall market.

The Cisco PIX Firewall is built around a non-UNIX, secure, real-time, embedded operating system, which leads to excellent performance without comprising security. This high level of performance is the result of the hardware architecture of the PIX Firewall, compared with operating system-based firewalls.

The Cisco PIX Firewall encompasses the Internet Engineering Task Force (IETF) IPSec standard for secure private communications over the Internet or any IP network. This makes the Cisco Secure PIX Firewall an excellent and logical choice to terminate IPSec Virtual Private Network (VPN) traffic from IPSec-compliant network equipment.

Currently, there are four versions of the PIX Firewall:

- **PIX 506**—The PIX 506 is the entry-level firewall designed for high-end small office, home office (SOHO) installations. The throughput has been measured at 10 Mbps and reflects the market at which the product is aimed.

- **PIX 515**—The PIX 515 is the midrange firewall designed for the small or medium business and remote office deployments. It occupies only one rack unit and offers a throughput of up to 120 Mbps with a maximum of 125,000 concurrent sessions. The default configuration is two Fast Ethernet ports, and it is currently upgradable by two onboard PCI slots.

- **PIX 520**—The PIX 520 is the high-end firewall designed for enterprise and service provider use. The unit occupies three rack units and offers a throughput of up to 370 Mbps with a maximum of 250,000 concurrent sessions. The default configuration consists of two Fast Ethernet ports, and it is currently upgradable by four onboard PCI slots. The end-of-life date of 23 June 2001 has been announced for the PIX 520. The replacement for the PIX 520 is the PIX 525.

- **PIX 525**—The PIX 525 is intended for enterprise and service provider use. It has a throughput of 370 Mbps with the ability to handle as many as 280,000 simultaneous sessions. The 600 MHz CPU of the PIX 525 can enable it to deliver an additional 25–30% increase capacity for firewalling services.

- **PIX 535**—The Cisco Secure PIX 535 is the latest and largest addition to the PIX 500 series. Intended for enterprise and service provider use, it has a throughput of 1.0 Gbps with the ability to handle up to 500,000 concurrent connections. Supporting both site-to-site and remote access VPN applications via 56-bit DES or 168-bit 3DES, the integrated VPN functionality of the PIX 535 can be supplemented with a VPN Accelerator card to deliver 100 Mbps throughput and 2,000 IPSec tunnels

There is also a dedicated PIX Firewall VPN Accelerator Card (VAC) that can be used in the PIX 515, 520, 525, and 535 units. This card performs hardware acceleration of VPN traffic encryption/decryption providing 100 Mbps IPSec throughput using 168-Bit 3DES.

The PIX Firewall is configured using a command-line editor. The commands are similar to those used in the standard Cisco IOS, but they vary in whether they permit inbound and outbound traffic.

Further information on the Cisco Secure PIX Firewall can be found at www.cisco.com/go/pix.

Cisco IOS Firewall

The Cisco IOS Firewall is an IOS-based software upgrade for a specific range of compatible Cisco routers.

The Cisco IOS Firewall provides an extensive set of new CLI commands that integrate firewall and intrusion detection functionality into the IOS of the router. These added security features enhance the existing Cisco IOS security capabilities, such as authentication and encryption. These added security features also add new capabilities, such as defense against network attacks; per-user authentication and authorization; real-time alerts; and stateful, application-based filtering.

VPN support is provided with the Cisco IOS Firewall utilizing the IETF IPSec standard as well as other IOS-based technologies such as L2TP tunneling.

Cisco IOS Firewall also adds limited intrusion detection capabilities. Traffic is compared to 59 default intrusion detection signatures, and output can be directed to the Cisco Secure IDS Director.

Although performance of the Cisco IOS Firewall will never compete with that of the Cisco PIX Firewall, Cisco IOS Firewall still has a place in the portfolio of most modern organizations. There might be times when the full power and associated cost of a PIX

Firewall is not required because of the low throughput or an operational requirement. For example, a SOHO worker with a 64-kbps ISDN Internet connection is not going to be concerned about the reduction in throughput offered by using the Cisco IOS Firewall instead of the PIX Firewall.

The features available with Cisco IOS Firewall are configurable using the Cisco ConfigMaker software. This eases the administrative burden placed on the network professional, because a full understanding of the CLI commands is not required to configure the security features and deploy the configurations throughout the required devices.

More information on ConfigMaker can be found at www.cisco.com/go/configmaker.

Further information on the Cisco IOS Firewall can be found at www.cisco.com/go/firewall.

Cisco Secure Intrusion Detection System (IDS)

Intrusion detection is key in the overall security policy of an organization. Intrusion detection can be defined as detecting, reporting, and terminating unauthorized activity on the network.

The Cisco Secure Intrusion Detection System (IDS) (formerly NetRanger) is the dynamic security component of Cisco's end-to-end security product line. IDS is a real-time intrusion detection system designed for enterprise and service provider deployment. IDS detects, reports, and terminates unauthorized activity throughout the network.

Cisco Secure IDS consists of three major components:

- The Intrusion Detection Sensor
- The Intrusion Detection Director
- The Intrusion Detection Post Office

Intrusion Detection Sensor

The Intrusion Detection Sensor is a network "plug-and-play" device that interprets IP traffic into meaningful security events. These events are passed to the Intrusion Detection Director for analysis and any required further action.

The main features of the Intrusion Detection Sensor are

- **Network sensing**—The sensor captures packets on one of its interfaces, reassembles the packets, and compares the data received against a rule set that contains signatures of the common network intrusions. Both the packet header and packet data are examined against the rule set to catch the varying types of attacks.

- **Attack response**—If the sensor identifies an attack, the sensor will respond to the attack in the following user-configurable ways:
  - *Generate an alarm*—The sensor will generate an alarm and notify the Intrusion Detection Director immediately.
  - *Generate IP session logs*—A session log will be sent to the configurable log type and location. This session log will contain detailed information about the attack and will record the time of day along with any captured IP address information.
  - *Reset TCP connections after an attack begins*—The sensor can terminate individual TCP connections if it senses that they have been involved in an actual or attempted attack. All other connections go on as usual.
  - *Shun the attack*—The term shunning describes the sensor's ability to automatically reconfigure an access control list on a router, if the sensor detects suspicious activity. To implement shunning, the sensor changes the access control list on the device to block the attacker at the perimeter entry point to the network.
- **Device management**—If the sensor detects suspicious activity, it has the ability to dynamically reconfigure a networking device's access control lists to shun the source of an attack in real time.

Intrusion Detection Director

The Intrusion Detection Director is the software application that monitors and controls the behavior of the sensors. There is usually only one Intrusion Detection Director on any given network, and all sensors direct their alarms and notifications to it. The Intrusion Detection Director software currently supports only the Solaris platform.

The main functions of the Intrusion Detection Director are

- **Initial configuration of the Intrusion Detection Sensor**—Once the sensor has been configured on its own, the director will complete the configuration of the sensor and will start receiving alarms and notifications from it.
- **Intrusion Detection Sensor monitoring**—The sensors send real-time security information to the director, and the director is responsible for collating and representing this data graphically on the director console.
- **Intrusion Detection Sensor management**—The director can remotely manage the configuration of services on a sensor. This enables you to use the built-in embedded signatures or to create your own signatures to match the needs of your network.

- **Collection of the Intrusion Detection Sensor data**—Every sensor sends its data to the director. The Intrusion Detection Director ships with drivers for Oracle and Remedy, enabling the administrator to write the data to an external data source for storage.

- **Analysis of the Intrusion Detection Sensor data**—The Intrusion Detection Director software has a built-in set of SQL-compliant queries that can be run against data collected from the sensors. Many third-party tools can be integrated into the Intrusion Detection Director to provide more detailed analysis of the data presented.

- **Network Security Database**—The Network Security Database (NSDB) is an HTML-based encyclopedia of network security information. This information includes the current vulnerabilities, their associated exploits, and preventive measures you can take to avoid them. This database is upgradable with a download from Cisco Connection Online (CCO), www.cisco.com, for customers with a maintenance agreement with Cisco. User-defined notes can be added to each vulnerability.

- **Support for user-defined actions**—The Intrusion Detection Director can be programmed with user-defined actions. This can be as simple as sending specific people an e-mail if a certain condition is met or as complex as running a UNIX script to lock down a specific service.

Intrusion Detection Post Office

The IDS Post Office is the communications backbone that allows Cisco Secure IDS services and hosts to communicate with each other. All communications between the Intrusion Detection Sensor and Director use a proprietary connection-based protocol that can switch between alternate routes to maintain point-to-point connections.

Further information on the Cisco Secure Intrusion Detection System can be found at www.cisco.com/go/netranger.

Cisco Secure Scanner

The Cisco Secure Scanner (formerly Cisco NetSonar) is a software application that offers a complete suite of network scanning tools designed to run on either Windows NT or Solaris.

Network scanning is the process in which a specific host is configured as a scanner and it scans all or just configurable parts (depending on the scanner) of the network for known security threats. The design and operation of the scanner makes it a valuable asset to have in your quest for Internet security.

The Cisco Secure Scanner follows a four-step process to identify any possible network vulnerabilities:

Step 1 Gather information.

> The user instructs the scanner to scan a network or various networks based on provided IP address details. The scanner identifies all active devices.

Step 2 Identify potential vulnerabilities.

> The detailed information that is obtained from the active devices is compared against well-known security threats appertaining to the specific host type and version number.

Step 3 Confirm selected vulnerabilities.

> The scanner can take action to confirm vulnerabilities by using active probing techniques to ensure that no damage to a network occurs.

Step 4 Generate reports and graphs.

> Once all of the information has been gathered and potential vulnerabilities have been identified, full reports can be created. These reports can be geared toward specific organizational roles, ranging from the system administrators to senior management.

The Cisco Secure Scanner identifies information about the network hosts for a given network. For example, you might scan your public IP address allocation of 212.1.1.0/24. The scanner will identify which IP addresses are live and will also extract the operating system, version number, domain name, and IP settings for all hosts, including internetworking devices such as routers, switches, and remote access servers. Key Internet servers such as Web, FTP, and SMTP servers will also be identified.

Once this information has been obtained, the list of hosts is compared against common vulnerabilities. These vulnerabilities are in the following categories:

- TCP/IP
- UNIX
- Windows NT
- Web servers (HTTP, HTTPS)
- Mail servers (SMTP, POP3, IMAP4)
- FTP servers
- Firewalls
- Routers
- Switches

This vulnerability information is collated from the Network Security Database (NSDB). The NSDB contains the current well-known security vulnerabilities grouped by operating system. The Cisco Countermeasures Research Team (C-CRT) frequently updates the database, and the updated database is posted on Cisco Connection Online (CCO). Customers with maintenance contracts can download the latest database to update the scanning host with the most recent revision.

Figure 3-2 shows the scanner performing a scan for a given network.

Figure 3-2   *Cisco Secure Scanner*

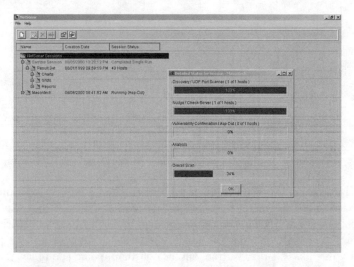

Once the data has been collated and any vulnerability identified, the application allows you to create numerous charts and reports within three report formats. The reports are configurable for an Executive Report, Brief Technical Report, and Full Technical Report.

Figure 3-3 shows a sample Executive Summary from a Full Technical Report.

Figure 3-3   *Cisco Secure Scanner Reporting*

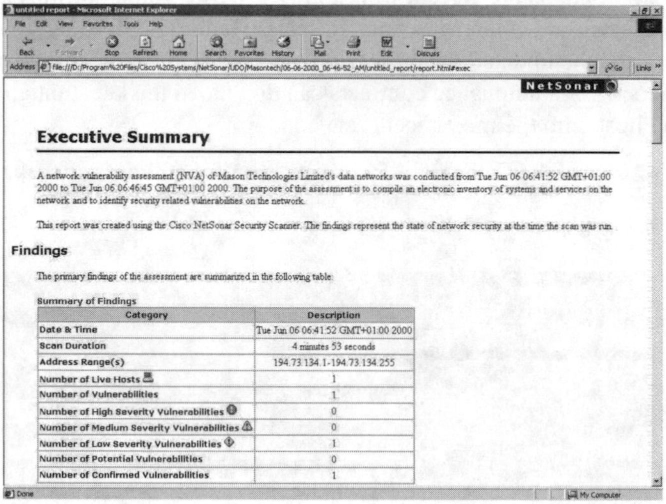

The Cisco Secure Scanner is a key component in the Cisco Security Solution. The product falls into the security monitoring category discussed in the previous "Security Monitoring" section, and it is a key element of the constant review of Internet security. As a network designer, you might feel that you have protected your network against all current Internet security threats. This may be true, but the constant update and renewal of the NSDB may introduce new threats that you have not considered or vulnerabilities that were not exploited before. This constant evolution makes Internet security a constant task and the security scanner an invaluable tool for the modern network engineer.

Further information on the Cisco Secure Scanner can be found at www.cisco.com/go/netsonar.

Cisco Secure Policy Manager

Cisco Secure Policy Manager (formerly Cisco Security Manager) is a very powerful security policy management application designed around the integration of Cisco Secure PIX Firewalls, IPSec VPN-capable routers, and routers running the Cisco IOS Firewall feature set.

Currently, Cisco Secure Policy Manager is available only on the Windows NT platform.

The Policy Manager provides a tool that enables the security administrator to define, enforce, and audit security policies. The administrator is able to formulate complex security policies based on organizational needs. These policies are then converted to detailed configurations by the Policy Manager and distributed to the specific security devices in the network.

The main features of Cisco Secure Policy Manager are

- **Cisco firewall management**—Cisco Secure Policy Manager empowers the user to define complex security policies and then distribute these to several hundred PIX Firewalls or routers running the Cisco IOS Firewall. Full management capabilities are available for the firewalls.

- **Cisco VPN router management**—IPSec-based VPNs can be easily configured by using the simple GUI. As with the firewall management, this VPN configuration can be distributed to several hundred PIX Firewalls or routers running the Cisco IOS Firewall.

- **Security policy management**—The GUI enables the creation of network-wide security policies. These security policies can be managed from a single point and delivered to several hundred firewall devices without requiring extensive device knowledge and dependency on the command-line interface.

- **Intelligent network management**—The defined security policies are translated into the appropriate device commands to create the required device configuration. The device configuration is then securely distributed throughout the network, eliminating the need for device-by-device management.

- **Notification and reporting system**—Cisco Secure Policy Manager provides a basic set of tools to monitor, alert, and report activity on the Cisco Secure devices. This provides the security administrator with reporting information that can be used to ascertain the current state of the security policy as well as a notification system to report various conditions. Along with the built-in notification and reporting tools, the product also implements and integrates with leading third-party monitoring, billing, and reporting systems.

Figure 3-4 shows the main configuration screen of the Cisco Secure Policy Manager.

Figure 3-4 *Cisco Secure Policy Manager*

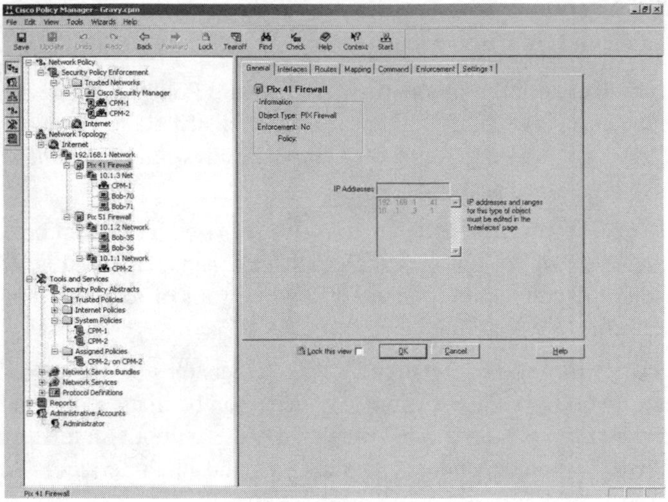

The following devices and software revisions are supported by Cisco Secure Policy Manager:

- Cisco Secure PIX Firewall
  - PIX OS 4.2.4, 4.2.5, 4.4.x, 5.1.x, 5.2.x, 5.3.x
- Cisco 1720 Series running Cisco IOS Firewall
- Cisco 2600 Series running Cisco IOS Firewall
- Cisco 3600 Series running Cisco IOS Firewall
- Cisco 7100 Series running Cisco IOS Firewall
- Cisco 7200 Series running Cisco IOS Firewall

NOTE   Though not documented at the time this book was written, Cisco Secure Policy Manager can be expected to support the Cisco PIX 525.

Further information on the Cisco Secure Policy Manager can be found at www.cisco.com/go/policymanager.

Cisco Secure Access Control Server (ACS)

Cisco Secure Access Control Server (ACS) (formerly known as Cisco Secure) is a complete network control solution built around the authentication, authorization, and accounting (AAA) standards. Currently, Cisco Secure ACS is available on Windows NT and Solaris platforms. Both versions have similar features and operate using industry-standard protocols.

AAA functions are available on most Cisco devices, including routers and the Cisco Secure PIX Firewall. The two main AAA protocols used are RADIUS and TACACS+. Figure 3-5 shows the main configuration screen of Cisco Secure ACS for Windows NT.

Figure 3-5   *Cisco Secure ACS*

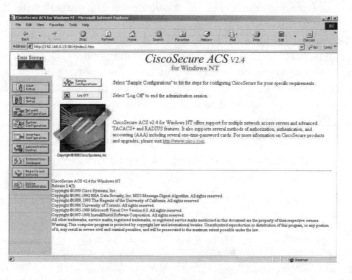

Authentication

Authentication is the determination of a user's identity and the verification of the user's information, similar to the username and password pair utilized by most common network operating systems. Cisco Secure ACS provides a secure authentication method for dealing with access to your corporate network. This access might include remote users logging in over a VPN or the corporate RAS system or network administrators gaining access to internetworking devices such as routers or switches. Authentication can be enabled against numerous data sources; for example, with the Windows NT version of Cisco Secure ACS, you can enable authentication against the Windows NT User Domain. All leading crypto card manufacturers are also supported.

Authorization

With authorization, you can specify what users can do once they are authenticated. You create user profile policies on the ACS server that are enforced when the user logs in. This is useful for allowing specific groups of users access to specific areas on the network. For example, you can restrict access to the Internet for all users unless they are in the Internet Access user group on the ACS server.

Accounting

Accounting can be defined as recording what a user is doing once authenticated. This is extremely useful to implement on the internetworking devices within your operation. Unplanned changes occurring on the configuration of a mission critical router are common in every organization. These changes disrupt service, cause network downtime, and cost the company money. When it comes to identifying the culprit, you can expect that nobody will own up to making the changes. With the accounting features of Cisco Secure ACS, you can log every single command that a user enters on a supporting device to either a comma-separated value (CSV) file or a syslog server. This information is held along with the logged-in username and the date and time. This preventive system is excellent to stop budding CCIE engineers from tweaking various configuration settings without really knowing or understanding the ramifications.

Further information on the Cisco Secure ACS can be found at www.cisco.com/go/ciscosecure.

Summary

This chapter has provided an overview of the Cisco Security Solution and has introduced you to the Cisco Secure product family. As you can see, each product in the family fits into a specific role in the Cisco Security Solution. Security is more than just implementing a PIX Firewall or occasionally scanning your network with the Cisco Secure Scanner. It should be clear in your mind that the correct security approach is one that looks at all angles of security, as outlined in the Cisco Security Solution. Multiple products are required to facilitate this, and an intrinsically sound security policy that is implemented and understood by all is key to the success of your endeavors.

Frequently Asked Questions

Question: What Cisco product provides intrusion detection capabilities?

Answer: The dedicated intrusion detection solution from Cisco Systems is the Cisco Secure IDS. Keep in mind that Cisco IOS Firewall also has intrusion detection features built in.

Question: Is it necessary to perform security scanning on your network?

Answer: Yes, security scanning with a product such as the Cisco Secure Scanner is an excellent way to measure the security of your network. Every network that is designed must have a benchmark to measure itself against concerning the security safeguards that have been implemented. A security scanner uses the same techniques that common hackers employ to test the vulnerability of the network. It is better for you to discover the vulnerability rather than for a potential attacker to do so.

Glossary

AAA (authentication, authorization, accounting)—Often pronounced "triple a."

ACS (Access Control Server)—The Cisco Secure ACS is an integrated RADIUS and TACACS+ server for authentication, authorization, and accounting.

CCO (Cisco Connection Online)—The Cisco Systems home page on the Internet. Located at http://www.cisco.com.

IDS (Intrusion Detection System)—Scans the network in real time to intercept attempted breaches of security.

ISP (Internet service provider)—A service provider that provides a connection to the public Internet.

IPSec (Internet Protocol Security)—A standards-based method of providing privacy, integrity, and authenticity to information transferred across IP networks.

NSDB (Network Security Database)—The security database of known security vulnerabilities, their exploits, and associated remedies. Used by security scanners and intrusion detection systems.

PIX (Private Internet Exchange)—The Cisco range of leading hardware-based firewalls.

RADIUS (Remote Access Dial-In User Service)—A protocol used to authenticate users on a network.

TACACS+ (Terminal Access Controller Access Control System Plus)—A protocol used to authenticate users on a network. Also provides authorization and accounting facilities.

VPN (Virtual Private Network)—A secure connection over an unsecured medium. The connection is secured by the use of tunneling protocols and encryption.

Bibliography

Designing Network Security by Merike Kaeo, Cisco Press 1999. (ISBN 1-57870-043-4)

URLs

Cisco Connection Online

www.cisco.com

Cisco Secure home page

www.cisco.com/warp/public/44/jump/secure.shtml

Security products and technologies

www.cisco.com/warp/public/cc/cisco/mkt/security/

Cisco Secure ACS

www.cisco.com/warp/public/cc/cisco/mkt/access/secure/

Cisco IOS Firewall

www.cisco.com/warp/public/cc/cisco/mkt/security/iosfw/

Cisco Secure IDS

www.cisco.com/warp/public/cc/cisco/mkt/security/nranger/

Cisco Secure PIX Firewall

www.cisco.com/go/pix

Cisco Secure Policy Manager

www.cisco.com/warp/public/cc/pd/sqsw/sqppmn/index.shtml

Cisco Secure Scanner

www.cisco.com/warp/public/cc/pd/sqsw/nesn/index.shtml

127This chapter contains the following sections:

- PIX Models
- PIX Features
- PIX Configuration
- VPN with Point-to-Point Tunneling Protocol (PPTP)
- VPN with IPSec and Manual Keys
- VPN with Preshared Keys
- Obtaining Certificate Authorities (CAs)
- PIX-to-PIX Configuration
- Summary

CHAPTER 4

Cisco Secure PIX Firewall

This chapter focuses on the Cisco Secure Private Internet Exchange (PIX) Firewall. The strength of the security features within the PIX lay in the fact that it was designed solely as a firewall. Although a PIX Firewall will do a limited amount of routing, the real purposes of the PIX are to deny unrequested outside traffic from your LAN and to form secure Virtual Private Networks (VPNs) between remote locations. A router requires a great deal of configuration to act effectively as a firewall. The PIX, however, only requires six commands before it can be placed into service. The PIX is easy to configure and generally requires no routine maintenance once configured.

The larger a sphere is, the larger the surface area of that sphere. If you analogize the security concerns of an operating system to a sphere, you soon realize that the larger the operating system, the larger the "surface area" that must be defended. A router with a much larger operating system must be carefully configured to stop intruders, prevent denial of service (DoS) attacks, and secure the LAN. The PIX operating system, originally designed as a Network Address Translation (NAT) device, is not a general-purpose operating system and operates in real time, unlike both Windows NT and UNIX. Therefore, the PIX has a very small operating system that presents fewer opportunities for a security breach. The smaller the operating system, the less chance that an area has been overlooked in the development process.

The PIX does not experience any of the many security holes present within either UNIX or Windows NT. The operating system is proprietary, and its inner workings are not published for use outside of Cisco Systems. The general networking public does not have access to the source code for the PIX, and therefore, the opportunities for exploiting a possible vulnerability are limited. The inner workings of the PIX Firewall are so secret that the authors of this book were not able to gain access to them.

Several advantages to using the PIX over a router or a UNIX, Linux, or Windows NT-based firewall exist. The benefits of using a PIX include the following:

- PIX's Adaptive Security Algorithm (ASA), combined with cut-through proxy, allows the PIX to deliver outstanding performance
- Up to 500,000 connections simultaneously
- Throughput speeds up to 1000 Mbps
- Failover capabilities on most models

- An integrated appliance
- IPSec VPN support
- NAT and Port Address Translation (PAT) fully supported
- Low packet delay
- Low cost of ownership due to no OS maintenance
- Integrated Intrusion Detection System (IDS)
- High reliability, no hard disk, Mean Time Between Failure greater than 60,000 hours
- Common criteria EAL 2 certification

PIX Models

The PIX Firewall comes in four main models, with an additional model that's being phased out. Ranging in size from models designed for the home or small office through enterprise level firewalls, the PIX models allow for virtually any size of organization to be protected. The models are as follows:

- PIX 506
- PIX 515
- PIX 520/525
- PIX 535

The features of each model follow.

PIX 506

The PIX 506 is the smallest of the PIX Firewalls available. Currently list-priced at less than U.S. $2000, the 506 is designed for firewall protection of the home or small business office. The 506 is approximately one-half the width of the rest of the PIX models. The capabilities and hardware features of the 506 are as follows:

- 10 Mbps throughput
- 7 Mbps throughput for Triple Data Encryption Standard (3DES) connections
- Up to ten simultaneous IPSec Security Associations (SAs)
- 200 MHz Pentium MMX processor
- 32 MB SDRAM
- 8 MB Flash memory
- Two integrated 10/100 ports

A picture of the PIX 506 is shown in Figure 4-1.

Figure 4-1   *PIX 506*

PIX 515

The PIX 515 is designed for larger offices than those of the 506. There are three main advantages of the 515 over the 506. The first advantage is the ability to create demilitarized zones (DMZs) through the use of an additional network interface. The second advantage is the throughput speed and number of simultaneous connections supported. The third advantage is the ability to support a failover device that will assume the duties of the primary PIX should there be a failure. The PIX 515 comes in two models, the 515 Restricted (515-r) and the 515 Unrestricted (515-ur). The characteristics of these two models follow.

PIX 515-r:

- No failover devices supported.
- A single DMZ can be used.
- Ethernet must be the LAN protocol.
- Maximum of three interfaces may be used.
- 32 MB RAM.

PIX 515-ur:

- Failover devices are supported.
- Two DMZs may be implemented.
- Ethernet must be the LAN protocol.
- Maximum of six interfaces may be used.
- 64 MB RAM.

These two models are essentially the same hardware with different memory and software. It is possible to purchase a 515-r and upgrade it to a 515-ur by adding more memory and updating the operating system. The net cost to the user is very close to the purchase price of a 515-ur. The capabilities and hardware features of the 515 follow:

- Rack mountable
- Up to 100,000 simultaneous connections
- Up to 170 Mbps throughput
- Up to four interfaces
- Up to 64 MB SDRAM
- 16 MB Flash memory
- 200 MHz Pentium MMX processor

A picture of the PIX 515 is shown in Figure 4-2.

Figure 4-2   *PIX 515*

PIX 520/525

The PIX 520, sometimes called the classic PIX, is in the process of being phased out in favor of the newer design of the model 525. Both of these firewalls have the same underlying hardware.

The PIX 525 is designed for a large organization and has the following capabilities and hardware features:

- Rack mountable
- More than 256,000 simultaneous connections
- Six to eight integrated Ethernet cards
- Up to four Token Ring cards
- Up to four FDDI or four Gigabit Ethernet cards
- More than 240 Mbps throughput
- Up to 256 MB RAM

A picture of the PIX 525 is shown in Figure 4-3.

Figure 4-3   *PIX 525*

PIX 535

The PIX 535 is designed for large enterprise and Internet service provider (ISP) environments where an extreme amount of traffic must be secured. This is presently the largest PIX Firewall available and has the following capabilities and hardware features:

- Rack mountable
- More than 500,000 simultaneous connections
- Six to eight integrated Ethernet cards
- Up to four Token Ring cards
- Up to four FDDI or eight Gigabit Ethernet cards
- More than 1,000 Mbps throughput
- 512 to 1024 MB RAM

A picture of the PIX 535 is shown in Figure 4-4.

Figure 4-4   *PIX 535*

PIX Features

The PIX Firewalls, regardless of model number, all provide the same security features. The PIX is a stateful firewall that delivers full protection to the corporate network by completely concealing the nature of the internal network to those outside. The main operating features of the PIX follow:

- **Sequence random numbering**—IP spoofing generally relies on the ability to guess a sequence number. The PIX randomizes the IP sequence numbers for each session. This makes IP spoofing much more difficult to accomplish.

- **Stateful filtering**—This is a secure method of analyzing data packets that is also known as the Adaptive Security Algorithm (ASA). When data traverses from the trusted interface on the PIX to a less trusted interface, information about this packet is entered into a table. When the PIX receives a data packet with the SYN bit set, the PIX checks the table to see if, in fact, the destination host has previously sent data out to the responding host. If the table does not contain an entry showing that the local host has requested data, the packet is dropped. This technique virtually eliminates all SYN-based DoS attacks.

- **Network Address Translation (NAT)**—NAT is the process of changing the source IP address on all packets sent out by a host and changing the destination IP address of all incoming packets for that host. This prevents hosts outside of the LAN from knowing the true IP address of a local host. NAT uses a pool of IP addresses for all local hosts. The IP address a local host will receive changes as addresses are used and returned to the pool.

- **Port Address Translation (PAT)**—PAT is similar to NAT except that all local hosts receive the same IP address. Using different ports for each session differentiates local host sessions. The IP address of the local host is still changed using PAT, but the ports associated with the session are also changed. Both PAT and NAT can be used concurrently on a PIX Firewall.

- **Embedded operating system**—A UNIX, Linux, or Windows NT machine can be used as a proxy server. However, the throughput of such a machine is slower by design than that available through the PIX. A proxy server receives an Ethernet packet, strips off the header, extracts the IP packet, and then moves that packet up through the OSI model until it reaches the application layer (Layer 7), where the proxy server software changes the address. The new IP packet is rebuilt and sent down to Layer 1 of the OSI model, where it is transmitted. This uses a large number of CPU cycles and introduces delay. Because the PIX is a proprietary system, the OSI model constraints can be bypassed and made to allow cut-through proxy to operate.

- **Cut-through proxy and ASA**—The combination of cut-through proxy and ASA allows the PIX to process more than 500,000 connections simultaneously with virtually no packet delay. Cut-through proxy is the process where the first packet in a session is checked as in any proxy server, but all subsequent packets are passed through. This technique allows the PIX to transfer packets extremely efficiently.

- **DNS guard**—By default, all outgoing DNS requests are allowed. Only the first response is allowed to enter the LAN.

- **Mail guard**—Only RFC 821-specific commands are allowed to a Simple Mail Transfer Protocol (SMTP) server on an inside interface. These commands are **HELLO, MAIL, RCPT, DATA, RSET, NOOP,** and **QUIT.** The PIX responds with an OK to all other mail requests to confuse attackers. This is configured with the **fixup** command.

- **Flood defender**—This limits the total number of connections and the number of half-open connections. User Datagram Protocol (UDP) response packets that either have not been requested or arrive after a timeout period are also dropped.

- **ICMP deny**—By default, all Internet Control Message Protocol (ICMP) traffic does not get sent over the inside interface. The administrator must specifically allow ICMP traffic to enter if needed.

- **IP Frag Guard**—This limits the number of IP full-fragment packets per second per internal host to 100. This prevents DoS attacks such as LAND.c and teardrop. Additionally, this ensures that all responsive IP packets are let through only after an initial IP packet requesting the response has traversed the PIX.

- **Flood guard**—This feature is designed to prevent DoS attacks that continuously request an authentication of a user. The repetitive requests for authentication in this type of DoS attack are designed to use memory resources on a network device. The PIX relies on a subroutine that uses its own section of memory. When an excessive number of authentication requests are received, the PIX starts dropping these requests and reclaiming memory, thus defeating this form of attack.

- **Automatic Telnet denial**—By default, the PIX Firewall will not respond to any Telnet request except through the console port. When enabling Telnet, set it to allow only those connections that are actually necessary.

- **Dynamic Host Configuration Protocol (DHCP) client and server support**—The PIX can rely on a DHCP server to gain an IP address for an interface. As a DHCP server, the PIX provides IP addresses for hosts attached to one of the interfaces.

- **Secure Shell (SSH) support**—The PIX supports the SSH remote shell functionality available in SSH version 1. SSH is an application that runs on top of a connection-oriented Layer 3 protocol such as TCP. SSH provides encryption and authentication services for Telnet sessions. Support for SSH requires third-party software, which may be obtained at the following sites:

  — Windows client:

hp.vector.co.jp/authors/VA002416/teraterm.html

  — Linux, Solaris, OpenBSD, AIX, IRIX, HP/UX, FreeBSD, and NetBSD client:

www.openssh.com

— Macintosh client:

www.lyastor.liu.se/~jonasw/freeware/niftyssh

- **Intrusion Detection System (IDS)**— The PIX integrates the same IDS features that are available on routers through the Cisco Secure IOS. The IDS detects 53 specific types of intrusion. See Chapter 6, "Intrusion Detection Systems," for more details on IDS.

- **TCP intercept**—The PIX can act like a TCP intercept device, isolating protected hosts from direct contact through TCP connections. TCP intercept is discussed in Chapter 2, "Basic Cisco Router Security."

PIX Configuration

This section explores how to configure a PIX Firewall for a number of different scenarios. This section defines terms and gives explanations of how different scenarios require different hardware and software configurations.

The basic PIX configuration is extremely simple. By default, this configuration allows outgoing packets and responsive packets into the LAN. This configuration also denies all ICMP packets traversing the PIX from the outside to the inside, even when such a packet is in response to a ping issued from the inside.

Like any other Cisco IOS, the Cisco PIX has a command-line interface (CLI). There is a user mode and an enable mode. For the moment, you will configure the PIX by connecting the console port on the PIX to a serial port on a computer using the cable you received with the PIX Firewall. Some of the commands will be familiar and some will be new. Each scenario in this section builds on the previous scenario.

If by issuing a **show config** command you see a number of items not shown on a particular configuration, do not panic. The PIX enters a number of defaults into the configuration when booting. These defaults can be changed. This chapter will deal with the most frequently used commands first. If you simply cannot wait to see what a command does, look in the index and jump ahead to the section concerning that command.

Basic Configuration

The basic configuration for the PIX is illustrated in Figure 4-5. In this scenario, the PIX is used to protect a single LAN from the Internet. Notice in Figure 4-5 that the perimeter router and the connection between the perimeter router and the outside interface of the PIX are unprotected. The perimeter router should be hardened against attacks—especially DoS attacks—because it is not protected by the PIX Firewall. Chapter 10, "Securing the Corporate Network," deals with securing a perimeter router. Any device that is outside of the PIX Firewall cannot be protected by the PIX. If possible, only the perimeter router should reside on the unprotected side of the network. Take a few minutes to study Figure 4-5, which you can use to define terms such as *inside, outside, protected,* and *unprotected.*

Figure 4-5   *Basic PIX Configuration Sample Network*

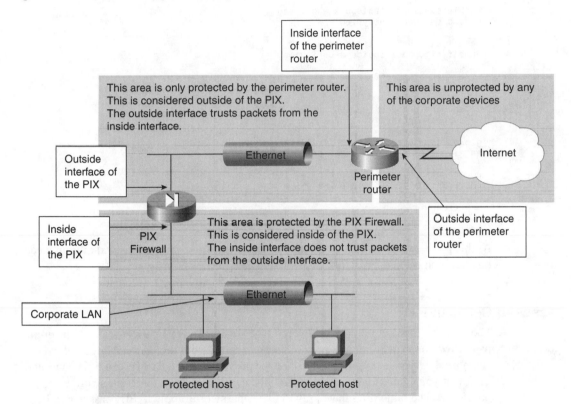

As shown in Figure 4-5, there is an inside and an outside interface on the PIX. The outside interface is less trusted than the inside interface. The inside interface has a security level of 100. The outside interface has a security level of 0. The security level is what determines whether packets originating from a particular interface are trusted by another interface. The higher the security level, the more an interface is trusted. This premise becomes more important as you build systems with multiple DMZs. When packets are trusted, they are allowed through an interface by default. When packets are not trusted, they are not allowed through by default.

For the basic configuration, you only need to add a few commands. This section takes much longer to read than it will actually take to configure the PIX. Start up the PIX Firewall and connect the inside interface into your local network. Connect the outside interface to the inside interface of your perimeter router. Do *not* connect these through the same switch or hub that runs your local network. The only path from the perimeter router to your LAN must travel through the PIX Firewall. Companies with multiple paths to the Internet should employ a PIX Firewall between each perimeter router and the LAN.

After showing you how to configure the PIX, the chapter explains what has been done. Using Telnet, enter the following commands. The lines are separated for clarity.

```
enable password enablepass encrypted
passwd password encrypted

nameif ethernet0 outside security0
nameif ethernet1 inside security100

interface ethernet0 10baset
interface ethernet1 10baset

ip address outside 192.168.1.1 255.255.255.0
ip address inside 10.1.1.254 255.255.255.0

global (outside) 1 192.168.1.100 255.255.255.0
nat (inside) 1 10.1.1.0 255.255.255.0 0 0

route outside 0.0.0.0 0.0.0.0 192.168.1.254 1
route inside 10.1.1.0 255.255.255.0 10.1.1.1 1

arp timeout 7200

write mem
```

At this point, you have your basic configuration set. The next sections walk through each line that you entered and explain the significance of the commands.

password Commands

The first two lines set up your passwords. The first password line was set with the **enable password** command to **enablepass**. This was entered with the optional keyword **encrypted**. Using **encrypted** ensures that the password will not be revealed if you print out a copy of your configuration. The second line configures your Telnet password to **password**. The same rules that apply to router passwords apply to PIX passwords. For example, the enable password controls access to the enable commands.

nameif Command

The **nameif** command is used to label your interfaces and set the security levels for each of your interfaces. The first line sets the Ethernet0 interface to be called **outside** and to have a security level of zero. The next line labels the Ethernet1 interface as **inside** with a security level of 100. In other words, Ethernet0 is from now on called **outside** instead of Ethernet0 and is completely untrusted because it has a security level of zero. Ethernet1 is now called **inside** and is completely trusted. These are both the defaults and are necessary to the configuration. Ethernet0 is always **outside** and Ethernet1 is always **inside. outside** always has a security level of zero, and **inside** always has a security level of 100. Except for the inside and outside interfaces, an interface may be named anything you desire and will have a security level somewhere between 0 and 100. Remember that the higher a security level, the more it is trusted.

This is important because the default behavior of the PIX Firewall is relative to the security levels associated with the interfaces in question. Every interface has a higher security level than the outside interface. Therefore, by default, packets from any interface can travel through the outside interface. Conversely, no packets from the outside interface by default can travel to any other interface.

Suppose that your PIX had two additional interfaces, Ethernet2 and Ethernet3. You enter the following two lines:

```
nameif ethernet2 joe security16
nameif ethernet3 nancy security45
```

The **joe** interface (Ethernet2) has a security level of 16 and the **nancy** interface (Ethernet3) has a security level of 45. This is feasible because you can assign any security level to an interface and can call the interface anything you choose. In this scenario, packets from nancy could travel through the joe interface without any special configurations. Packets originating at joe cannot by default travel through the nancy interface because the nancy interface has a higher security level. The advanced configurations later in this chapter expand on this concept and use more realistic names for the interfaces.

interface Command

The lines starting with **interface** accomplish two tasks. The first task is to set the speed and type of the interface. If you set interface Ethernet0 to 100BaseT, you would use the following line:

```
interface Ethernet0 100baset
```

Alternatively, if you want to set the first Token Ring interface at 16 Mbps, you would enter:

```
interface tokenring0 16
```

The second accomplishment of this line is to turn up the interface. This is the equivalent of issuing a **no shut** command on a router. The **interface** command is also the exception to the rule that you can use **inside** or **outside** instead of **Ethernet0**. The actual hardware identification must be used with the **interface** command.

Assigning IP Addresses

The next two lines assign an IP address and subnet mask to the inside and outside interfaces. The words *inside* and *outside* are used because that is what you have named with the **nameif** command. Substitute whatever name you have given to this particular interface. The IP addresses on each interface must reside on different subnets.

The full **ip address** command follows:

```
ip address interface_name ip_address subnet_mask
```

global Command

One of the strengths of the PIX Firewall is its ability to support NAT and PAT. The **global** command, in conjunction with the **nat** command, is used to assign the IP addresses that packets receive as they cross the interface. The **global** command defines a pool of global addresses. This pool provides an IP address for each outbound connection and for inbound connections resulting from these outbound connections. Whether NAT or PAT is used depends on how the **global** command is used. If you are connecting to the Internet, the global addresses should be registered. Nonroutable IP addresses are used here for illustrative purposes only. Using routable IP addresses becomes a vital consideration when using VPNs that terminate on the PIX Firewall, because without a routable IP address the VPN will never travel over the Internet. The syntax for the **global** command follows:

```
global [(interface_name)] nat_id global_ip[-global_ip]
    [netmask global_netmask]
```

The *interface_name* is the name assigned with the **nameif** command. The *nat_id* is an integer. The *nat_id* must match the number used in the **nat** command. Although almost any number can be used (as long as the number is consistent between the **global** and **nat** commands), the number 0 is reserved for special cases. The use of 0 is covered in the section "**nat** Command."

The *global-ip* can take one of two forms. The form chosen determines whether NAT or PAT is used. If PAT is to be used, enter a single IP address. All packets from all hosts will receive this address as they cross the interface. If NAT is to be used, enter an address range for the IP addresses to be seen from the outside. For example, if you wish to use the single address of 192.10.10.1, you would enter the following:

```
global (outside) 1 192.10.10.1 255.255.255.0
```

If, on the other hand, you wish to use NAT and use a whole Class C subnet, you would enter the following:

```
global (outside) 1 192.10.10.1-192.10.10.254 255.255.255.0
```

You could also use more than a Class C network by adjusting the IP addresses entered and the subnet mask. The following example uses a 23-bit subnet mask and allows you to use all IP addresses between 192.10.10.1 and 192.10.11.254. When an address range overlaps subnets, the broadcast and network addresses are not used by the **global** command.

```
global (outside) 1 192.10.10.1-192.10.11.254 255.255.254.0
```

When you want to use PAT, you use a single address instead of a range. PAT supports up to 65,535 concurrent translations. There are some limitations in the use of PAT. For example, PAT cannot be used with H.323 and multimedia applications. These types of applications expect to be able to assign certain ports within the application. PAT also does not work in conjunction with the **established** command. Because the ports are changed when using PAT, these applications fail. As in the basic configuration, the following line sets a single IP address:

```
global (outside) 1 192.168.1.100 255.255.255.0
```

The use of the **global** command requires reverse DNS PTR entries to ensure that external network addresses are accessible through the PIX Firewall. Without these PTR entries, you will see slow or intermittent Internet connectivity and File Transfer Protocol (FTP) requests consistently failing. DNS servers on a higher security level needing updates from a name server on an outside interface must use the **static** command, which will be explained in the "Realistic Configuration" section.

The subnet mask should match the subnet mask on the network segment. Use the ranges of IP addresses to limit the hosts used, not the subnet mask. In more advanced configurations later in this chapter, you will see how to use NAT and PAT together and how to use multiple global ranges.

nat Command

The **nat** command is used in conjunction with the **global** command. The **nat** command specifies from which interface connections can originate. The syntax for the **nat** command follows:

```
nat [(interface_name)] nat_id local_ip [netmask [max_connections
[em_limit]]] [norandomsequence]
```

The *nat_id* number must be the same on the **nat** and **global** command statements. Although you might have multiple **global** commands associated with an interface, only a single **nat** command can be used. Use the **no** form of the **nat** command to remove the **nat** entry, or rewrite the **nat** command with the same *nat_id* to overwrite the existing **nat** command. After issuing a **nat** command, you should enter the **clear xlate** command. This command clears all present NAT and PAT connections, which are then reestablished with the new parameters. This section will deal with using the number 0 for the *nat_id* after you have seen the other parameters within the **nat** command and the discussion on using the **nat** command with access lists.

The *local_ip* parameter can be set to a single IP address or to a whole network by adjusting the *netmask* parameter. The *local_ip* parameter specifies the internal network address to be translated. Using 0.0.0.0 allows all hosts to start outbound connections. Instead of using 0.0.0.0, you can abbreviate by using simply 0.

Use the *netmask* parameter as you would use any subnet mask. The exception is when you use 0.0.0.0 as the *netmask*. Using 0.0.0.0 means that you want to allow all hosts on the local network through. This can be abbreviated as simply 0. When allowing all hosts through, you can use 0 for both the *local_ip* and the *netmask*. Within the PIX, 0 can be substituted for where the word *any* would be used on a Cisco router. The command line might look like any of the following lines, assuming that the local inside network is 10.1.1.0 with a Class C subnet mask:

```
nat (inside) 1 0 0 0 0
nat (inside) 1 10.1.1.0 255.255.255.0 0 0
nat (inside) 1 0 255.255.255.0 0 0
nat (inside) 1 10.1.1.0 0 0 0
```

The *max connections* parameter limits the number of concurrent TCP connections through an interface. Using 0 makes the number of connections limited only by the license agreement and software installed on the PIX Firewall.

Embryonic connections are half-open TCP connections. The default of 0 does not limit the number of embryonic connections. On slower systems, entering a number for *em_limit* ensures that the system does not become overwhelmed trying to deal with embryonic connections.

The **norandomsequence** keyword is used to disable the default random sequencing of TCP packet numbers. Although usually not added to the **nat** command, this can be useful for debugging and in certain other circumstances. For example, if traffic must travel through two PIX Firewalls, the dual randomization of sequence numbers might cause the application to fail. In this case, adding the **norandomsequence** keyword to one of the PIX Firewalls should resolve the problem.

There are some special considerations for using the **nat** and **global** commands with a *nat_id* of 0. The first consideration is when using an access list to prevent NAT from occurring. For example, the following lines allow the hosts at IP addresses 10.1.1.54 and 10.1.1.113 to traverse the PIX without changing their IP addresses. All other addresses on the inside network receive translation services. The access list associated with a **nat 0** command merely prevents NAT; it does not limit accessibility to the outside.

```
access-list prevent_nat tcp host 10.1.1.54
access-list prevent_nat tcp host 10.1.1.113
nat (inside) 0 access-list prevent_nat
```

The access list should not attempt to prevent specific ports, because this causes the addresses to become translated. The ASA remains in effect, watching packets and preventing unauthorized access. However, the addresses within the access list are available through the outer interface without translation.

The **nat 0** command can also be used without an access list as any other *nat_id* could be used. However, using a *nat_id* of 0 without an access list causes all hosts on the network specified with the *netmask* to avoid being translated by the NAT functionality of the PIX. Previous versions of the PIX software experienced an issue when using 0 as the *nat_id*. This issue was that using 0 would cause the PIX to use proxy Address Resolution Protocol (ARP) for all inside addresses. PIX IOS versions 5.0 and above disable this behavior. If no addresses are to be translated, the **global** command is not necessary. The following example shows how all inside addresses can be prevented from being translated:

```
nat (inside) 0 0 0 0 0
```

route Command

The **route** command is used by the PIX in the same manner that static routes and default routes are used on a router. The PIX has limited routing capabilities. It is necessary for you to specify routes. As in a router, the most specific route listed takes precedence. The syntax for the route command follows:

```
route interface_name ip_address netmask gateway_ip [metric]
```

The *interface_name* is any name previously defined by the **nameif** command. The *ip_address* is the address of the internal or external network. A default route can be set with either 0.0.0.0 or 0. The *netmask* is the subnet mask of the route. A default route can use either 0.0.0.0 or 0.

The *gateway_ip* is the IP address of the next hop for the network to which you are adding a route. For example, if your inside interface supported multiple networks connected with a router whose interface is 10.1.1.20, your route statements might appear as follows:

```
route inside 10.1.2.0 255.255.255.0 10.1.1.20 2
route inside 10.1.8.0 255.255.255.0 10.1.1.20 2
route inside 10.2.13.0 255.255.255.0 10.1.1.20 2
route inside 10.11.7.0 255.255.255.0 10.1.1.20 2
```

Version 5.1 has been improved to specify automatically the IP address of a PIX Firewall interface in the **route** command. Once you enter the IP address for each interface, the PIX creates a **route** statement entry that is not deleted when you use the **clear route** command. If the **route** command uses the IP address from one of the PIX's own interfaces as the gateway IP address, the PIX uses ARP for the destination IP address in the packet instead of issuing an ARP for the gateway IP address.

The *metric* parameter is used to specify the number of hops to *gateway_ip*, not to the ultimate destination of the IP packet. A default of 1 is assumed if this parameter is not used. If duplicate routes are entered with different metrics for the same gateway, the PIX changes the metric for that route and updates the metric for the route.

arp timeout Command

The **arp timeout** command is used to specify the time that an ARP entry remains in the ARP cache before it is flushed. The number shown is the time in seconds that an ARP entry remains in the cache. The default time is 14,400 seconds, or 4 hours. In the configuration, you change the default to 2 hours with the following:

```
arp timeout 7200
```

write Command

The **write** command works in the same way that the **write** command operates in a Cisco router. For those of you relatively new to Cisco equipment, this command has largely been replaced on routers with the **copy** command. The **write** command can take any of the following formats:

```
write net [[server_ip_address]:[filename]]
write erase
write floppy
write memory
write terminal
write standby
```

The **write net** command writes across a network to a Trivial File Transfer Protocol (TFTP) server with the filename specified. If no server IP address or filename is entered, the user is prompted.

The **write erase** command clears the Flash memory configuration. The **write floppy** command writes the configuration to the floppy disk, if the PIX has a floppy. The **write memory** command stores the configuration in RAM memory. The **write terminal** command shows the current configuration on the terminal. The **write standby** command is used to write the configuration to either a failover or standby, PIX'S RAM memory.

At this point, you have completed a basic configuration. You are ready to move toward a more realistic situation, such as a network with a mail server and an FTP server.

Realistic Configuration

Although the basic configuration suffices to illustrate how simple it is to configure the PIX, there are a few more items that almost all systems need. Three examples are Web services, e-mail services, and FTP services. This configuration will show how access from the outside to the inside of the PIX can be allowed.

The default configuration for the PIX Firewall is to prevent all access from an interface with a lower security level through an interface with a higher security level. The configuration in this section shows how access can be allowed without losing security protection on the whole network subnet, or even on the hosts that you allow to be seen from the outside.

Figure 4-6 shows the layout for this scenario. Note that the 192.168.1.0 /24 network has been used on the interfaces between the PIX and the perimeter router. In real life, these should be routable IP addresses, because you need people on the Internet to be able to browse your Web server, download files from your FTP server, and send and receive from your e-mail server.

Figure 4-6   *Realistic PIX Configuration*

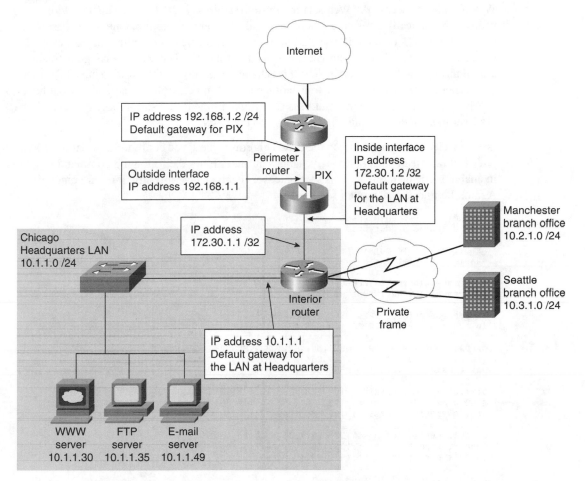

As shown in Figure 4-6, the interior router and the inside interface of the PIX are on a separate network. This is not mandatory. However, if there is a spare Ethernet interface on the interior router and plans to use a **nat 0** command, using a spare interface on the inside router is advised, because the PIX will use ARP to a router for the address of each request. Repeated ARP requests can cause an excessive load on an overtaxed network. Connecting the PIX to a router's interface also ensures that all packets from and to the PIX are not delayed because of issues such as collisions and broadcast storms. Finally, the interior router can and should be configured with at least simple access lists to ensure that only authorized traffic is traversing the network. This might seem like too much trouble for some administrators. However, security should become a pervasive attitude throughout the network engineering staff. Having an extra layer of protection is never a waste of effort.

You now have three major design changes to make to your system. You must first allow WWW traffic to access the Web server, whose IP address is 10.1.1.30. This IP address needs to be statically translated to a routable address on the Internet. One of the easiest ways to keep track of static IP translations is to use the same last octet in both addresses. In the case of the Web server, you will use 30 as the last octet. The second change is to allow e-mail through to the mail server. The third change is to allow FTP traffic to the FTP server. All of these servers need a static translation because you cannot be guaranteed what host will be using a given outside IP address at any given time if you simply rely on the default NAT settings on the PIX and allow traffic into the LAN.

Issue a **write erase** command on the PIX. This erases the saved configuration. Turn the PIX power off and then back on to arrive at a clean state. Enter the following commands while in enable mode on the PIX. This section covers each change after the lines are entered. Again, the lines are separated for clarity.

```
enable password enablepass encrypted
passwd password encrypted

nameif ethernet0 outside security0
nameif ethernet1 inside security100

interface ethernet0 10baset
interface ethernet1 10baset

ip address outside 192.168.1.1 255.255.255.0
ip address inside 172.30.1.2 255.255.255.252

global (outside) 1 192.168.1.50-192.168.1.253 255.255.255.0
global (outside) 1 192.168.1.254 255.255.255.0
nat (inside) 1 10.1.1.0 255.255.255.0 0 0

static (inside, outside) 192.168.1.30 10.1.1.30 netmask 255.255.255.255 0 0
static (inside, outside) 192.168.1.35 10.1.1.35 netmask 255.255.255.255 0 0
static (inside, outside) 192.168.1.49 10.1.1.49 netmask 255.255.255.255 0 0

conduit permit tcp host 192.168.1.30 eq http any
conduit permit tcp host 192.168.1.35 eq ftp any
conduit permit tcp host 192.168.1.49 eq smtp any

route outside 0 0 192.168.1.2 1
route inside 10.1.1.0 255.255.255.0 172.30.1.1 1

arp timeout 7200

write mem
```

There are only a few changes from the basic configuration. You first changed the inside IP address to reflect the separate network between the PIX and the interior router. The two **global** commands shown next assign both NAT and PAT to be used by the inside hosts. Because you used a range of IP addresses, the first **global** command allows for each host on the LAN to get a dynamically assigned global address, or NAT. Once all of the available global IP addresses are in use, any hosts attempting to connect to the outside will use PAT. The second **global** line is critical because it assigns one address for use with PAT. If a single address is not reserved for use by PAT, hosts will simply not be able to get through the PIX.

The users will think that the Internet connection has been dropped, because they will receive no indication of a problem other than a lack of connection.

You might wonder why the range of IP addresses starts at 50 in the first **global** command. This allows servers to have static IP addresses. The number 50 was arbitrarily chosen. Whatever number is chosen ensures that there are sufficient reserved IP addresses for all servers on the network. You could have also reserved a set of IP addresses on the upper end of the network. The inside and outside routes were also changed to reflect the network as shown in Figure 4-6. You are now actually ready to allow users on the Internet to access your e-mail, FTP, and Web services.

Setting up to allow e-mail to traverse the PIX requires a few new commands. This replaces the **mailhost** command in previous versions of the PIX. These commands are covered later in this section. Enter the following lines into the PIX configuration.

```
static (inside, outside) 192.168.1.49 10.1.1.49 netmask 255.255.255.255 0 0
conduit permit tcp host 192.168.1.49 eq smtp any
```

That is all that is required to allow SMTP packets to traverse the PIX to the server with the 10.1.1.49 IP address. Users outside the PIX will see this server as 192.168.1.49. Packets sent to 192.168.1.49 will have NAT applied to them and will be forwarded to 10.1.1.49. Only the SMTP commands **HELLO, MAIL, RCPT, DATA, RSET, NOOP,** and **QUIT** are allowed through the PIX. The response to all other SMTP commands is an OK packet from the PIX. You added two new commands here, the **static** and the **conduit** commands. Each of them will be examined before moving on to the FTP and Web servers.

static Command

The **static** command is actually a very simple command once you are familiar with it. The purpose of the **static** command is to apply NAT to a single host with a predefined IP address. The syntax is as follows:

```
static [(internal_interface, external_interface)] global_ip local_ip [netmask
    subnet_mask] [max_connections [em_limit]] [norandomsequence]
```

The *internal_interface* and *external_interface* are names defined by the **nameif** command. The *global_ip* is the IP address seen on the outside, after NAT has been applied. The *local_ip* is the IP address used on the local host before NAT is applied. The *subnet_mask* should always be 255.255.255.0 when applied to a single host. If a network is being assigned to a single address, use the subnet mask for the network. For example, if you want the whole 10.1.4.0 network to be translated using PAT to 192.168.1.4, you use the following line:

```
static (inside, outside) 192.168.1.4 10.1.4.0 netmask 255.255.255.0 0 0
```

In this case, you also need to associate an access list with the **conduit** command. This will be covered under a more advanced configuration entitled "Dual DMZ with AAA Authentication" later in this chapter.

The *max_connections* and *em_limit* (embryonic limit) work in the same manner as with the **global** command. Using the **no** form of the command removes the **static** command. Using a **show static** command displays all of the statically translated addresses.

The **static** command is simple if you remember the order in which interface names and IP addresses appear. The order is:

```
static (high, low) low high
```

In other words, the name of the interface with the higher security level is shown first within the parenthesis, followed by the name of the lower security level interface and a closing parenthesis. This is followed by the IP address as seen on the lower security interface, then the IP address as seen on the higher security level interface. The authors remember this with the phrase "high, low, low, high." When you start looking at PIX Firewalls using one or more DMZs, the principle will hold true. Because every interface must have a unique security level, one interface must be more trusted than the other. You will still place the name of the interface with the higher security level first, followed by the less trusted interface name inside the parenthesis. Outside the parenthesis, you will show the IP address as seen on the lower security level interface, followed by the IP address as seen on the higher security level interface.

If you choose to use **nat 0** to avoid translating the IP address, you still use "high, low, low, high," but the IP addresses are the same for the global and local IP. The following is an example for when you do not use NAT on the IP address:

```
static (inside, outside) 10.1.1.49 10.1.1.49 netmask 255.255.255.255 0 0
```

conduit Command

The **conduit** command is necessary to allow packets to travel from a lower security level to a higher security level. The PIX Firewall allows packets from a higher security level to travel to a lower security level. However, only packets in response to requests initiated on the higher security level interface can travel back through from a lower security level interface. The **conduit** command changes this behavior. By issuing a **conduit** command, you are opening a hole through the PIX to the host that is specified for certain protocols from specified hosts.

The **conduit** command acts very much like adding a **permit** statement to an access list. The default behavior of the PIX is to act as if there were a deny all access list applied. Because you must allow e-mail to reach your server, you need to use the **conduit** command. The rule for access from a higher security level interface to a lower security level interface is to use the **nat** command. For access from a lower security level interface to a higher security level interface, use the **static** and **conduit** commands. As with any opening into the corporate network, this opening should be as narrow as possible. The following allows any host on the Internet to send mail to the host:

```
conduit permit tcp host 192.168.1.49 eq smtp any
```

If you wish to limit the originating IP address for e-mail, you could simply add an IP address and network mask to the end of the preceding line. You are allowed to have as many **conduit** statements as required. The following example allows SMTP traffic to enter the network from one of three networks—two with Class C subnets and the final one with a Class B subnet:

```
conduit permit tcp host 192.168.1.49 eq smtp 10.5.5.0 255.255.255.0
conduit permit tcp host 192.168.1.49 eq smtp 10.15.6.0 255.255.255.0
conduit permit tcp host 192.168.1.49 eq smtp 10.19.0.0 255.255.0.0
```

The combination of the **static** declaration and the **conduit** command can allow FTP traffic through your network. You have allowed FTP traffic to the FTP server with the following two lines:

```
static (inside, outside) 192.168.1.35 10.1.1.35 netmask 255.255.255.255 0 0
conduit permit tcp host 192.168.1.35 eq ftp any
```

It is possible to have multiple **conduit** commands associated with a single IP address. For example, the following lines allow SMTP, FTP, and HTTP services to gain access to a single server:

```
static (inside, outside) 192.168.1.35 10.1.1.35 netmask 255.255.255.255 0 0
conduit permit tcp host 192.168.1.35 eq ftp any
conduit permit tcp host 192.168.1.35 eq http any
conduit permit tcp host 192.168.1.35 eq smtp any
```

Notice that there is a single **static** statement for the host. Although some versions of the PIX IOS will allow you to enter multiple **static** commands for a single address, only the first **static** command is used. The PIX only allows the use of the host in the first **static** command. If you are using multiple **conduit** commands, you might deny some networks while allowing others. Alternatively, you might allow traffic from some networks, but not from others. In the following example, you deny FTP traffic from the 10.5.1.0/24 network, while allowing traffic from all other networks:

```
static (inside, outside) 192.168.1.35 10.1.1.35 netmask 255.255.255.255 0 0
conduit deny tcp host 192.168.1.35 eq ftp 10.5.1.0 255.255.255.0
conduit permit tcp host 192.168.1.35 eq ftp any
```

Remote Site Configuration

At this point, you have a configuration that allows the main office to communicate through the Internet. You allowed access to the Web, FTP, and mail servers. What you do not have is access from the remote sites in Manchester and Seattle. The reason you do not have access is that the **nat** statement only applies to the Chicago LAN. You can easily add access to the Seattle and Manchester offices by adding the following lines:

```
nat (inside) 1 10.2.1.0 255.255.255.0 0 0
nat (inside) 1 10.3.1.0 255.255.255.0 0 0
route inside 10.2.1.0 255.255.255.0 172.30.1.1 1
route inside 10.3.1.0 255.255.255.0 172.30.1.1 1
```

The next configuration adds a DMZ and allows configuration of the PIX through something other than the console. The configuration also enables SNMP, a syslog server, and filter URLs.

Single DMZ Configuration

This configuration moves the FTP, Web, and e-mail servers to a DMZ. All traffic destined for these servers will not touch the LAN. When using a DMZ, it is critical that no connection between the LAN and the DMZ be maintained except through the PIX Firewall. Connecting the LAN to the DMZ in any way except through the firewall defeats the purpose of the DMZ. Figure 4-7 shows that a third interface has been added to the PIX. This interface will be used as a DMZ.

Figure 4-7 *Single DMZ Configuration*

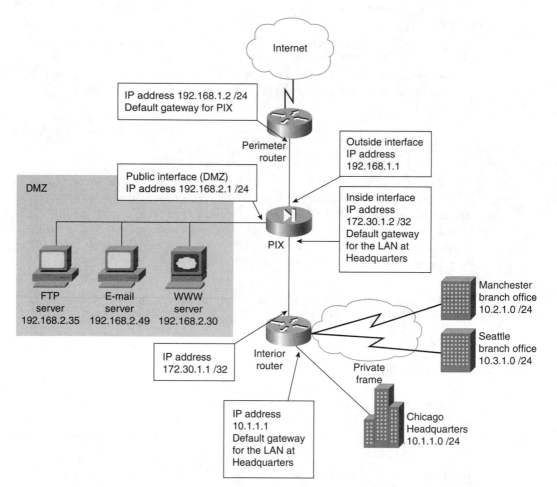

The configuration will need a few changes from the previous one. Look through the following configuration. This section will discuss where changes have been made and the ramifications of those changes after the configuration. As before, the blank lines are for clarity.

```
hostname pixfirewall

enable password enablepass encrypted
passwd password encrypted

nameif ethernet0 outside security0
nameif ethernet1 inside security100
nameif ethernet2 public security 50

interface ethernet0 auto
interface ethernet1 auto
interface ethernet2 auto

ip address outside 192.168.1.1 255.255.255.0
ip address inside 172.30.1.2 255.255.255.252
ip address public 192.168.2.1 255.255.255.0

fixup protocol http 80
fixup protocol http 10120
fixup protocol http 10121
fixup protocol http 10122
fixup protocol http 10123
fixup protocol http 10124
fixup protocol http 10125
fixup protocol ftp 21
fixup protocol ftp 10126
fixup protocol ftp 10127

snmp-server community ourbigcompany
snmp-server location Seattle
snmp-server contact Mark Newcomb Andrew Mason
snmp-server host inside 10.1.1.74
snmp-server enable traps

logging on
logging host 10.1.1.50
logging trap 7
logging facility 20
no logging console

telnet 10.1.1.14 255.255.255.255
telnet 10.1.1.19 255.255.255.255
telnet 10.1.1.212 255.255.255.255

url-server (inside) host 10.1.1.51 timeout 30
url-server (inside) host 10.1.1.52
filter url http 0 0 0 0

global (outside) 1 192.168.1.50-192.168.1.253 255.255.255.0
global (outside) 1 192.168.1.254 255.255.255.0
nat (inside) 1 10.1.1.0 255.255.255.0 0 0
nat (inside) 1 10.2.1.0 255.255.255.0 0 0
nat (inside) 1 10.3.1.0 255.255.255.0 0 0
nat (public) 1 192.168.2.1 255.255.255.0 0 0

static (public, outside) 192.168.1.30 192.168.2.30
static (public, outside) 192.168.1.35 192.168.2.35
static (public, outside) 192.168.1.49 192.168.2.49

conduit permit tcp host 192.168.1.30 eq http any
conduit permit tcp host 192.168.1.35 eq ftp any
conduit permit tcp host 192.168.1.49 eq smtp any
conduit permit tcp any eq sqlnet host 192.168.1.30
```

```
route outside 0 0 192.168.1.2 1
route inside 10.1.1.0 255.255.255.0 172.30.1.1 1
route inside 10.2.1.0 255.255.255.0 172.30.1.1 1
route inside 10.3.1.0 255.255.255.0 172.30.1.1 1
route public 192.168.2.0 255.255.255.0 192.168.2.1

arp timeout 7200

clear xlate
write mem
```

The **hostname** command has been added as the first line in this configuration. This merely identifies the host when you Telnet in for configuration.

You add a new interface, name it **public**, and assign a security level of 50 with the following line:

```
nameif ethernet2 public security 50
```

Because the security level of this interface is less than the inside and greater than the outside, some default behaviors come into play. By default, packets from the outside interface are not allowed into this network. Packets from the inside are, by default, allowed into this network.

You also changed the speeds for all of the interfaces. You are now using the keyword **auto** with the **interface** command. This allows the interface to connect in whatever form is most appropriate, based on the equipment to which it is connected. You added an IP address for the new network card and a subnet mask for the network.

fixup Command

Several **fixup** commands were entered. Some **fixup** commands appear in the configuration by default, others are added as needed. The **fixup protocol** commands allow changing, enabling, and disabling the use of a service or protocol through the PIX Firewall. The ports specified for each service are listened to by the PIX Firewall. The **fixup protocol** command causes the ASA to work on port numbers other than the defaults. The following **fixup protocol** commands are enabled by default:

```
fixup protocol ftp 21
fixup protocol http 80
fixup protocol smtp 25
fixup protocol h323 1720
fixup protocol rsh 514
fixup protocol sqlnet 1521
```

You added the following lines regarding the HTTP protocol:

```
fixup protocol http 10120
fixup protocol http 10121
fixup protocol http 10122
fixup protocol http 10123
fixup protocol http 10124
fixup protocol http 10125
```

These lines accomplish a very specific task. When HTTP traffic is seen by the PIX, it can now be on any of the previously listed ports. Before these lines were entered, the PIX would have seen what looked like HTTP traffic entering the PIX. Because the destination port was set to something other than the default of 80, that traffic would be denied. For example, if an outside user tried to connect to the Web server with the following URL, the user would be denied:

http://www.ourcompany.com:10121

The reason for the denial is that the **:10121** at the end of the URL specifies that the connection should be made on port 10121, rather than on the default port of 80. The Web developers have specific reasons for wanting to allow users to connect to these ports. The configuration allows the users to connect with these ports, and you still maintain the same safeguards regarding HTTP traffic that is true for port 80.

Similarly, the developers have specific reasons for wanting to change the defaults. The developers decided that users requiring FTP access should be able to gain access through the default port of 21 or ports 10126 and 10127. You have no idea why they want to do this, nor do you really care. What you care about is that you can open these ports to FTP traffic, and only FTP traffic, without compromising the network security. To accomplish this, you add the following lines:

```
fixup protocol ftp 21
fixup protocol ftp 10126
fixup protocol ftp 10127
```

It should be noted that the **fixup protocol** command is global in nature. For example, when you told the PIX that port 10121 was part of the HTTP protocol, this applied to all interfaces. You cannot selectively cause port 10121 to be regarded as HTTP traffic on one interface, but not on another interface.

There might be times when it is necessary to disable one of the default **fixup protocol** commands. For example, if your company develops e-mail software and the PIX is used to separate the test network from the corporate network. In this case, you might want to allow more commands than **HELLO, MAIL, RCPT, DATA, RSET, NOOP,** and **QUIT** to travel through the PIX. In this case, using the **no** form of the **fixup protocol** command will disable the feature. An example of removing the Mailguard feature is as follows:

```
no fixup protocol smtp 25
```

SNMP Commands

You add SNMP to the PIX because you want to be informed when errors occur. You can browse the System and Interface groups of MIB-II. All SNMP values within the PIX Firewall are read-only (RO) and do not support browsing (SNMPget or SNMPwalk) of the Cisco syslog Management Information Base (MIB). Traps are sent to the SNMP server. In other words, SNMP can be used to monitor the PIX but not for configuring the PIX. The syntax for the commands is essentially the same as when working on a Cisco router. The following lines set the community string, the location, the contact, and the interface and IP address of the SNMP server. Because you have specified **inside** on the **snmp-server host** command, the PIX knows which interface to send SNMP traps out without the need for a specific route to this host.

```
snmp-server community ourbigcompany
snmp-server location Seattle
snmp-server contact Mark Newcomb Andrew Mason
snmp-server host inside 10.1.1.74
```

logging Commands

The following **logging** commands allow you to use a syslog server for recording events. These commands are similar to those used on a Cisco router. The **logging on** command is used to specify that logging will occur. The **logging host** command is what actually starts the logging process on the host at 10.1.1.50. The **logging trap** command sets the level of logging to be recorded, which is all events with a level of 7. Finally, the **no logging console** command is used to prevent the log messages from appearing on the console. For this to work, the PIX must know how to find the host at 10.1.1.50. Ensure that a route to this host exists.

```
logging on
logging host 10.1.1.50
logging trap 7
logging facility 20
no logging console
```

telnet Command

You added three lines to allow access to the PIX Firewall through Telnet in addition to the console port access. This is a major convenience and a major security risk. There are three reasons that we consider Telnet access a risk. The first is that Telnet limits access based on the IP address. It is very easy for a user to change the IP address on a computer, especially if the user is using an operating system such as Windows 95. This allows the possibility of a user gaining access where the user should not be able to gain access. The second concern regarding security is that, as hard as you may try to prevent it, you cannot always be sure that a user walking away from a desk will lock the terminal. Password-protected screensavers help minimize the issue, but they cannot completely resolve it. Because the PIX forms the corporation's major defense from outside intrusion, it is critical that access is limited as much as possible. The third concern regarding Telnet access is a misunderstanding on how it should be configured. This third issue is covered in this section, after examining the commands entered.

```
telnet 10.1.1.14 255.255.255.255
telnet 10.1.1.19 255.255.255.255
telnet 10.1.1.212 255.255.255.255
```

In the preceding lines, you specified a subnet mask of 32 bits for each of these IP addresses. Entering **255.255.255.255** is optional, because an IP address without a subnet mask is assumed to have a 32-bit mask associated with that address. The subnet mask used on the **telnet** command is the mask for those who should have access to the PIX, not the subnet mask for the network. Approximately 50 percent of the PIX Firewalls the authors of this book have examined have been incorrectly configured with the subnet mask of the LAN. In these cases, any user on the LAN can Telnet to the PIX Firewall. If one of these users is able to guess the password, the user can control the PIX. In the configuration section "Dual DMZ with AAA Authentication" later in this chapter, you will see how to use authentication, authorization, and accounting (AAA) services to ensure that unauthorized users cannot Telnet to the PIX Firewall.

URL Filtering

You added URL filtering for monitoring, reporting, and restricting URL access. Cisco Systems and Websense, Inc. have formed a partnership for joint marketing and coordination of technical information on a product called Websense, which is used to control the sites that users are allowed to access. For example, web sites classified as employment or violent can be blocked. Instructions on ordering Websense are included in the documentation of every PIX Firewall.

The PIX Firewall configuration for enabling URL filtering is very simple. The following three lines show the configuration. The first line tells the PIX to allow or block URL access based on the information received from the Websense server on the inside interface at the 10.1.1.51 IP address. Should a response to a request not be received within the timeout parameter of 30 seconds shown on this line, the next Websense server will be queried. The default timeout is 5 seconds. The second line shows the failover Websense server, which is also the Web server on the public interface. The third line defines that all HTTP requests will be watched. Multiple filter commands can be combined to refine what is monitored. The full syntax of the **filter** command will be shown after the command lines.

```
url-server (inside) host 10.1.1.51 timeout 30
url-server (public) host 192.168.2.30
filter url http 0 0 0 0
```

The full syntax of the **filter** command is as follows:

```
filter [activex http url] |except local_ip local_mask foreign_ip
    foreign_mask [allow]
```

The definitions of the parameters can be found in Table 4-1.

Table 4-1   **filter** *Command Parameters*

Command	Description
activex	Blocks outbound ActiveX, Java applets, and other HTML object tags from outbound packets.
url	Filters URL data from moving through the PIX.
http	Filters HTTP URLs.
except	Creates an exception to a previously stated filter condition.
local_ip	The IP address before NAT (if any) is applied. Use 0 for all IP addresses.
local_mask	The subnet mask of the local IP. Use 0 if 0 is used for the IP address.
foreign_ip	The IP address of the lower security level host or network. Use 0 for all foreign IP addresses.
foreign_mask	The subnet mask of the foreign IP. Use 0 if the foreign IP is 0.
allow	When a server is unavailable, this lets outbound connections pass through the PIX without filtering.

Additional Single-DMZ Configuration Considerations

The remaining changes to this configuration involve commands that were previously examined in this chapter. You added a new **nat** statement with the interface set as **public** to allow for translation of the public DMZ to global addresses. This eliminates the chance that anyone from the outside will see any traffic on the inside network. You can use NAT on all of the public hosts and add them to the common global pool. The command used is as follows:

```
nat (public) 1 192.168.2.1 255.255.255.0 0 0
```

Next, you change the static NAT for the Web, FTP, and e-mail servers from the inside interface to the public interface. The new lines read:

```
static (public, outside) 192.168.1.30 192.168.2.30
static (public, outside) 192.168.1.35 192.168.2.35
static (public, outside) 192.168.1.49 192.168.2.49
```

If you were using the previous configuration, you would have needed to remove the old static translations using the **no** form of the **static** command. You also added a new **conduit** statement. This statement allows any Oracle database traffic from the Web server on the public interface to enter into your inside LAN. The PIX Firewall uses port 1521 for SQL*Net. This is also the default port used by Oracle for SQL*Net, despite the fact that this value does not agree with Internet Assigned Numbers Authority (IANA) port assignments.

Because the Web server has a database running in the background, you need to allow traffic from this Web server to enter into the LAN and talk to the Oracle database servers. These tasks are accomplished with the following lines:

```
conduit permit tcp host 192.168.1.30 eq http any
conduit permit tcp host 192.168.1.35 eq ftp any
conduit permit tcp host 192.168.1.49 eq smtp any
conduit permit tcp any eq sqlnet host 192.168.1.30
```

You also added a few new **route** statements. You added routes for both the Seattle and Manchester networks as well as the public network. Finally, you made sure that the NAT changes would occur by issuing a **clear xlate** command and then writing the configuration.

Dual DMZ with AAA Authentication

This section introduces AAA authorization and creates two DMZs. Chapter 10 deals extensively with AAA. This section focuses on the PIX configuration aspects of AAA. This section also introduces a failover PIX and access lists into this configuration.

Figure 4-8 shows how this network is configured. Notice that there are two PIX Firewalls, a primary and a failover. Should the primary PIX fail, the failover PIX takes over all of the duties of the primary PIX. You also have two DMZs, the public and the accounting DMZs. The accounting DMZ is used for clients on the Internet to access the accounting data for the services.

Figure 4-8 *Dual DMZ Configuration*

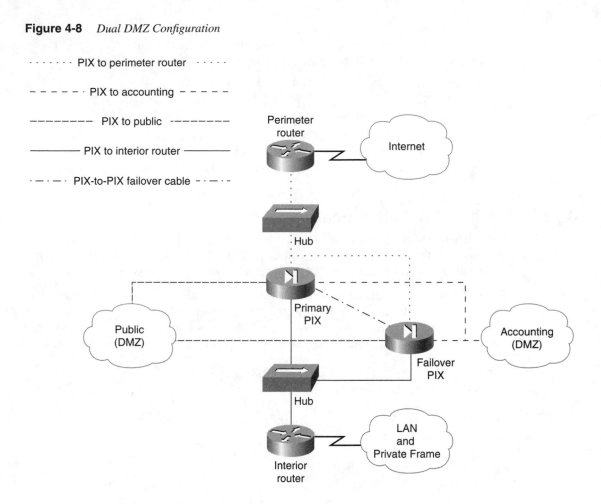

Although there is a failover cable that connects the serial ports on the firewalls, you also added a hub on the inside interfaces to allow connectivity between the firewalls and the interior router in order to save interfaces on the interior router. You did the same between the outside interfaces of the firewalls and the exterior router. Both PIX Firewalls must have connectivity to both DMZs for the failover PIX to operate correctly, should the primary fail.

The configuration of the primary PIX follows. This section discusses the changes made to this configuration after the listing. The blank lines were added for clarity.

```
hostname pixfirewall

enable password enablepass encrypted
passwd password encrypted

nameif ethernet0 outside security0
nameif ethernet1 inside security100
nameif ethernet2 public security 50
nameif ethernet3 accounting security 60
```

```
interface ethernet0 auto
interface ethernet1 auto
interface ethernet2 auto
interface ethernet3 auto

ip address outside 192.168.1.1 255.255.255.0
ip address inside 172.30.1.2 255.255.255.248
ip address public 192.168.2.1 255.255.255.0
ip address accounting 10.200.200.1 255.255.255.0

fixup protocol http 80
fixup protocol http 10120
fixup protocol http 10121
fixup protocol http 10122
fixup protocol http 10123
fixup protocol http 10124
fixup protocol http 10125
fixup protocol ftp 21
fixup protocol ftp 10126
fixup protocol ftp 10127

failover active
failover link failover

no rip inside passive
no rip outside passive
no rip public passive
no rip accounting passive
no rip inside default
no rip outside default
no rip public default
no rip accounting default

pager lines 24

aaa-server TACACS+ (inside) host 10.1.1.41 thekey timeout 20
aaa authentication include any outbound 0 0 0 0 TACACS+
aaa authorization include any outbound 0 0 0 0 TACACS+
aaa accounting include any outbound 0 0 0 0 TACACS+
aaa authentication serial console TACACS+

snmp-server community ourbigcompany
snmp-server location Seattle
snmp-server contact Mark Newcomb Andrew Mason
snmp-server host inside 10.1.1.74
snmp-server enable traps

logging on
logging host 10.1.1.50
logging trap 7
logging facility 20
no logging console

outbound limit_acctg deny 10.200.200.0 255.255.255.0
outbound limit_acctg except 10.10.1.51
outbound limit_acctg permit 10.200.200.66
outbound limit_acctg permit 10.200.200.67
apply (accounting) limit_acctg outgoing_dest

access-list acct_pub permit host 10.200.200.52
access-list acct_pub deny 10.200.200.0 255.255.255.0
access-group acct_pub in interface public
```

```
telnet 10.1.1.14 255.255.255.255
telnet 10.1.1.19 255.255.255.255
telnet 10.1.1.212 255.255.255.255

url-server (inside) host 10.1.1.51 timeout 30
url-server (inside) host 10.1.1.52
filter url http 0 0 0 0

global (outside) 1 192.168.1.50-192.168.1.253 255.255.255.0
global (outside) 1 192.168.1.254 255.255.255.0
nat (inside) 1 10.1.1.0 255.255.255.0 0 0
nat (inside) 1 10.2.1.0 255.255.255.0 0 0
nat (inside) 1 10.3.1.0 255.255.255.0 0 0
nat (public) 1 192.168.2.1 255.255.255.0 0 0
nat (accounting) 0 0 0

static (public, outside) 192.168.1.30 192.168.2.30
static (public, outside) 192.168.1.35 192.168.2.35
static (public, outside) 192.168.1.49 192.168.2.49

conduit permit tcp host 192.168.1.30 eq http any
conduit permit tcp host 192.168.1.35 eq ftp any
conduit permit tcp host 192.168.1.49 eq smtp any
conduit permit tcp any eq sqlnet host 192.168.1.30

route outside 0 0 192.168.1.2 1
route inside 10.1.1.0 255.255.255.0 172.30.1.1 1
route inside 10.2.1.0 255.255.255.0 172.30.1.1 1
route inside 10.3.1.0 255.255.255.0 172.30.1.1 1
route public 192.168.2.0 255.255.255.0 192.168.2.1
route accounting 10.200.200.0 255.255.255.0 10.200.200.1 1

arp timeout 7200

mtu inside 1500
mtu outside 1500
mtu public 1500
mtu accounting 1500

clear xlate
write mem
write standby
```

The first change made to this configuration is the added **nameif** command for the accounting DMZ, assigning a security level of 60. The next change is that you enabled this interface with the **interface** command. You then assigned an IP address to the interface. Next, you configured the failover parameters.

failover Commands

The **failover** commands are relatively simple to use. Before discussing the commands, this section takes a few moments and discusses the requirements for a failover PIX, how the primary and secondary PIX are connected, and how the failover PIX is configured.

When purchasing a PIX, consider purchasing a failover PIX at the same time. When both are purchased together, there is a significant price reduction on the failover unit. Because the PIX is generally used as the primary device protecting your network, it usually makes sense from both service and fiscal points of view to make this a redundant system.

For a PIX to failover to another PIX after failure, both firewalls must have identical hardware and identical software versions. There is a proprietary cable made specifically for connecting between PIX Firewalls. On the back of each PIX is a port labeled *failover*. The cable ends are labeled *primary* and *secondary*. Once the primary PIX is configured, turn the secondary PIX's power off. Connect the cable, and restore power to the secondary PIX. After a few seconds, the secondary PIX acquires a copy of the configuration on the primary PIX. Should the primary PIX fail, the secondary PIX starts establishing connections. However, any connections that exist when the primary PIX fails are dropped and need to be reestablished. After the secondary PIX is powered on with the failover cable connected, changes should only be made to the primary PIX. One limitation of the failover system on the PIX is the length of the failover cable. The length of the cable cannot be extended, and the cable is required to be used. Therefore, you cannot use a primary PIX in one physical location and the secondary PIX in another location.

The first command used is the **failover active** command. This command, like all commands, should only be entered on the primary PIX. This command establishes that failover is configured and that the present PIX is the primary PIX. Using the **no** form of this command forces the current PIX to become the secondary PIX.

The second command shown is the **failover link** command. You have specified that the port used for the failover is the failover port. There is one more command used regarding failover. This command, **write standby**, is shown at the bottom of the configuration. The **write standby** command should be used after each time the configuration is changed. This causes the secondary PIX to receive a copy of the current configuration.

Understanding Failover

The failover features of the PIX are similar to those used with the Hot Standby Router Protocol (HSRP) in that the standby device remains inactive until the primary device fails. The standby device, on activation, assumes the IP and Media Access Control (MAC) address of the primary unit. Likewise, the previously active device assumes the IP and MAC addresses of the formerly standby device. Because network devices do not see any change in these addresses, no new ARP entries need to be made on the hosts using the PIX Firewall.

Starting with the PIX IOS 5.0 software release, stateful failovers are supported. Prior to this release, the PIX did not maintain a copy of the connection state in the standby unit. When the primary device failed, network traffic needed to reestablish previous connections. Stateful failovers overcome this issue by passing data about the state of connections between the primary and the standby devices within *state update packets*. A single packet traversing the PIX can establish a new connection state. Because each connection state changes on a per-packet basis, every packet received by the currently active device requires a state update packet to be relayed to the inactive device. Although this process works very well, there are some latency-sensitive applications that will time out before the failover process is completed. In these cases, a new session will need to be established.

IP states are supported, as are TCP states, except those using HTTP. Almost no UDP state tables are transferred between the active and standby devices. Exceptions to this include dynamically opened ports used with multichannel protocols, such as H.323. Because DNS resolves use a single channel port, the state of DNS requests is not transferred between devices.

A dedicated LAN interface between the two PIX devices is required to achieve stateful failover. State update packets are transmitted asynchronously in the background from the active device to the standby device over the dedicated LAN interface. There are also a few configurations changes required when using stateful failover. These changes are covered in the section "Stateful Failover Configuration."

Several criteria are considered before a failover occurs. If the standby device detects that the active device is powered down, the standby device will take active control. If the failover cable is unplugged, a syslog entry is generated, but both devices maintain their present state. An exception to this is during the boot process. Should the failover cable be unplugged while the devices are booting, both devices will assume the same IP address, causing a conflict on your network. Even if you are configuring the PIX Firewalls for stateful failover using a dedicated LAN interface, the failover cable must be installed on both devices for failover to function properly.

Failover hello packets are expected on each interface every 15 seconds. When the standby device does not receive a failover hello packet within 30 seconds, the interface runs a series of tests to establish the state of the active device. If these tests do not reveal that the active device is present, the standby device assumes the active role.

A power failure on the active device is detected through the failover cable within 15 seconds. In this case, the standby device assumes the active role. A disconnected or damaged failover cable is detected within 15 seconds.

Stateful Failover Configuration

Only a few commands need to be added to a configuration to enable stateful failover. The following is a partial configuration, showing the commands necessary to enable stateful failover. After the configuration, the commands are discussed.

```
nameif ethernet0 outside security0
nameif ethernet1 inside security100
nameif ethernet2 failover security 60

ip address outside 192.168.1.1 255.255.255.0
ip address inside 172.30.1.1 255.255.255.0
ip address failover 10.200.200.1 255.255.255.0

failover active
failover ip address outside 192.168.1.2
failover ip address inside 172.30.1.2
failover ip address failover 10.200.200.2
failover link failover
```

Notice that the interfaces are named *failover,* and a security level is assigned to the interface with the **nameif** command. You could have named this interface anything, but for clarity, it is named failover here. This is the interface you will be using to transfer state update packets between the active and the standby devices.

After assigning IP addresses and netmasks to each of the interfaces, you are ready to start on the failover commands. Start failover with the **failover active** command. Next, use the **failover ip address** command on all of the interfaces.

When using the **failover ip address** command, you need to remember two things. First, every interface needs the **failover ip address** command entered for that interface. If an interface does not have an associated **failover ip address** command and the state of that interface is changed to down, failover will not occur. For example, if you did not add the **failover ip address** command for the outside interface and the cable connecting that interface broke, all data intended to travel through that interface will be lost. This defeats the purpose of having a failover device, because a failover device should allow all services to continue after the primary device has failed. Additionally, because both devices must have the same hardware installed, there is no reason not to enable failover to check all interfaces. The second item that you need to remember is that the **failover ip address** needs to be on the same subnet but with a different IP address than that to which the interface is set.

The final configuration required is to assign a dedicated interface to failover. Using the **failover link** command with the interface name assigned by the **nameif** command, Ethernet2 has been assigned as the failover interface in this example.

rip Commands

You added commands to disable RIP on all interfaces. Notice that each interface has two lines associated with that interface: a **no rip** *interface_name* **passive** and a **no rip** *interface_name* **default** command. Each one of these commands accomplishes a different objective. The **no rip** *interface_name* **passive** command causes the PIX to stop listening to RIP updates. The **no rip** *interface_name* **default** command causes the PIX to stop broadcasting known routes through RIP.

RIPv1 and RIPv2 are both available on the PIX through the **rip** command. Use the **no** form of the **rip** command to disable a portion of RIP. Use the **show rip** command to show the current RIP entries and the **clear rip** command to clear RIP tables. The full syntax of this command is:

```
rip interface_name default | passive [version [1 | 2]]
    [authentication [text | md5 key (key_id)]]
```

The parameters and keyword meanings are listed in Table 4-2.

Table 4-2   **rip** *Command Parameters*

Command	Description
interface_name	The interface to which this command should be applied.
default	Broadcasts a default route on the interface.
passive	Enables passive RIP (listening mode) and propagates the RIP tables based on these updates.
version	RIP version 1 or 2. Version 2 must be used if encryption is required.
authentication	Enables RIP version 2 authentication.
text	Sends RIP updates as clear text. This is not a recommended option.
md5	Sends RIP update packets using MD5 encryption. Version 2 only.
key	This is the key used to encrypt RIP updates for version 2.
key_id	The key identification value. Both sides must use the same key. Version 2 only.

pager lines Command

The **pager lines** command specifies how many lines are shown when a **show config** command is issued before a **more** prompt appears. Although this can be set to almost any value, 24 works well when using standard Telnet applications.

AAA Commands

You have enabled AAA using Terminal Access Controller Access Control System Plus (TACACS+) on your PIX for authenticating, authorizing, and accounting for users passing from the inside through the outside interface. You have also enabled TACACS+ authentication for those connecting to the PIX through the console.

The first command you need to look at is the **aaa-server** command. The example sets the server to TACACS+ on the inside interface with the IP address of 10.1.1.41. You are using **thekey** as your TACACS+ key and have set a timeout of 20 seconds. This command is also responsible for starting AAA on the PIX. The full syntax of the **aaa-server** command follows:

```
aaa-server group_tag (interface_name) host server_ip key timeout seconds
```

The parameters and keywords, along with their descriptions, are displayed in Table 4-3.

Table 4-3   aaa-server *Command Parameters*

Command	Description
group_tag	TACACS+ or RADIUS.
interface_name	Name of the interface where the server resides.
host	Keyword designating that a single host IP address follows.
server_ip	The IP address of the server.
key	The alphanumeric key expected at the server.
timeout	Keyword designating that the parameter following is the number of seconds.
seconds	The wait time in seconds that the PIX will wait after sending a request without receiving a response before another request is sent. The default time is 5 seconds. Four requests will be sent before timing out.

After starting AAA, you authenticated, authorized, and accounted for any outbound traffic. For a full description of these three processes, see Chapter 10. For the moment, it will suffice to say that when users attempt to send data outside, first they will be checked to ensure that they are who they claim to be, then a check will determine whether they are allowed to send the data outside, and then a record will be made that the users sent the data. You accomplish these three tasks in this example with the following three lines:

```
aaa authentication include any outbound 0 0 0 0 TACACS+
aaa authorization include any outbound 0 0 0 0 TACACS+
aaa accounting include any outbound 0 0 0 0 TACACS+
```

The key here is the word **outbound**, which means packets traversing from the inside interface through the outside interface. The **any** in these lines refers to the type of accounting service; possible values are **any**, **ftp**, **http**, **telnet**, or **protocol/port**. The four zeros refer, in order, to the local address, the local mask, the foreign IP address, and the foreign mask. The final parameter determines which service should be used, RADIUS or TACACS+. It is possible to run both TACACS+ and RADIUS at the same time. To accomplish this, merely add another **aaa-server** command with the other service.

The **aaa authentication** command has another form that allows you to authenticate connections for the serial port, the Telnet ports, and the enable mode. The full syntax of this command follows:

```
aaa authentication [serial | enable | telnet] console group_tag
```

outbound and apply Commands

Now that you have seen how AAA can limit outbound access through an interface, there is another way to control and limit access from a higher security level interface to a lower security level interface. This method uses PIX access lists configured with the **outbound** and **apply** commands. The first thing to remember about this type of PIX access list is that it operates in a totally different manner than a router's access list. If you are intimately familiar with router access lists, you might have a harder time accepting how PIX access lists work than those who are not so familiar with router access lists. The order of a router's access list is vitally important, because the first match will cause a rejection or acceptance. However, the PIX uses a best-fit mechanism for its access lists. This allows the administrator to deny whole ranges of IP addresses and then allow specific hosts through at a later date without having to rewrite the whole access list. The PIX access list is also neither a standard nor an extended access list, but rather a combination of the two forms.

Where a router uses two commands, **access-list** and **access-group** (or **access-class**), to define and apply an access list, the PIX uses the **outbound** and **apply** commands to define and apply an access list.

The full syntax of the **outbound** command follows:

```
outbound list_id permit | deny ip_address [netmask [java | port[-port]]]
    [protocol]
```

A description of the command parameters can be found in Table 4-4.

Table 4-4   **outbound** *Command Parameters*

Command	Description
list_id	This is an arbitrary name or number used to identify the access list. This is similar to a named access list on a router.
permit	Allows the access list to access the specified IP address and port.
deny	Denies access to the specified IP address and port.
except	Creates an exception to the previous **outbound** command.
	The IP address associated with an **except** statement changes depending on whether an **outgoing_src** or **outgoing_dest** parameter is used in the **apply** command.
	If the **apply** command uses **outgoing_src**, the IP address applies to the destination IP address.
	If the **apply** command uses an **outgoing_dest**, the IP address refers to the source IP address.
ip_address	The IP address associated with the **outbound permit**, **outbound deny**, or **outbound except** command.
netmask	The subnet mask associated with the IP address. Remember that this is a subnet mask, not a wildcard mask as used on routers. Where a router would have a wildcard mask of 0.0.0.255, the PIX would have a subnet mask of 255.255.255.0.
port	The port or range of ports associated with this command.
java	The keyword **java** is used to indicate port 80. When **java** is used with a **deny**, the PIX blocks Java applets from being downloaded from the IP address. By default, the PIX permits Java applets.
protocol	This limits access to one of the following protocols: UDP, TCP, or ICMP. TCP is assumed if no protocol is entered.

Now that you know how the command works, look at the effects of the commands. The first two lines of the configuration regarding access lists read:

```
outbound limit_acctg deny 10.200.200.0 255.255.255.0
outbound limit_acctg except 10.10.1.51
```

The first **outbound** command denies all packets from the Class C network at 10.1.1.0. When using the **deny** and **permit** forms of the **outbound** command, you are referring to the destination IP address. You could use the word **permit** in the example instead of **deny**, which would allow packets from these IP addresses. The effects of the second line cannot be fully determined until you look at the **apply** command. However, you can still see that an exception to the previous **deny** command exists. This exception allows packets associated with the IP address of 10.10.1.51 through the PIX. Here the word *associated* is used instead of *destination* or *source* because whether you are concerned about the source or the destination IP address is actually determined by the **apply** command. If the **apply** command specifies a source IP address, the packets from the source used with the **outbound** command are permitted or denied. If the **apply** command specifies a destination address, then packets whose destination address matches the IP address used with the **outbound** command are denied or permitted.

This is a two-step process that requires the administrator to ask two questions. First, look at the **outbound** command. Is this a permit or deny statement? Next, look at the **apply** command. Is the **apply** command concerned with the source or the destination address?

The next two lines are easy to understand. You permit access to the hosts at 10.200.200.66 and 10.200.200.67. At this point, you still do not have a definition as to whether the IP address associated with the **except** is a source or destination address. However, the **apply** command will resolve this outstanding issue. For review purposes, the two lines follow:

```
outbound limit_acctg permit 10.200.200.66
outbound limit_acctg permit 10.200.200.67
```

The **apply** statement is used to connect an access list with an interface and to define whether IP addresses specified with that access list are source or destination IP addresses. This example of the **apply** command follows:

```
apply (accounting) limit_acctg outgoing_dest
```

In this example, you applied an access list to the interface previously defined as **accounting** by the **nameif** command. The access list you connected is the one called **limit_acctg**. As with a router's access lists, only one access list can be applied in a given direction on any PIX interface.

This **apply** command has applied the **except** command to source packets. The alternative would be to apply the **except** command to destination packets by using the **outgoing_src** parameter. The application of this command has a distinct effect on the access list. This effect is that the IP address specified by the **except** command is a source address.

For review purposes, look at Figure 4-9. Refer to Figure 4-9 while reviewing the following discussion about the command lines used.

Figure 4-9 *PIX* **outbound** *Command Example*

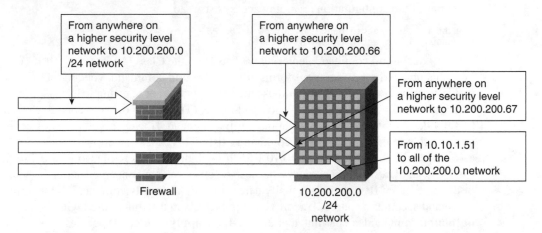

The following line prevents access to all of the 10.200.200.0/24 network from all hosts for all protocols. The PIX uses subnet masks, not wildcard masks.

```
outbound limit_acctg deny 10.200.200.0 255.255.255.0
```

The following line is an exception to the preceding line. Because the **apply** statement uses **outgoing_src**, the preceding denial of access to the 10.200.200.0 network does not apply to the host with the IP address of 10.10.1.51. Because the security level is higher on the network where this computer sits, this computer has access to the whole of the 10.200.200.0 network.

```
outbound limit_acctg except 10.10.1.51
```

The following line allows all hosts on all networks with a higher security level to have access to the host at 10.200.200.66.

```
outbound limit_acctg permit 10.200.200.66
```

The following line allows all hosts on all networks with a higher security level to have access to the host at 10.200.200.67.

```
outbound limit_acctg permit 10.200.200.67
```

The following line applies the access list called **limit_acctg** to the accounting interface and makes a definition for the **except** command, specifying that the IP addresses within the **except** command refer to a source address.

```
apply (accounting) limit_acctg outgoing_dest
```

It is important to remember that the order of the outbound statements is not a concern because the PIX uses a best-fit algorithm.

access-list and access-group Commands

There is another method of using access lists shown in this configuration. This method, heavily used in conjunction with crypto maps, will be explored further in the VPN sections later in this chapter. This section discusses the **access-list** and **access-group** commands as they relate to traffic other than encrypted traffic. Access lists on a PIX Firewall use either of these commands to limit connections between interfaces. When used to limit connections from a lower security level interface to a higher security level interface, the **access-list** command command can replace a **conduit** command. When used to limit connections from a higher security level interface to a lower security level interface, the access list can replace the **outbound** command.

Whether you are using the **access-list** command from a higher to lower or a lower to higher interface changes how you use this command. The following are some rules to keep in mind when designing PIX access lists.

For access from a higher security level interface to a lower security interface, always permit access first and then deny access afterward. Outbound connections are permitted by default. Therefore, the access list is used to limit this default behavior. Only **deny** statements need to be added, unless a **permit** is needed to override a **deny** command. Because PIX access lists are best-fit, this is a legitimate technique. In the configuration, you first allowed access for a single host at 10.200.200.52. You then denied access from all of those hosts on the 10.200.200.0 /24 network. Make sure that the netmask used on a PIX access list is really a subnet mask, and not the wildcard mask used on router access lists. This is shown in the configuration with the following two lines:

```
access-list acct_pub permit host 10.200.200.52
access-list acct_pub deny 10.200.200.0 255.255.255.0
```

When accessing from a lower to a higher security level, access is denied by default. Therefore, an access list would normally only contain **permit** statements. Again, you might have a situation where all except for a few hosts should be denied. In this case, you would use **permit** commands for the hosts to be let through the interface, along with a **deny** command for the specific hosts to be denied.

The full syntax for a PIX access list follows:

```
access-list name [deny | permit] protocol src_addr src_mask
    operator port dest_addr dest_mask operator port
```

On the PIX Firewall, access lists are applied to an interface with the **access-group** command. In the command, shown below, you apply the access list named **acct_pub** to the **public** interface.

```
access-group acct_pub in interface public
```

The **access-group** command always uses the keywords **in interface** before the interface name.

There are a few things to consider when working with PIX access lists. First, it is recommended that you do not use the **access list** command with the **conduit** and **outbound** commands. Technically, these commands will work together, however, the way these commands interact causes debugging issues. The **conduit** and **outbound** commands operate with two interfaces, while the **access-list** command applies only to a single interface. If you choose to ignore this warning, remember that the access list is checked first. The **conduit** and **outbound** commands are checked after the **access-list** command. Second, the masks used in the PIX access lists and the **outbound** command are subnet masks, not wildcard masks.

Additional Dual-DMZ Configuration Considerations

Notice that there is a **nat 0** command associated with the accounting DMZ. A **nat 0** command prevents any NAT or PAT from occurring. How could this be used to your advantage? Assuming that you do not use NAT and you assign nonroutable IP addresses to a DMZ, you can prevent anyone on the Internet from reaching this DMZ while still allowing the local LANs to reach the network. You can also provide additional protection when you are using routable IP addresses through the PIX. Whether or not you choose to use NAT on an interface does not really affect how that interface operates.

This concludes the configuration of the PIX Firewall, with the exception of VPNs. The remainder of this chapter covers VPNs, starting with Point-to-Point Tunneling Protocol (PPTP) and then moving on to IPSec VPNs.

VPN with Point-to-Point Tunneling Protocol (PPTP)

Starting with Version 5.1 of the PIX IOS, Cisco provides support for Microsoft PPTP VPN clients as an alternative to IPSec. Although PPTP is a less secure technology than IPSec, PPTP is easier to configure and maintain. PPTP also enjoys a great deal of support, especially from Microsoft clients. The PPTP is an OSI Layer 2 tunneling protocol that allows a remote client to communicate securely through the Internet. PPTP is described by RFC 2637. The PIX Firewall only supports inbound PPTP, and only a single interface can have PPTP enabled at any given time. PPTP through the PIX has been tested with Windows 95 using DUN1.3, Windows 98, Windows NT 4.0 with SP6, and Windows 2000.

The PIX Firewall supports Password Authentication Protocol (PAP), Challenge Handshake Authentication Protocol (CHAP), and Microsoft Challenge Handshake Authentication Protocol (MS-CHAP), using an external AAA server or the PIX local username and password database. Point-to-Point Protocol (PPP) with Combined Packet Protocol (CCP) negotiations with Microsoft Point-To-Point Encryption (MPPE) extensions using the RSA/RC4 algorithm and either 40- or 128-bit encryption is also supported. The compression features of MPPE are not currently supported.

To enable PPTP support, you first need to have the PIX configured to allow and deny packets in the normal fashion. The interfaces must be configured and the passwords set. After this is accomplished, you can add additional features. The sections regarding VPN in this chapter do not show all of the commands necessary to configure the PIX. Instead, this section concentrates on those commands that require configuration changes from previously shown examples or that are new commands.

Take a moment to look at Figure 4-10. Notice that the VPN tunnel is terminated on the outside interface of the PIX. Although you could terminate the VPN on the perimeter router, there are a few reasons why terminating at the PIX is preferred. The first reason is that the PIX is optimized for security operations, including VPN termination. The PIX is able to handle a much larger number of VPN terminations than most routers. The second reason is that if you terminate on the perimeter router, then only the perimeter router ensures security on the packets after the VPN tunnel has been decrypted. Because the PIX is considered the primary defense, it makes logical sense to keep packets encrypted all the way to the PIX, even if the perimeter router is running the PIX Firewall IOS.

Figure 4-10 *PIX PPTP VPN*

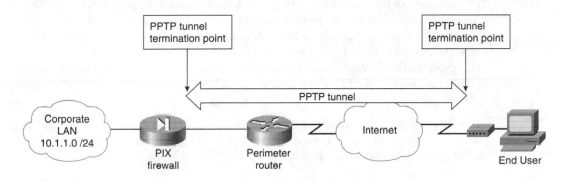

The sample configuration used throughout this chapter requires changes to enable PPTP. These are shown in the following configuration. This section examines each of the new commands, after the following new configuration:

```
ip local pool thelocalpool 10.1.1.50-10.1.1.75
vpdn enable outside
vpdn group 1 accept dialin pptp
vpdn group 1 ppp authentication mschap
vpdn group 1 client configuration address local thelocalpool
vpdn group 1 client configuration dns 10.1.1.41
vpdn group 1 client configuration wins 10.1.1.9
vpdn group 1 client authentication local
vpdn username joe password joespassword
vpdn username mary password marryspassword
sysopt connection permit-pptp
```

ip local pool Command

An IP local pool is used with VPNs to reserve a range of IP addresses that will be assigned to hosts using VPNs. The addresses in this range must not be in use by any other hosts and should not be used in any other commands. Use the **show** form of the command to display all of the IP addresses within a pool. The command, reserving IP addresses of 10.1.1.50 through 10.1.1.75 and using the name **thelocalpool** follows.

```
ip local pool thelocalpool 10.1.1.50-10.1.1.75
```

vpdn Command

The **vpdn** command takes many forms. The first line, the **vpdn enable outside** command, accomplishes two tasks. First, this enables virtual private dial-up network (VPDN) support on the PIX itself. Second, VPDN is enabled on the interface labeled **outside** by the **nameif** command. Multiple interfaces accepting PPTP traffic each require a separate **vpdn enable** *interface* command. Note that the PIX Firewall only accepts incoming PPTP traffic and cannot be used to initiate a PPTP tunnel.

The basic form of the command, **vpdn group 1 accept dialin pptp**, associates the VPDN group numbered 1 within other commands. Assuming that multiple PPTP tunnels are to be terminated on this interface, you might wish to set up some users on one tunnel and other users on a different tunnel. In this case, multiple tunnels allow you to accomplish such tasks as assigning different WINS or DNS severs to individuals. The **accept dialin pptp** portion of this command tells the PIX that it should accept PPTP connections requested by outside entities.

The **vpdn group 1 ppp authentication mschap** command shown next ensures that the password authentication protocol used within VPDN group 1 is **mschap**. The other options available on this command are **pap** and **chap**.

NOTE   You must also ensure that any associated Windows devices needing to use a PPTP tunnel into your network are also configured correctly. Unless you have set a Microsoft Windows client to require encrypted passwords, the client will first use a clear-text PAP password. This attempt will fail because of your PIX configuration that requires encryption. The client will then attempt to connect using the same password in an encrypted form, which will be successful. Even though the connection is ultimately successful, the password has been sent in clear text and might have been revealed to hackers. Therefore, ensure that encrypted passwords are required on all Microsoft Windows clients used with tunneled connections.

The **vpdn group 1 client configuration address local thelocalpool** command is used to assign the IP address used by the client while the client is connected through the PPTP connection. Because you created a group called **thelocalpool** and assigned the addresses of 10.1.1.50 through 10.1.1.75 to that pool, this command assigns the client to look to that pool for one of these available addresses. Limiting the total number of available IP addresses in the pool in turn limits the total number of PPTP connections that can be used simultaneously.

The **client configuration** form of the **vpdn** command is used to assign WINS and DNS servers for use by the PPTP client while the client is connected into your system. Both of these commands can take either one or two IP addresses. The order that these IP addresses are entered within the command reflects the order of their use by Windows clients.

The **vpdn group 1 client authentication local** command tells the PIX to look to the local user database to check passwords. If you are using a AAA server for client authentication, you would need to set up the PIX to recognize the AAA server and the need to authenticate PPTP users with lines similar to the following:

```
aaa-server TACACS+ (inside) host 10.1.1.41 thekey timeout 20
client authentication aaa TACACS+
```

The **vpdn username joe password joespassword** command enters Joe as a user within the local database and assigns **joespassword** to Joe. This is the password whose hash result will be sent over the connection through the MS-CHAP authentication process. You have also enabled Mary as a user with a unique password. Once the system is configured to allow one user, allowing other users involves adding a username and password to the PIX configuration.

sysopt Command

The previous commands shown in this example have set up the PPTP tunnel and users. What has not been done is to allow the users access through the firewall. The **sysopt connection permit-pptp** command allows for all authenticated PPTP clients to traverse the PIX interfaces. The **sysopt** command is used to change the default security behavior of the PIX Firewall in a number of different ways. There are many forms of this command, each acting slightly differently. Table 4-5 contains a list of the **sysopt** commands and a description of each of their functions. Each of these commands also has an associated **no** form of the command, which is used to reverse the behavior associated with the command.

Table 4-5   sysopt *Commands*

Command	Description
sysopt connection enforcesubnet	Prevents packets with a source address belonging to the destination subnet from traversing an interface. A packet arriving from the outside interface having an IP source address of an inside network is not allowed through the interface.
sysopt connection permit-ipsec	Allows traffic from an established IPSec connection to bypass the normal checking of access lists, **conduit** commands, and **access-group** commands. In other words, if an IPSec tunnel has been established, this command means that the traffic will be allowed through the interface on which the tunnel was terminated.
sysopt connection permit-pptp	Allows traffic from an established PPTP connection to bypass **conduit** and **access-group** commands and access lists.
sysopt connection tcpmss *bytes*	Forces TCP proxy connections to have a maximum segment size equal to the number specified by the parameter *bytes*. The default for *bytes* is 1380.
sysopt connection timewait	Forces TCP connections to stay in a shortened time-wait state of at least 15 seconds after the completion of a normal TCP session ends.
sysopt ipsec pl-compatible	Enables IPSec packets to bypass both NAT and the ASA features. This also allows incoming IPSec tunnels to terminate on an inside interface. For a tunnel crossing the Internet to terminate on the inside interface, the inside interface must have a routable IP address.
sysopt nodnsalias outbound	Denies outbound DNS A record replies.
sysopt noproxyarp *interface_name*	Disables proxy ARPs on the interface specified by *interface_name*.
sysopt security fragguard	Enables the IP Frag Guard feature, which is designed to prevent IP fragmentation attacks such as LAND.c and teardrop. This works by requiring responsive IP packets to be requested by an internal host before they are accepted and limits the number of IP packets to 100 per second for each internal host.

VPN with IPSec and Manual Keys

IOS versions of the PIX prior to 5.0 used a connection method involving the Private Link Encryption Card to connect between two PIX Firewalls. This method is no longer supported; IPSec is used as the alternative. If your system is still using Version 4 or earlier of the Cisco PIX IOS, it is time to upgrade.

In this configuration, you will use IPSec to connect two networks over the Internet. You will also use manual keys for this example. In this example, your main corporate office uses an internal IP address of 10.1.1.0 with a 24-bit subnet mask, while your branch office uses 10.1.2.0 with a 24-bit subnet mask. (As with any interface accessible from the Internet, the outside interface of the PIX must have a routable IP address.) Figure 4-11 shows a diagram of how these networks are connected.

Figure 4-11 *VPN with IPSec*

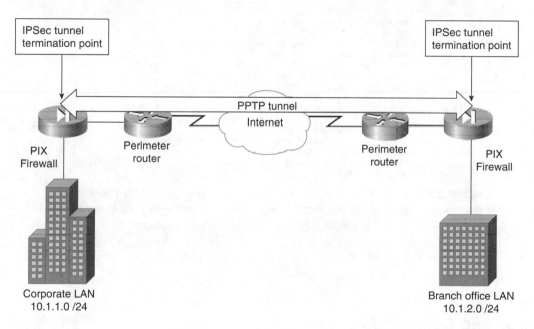

You need to configure both PIX Firewalls to enable a secure tunnel between them. The configurations that follow show only the items associated with setting up the IPSec tunnels. You will see both configurations and then a discussion of the ramifications of using the commands. Keep in mind that these are examples and, therefore, do not have routable IP addresses on the outside interfaces. In real life, the outside interfaces would need routable IP addresses; inside the corporate LANs, the IP addresses do not need to be routable. The corporate PIX configuration changes are as follows:

```
ip address outside 172.30.1.1 255.255.255.252
access-list 20 permit 10.1.2.0 255.255.255.0
crypto map mymap 10 ipsec-manual
crypto map mymap 10 set transform-set myset
crypto ipsec transform-set myset ah-md5-hmac esp-des
crypto map mymap 10 match address 20
crypto map mymap 10 set peer 172.30.1.2
crypto map mymap 10 set session-key inbound ah 400
     aaaaaaaaaaaaaaaaaaaaaaaaaaaaaaaa
crypto map mymap 10 set session-key outbound ah 300
     bbbbbbbbbbbbbbbbbbbbbbbbbbbbbbbb
crypto map mymap 10 set session-key inbound esp 400 cipher
     cccccccccccccccccccccccccccccccc
crypto map mymap 10 set session-key outbound esp 300 cipher
     dddddddddddddddddddddddddddddddd
crypto map mymap interface outside
sysopt connection permit-ipsec
```

The branch office PIX configuration changes are as follows:

```
ip address outside 172.30.1.2 255.255.255.252
access-list 20 permit 10.1.1.0 255.255.255.0
crypto map mymap 10 ipsec-manual
crypto map mymap 10 set transform-set myset
crypto ipsec transform-set myset ah-md5-hmac esp-des
crypto map mymap 10 match address 20
crypto map mymap 10 set peer 172.30.1.1
crypto map mymap 10 set session-key inbound ah 300
     bbbbbbbbbbbbbbbbbbbbbbbbbbbbbbbb
crypto map mymap 10 set session-key outbound ah 400
     aaaaaaaaaaaaaaaaaaaaaaaaaaaaaaaa
crypto map mymap 10 set session-key inbound esp 300 cipher
     dddddddddddddddddddddddddddddddd
crypto map mymap 10 set session-key outbound esp 400 cipher
     cccccccccccccccccccccccccccccccc
crypto map mymap interface outside
sysopt connection permit-ipsec
```

In this example, after assigning your outside IP addresses, you added an access list. Because you decided to use manual keys, this access list might contain only a single **permit**. If you used preshared keys, the access list could contain multiple **permit** statements. The access list is used to invoke your IPSec connection. When packets are sent to this address, your PIX establishes a connection with the peer, and all data traveling between the two is carried over your tunnel.

crypto map Commands

The **crypto map** command is used extensively with IPSec. This section examines the forms of this command in Table 4-6 before examining exactly what has to be configured in the examples. The **crypto map** command's first parameter is always the *mapname*. The *mapname* parameter is an arbitrary name assigned to distinguish one map from another. Table 4-6 assumes that **crypto map** *mapname* precedes the command. As with most commands, the **no** form of a command removes the configuration.

Table 4-6   **crypto map** *mapname Parameters*

Crypto Command	Description
client authentication *aaa-server*	This is the name of a AAA server that authenticates the user during Internet Key Exchange (IKE) negotiations.
client configuration address initiate	This forces the PIX to attempt to set the IP address for each peer.
client configuration address respond	This forces the PIX to attempt to accept requests from any requesting peer.
interface *interfacename*	This specifies the interface, as defined by the **nameif** command, that the PIX will use to identify peers. When IKE is enabled and a certificate authority (CA) is used to obtain certificates, this must be the interface specified within the CA certificate.
seq-num **ipsec-isakmp** | **ipsec-manual** [**dynamic** *dynamic-map-name*]	The *seq-num* (sequence number) is the number assigned to the map entry. The *seq-num* is used in a number of forms of the **crypto map** command. **ipsec-isakmp** indicates that IKE is used to establish the security association (SA). **ipsec-manual** indicates that IKE should not be used. **dynamic** *dynamic-map-name* is an optional keyword and parameter. The keyword **dynamic** indicates that the present **crypto map** entry references a preexisting dynamic crypto map. The parameter *dynamic-map-name* is the name of the preexisting map.
seq-num **match address** *acl_name*	Traffic destined for the IP addresses with a **permit** statement within the access list defined by *acl_name* will be encrypted.
seq-num **set peer** *hostname* | *ipaddress*	This specifies the peer for this SA. A host name might be specified if the **names** command has been used. Otherwise an IP address is used.
seq-num **set pfs** [**group1** | **group2**]	Specifies that IPSec will ask for Perfect Forward Secret (PFS). **group1** and **group2** are optionally used to specify whether a 768-bit Diffie-Hillman prime modulus group (**group1**) or a 1024-bit Diffie-Hillman prime modulus group (**group2**) will be used on new exchanges.

Table 4-6   **crypto map** *mapname Parameters (Continued)*

Crypto Command	Description
seq-num **set session-key inbound** | **outbound ah** *spi hex-key-string*	This sets the session keys within a **crypto map** entry. Using the keyword **inbound** specifies that the following *key-string* is for inbound traffic. Specifying the keyword **outbound** specifies that the *key-string* is for outbound traffic. One peer's outbound key string must match the other peer's inbound key string and vice versa.
	The *spi* parameter is used to specify the Security Parameter Index (SPI). The SPI is an arbitrarily assigned number ranging from 256 to more than 4 billion (OxFFFFFFFF).
	The *hex-key-string* is an arbitrary hexadecimal session key. The length of this key is determined by the transform set in use. DES uses 16 digits, MD5 uses 32, and SHA uses 40 digits.
seq-num **set session-key inbound** | **outbound esp** *spi* **cipher** *hex-key-string* [**authenticator** *hex-key-string*]	This is very similar to the previous command, except that it is used with encapsulating security payload (ESP) instead of authentication header (AH). The keyword **esp** specifies that the ESP protocol will be used.
	The keyword **cipher** indicates that the following *hex-key-string* is to be used with the ESP encryption transform.
	The optional authenticator string is used with the ESP authentication transform.

crypto ipsec Command

You have also seen the **crypto ipsec** command used within the configurations. There are two major forms of this command, the **crypto ipsec transform-set** and the **crypto ipsec security-association lifetime** forms. Both of these can be removed with the **no** form of the command. These commands are explained in Table 4-7.

Table 4-7   crypto ipsec *Commands*

Crypto Command	Description
crypto ipsec set security-association lifetime seconds *seconds* | **kilobytes** *kilobytes*	If the keyword **seconds** is used, the *seconds* parameter specifies how many seconds before an SA will remain active without renegotiation. The default is 28,800 seconds, which is 8 hours. If the keyword **kilobytes** is used, the *kilobytes* parameter specifies how many kilobytes of data can pass between peers before a renegotiation must occur. The default value is 4,608,000 KB, which is approximately 4.5 GB.
crypto ipsec transform-set *transform-set-name*	This command defines the transform sets that can be used with the map entry. There can be up to a total of six *transform-set-names* used within a single line. The transform set attempts to establish an SA in the order that the sets are specified.

Now that you have seen the syntax and uses of the **crypto map** and **crypto ipsec** commands, look again at the sample configurations.

You tell the PIX that your crypto map is named **mymap** with a map number of 10 and that IKE should not be used. This is done with the following line:

```
crypto map mymap 10 ipsec-manual
```

Next, you define the name of the transform with the following:

```
crypto map mymap 10 set transform-set myset
```

The transform set is defined with the following line:

```
crypto ipsec transform-set myset ah-md5-hmac esp-des
```

You previously created an access list 20 and permitted packets originating from the remote site's network. You then set the PIX to look at access list 20. If the packets are traveling to or from an address within this access list, they will be encrypted.

```
crypto map mymap 10 match address 20
```

Set the other end of the IPSec tunnel to terminate at 172.30.1.2, which is the outside interface of the branch office's PIX:

```
crypto map mymap 10 set peer 172.30.1.2
```

Set up the inbound and outbound session keys:

```
crypto map mymap 10 set session-key inbound ah 400
    aaaaaaaaaaaaaaaaaaaaaaaaaaaaaaaaaaaa
crypto map mymap 10 set session-key outbound ah 300
    bbbbbbbbbbbbbbbbbbbbbbbbbbbbbbbbbbbb
crypto map mymap 10 set session-key inbound esp 400 cipher
    cccccccccccccccccccccccccccccccc
crypto map mymap 10 set session-key outbound esp 300 cipher
    dddddddddddddddddddddddddddddddd
```

Associate the crypto map with the outside interface.

```
crypto map mymap interface outside
```

Finally, permit IPSec packets into the network with the **sysopt** command.

```
sysopt connection permit-ipsec
```

The branch office PIX configuration is almost identical. The following section points out where it differs.

The branch office PIX has a different outside IP address.

```
ip address outside 172.30.1.2 255.255.255.252
```

The access list must reflect the main office's IP addresses.

```
access-list 20 permit 10.1.1.0 255.255.255.0
```

The peer is the outside IP address of the main office's PIX.

```
crypto map mymap 10 set peer 172.30.1.1
```

The session keys for the branch office are configured in the opposite order of what is configured on the main office's PIX. The inbound key on one side of a connection must equal the outbound key on the opposite side of the connection. The inbound AH session key on the Branch office is equal to the outbound AH session key on the main office's PIX. The inbound AH session key must match the main office's outbound AH session key in order for the connection to be established. The inbound ESP session key matches the main office's inbound ESP session key and the outbound ESP session key matches the main office's inbound ESP session key:

```
crypto map mymap 10 set session-key inbound ah 300
    bbbbbbbbbbbbbbbbbbbbbbbbbbbbbbbbbbbb
crypto map mymap 10 set session-key outbound ah 400
    aaaaaaaaaaaaaaaaaaaaaaaaaaaaaaaaaaaa
crypto map mymap 10 set session-key inbound esp 300 cipher
    dddddddddddddddddddddddddddddddd
crypto map mymap 10 set session-key outbound esp 400 cipher
    cccccccccccccccccccccccccccccccc
```

VPN with Preshared Keys

Using preshared keys is easy, once you understand the concepts presented in the previous example. The difference between this configuration and the previous one is that you are now relying on the Internet Security Association and Key Management Protocol

(ISAKMP) for exchanging keys. This section presents the configuration before exploring how it has changed. The main office's configuration is as follows:

```
hostname chicago
domain-name bigcompany.com
isakmp enable outside
isakmp policy 15 authentication pre-share
isakmp policy 15 encr 3des
crypto isakmp key isakmpkey address 172.30.1.2
crypto ipsec transform-set strong esp-sha-hmac esp-3des
access-list myaccesslist permit ip 10.1.2.0 255.255.255.0
crypto map seattletraffic 29 ipsec-isakmp
crypto map seattletraffic 29 match address myaccesslist
crypto map seattletraffic 29 set transform-set strong
crypto map seattletraffic 29 set peer 172.30.1.2
crypto map seattletraffic interface outside
sysopt connection permit-ipsec
```

The branch PIX Firewall configuration looks like this:

```
hostname seattle
domain-name bigcompany.com
isakmp enable outside
isakmp policy 21 authentication pre-share
isakmp policy 21 encryption 3des
crypto isakmp key isakmpkey address 172.30.1.1
crypto ipsec transform-set strong esp-3des esp-sha-hmac
access-list chicagolist permit ip 10.1.1.0 255.255.255.0
crypto map chicagotraffic 31 ipsec-isakmp
crypto map chicagotraffic 31 match address chicagolist
crypto map chicagotraffic 31 set transform-set strong
crypto map chicagotraffic 31 set peer 172.30.1.1
crypto map chicagotraffic interface outside
sysopt connection permit-ipsec
```

isakmp Commands

Before explaining the example, review Table 4-8 concerning the **isakmp** commands. The **isakmp** commands are very similar in syntax to the **vpdn** commands. As with most commands, using the **no** form of the command removes the configuration.

Table 4-8   **isakmp** *Commands*

Command	Description
isakmp client configuration address-pool local *localpoolname*	This command assigns a VPN client an address from within the addresses set aside by the **ip local pool** command.
isakmp enable *interfacename*	This enables ISAKMP on the interface specified by the parameter *interfacename*.
isakmp identity *address* | *hostname*	This identifies the system for IKE participation.
isakmp key *keystring* **address** *peer-address*	The *keystring* specifies the preshared key. The *peer-address* specifies the IP address of the peer.

Table 4-8   **isakmp** *Commands (Continued)*

Command	Description
isakmp peer fqdn *fqdn* **no-xauth no-config-mode**	The *fqdn* (fully qualified domain name) is the full DNS name of the peer. This is used to identify a peer that is a security gateway.
	The **no-xauth** option is to used if you enabled the Xauth feature and you have an IPSec peer that is a gateway.
	The **no-config-mode** option is used if you enabled the IKE Mode Configuration feature and you have an IPSec peer that is a security gateway.
isakmp policy *priority* **authentication pre-share | rsa-sig**	This sets the priority for the authentication and defines whether you are using pre-shared keys or RSA signatures.
isakmp policy *priority* **group1 | group2**	**group1** and **group2** are optionally used to specify whether a 768-bit Diffie-Hillman prime modulus group (**group1**) or a 1024-bit Diffie-Hillman prime modulus group (**group2**) will be used on new exchanges.
isakmp policy *priority* **hash md5 | sha**	Specifies MD5 or SHA as the hash algorithm to be used in the IKE policy.
isakmp policy *priority* **lifetime** *seconds*	Specifies how many seconds each SA should exist before expiring.

Explanation of VPN with Preshared Keys

Going back to the configuration, you can see that it is really quite simple to enable preshared keys. The following section will walk you through the configuration and explain what has been configured.

First, set the host name. The fully qualified domain name (FQDN) is set with the **domain-name** command.

```
hostname chicago
domain-name bigcompany.com
```

Then set ISAKMP to the outside interface and define that you use preshared keys and 3DES encryption.

```
isakmp enable outside
isakmp policy 15 authentication pre-share
isakmp policy 15 encr 3des
```

The ISAKMP key, whose value is **isakampkey**, is set, along with the IP address of the outside interface of the peer. Then set **transform-set** to first use **esp-sha-hmac** and then **esp-3des**.

```
crypto isakmp key isakmpkey address 172.30.1.2
crypto ipsec transform-set strong esp-sha-hmac esp-3des
```

Define an access list for use with the **crypto map** command, setting the permitted IP addresses to match the remote site's IP address.

```
access-list myaccesslist permit ip 10.1.2.0 255.255.255.0
```

Next, map the traffic to be encrypted, set the peer, and set the interface.

```
crypto map seattletraffic 29 ipsec-isakmp
crypto map seattletraffic 29 match address myaccesslist
crypto map seattletraffic 29 set transform-set strong
crypto map seattletraffic 29 set peer 172.30.1.2
crypto map seattletraffic interface outside
```

Finally, set the PIX to allow IPSec traffic through the interfaces.

```
sysopt connection permit-ipsec
```

The only real differences between the branch office and the main office configurations are that the peers are set to the other office's PIX outside interface, and the traffic to be encrypted is set to the other office's LAN.

Obtaining Certificate Authorities (CAs)

Retrieving certificate authorities (CAs) with the PIX Firewall uses almost exactly the same method as that used on routers. The following are the commands used to obtain a CA. Note that these commands might not show in a configuration. The administrator should avoid rebooting the PIX during this sequence. The steps are explained as they are shown.

First, define your identity and the IP address of the interface to be used for the CA. Also configure the timeout of retries used to gain the certificate and the number of retries.

```
ca identity bigcompany.com 172.30.1.1
ca configure bigcompany.com ca 2 100
```

Generate the RSA key used for this certificate.

```
ca generate rsa key 512
```

Then get the public key and certificate.

```
ca authenticate bigcompany.com
```

Next, request the certificate, and finally, save the configuration.

```
ca enroll bigcompany.com enrollpassword
ca save all
```

At this point, you have saved your certificates to the flash memory and are able to use them. The configuration for using an existing CA is as follows:

```
domain-name bigcompany.com
isakmp enable outside
isakmp policy 8 auth rsa-signature
ca identity example.com 172.30.1.1
ca generate rsa key 512
```

```
access-list 60 permit ip 10.1.2.0 255.255.255.0
crypto map chicagotraffic 20 ipsec-isakmp
crypto map chicagotraffic 20 match address 60
crypto map chicagotraffic 20 set transform-set strong
crypto map chicagotraffic 20 set peer 172.30.1.2
crypto map chicagotraffic interface outside
sysopt connection permit-ipsec
```

PIX-to-PIX Configuration

One advantage of using the PIX Firewall is that it has become a standard within the industry. As time passes, your business might acquire or become acquired by another company. To provide connectivity, you are faced with two choices: enabling VPNs over the Internet or using dedicated connections. Because one of the benefits of the PIX box is to allow secure VPNs, this section explores how to set up two PIX Firewalls between different locations through the Internet.

In this scenario, shown in Figure 4-10, assume that both companies trust each other totally. This means that you will not filter any traffic between the sites, and all hosts on both sites will be able to see all hosts on the other site. The peers use ISAKMP in Phase 1 to negotiate an IPSec connection in Phase 2.

Figure 4-12 *PIX-to-PIX IPSec with ISAKMP Example*

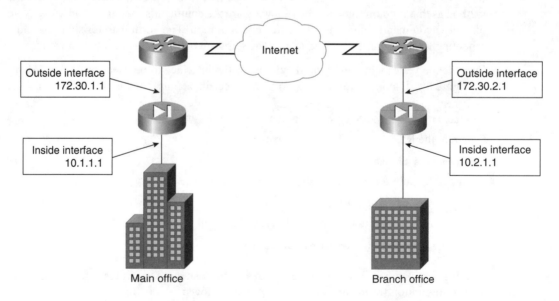

As shown in Figure 4-12, the main office uses an internal IP address of 10.1.1.1/24 with an IP address of 172.30.1.1 on the outside interface. The branch office uses an internal IP address of 10.2.1.1/24 and an IP address of 172.30.2.1 on the outside interface. The following is the configuration for the PIX Firewall at the main office. After the configuration, you will see a discussion of the commands used.

```
hostname mainofficepix
nameif ethernet0 outside security0
nameif ethernet1 inside security100
interface ethernet0 auto
interface ethernet1 auto
mtu outside 1500
mtu inside 1500
ip address outside 172.30.1.1 255.255.255.0
ip address inside 10.1.1.1 255.255.255.0
access-list 100 permit ip 10.1.1.0 255.255.255.0 10.2.1.0 255.255.255.0
nat (inside) 0 access-list 100
sysopt connection permit-ipsec
crypto ipsec transform-set maintransformset esp-des esp-md5-hmac
crypto map mymap 10 ipsec-isakmp
crypto map mymap 10 match address 100
crypto map mymap 10 set peer 172.30.2.1
crypto map mymap 10 set transform-set maintransformset
crypto map mymap interface outside
isakmp enable outside
isakmp key mysharedkey address 172.30.2.1 netmask 255.255.255.255
isakmp policy 10 authentication pre-share
isakmp policy 10 encryption des
isakmp policy 10 hash md5
isakmp policy 10 group 1
isakmp policy 10 lifetime 768
```

All of the preceding commands have been discussed previously within this chapter. There are only a few new items that you need to watch carefully to ensure that this configuration will work.

First, access list 100 must allow hosts from the branch office through the PIX Firewall. Limiting who is allowed through on the branch office network or which hosts that the branch office hosts are allowed to see is controlled through this access list. For example, assume that everyone except the branch manager in the branch office is allowed to connect only to the hosts at 10.1.1.14, 10.1.1.15, and 10.1.1.200. The branch manager, whose IP address is 10.2.1.53, is allowed to access all hosts on the main office network. In this case, your access list would be as follows:

```
access-list 100 permit ip 10.1.1.0 255.255.255.0 10.1.2.1.53 255.255.255.255
access-list 100 permit ip 10.1.1.14 255.255.255.255 10.2.1.0 255.255.255.0
access-list 100 permit ip 10.1.1.15 255.255.255.255 10.2.1.0 255.255.255.0
access-list 100 permit ip 10.1.1.200 255.255.255.255 10.2.1.0 255.255.255.0
```

Now take note of the use of the **nat 0** command to prevent NAT from occurring. In some cases, you need to enable NAT because both sites are using the same nonroutable IP addresses. This is actually a common scenario. For example, without NAT enabled and both sites using the 10.1.1.0/24 network, both PIX Firewalls will not know which network to respond to when a packet is received.

Next, you set up the Phase 2 connection. Use the **sysopt** command with the *permit-ipsec* parameter to allow packets associated with this SA through the PIX Firewall. Set up the transform set for IPSec, assign a map to the access list, and set the interface for the crypto connection. You also use the **crypto map** command to set the peer for this connection. As always, the IP address of the peer should be the outside interface of the remote PIX Firewall.

As with any ISAKMP key exchange, you need to ensure that the interface chosen is appropriate, that the key is exactly the same on both peers, and that the encryption and hash types are identical between peers.

PIX-to-PIX with Identical Internal IP Addresses

One of the issues raised by using a nonroutable IP address is the use of the IP address while another connected location is using that same address. This is a common issue when two companies connect to each other for the first time. Looking at Figure 4-13, notice that both the main and branch offices use the same internal IP address. In this situation, you will need to translate the addresses of both internal networks.

Figure 4-13 *PIX-to-PIX with Identical Internal Network Addresses*

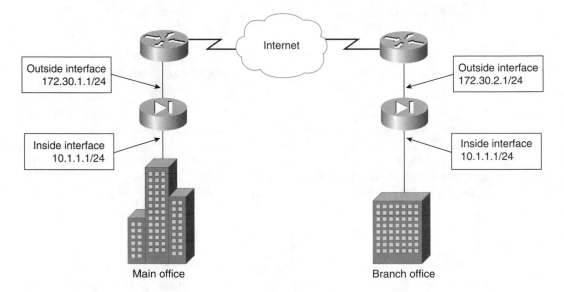

On the PIX at the main office, you will use NAT to translate all data destined for the branch office to the 192.168.1.0/24 network. The branch office translates all data destined for the main office to use 192.168.2.0/24 addresses. Therefore, from the point of view of the main office, the branch office appears to use 192.168.2.0/24. From the point of view of the branch office, the main office appears to use 192.168.1.0 as its internal IP addresses. Each PIX Firewall needs to be configured in a similar manner. Figure 4-14 shows how each office sees the other.

Figure 4-14 *PIX-to-PIX with Each Side Using NAT*

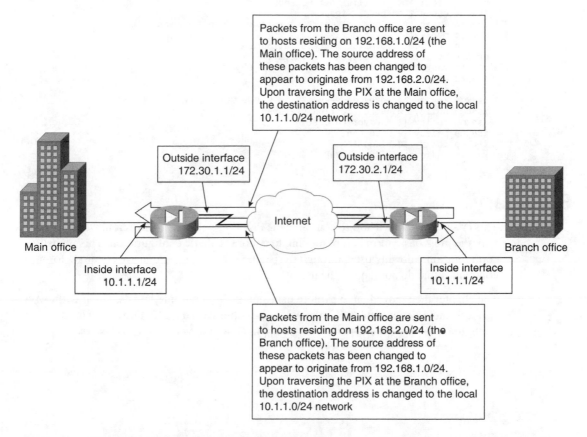

Packets from the Branch office are sent
to hosts residing on 192.168.1.0/24 (the
Main office). The source address of
these packets has been changed to
appear to originate from 192.168.2.0/24.
Upon traversing the PIX at the Main office,
the destination address is changed to the local
10.1.1.0/24 network

Outside interface
172.30.1.1/24

Outside interface
172.30.2.1/24

Internet

Main office

Branch office

Inside interface
10.1.1.1/24

Inside interface
10.1.1.1/24

Packets from the Main office are sent
to hosts residing on 192.168.2.0/24 (the
Branch office). The source address of
these packets has been changed to
appear to originate from 192.168.1.0/24.
Upon traversing the PIX at the Branch office,
the destination address is changed to the local
10.1.1.0/24 network

The listing of this configuration follows. This is virtually the same configuration as the
previous example, with a few minor changes. First, you have to implement a global pool
for use with NAT for data traveling to the branch office. Second, you have to remove
the lines associated with the **nat 0** command for data traveling to the branch office.
Third, you have to create a new access list called *nattobranch*, which is used by NAT to
change the source address of the packets so that these packets appear to originate from
the 192.168.1.0/24 network.

```
hostname mainofficepix
nameif ethernet0 outside security0
nameif ethernet1 inside security100
interface ethernet0 auto
interface ethernet1 auto
mtu outside 1500
mtu inside 1500
ip address outside 172.30.1.1 255.255.255.0
ip address inside 10.1.1.1 255.255.255.0
global (outside) 1 192.168.1.1-192.168.1.253
global (outside) 1 192.168.1.254
```

```
access-list nattobranch permit ip 10.1.1.0 255.255.255.0 192.168.2.1 255.255.255.0
nat (inside) 1 access-list nattobranch
sysopt connection permit-ipsec
crypto ipsec transform-set maintransformset esp-des esp-md5-hmac
crypto map mymap 10 ipsec-isakmp
crypto map mymap 10 match address nattobranch
crypto map mymap 10 set peer 172.30.2.1
crypto map mymap 10 set transform-set maintransformset
crypto map mymap interface outside
isakmp enable outside
isakmp key mysharedkey address 172.30.2.1 netmask 255.255.255.255
isakmp policy 10 authentication pre-share
isakmp policy 10 encryption des
isakmp policy 10 hash md5
isakmp policy 10 group 1
isakmp policy 10 lifetime 768
```

Summary

This chapter has shown how to configure the PIX Firewall in many different ways. It started with the most basic form before moving to a more realistic configuration. This realistic configuration, allowing users through to specific services, should prove adequate for most companies that do not require the use of a DMZ.

The chapter then moved on to explore using single and multiple DMZs, along with AAA services and other examples of connections possible with the PIX Firewall. These configurations provide examples that are applicable to larger organizations.

This chapter contains the following sections:

- Access Lists
- Dynamic Access Lists
- Time-Based Access Lists
- Reflexive Access Lists
- Cisco IOS Firewall Features
- How Context-Based Access Control (CBAC) Works
- Configuring Context-Based Access Control (CBAC)
- Summary

CHAPTER 5

Cisco IOS Firewall

Cisco IOS Firewall is an add-on component of the Cisco IOS that provides functionality similar to that found on the Cisco PIX. Designed to allow the administrator to leverage existing hardware, Cisco IOS Firewall allows the administrator to effectively secure the network without the added cost of a separate firewall.

This chapter explores the features of Cisco IOS Firewall and discusses configuration choices associated with using this software. Before exploring Cisco IOS Firewall, this chapter will discuss advanced access lists to ensure that you have the solid foundation needed to work with Cisco IOS Firewall.

Access Lists

Chapter 2, "Basic Cisco Router Security," explored standard and extended access lists. This chapter explores more advanced forms of access lists. The act of creating and removing entries in access lists without administrator intervention is the basis for advanced access lists. Security on a network should be as tight as is reasonable at any given time. Advanced access lists, such as dynamic, reflexive, and Context-based Access Control (CBAC), all change the existing access lists to create openings in real time without changing any configurations. These openings are usually created in response to a request made from the inside (trusted side) of the corporate network. The newly created opening is closed after a period of time with no activity or when the session initiating the opening ends. Creating openings only when initiated from inside of the network and closing them when they are not needed limits the time when an outside entity can exploit these openings.

Dynamic Access Lists

Dynamic access lists permit dynamic entries to be made into standard or extended access lists by users after authentication. This authentication comes through the use of a Telnet session to the router initiated by the user. Once the user successfully initiates a Telnet session to the router, the Telnet session is ended by the router and a dynamic entry is added to the access list. The user can then use the newly created opening through the router. Using dynamic access lists requires that usernames and passwords are entered into the router, and that the access list has a statement reflecting the username that is mapped to a permission statement. There are four steps required to use a dynamic access list:

- The extended access list must be created.

- The access list must be assigned to an interface.

- The user must be authenticated through TACACS+, RADIUS, or through a username and password on the router.

- The user must be able to Telnet to the virtual terminal.

The following is an example of a dynamic access list. Note that the use of an exclamation mark (!) at the beginning of a line indicates that the line is a comment.

```
access-list 109 permit telnet any host 172.31.10.2 eq telnet
access-list 109 dynamic testdynamic timeout 10 permit ip any any
deny any any
!Set up the access list with a dynamic entry called "testdynamic."
!This is the same name as is used in the Telnet session.
!The timeout is set to 10 minutes.
!The dynamic list entry permits ip traffic from and to any host.
!As with any extended access list, you could allow only certain protocols or
!ports to be available through this access list entry.

interface serial 1
 ip address 172.30.1.1 255.255.255.0
 ip access-group 109 in
!Assigns the access list number 109 to the interface.

Username testdynamic password iwanttotelnet
!This sets up the user with a password.

line vty 0 4
  login local
!Use the local login.
auto-command access-enable host timeout 5
!This is the line that tells user to create the dynamic entry.
password mypassword
rotary 1
!You need a way for the administrator to access the router.
!Using "rotary 1" says that admin Telnets should occur on port 3001.
!"rotary 2" would mean port 3002. And so on.
```

Three **show access-list** commands follow. The first one is from before the user Telnets to the router. The second one is from during the timeout period that the new opening exists. The last one is from after the opening has closed.

Before the user Telnets to the router:

```
routera:#show access-list
  Extended IP access-list 109
    permit telnet any host 172.31.10.2 eq telnet
    dynamic testdynamic timeout 10 permit ip any any
```

During the timeout period:

```
routera#show access-list
  Extended access-list 109
```

```
permit telnet any host 172.31.10.2 eq telnet
dynamic testdynamic timeout 10 permit ip any any
   permit ip host 192.168.1.2 any idle-time 5 min.
```

After the opening has closed:

```
routera:#show access-list
  Extended IP access-list 109
    permit telnet any host 172.31.10.2 eq telnet
    dynamic testdynamic timeout 10 permit ip any any
```

In the preceding examples, the user at host 192.168.1.2 created the dynamic permit statement in the access list by Telnetting to the router. In response, the dynamic access list opened all traffic to that host from the outside. This opening will remain for as long as data is traveling to and from the local host. When activity ceases for the amount of time specified within the dynamic statement, 5 minutes in this example, packets destined for 192.168.1.2 will again be denied.

Figure 5-1 shows how under normal circumstances access from the outside to the host at 192.168.1.2 is prevented.

Figure 5-1   *Before User Authenticates with Router*

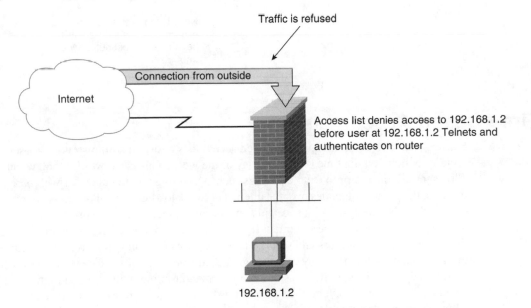

Once the user at host 192.168.1.2 is authenticated by the router, a new entry opens in the router, allowing access to host 192.168.1.2. This is illustrated in Figure 5-2.

This is not an ideal situation because you do not necessarily want all traffic to be able to enter; you only want the traffic that is directly related to the type of connection the user wishes to establish. Although you could limit the type of traffic available through this opening by adjusting the **dynamic** statement, this presupposes that you know exactly what type of traffic a user will want. CBAC was designed for this purpose and is covered later in this chapter, in the section "How Context-Based Access Control (CBAC) Works."

Figure 5-2   *After User Authenticates with Router*

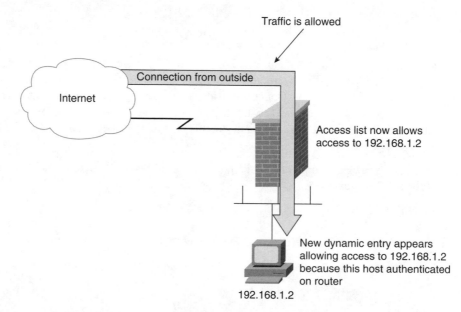

Time-Based Access Lists

Starting with IOS version 12.0, time-based access lists allow an administrator to base security policies on the time of day and day of the week. This is a powerful tool, which allows the administrator to enable policies such as limiting the download of Web-based music or the playing of games over the internal network to after normal business hours. The end result is that the system users can play music and games when network response times are not an issue. This can be important from a political viewpoint, because a lot of users think that the administrators and security administrators prevent them from having fun, even when it does not affect any company goal. Additional benefits can be realized by using time-based access lists in the areas of dial-on-demand routing, policy-based routing, and queuing. These are all beyond the scope of this book, but are still useful in the daily administration of a network.

To establish time-based access lists, three steps are necessary:

Step 1   Accurate times must be established on all affected routers. Generally speaking, the easiest way to accomplish this is by using Network Time Protocol (NTP).

Step 2   Time ranges must be established. This is done by one of two methods. The first method is to use the **periodic** statement. The syntax for the **periodic** command is shown below:

```
periodic day-of-week hh:mm to day-of-week hh:mm
```

In the preceding command syntax, a number of substitutions are available for the *day-of-week* variable. The *day-of-week* can be any individual day; a selection of days separated by spaces; or the words **daily** to represent every day, **weekday** to represent Monday through Friday, or **weekend** to represent Saturday and Sunday. If the time to be specified traverses specific days, a second *day-of-week* is used after the **to** keyword. The *hh:mm* variable is the time entered in military time. The following two examples show how to use the **periodic** statement. The first example will set the time of the permissions for the time range named "firsttime" between 08:00 (8 a.m.) and 13:00 (1 p.m.) on Tuesday, Wednesday, and Thursday:

```
time-range firsttime
periodic Tuesday Wednesday Thursday 08:00 to 13:00
```

The second example sets the time for the time range named "secondtime" of the permissions to be checked between 22:00 (10 p.m.) on Friday and 23:30 (11:30 p.m.) on Saturday:

```
time-range secondtime
periodic friday 22:00 to saturday 23:30
```

Another method for setting a time range is to use the **absolute** command, which is used to assign specific hours and dates to a named time range. The following example assigns the time of 11:00 on January 1, 2001 through 14:00 on January 2, 2002 to the time range named "absolutetime."

```
time-range absolutetime
absolute start 11:00 1 january 2001 end 14:00 2 january 2002
```

Step 3   Once a time range is defined, it can be used within an extended access list. The following is an example of using the "firsttime" time range to limit Telnet access. In this example, Telnet is only permitted between 08:00 on Tuesday through 13:00 on Thursday:

```
access-list 110 permit any any eq telnet time-range firsttime
access-list 110 deny any any
```

Time-based access lists allow the administrator to allow or deny traffic based on the current time. Another tool available to the administrator is a reflexive access list, which will be discussed next.

Reflexive Access Lists

Reflexive access lists are a type of extended access list that allow two access lists to work together dynamically. When the outbound access list senses a connection to a remote site, the inbound access list is opened up to allow two-way communications to occur. Once this two-way session is completed, the inbound access list is again closed to the remote site. The characteristics of reflexive access lists are as follows:

- There are no implied deny any statements at the end of the reflexive access control list.
- A reflexive access list entry is always a permit entry.
- Named access lists are used in pairs and relate to each other while using reflexive access lists.
- The inbound interface access list is dynamically changed in relation to sessions initiated from the inside of the network.

  These dynamic changes are created and removed as sessions are initiated and closed from hosts on the internal network or after a specified time of inactivity. In the case of TCP, the FIN or RST bit is used. In UDP connections, or when a TCP session is not properly ended, the timeout is used.

- Reflexive access lists support TCP and UDP sessions.
- Reflexive access lists are built within extended access lists and are not applied directly to an interface.
- Reflexive access lists provide security greater than that experienced with extended access lists, especially in the area of spoofed addresses and certain DoS attacks.
- Reflexive access lists are a type of named access list that allows two access lists to work together dynamically, creating Layer 4 session-based filtering.

Reflexive access lists are similar to dynamic access lists, as both dynamically open pathways through the router based on the needs of a user at a given time. These pathways are closed once the initiating application has terminated. The advantage of reflexive access lists is that the user does not need to be authenticated on the router by initiating a Telnet session. This allows a transparent operation, where the user is not even aware that an access list is controlling availability. Additionally, reflexive access lists are much easier to use with mass-produced and system-based software because no additional steps are required to allow additional access.

When setting up reflexive access lists, two access lists must be created: one for the inbound packets, and one for the outbound packets. The following is an example of two access lists without any reflexive properties. After the example, you will see these access lists with changes to incorporate reflexive properties.

```
interface Serial 0
    ip access-group inbound in
    ip access-group outbound out
```

```
ip access list extended inbound
permit ip 10.1.1.0 0.0.0.255 172.30.1.0 0.0.0.255
deny ip any any

ip access list extended outbound
deny ip 172.30.1.18 0.0.0.0 10.1.1.0 0.0.0.255
permit ip any any
```

In the preceding configuration, any IP packet destined for the 172.30.1.0/24 network with a source address on the 10.1.1.0/24 network is allowed into the router. All packets from inside the network are allowed out except for those originating from 172.30.1.18 and destined to the 10.1.1.0/24 network.

The problem with this list becomes apparent when someone inside the corporate network wants to establish a connection to another network that is not on the access list. For example, if a user wants to establish a connection to the 10.10.10.0/24 network, the inbound access list will prevent the receipt of responses. Reflexive access lists were designed with this particular situation in mind. You can easily change the access lists to allow a connection initiated on the inside of the network to be available as needed. The following is an example of how the access lists changes to allow this:

```
interface Serial 0
    ip access-group inbound in
    ip access-group outbound out

ip access list extended inbound
permit ip 10.1.1.0 0.0.0.255 172.30.1.0 0.0.0.255
evaluate packetssent
deny ip any any

ip access list extended outbound
deny ip 172.30.1.18 0.0.0.0 10.1.1.0 0.0.0.255
permit tcp any any reflect packetssent timeout 90
permit udp any any reflect packetssent timeout 60
permit icmp any any reflect packetssent timeout 30
permit ip any any
```

A total of four lines have been added to the configuration. The first line, **evaluate packetssent,** is applied on the inbound filter. The next three lines are applied to the outbound filter. When an outbound packet is seen on the interface, the outbound access list is checked. If the packet meets any of the criteria, it is allowed through. The following paragraph contains a specific example to help you understand exactly what happens to the access lists. If no activity is present on the connection for the period in seconds specified by the **timeout** parameter, the reflexive access list will automatically be discontinued.

Assume that a user on host 172.30.1.18 initiates a Telnet connection to 10.10.10.10. The outbound access list sees the Telnet packets and mirrors them on the inbound filter to allow responses. In fact, the inbound filter dynamically changes to allow responses to travel through the interface in response to the connection initiated from 172.30.1.18. Using the **show access-list** command proves this. Three examples of the **show access-list** command follow, one before the connection is initiated, one while the connection session is running, and one after the connection has terminated. Notice that while the session is running, the "packetssent" reflexive access list is visible and contains a permit statement allowing Telnet traffic from the remote host with the appropriate port number. The inbound filter evaluates the inbound traffic against this temporary access list and permits the packets that match the criteria.

Before the connection is initiated:

```
routera#show access-list
Extended ip access list inbound
  permit ip 10.1.1.0 0.0.0.255 172.30.1.0 0.0.0.255
  evaluate packetssent
  deny ip any any
extended ip access list outbound
  deny ip host 172.30.1.18 10.1.1.0 0.0.0.255
  permit tcp any any reflect packetssent timeout 90
  permit udp any any reflect packetssent timeout 60
  permit icmp any any reflect packetssent timeout 30
  permit ip any any
```

During the connection session:

```
routera#show access-list
Extended ip access list inbound
  permit ip 10.1.1.0 0.0.0.255 172.30.1.0 0.0.0.255
  evaluate packetssent
  deny ip any any
extended ip access list outbound
  deny ip host 172.30.1.18 10.1.1.0 0.0.0.255
  permit tcp any any reflect packetssent timeout 90
  permit udp any any reflect packetssent timeout 60
  permit icmp any any reflect packetssent timeout 30
  permit ip any any
reflexive access list packetssent
  permit tcp host 10.10.10.10 eq telnet host 172.30.1.18 eq 1045
  (15 matches) (time left 23 seconds)
```

After the connection has terminated:

```
routera#show access-list
Extended ip access list inbound
  permit ip 10.1.1.0 0.0.0.255 172.30.1.0 0.0.0.255
  evaluate packetssent
  deny ip any any
extended ip access list outbound
  deny ip host 172.30.1.18 10.1.1.0 0.0.0.255
  permit tcp any any reflect packetssent timeout 90
  permit udp any any reflect packetssent timeout 60
  permit icmp any any reflect packetssent timeout 30
  permit ip any any
```

Figure 5-3 shows the sequence of the reflexive access list example.

As with all access lists, placements of permit and deny statements are crucial to proper functioning. If the user chose to Telnet to a host on the 10.1.1.0/24 network, the request would still have been denied, because the deny statement for that network would have been evaluated before reaching the reflexive access list statements.

Figure 5-3   *Reflective Access Lists Open the Router in Response to Connections Initiated from Inside the Network*

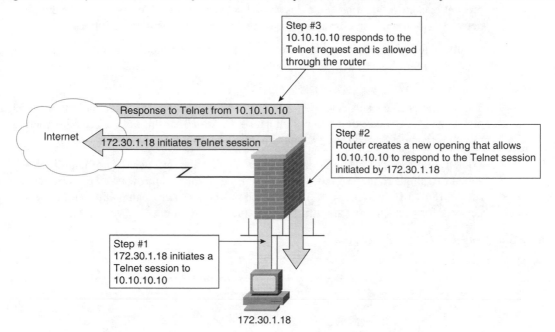

Although a reflexive access list is a very powerful and useful tool, there are still some limitations. Reflexive access lists do not have the ability to handle multiple channel applications. Context-based Access Control (CBAC), which will be discussed later in this chapter in the section "How Context-Based Access Control (CBAC) Works," was designed to provide security support for multiple channel applications.

Null Route

An alternative to access lists is the null route command. This is actually a static route that directs packets to the null interface. The null interface, also known as the *bit bucket*, simply drops packets instead of forwarding them to the next hop.

Using this command has a number of advantages. The first is that very few CPU cycles are required to implement this method. Unlike an access list, which can consume an unacceptable number of CPU cycles, using the null route command consumes no more cycles than any other static route. The next advantage is that a single entry can be used to control access to both inbound and outbound packets. The third advantage is that a null route can be redistributed, and therefore, a single entry can drop data destined for any given network as soon as that data attempts to traverse a router.

A drawback to using the null route command for security purposes is that using it does *not* prevent packets originating at the designated network from entering your company's network. However, responses destined to the designated network are dropped.

A null route is entered as a static route with the next-hop router entered as **null**. For example, if you wish to deny access to the 184.15.10.0/24 network, use the following:

```
ip route 184.15.10.0 255.255.255.0 null 0
```

This forwards all packets destined for the 184.15.10.0/24 network to the null bit bucket. In other words, the router throws away all packets destined for this network. Redistributing this static route allows all routers on the network to drop these packets.

Look at Figure 5-4 to see an example of how a null route operates. After the null route is added to a single router and redistributed, all routers know to throw away packets destined for the 184.15.10.0/24 network. This method prevents wasting bandwidth within the network for packages that are ultimately destined to be dropped.

Figure 5-4   *Null Route with Redistribution*

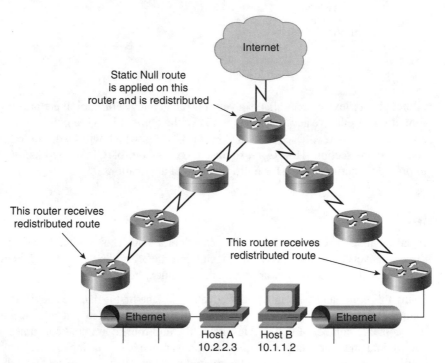

In the Figure 5-4 example, if Host A tries to send information to the 182.15.10.0/24 network, the first router drops this packet. Likewise, if Host B tries to send data to the 182.15.10.0/24 network, the first router drops the packet.

Cisco IOS Firewall Features

Cisco IOS Firewall combines firewall features, routing services, and intrusion detection within a single router IOS. Formerly called the Cisco IOS Firewall Feature Set, Cisco IOS Firewall provides security and policy enforcement on a wide range of routers.

Cisco IOS Firewall adds functionality to the existing Cisco IOS security capabilities. These enhancements include encryption, failover services, authentication, encryption, per-user authentication, real-time intrusion alerts, and application-based filtering through CBAC.

In Chapter 6, "Intrusion Detection Systems," Table 6-1 contains the Cisco IOS intrusion-detection signatures that are used in conjunction with CBAC. There are a total of 59 distinctive signatures recognized by Cisco IOS Firewall. These signatures are listed in the same numerical order as listed by their signature number in the NetRanger Network Security Database.

These intrusion-detection signatures were chosen as representative of the most common network attacks and information gathering scans not commonly found in an operational network.

Included in Table 6-1 is an indication of the type of signature: Info or Attack, Atomic or Compound. Atomic signatures that show as Atomic* are allocated memory for session states by CBAC.

Port Application Mapping (PAM)

Port Application Mapping (PAM) gives the administrator the ability to customize TCP and UDP port numbers in relation to access lists. PAM allows support of services using ports different from the registered and well-known ports associated with an application.

PAM creates a table of default port-to-application mapping information at the firewall router. This table is populated with system-defined maps when the IOS is booted. The administrator can modify this table to include host-specific and user-defined mappings. The PAM table works with CBAC-supported services to allow applications through the access list while still running on nonstandard ports. Without the use of PAM, CBAC is limited to inspecting traffic using only the standard application ports. CBAC will use the PAM table to identify a service or application. CBAC associates the nonstandard port numbers entered through PAM with specific protocols. The mappings serve as the default port mapping for traffic passing through the router.

System-Defined Port Mapping

When the system starts, the PAM table is created, and the system-defined variables are entered into the table. The PAM table contains entries comprising all the services supported by CBAC, which requires the system-defined mapping information to function properly.

These system-defined mappings cannot be deleted or changed. It is possible, however, to override the system-defined entries for specific hosts using the PAM host-specific option.

Table 5-1 lists the system-defined services, port mappings, and protocol descriptions.

Table 5-1 *PAM System-Defined Services*

System-Defined Service	Port	Protocol
cuseeme	7648	CU-SeeMe
exec	512	Remote Process Execution
ftp	21	File Transfer Protocol control port
http	80	Hypertext Transfer Protocol
h323	1720	H.323 protocol used by MS NetMeeting and Intel Video Phone
msrpc	135	Microsoft Remote Procedure Call
netshow	1755	Microsoft NetShow
real-audio-video	7070	RealAudio and RealVideo
smtp	25	Simple Mail Transport Protocol
sqlnet	1521	SQL*Net
streamworks	1558	StreamWorks Protocol
sunrpc	111	SUN Remote Procedure Call
tftp	69	Trivial File Transfer Protocol
vdolive	7000	VDOLive

User-Defined Port Mapping

Using applications with nonstandard ports requires the addition of user-defined entries into the PAM table. Each instance of a nonstandard application is entered into the table. Applications can be enabled to use multiple ports or a range of ports by entering each port in succession. Entering a port number a second time with a new application overwrites the original entry. Attempting to enter an application using a system-defined port results in an error message and an unsuccessful mapping. Save mappings by writing the router configuration.

Host-Specific Port Mapping

User-defined entries can include host-specific mapping information, which establishes port mapping information for specific hosts or subnets. Host-specific port mapping overrides system-defined entries in the PAM table. It might be necessary to override the default port mapping information for a specific host or subnet.

Using host-specific port mapping, the same port number can be used for different services on different hosts. For example, it is possible to assign port 6565 to Telnet on one host while assigning the same port (6565) to HTTP on another host.

Host-specific port mapping also allows PAM to be applied to individual subnets. Similar to host-specific port mapping, you can assign port 6565 to Telnet on one network while assigning the same port (6565) to HTTP on another network.

Configuring PAM

The **ip port-map** command is used to configure PAM. The following example sets HTTP to ports 8000, 8001, 8002, and 8003. After this command is run, the keyword **http** in an access list will relate not only to the default port 80, but also to the ports 8000, 8001, 8002, and 8003. This example is entered in the global configuration mode and applies globally:

```
ip port-map http 8000
ip port-map http 8001
ip port-map http 8002
ip port-map http 8003
```

If PAM is to be applied to only a specific access list, the entries are made with the additional keyword **list** and the access list number for the affected access list. The following example shows HTTP ports mapped to an access list 101. In this case, HTTP for access list 101 includes port 80 (the default), as well as port 8000:

```
access-list 101 permit ip any any eq http
ip port-map http port 8000 list 101
```

In the following example, a specific host runs HTTP services on port 21, which is a system-defined port for FTP data. Therefore, it requires a host-specific entry:

```
access-list 55 permit 172.30.1.2
!define the host that will have the default mapping changed
ip port-map http port 21 list 55
!map HTTP to port 21, replacing the default usage for port 21
```

How Context-Based Access Control (CBAC) Works

Context-based Access Control (CBAC) was designed for use with multiple port protocols that are unable to be processed with reflexive access lists. Since standard and extended access lists work at the network (Layer 3) or transport (Layer 4) layers of the OSI model, their ability to work with some applications is limited. CBAC loosens these limitations by filtering packets based on the application (Layer 7) layer of the OSI model. Version 11.2 of the firewall feature set IOS includes CBAC for 1600 and 2500 series routers. IOS Version 12.0 expands the covered routers to include 1700, 2600, and 3600 series routers.

The major additional features enabled through the use of CBAC are as follows:

- **Application-layer filtering**—CBAC filters TCP and UDP packets based on application-layer protocol session information. CBAC can be configured to inspect traffic for sessions that originate from either inside or outside of the corporate network. By watching not only Layers 3 and 4, but also Layer 7, CBAC learns the state of connection sessions and filters based upon that state. When a protocol, such as RPC or SQL*NET, requires negotiation of multiple channels, CBAC is still able to filter effectively where a standard or extended access list could not.

- **IP packet fragmentation prevention and DoS defenses**—CBAC can detect and prevent certain types of network attacks, such as SYN-flooding. SYN-flooding is a type of DoS attack where multiple sync requests are sent to a router. The router holds these connections open until they time out or are completed. CBAC watches the packet sequence numbers for all connections and drops those that are of a suspicious origin. Suspicious packets are those outside of the expected range of sequence numbers. Additionally, CBAC detects and sends alert messages when an inordinately high number of new connections are seen.

- **Administrative alerts and audit trails**—CBAC creates audit trails and real-time alerts based on the events tracked by the firewall. Audit trails use syslog to track network transactions. The data included in this tracking contains source and destination address, source and destination port, and time stamps. Real-time alerts occur by sending syslog error messages to central management consoles.

- **Support for the Cisco IOS Intrusion Detection System (IDS)**—The Cisco IOS Firewall's Intrusion Detection System (Cisco IOS IDS) identifies a total of 59 of the most common attacks using the distinctive signatures of these attacks to detect patterns. CBAC has the ability to send data directly to a Cisco IDS component.

CBAC Operation

CBAC works in much the same manner as reflexive access lists. Both create temporary openings in access lists based on traffic traversing the external interface outbound from the router. These openings allow the returning traffic to enter the internal network back through the firewall. This traffic, normally blocked, is then allowed back through the router. In CBAC, only data from the same session that originally triggered the opening is allowed back through.

CBAC inspects traffic traveling through the router in order to discover and manage information about the state of TCP and UDP sessions. This information is used to create a temporary opening in access lists, allowing return traffic and additional data connections. These temporary access entries are never saved to NVRAM.

CBAC is limited in its ability to work with certain protocols. Not all protocols are supported, only those specified. If a protocol is not specified, no CBAC inspection will occur. As with all security methods, complete security cannot be guaranteed. CBAC excels in the detection and prevention of the most popular forms of attack.

CBAC is usable only with IP protocol traffic, and only TCP and UDP packets are inspected. ICMP is not inspected with CBAC. Use standard or extended access lists instead of CBAC for ICMP. CBAC also ignores ICMP Unreachable messages.

Figure 5-5 shows an example of CBAC in action. When the user on the host initiates a connection to another host on the opposite side of the router, an opening is created on the outside of the router to allow the responding packets for this connection to travel through the router. Once this session has ended, this newly created opening will again be closed.

Figure 5-5   *CBAC Creating a Temporary Opening Through the Firewall Router*

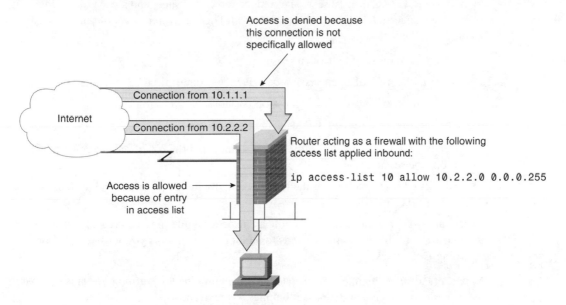

The administrator must specify which protocols are to be inspected, as well as the interfaces and direction on which the inspection of these protocols occurs. Only the protocols specified will be inspected. The selected protocols will be inspected in both directions as they traverse the interface.

The inspection of the control channel allows CBAC to detect and prevent certain types of application-based attacks. Packets are inspected by the access list first. CBAC then inspects and monitors the control channels of the connections. For example, when using FTP, CBAC parses the FTP commands and responses to those commands, but the actual data being transferred within the FTP program is not inspected. This is an important point, because only the control channels are monitored for state changes, not the data channels. Sequence numbers are tracked, and packets without the expected sequence number are dropped.

CBAC has knowledge of application-specific commands and will detect and prevent some forms of attacks based on the nuances of applications. On detection of an attack, the DoS feature built into CBAC responds in one of three ways:

- Protect system resources
- Block packets from the source of the suspected attack
- Generate alert messages

This feature protects system resources by determining when to drop sessions that have not become fully established. Timeout values for network sessions are set in order to free up system resources by dropping sessions after the specified time. Threshold values for network sessions are set in order to prevent DoS attacks by controlling the number of half-open sessions. CBAC drops a session to reduce resource usage, and a reset message is sent to both the source and destination for that session. There are three thresholds used by CBAC in relation to DoS attacks:

- The total number of half-open sessions
- The number of half-open session per given amount of time
- The number of half-open TCP session per host

When a threshold is exceeded, CBAC acts in one of two ways:

- Sends a reset message to source and destination of the oldest half-open session and drops the session.
- Blocks all SYN packets for the time specified with the *threshold* value. This is only used on TCP sessions.

To activate DoS prevention and detection, an inspection rule must be created and applied to an interface. This inspection rule needs to include the protocols you wish to monitor regarding DoS attacks.

As packets traverse the interface, a state table is maintained. Returning traffic is compared to this table to ensure that the packet belongs to a current session.

UDP is a connectionless service. Therefore, no session information is carried in UDP packets. CBAC uses a method of approximation to ensure reasonable care is used when allowing UDP packets through an interface. Each UDP packet is compared to previous UDP packets to see whether the source and destination addresses match, the port numbers match, and so on. Additionally, inbound UDP packets must be received after an outbound UDP packet within the time specified by the **udp idle timeout** command.

Sequence of CBAC Events

CBAC follows a defined flow of events when dealing with packets. Figure 5-6 shows the logical flow for these events. Take a few moments to view this logical flowchart before moving through the supported protocols.

Figure 5-6   *Sequence of CBAC Events*

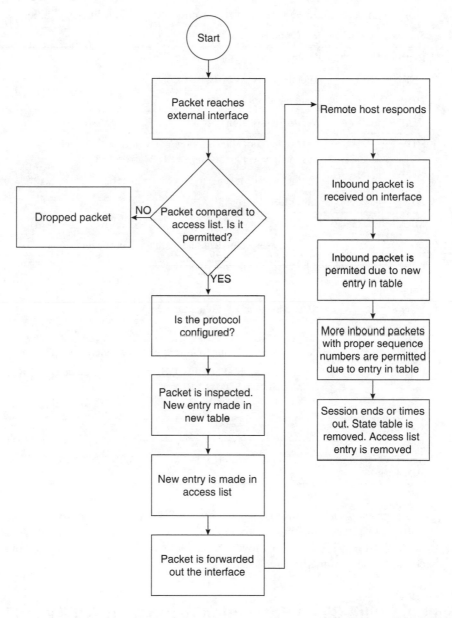

Protocol Sessions Supported by CBAC

CBAC can be configured to support the protocol sessions outlined in Table 5-2.

Table 5-2   *Supported CBAC Session Protocols*

Protocol	Notes
TCP	Handles all types of TCP session
UDP	Handles all types of UDP sessions
CU-SeeMe	White Pine version only
FTP	CBAC does not allow third-party connections. Data channels must have the destination port in the range of 1024 to 65,535 only
H.323	Microsoft NetMeeting and ProShare use H.323
HTTP	Java blocking
Microsoft NetShow	
Java	Protects against unidentified, malicious Java applets
UNIX R commands	rsh, rexec, rlogin, and so on
RealAudio	
SUN RPC	SUN compliant RPC, does not handle DCE RPC
Microsoft RPC	
SMTP	Any packet not on the following list is considered illegal: DATA, EHLO, EXPN, HELO, HELP, MAIL, NOOP, QUIT, RCPT, RSET, SAML, SEND, SOML, VRFY
SQL*Net	
StreamWorks	
TFTP	
VDOLive	

The term *supported* means that when a protocol is configured for CBAC, that protocol traffic is inspected, state information is maintained, and packets are allowed back through the firewall only if they belong to a permissible session (with the exception of connectionless protocols, such as UDP).

Compatibility with Cisco Encryption Technology (CET) and IPSec

When three routers are connected, the middle router is using CBAC, and the outside routers are running encryption, the results might not be what you expect. The reason is that CBAC cannot accurately inspect payloads that have been encrypted. This should be an expected occurrence, because encryption is specifically designed to prevent any but the end routers from being able to decipher the data. This situation is presented in Figure 5-7.

Figure 5-7   *Compatibility with CET*

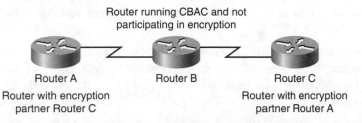

Router running CBAC and not
participating in encryption

Router A   Router B   Router C
Router with encryption   Router with encryption
partner Router C   partner Router A

Additionally, configuring both CBAC and encryption on the same router causes CBAC to stop working with some protocols. CBAC will still work with single-channel TCP and UDP, with the exception of Java and SMTP. CBAC will not work with any multiple channel protocols, except StreamWorks and CU-SeeMe. Therefore, when configuring both encryption and CBAC on the same router, configure Generic TCP, Generic UDP, CU-SeeMe, and StreamWorks as the only protocols.

CBAC is compatible with IPSec under limited circumstances. If the router running CBAC is the endpoint of an IPSec connection, there are no known compatibility issues. However, if the router running CBAC is not the endpoint of an IPSec connection, the same problem as with encryption occurs. For CBAC to run properly, the data within individual packets must be examined. Any time that this data is encrypted, CBAC will not work. Additionally, IPSec packets are not IP or UDP packets, which are the only types of packets CBAC is able to process.

Configuring CBAC

This section will discuss the configuration of CBAC.

Several steps are required to make CBAC effectively secure the corporate network:

Step 1   Choose an interface.

Step 2   Configure IP access lists on the interface.

Step 3   Configure global timeouts and thresholds.

Step 4   Define inspection rules and apply the inspection rule to the interface.

Step 5   Configure logging and audit trail.

Each of these will be discussed in turn.

Choose an Interface

The first step of configuring CBAC poses the administrator with a dilemma: Should CBAC be configured on the inside or outside interface? Should a demilitarized zone (DMZ) be created? No matter what configuration is ultimately chosen, one direction should always be configured first. Only after this configuration is thoroughly tested should a second interface be added.

The outside interface is the interface that connects to the Internet. An inside interface is an interface that connects directly to the corporate LAN. A DMZ is a network that is owned and controlled by a company and is not directly connected to either the Internet or the company LAN.

The most common configuration is shown in Figure 5-8. In this configuration, the CBAC is enabled on the external interface to prevent unauthorized access into the corporate network. In this configuration example, the only traffic allowed in from the Internet is in response to traffic initiated within the corporate network.

Figure 5-8   *Protecting the Corporate Network with CBAC*

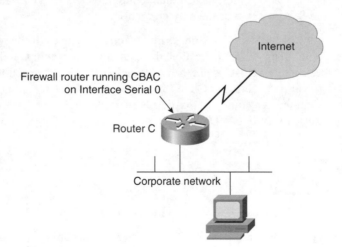

Figure 5-9 shows a different and slightly more complex configuration. In this configuration you build a DMZ to allow some access from the Internet to services provided to the general public. Examples of these services could include DNS, Web, or FTP servers.

When enabling CBAC as in the example in Figure 5-9, configure it on the internal Ethernet 0 interface. This method allows access to the DMZ from the Internet while still allowing access to the internal network in response to sessions initiated from within the corporate network.

No matter which interface is chosen for CBAC configuration, some basics regarding applying access lists in relation to CBAC need to be discussed.

Figure 5-9   *CBAC with a DMZ*

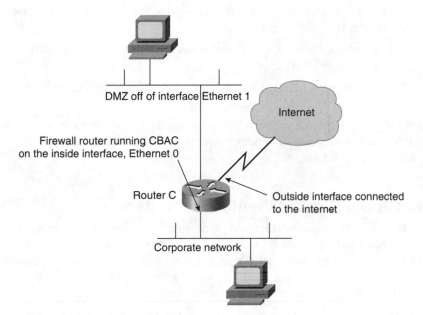

Configure IP Access Lists on the Interface

To maximize the benefits of CBAC, IP access lists need to be correctly configured. Some general rules should be followed when designing access lists for use with CBAC:

- Start with the basics. Make the initial access list as simple as possible and expand after it is thoroughly tested.

- Permit those protocols you wish CBAC to inspect to leave the network. For example, if TFTP traffic is prohibited from leaving the network, CBAC will never evaluate TFTP traffic.

- Deny returning CBAC traffic from entering through the router through an extended access list. This may sound wrong at first, but CBAC will create the temporary holes to allow data through in response to a valid request.

- Do not initially configure an access list preventing traffic from the internal side to the external side of the network. All traffic should flow freely out of the network until CBAC is fully functional. This is invaluable for troubleshooting purposes.

- Allow ICMP messages to flow freely in the initial configuration. ICMP traffic is not inspected by CBAC, therefore, entries are needed in the access list to permit return traffic for ICMP commands.

- Add an access list entry denying any network traffic from a source address matching an address on the protected network. This should really be done on all routers.

- An outbound access list on an external interface should permit traffic that you want to be inspected by CBAC. If traffic is not permitted, it will be dropped before getting to the CBAC.
- The inbound IP access list at the external interface must deny traffic destined to be inspected by CBAC.
- The inbound IP access list at the internal interface must permit traffic destined for inspection by CBAC.

In essence, you need to allow the CBAC to see the packets from the trusted side of the network. You also need to prevent returning packets and rely on CBAC to allow them to traverse the interface.

Configure Global Timeouts and Thresholds

CBAC uses timeouts and thresholds in conjunction in order to determine how long to manage state information for a session. Timeouts and thresholds are also used to determine when to drop sessions that are not fully established. Because timeouts and thresholds are so closely related, they are usually configured at the same time. These are global, so they apply to all CBAC configurations on the router.

The easiest way to configure the timeouts and thresholds is simply to use the default values. In this case, no changes to the configuration are necessary. However, this section will still explore timeouts and thresholds in case optimizations are necessary based on your individual corporate needs.

All of the threshold and timeouts available for changing, as well as their default values and a short description of the effect when they are changed, are listed in Table 5-3.

Table 5-3 *CBAC Timeouts and Thresholds*

Command	Default	Use
ip inspect dns-timeout *seconds*	5 seconds	The length of time a DNS name lookup session remains active after no activity
ip inspect max-incomplete high *number*	500 concurrent half-open sessions	The number of concurrent half-open sessions that causes the software to start deleting half-open sessions
ip inspect max-incomplete low *number*	400 concurrent half-open sessions	The number of concurrent half-open sessions that causes the software to stop deleting half-open sessions
ip inspect one-minute high *number*	500 half-open sessions per minute	The rate of new sessions at which CBAC starts deleting half-open sessions
ip inspect one-minute low *number*	500 half-open sessions per minute	The rate of new sessions at which CBAC stops deleting half-open sessions

Table 5-3   *CBAC Timeouts and Thresholds*

Command	Default	Use
ip inspect tcp finwait-time *seconds*	5 seconds	The length of time a TCP session stays active after the firewall detects a FIN-exchange
ip inspect tcp idle-time *seconds*	3600 seconds (1 hour)	The length of time a TCP session stays active after no activity (the TCP idle timeout)
ip inspect tcp max-incomplete host number block-time *minutes*	50 existing half-open TCP sessions; 0 minutes	The number of existing half-open TCP sessions with the same destination host address that causes CBAC to start dropping half-open sessions to the same destination host address
ip inspect tcp synwait-time *seconds*	30 seconds	The length of time CBAC waits for a TCP session to reach the established state before dropping the session

As with most commands, the **timeout** and **threshold** commands can be reset to the default by entering the **no** form of the command.

Define Inspection Rules

After the timeouts and thresholds are set, the inspection rules are defined. The inspection rules delineate which packets will be inspected by CBAC for a given interface. Unless you are configuring two separate interfaces both to use CBAC, only a single inspection rule is defined. The inspection rules define which application-layer protocols relying on IP will be inspected by CBAC. The inspection rules also include options for audit trail messages, alert messages, and packet fragmentation.

Two variations of the **ip inspect name** command are available for setting inspection of an application-layer protocol. The following are the two variations:

```
ip inspect name inspection-name protocol [alert {on | off}]
    [audit-trail {on | off}] [timeout seconds]
```

and

```
ip inspect name inspection-name rpc program-number number [wait-time minutes]
    [alert {on | off}] [audit-trail {on | off}] [timeout seconds]
```

The first instance of the command configures CBAC inspection for application-layer protocols, except for RPC and Java. The *protocol* keywords will be discussed in the next section. This command is repeated for each desired protocol, using the same inspection name each time. If more than one interface is using CBAC, this command is repeated for each protocol used with each interface, associating one name for each interface.

The second variation is used to enable CBAC inspection for the RPC application-layer protocol. As with the first instance, this command is specified multiple times, once for each program number.

Protocol Keywords

Table 5-4 contains a list of the keywords used for the *protocol* argument in the **ip inspect name** command.

Table 5-4   **ip inspect name** *Command protocol Keywords*

Keyword	Protocol
cuseeme	CU-SeeMe
h323	H.323
netshow	Microsoft NetShow
rcmd	UNIX R commands (rlogin, rexec, rsh, and so on)
realaudio	RealAudio
rpc	RPC
sqlnet	SQL*Net
streamworks	StreamWorks
tftp	TFTP
vdolive	VDOLive

A note concerning Microsoft NetMeeting 2.0: NetMeeting is an H.323 application-layer protocol that operates slightly outside of the normally accepted mode. Specifically, NetMeeting uses an additional TCP channel that is not defined within the H.323 specifications. To use NetMeeting and CBAC effectively, TCP inspection must also be enabled.

Java Blocking

CBAC filters Java applets by relying on a list of sites designated as friendly. In this method, a Java applet from a friendly site is allowed through, while all others are blocked. Java applets from sites other than friendly ones are not allowed through. The **ip inspect-name** command is used to block Java applets:

```
ip inspect name inspection-name http [java-list access-list]
    [alert {on | off}] [audit-trail {on | off}] [timeout seconds]
```

Use the same *inspection-name* as the other protocols checked by CBAC, unless you intend to use CBAC on more than one interface. CBAC does not detect or block Java applets that are encapsulated within another format. CBAC also does not detect or block Java applets loaded through HTTP on a nonstandard port or through the use of FTP, Gopher, or any other protocol where it cannot be determined that the Java applet is within the data.

Fragmentation Inspection

CBAC can be used to help protect against DoS attacks that use fragmented packets by maintaining an interfragment state table for IP packets. When a packet is received that has the fragment bit set, is not the first packet of a sequence of packets, and is not received in the proper order, CBAC will drop the packet.

This can cause problems in situations where it would normally be acceptable to accept packets out of order. When the sending host fails to receive an acknowledgement that all packets were received, another set of packets is sent. This can affect performance extremely. If it is acceptable to receive packets out of order, the default settings should be left as they are. If, however, receiving packets out of order is unacceptable, use the following form of the **ip inspect name** command:

```
ip inspect name inspection-name fragment [max number timeout seconds]
```

Generic TCP and UDP

Inspecting TCP and UDP packets is possible even if the application-layer protocol has not been configured for inspection. Doing this, however, means that CBAC does not recognize commands that are specific to the application. In this case, CBAC does not necessarily allow all packets of an application through the interface. This usually happens when the returning packets have a different port number than that associated with the packet previously sent out this interface. Because a defined application-layer protocol takes precedence over the TCP or UDP packet inspection, the more protocols that are defined, the less likely that this problem will be seen.

When using TCP and UDP inspection, packets attempting to enter the network must match the corresponding packet that previously exited the network in the source and destination addresses and ports. Failure to match results in the packet being dropped. UDP packets must also be received within the time specified by the **ip inspect udp idle-time** command. TCP packets must have the proper sequence number before being allowed to enter the interface. Inspection of TCP and UDP packets is enabled with the following commands:

```
ip inspect name inspection-name tcp [timeout seconds]
ip inspect name inspection-name udp [timeout seconds]
```

The next step in the configuration process is to configure logging and the audit trail.

Configure Logging and Audit Trail

Turning on logging and audit trails provides a record of all access through the firewall. Logging and audit trails are extremely simple to implement. The following is a small sample configuration that turns on both logging and audit trails:

```
service timestamps log datetime
!Adds the date and time to syslog and audit messages
logging 172.30.1.8
!Specifies that syslog messages are sent to 172.20.1.8
logging facility syslog
!Configures the syslog facility in which error messages are sent
!Valid options instead of syslog are: auth, cron, kern, local0-7, lpr, mail,
!news, sys9, sys10, sys11, sys12, sys13, sys14, daemon, user, and uucp.
logging trap 7
!Sets logging to level 7 (informational)
ip inspect audit-trail
!Turns on CBAC audit trail messages
```

CBAC Configuration Example

In the configuration example at the end of this section, a company, Bigg Incorporated, has a connection to a parts distributor on the 10.1.1.0/24 network through interface Serial 0.1. It also has a connection to one of its branch offices through interface Serial 0.2. The branch office is running on network 172.31.1.0/24. Figure 5-10 shows a logical view of these connections.

Because Bigg Inc. has no control over the network practices at the parts distributor, it enabled CBAC security between its main site and the distributor. All information exchanges, with the exception of ICMP messages, are denied by default. When a connection is initiated from within the corporate network, the CBAC will evaluate and allow a connection to be made.

In this configuration, Bigg Inc. set the CBAC to examine seven protocols and set the timeout on each to 30 seconds. Next, the company created an extended access list numbered 111. This access list, working in conjunction with CBAC, allows only ICMP messages through, unless the connection is initiated from within the network.

Bigg Inc. has added a named access list to the inbound and outbound sides of the serial interface connected to the branch office. This access list, in conjunction with the **reflect** statement, prevents all traffic from going to the branch office, except when in response to a session initiated from within the branch. Bigg Inc. could have added this prevention within the extended access list. However, this configuration illustrates how you can use CBAC on one interface without interfering with any other interface.

Interface Serial 0.1, which connects to the distributor's office, is set up with an IP address, an access list, and a call to the CBAC to inspect outgoing packets. Bigg Inc. allows HTTP (Web server) access to the host at 10.1.1.34 for ports 80 (the default) and ports 8001, 8002, 8003, and 8004.

Figure 5-10 *Connection to Branch Office and Distributor*

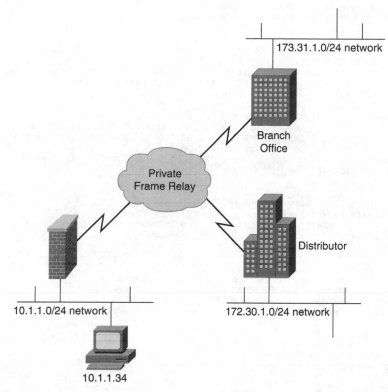

Interface Serial 0.2 is then set up with an IP address and a standard access list that limits packets to the 172.31.1.0/24.

Finally, Bigg Inc. set up an Ethernet interface that connects to the local network and the static IP routes. The company could alternatively use a routing protocol instead of static routes.

The following is the configuration:

```
ip port-map http 8001
ip port-map http 8002
ip port-map http 8003
ip port-map http 8004
!Sets HTTP to equal ports 8001, 8002, 8003 and 8004 in addition
!to the default port 80


ip inspect name test cuseeme timeout 30
ip inspect name test ftp timeout 30
ip inspect name test h323 timeout 30
ip inspect name test realaudio timeout 30
ip inspect name test rpc program-number 100000
ip inspect name test streamworks timeout 30
ip inspect name test vdolive timeout 30
```

```
time-range httptime
periodic weekday 08:00 to 17:00
!Set the httptime to occur between 08:00 and 17:00
!(8 a.m. till 5 p.m.) on weekdays

access-list 111 permit ip any host 10.1.1.34 eq http time-range httptime
!Because they added a port map earlier, this allows the new ports
!to have http access as well as the default port.  Additionally, they
!limit HTTP access to weekdays (mon-fri) at certain hours
access-list 111 deny TCP any any
access-list 111 deny UDP any any
access-list 111 permit icmp any any echo-reply
access-list 111 permit icmp any 172.30.1.0 0.0.0.255 time-exceeded
access-list 111 permit icmp any 172.30.1.0 0.0.0.255 packet-too-big
access-list 111 permit icmp any 172.30.1.0 0.0.0.255 traceroute
access-list 111 permit icmp any 172.30.1.0 0.0.0.255 unreachable
access-list 111 deny ip any any


ip access list extended inbound
evaluate packetssent
!The only packets allowed to enter are in response to connections
!initiated from within the corporate network
deny ip any any

ip access list extended outbound
permit tcp any any reflect packetssent timeout 90
permit udp any any reflect packetssent timeout 60
permit icmp any any reflect packetssent timeout 30
permit ip any any

interface s0.1
ip address 192.168.1.1 255.255.255.252
ip access-group 111 in
ip inspect test out

interface s0.2
ip address 192.168.1.5 255.255.255.252
ip access-group inbound in
!Set the named access list "inbound" to packets entering the
!interface
ip access-group outbound out
!Set the named access list "outbound" to packets leaving the
!interface for use with the reflect statement

interface e0
ip address 10.1.1.1 255.255.255.0

ip route 172.30.1.0 255.255.255.0 192.168.1.2
ip route 172.31.2.0 255.255.255.0 192.168.1.6
```

Summary

The preceding configuration combines most of the issues discussed in this chapter. Chapter 6 will discuss how the Intrusion Detection System works as a standalone option, as well as in conjunction with CBAC. Review the preceding configuration example before moving on to Chapter 6.

This chapter contains the following sections:

- Overview of Intrusion Detection
- Intrusion Detection Systems
- Cisco Secure Intrusion Detection System (CSIDS)
- Cisco IOS Firewall IDS
- Cisco Secure PIX Firewall IDS
- Cisco Intrusion Detection System (IDS) Configuration
- Summary
- Frequently Asked Questions
- Glossary

Intrusion Detection Systems

With the growth of the Internet, and the reliance of industry on it for revenue through business and e-commerce, come new challenges. A great deal of this book covers these new challenges and the risks associated with them. One area of network security that is becoming increasingly important is intrusion detection. You can spend tens of thousands of dollars implementing a corporate security policy that deploys technologically advanced hardware devices such as stateful firewalls and VPN terminators, but how can you actively monitor the data flow on your network to ensure that these devices are doing their jobs? One way to test the network integrity is to use a port scanner or vulnerability scanner from an outside interface to ascertain what is visible on the inside from the outside world. These devices are excellent tools, but they only inform network administrators of what they really should already know. A lot of attacks, especially denial of service (DoS) attacks, masquerade as legitimate session traffic. These attacks can bypass the common firewall technologies, because the firewall presumes that they are genuine users with genuine service requests. This is where intrusion detection plays a part in the total security solution. The intrusion detection system (IDS) passively listens to data on the network segment and matches the traffic pattern against known security signatures. Once this data is collected and interpreted, actions can be taken.

This chapter provides a basic introduction to intrusion detection. This overview looks at the two basic types of intrusion detection systems, host-based systems and network-based systems. The chapter then looks at the intrusion detection offerings from Cisco Systems that form part of the Cisco Secure product family. These offerings include the Cisco Secure Intrusion Detection System (CSIDS), the Cisco Secure PIX Firewall, and Cisco IOS Firewall. A sample configuration of the intrusion detection capabilities for both the PIX Firewall and the router running Cisco IOS Firewall is also provided.

Overview of Intrusion Detection

Intrusion detection works in a similar manner to virus protection software applications. The virus scanner scans files within a given operating system and tries to match the file against a database of known viruses. If the file is matched against the database, the software application interacts and takes action. This action can be to remove the virus from the file or to delete the file from the file system of the operating system. Intrusion detection works in a similar way. Instead of checking files for viruses, an intrusion detection system monitors the flow of network traffic and compares this flow to the database of security signatures that have been configured on the intrusion detection device. When a match is made, the intrusion detection system usually can alarm, drop the packet, or reset the connection.

This provides an excellent security tool that can scan the traffic on the network in real time and take action against any suspect activity.

Two main types of intrusion detection systems are commonly available and in use in today's networks:

- Host-based intrusion detection systems
- Network-based intrusion detection systems

Host-Based Intrusion Detection Systems

Host-based intrusion detection systems exist on the actual hosts or servers that they are protecting. They use resources on the host, such as disk space, RAM, and CPU time, and run as any other application would. The IDS application installed on the host is referred to as an *agent*. The agent collects data by analyzing the operating system, applications, and system audit trails and compares this data to a predefined set of rules. These rules indicate whether a security breach or intrusion has been attempted. Because the agents actually run on the host, they can be fine-tuned to detect operating system intrusion attempts and offer greater flexibility in this area than network-based intrusion detection systems.

The host agents can usually be configured to report intrusion attempts locally by some client application or centrally to an enterprise monitoring system. Scalability always becomes an issue with host-based agents, as you must install an agent on each protected host. Figure 6-1 displays the deployment of host-based intrusion detection systems.

Network-Based Intrusion Detection Systems

Network-based intrusion detection systems are physical devices that are connected to various network segments within the protected network. Network-based intrusion detection systems usually comprise two components that work together to provide the IDS service. These two components are an IDS sensor (Cisco's is the Intrusion Detection Sensor) and an IDS management platform (Cisco's is the Intrusion Detection Director).

Figure 6-1   *Host-Based Intrusion Detection*

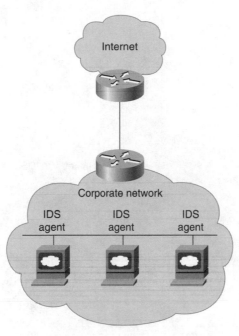

The IDS sensors are hardware devices that passively monitor and analyze the traffic flow within a network segment. The sensor monitors the traffic and compares the collected data to prebuilt IDS signatures, to build up a profile of activity on the network segment. One problem with the IDS sensors is their placement. They can only monitor traffic that their network connection sees. The network interface listens in promiscuous mode to process all network traffic, even that not destined for the sensor itself. The obvious problem is that a normal switch port creates a separate collision domain and a shared broadcast domain throughout the VLAN to which the switch port is connected. Therefore, the sensor only receives unicast traffic destined for the sensor itself and broadcast traffic on that VLAN. To get around this, you should connect the IDS sensor to what is called a Switched Port Analyzer (SPAN) port on the switch. SPAN ports can be configured on all of the Cisco Catalyst range of switches. A SPAN port can be configured to listen to all unicasts and broadcasts for specific VLANs on one port. This is ideal for the IDS sensor, as it can then passively monitor and analyze all unicast traffic on the network segment across multiple VLANs. Figure 6-2 shows a network-based intrusion detection system.

The second component of the network-based intrusion detection system is the IDS management platform. The IDS sensor sends notification messages to the IDS management platform, which can be configured to interpret these results and take necessary action on them.

Figure 6-2 *Network-Based Intrusion Detection*

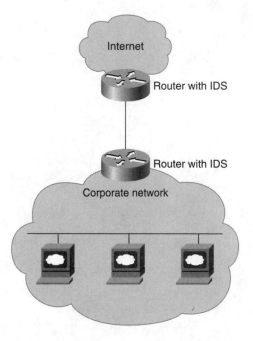

Intrusion Detection Systems

Now that you have a brief explanation of intrusion detection, the remainder of this chapter covers the current intrusion detection offerings from Cisco Systems. There are three main offerings from Cisco across differing platforms:

- Cisco Secure Intrusion Detection System (CSIDS)
- Cisco IOS Firewall IDS
- Cisco Secure PIX Firewall IDS

Cisco Secure Intrusion Detection System (CSIDS)

Most of this book focuses on ways to prevent outside unauthorized entities from connecting to your network. This section differs in that the focus is on how patterns of abuse are detected from both internal and external sources. After a pattern of abuse is noted, you can respond in real time to the threat. The phrase *patterns of abuse* is used because the Cisco Secure Intrusion Detection System (CSIDS) looks at the format and the amount of data traversing your network to determine the likelihood and severity of threats. The patterns within the data traversing the network are analyzed to determine whether an attack has been launched.

This section covers the CSIDS. The CSIDS is differentiated from the Cisco IOS Firewall IDS and the Cisco Secure PIX Firewall IDS in that the CSIDS is designed to run both independently and in conjunction with the existing hardware on a network. Additionally, the abilities of the CSIDS to detect and respond to threats are much greater than those built into either the Cisco IOS Firewall or the Cisco Secure PIX Firewall. These additional abilities are available because routing or performing firewall functions is not the main purpose of the CSIDS. The main purpose of the CSIDS is to detect and respond to patterns of abuse in real time.

A full explanation of the details of installation, maintenance, and configuration of the CSIDS is beyond the scope of this book. However, this section gives you the theory necessary to begin your investigations into the CSIDS. This section provides an overview of the most important features and issues involved with the CSIDS, the basics of Sensor deployment, Director deployment, signatures, alarms, and log files.

Intrusion detection monitors against three forms of attack.

- **Reconnaissance attacks**—A reconnaissance attack is where an attempt is made to discover and map services, vulnerabilities, and systems for purposes of later access or denial of service (DoS) attacks. As little information about your network should be revealed as possible, because excessive revelations might show possible weaknesses that have not yet been addressed. For example, an internal user might scan the ports on a server to prepare for breaking into that server for confidential information.

- **Access attacks**—An access attack occurs when users actively attempt to access services to which they do not have authority. For example, an internal user sitting at a desk and repeatedly trying to log into a server with another user's name and different passwords is considered an access attack.

- **Denial of service (DoS) attacks**—A DoS attack occurs when an attempt is made to prevent valid use of a network or system. Many examples of DoS attacks, including the ping of death attack, are discussed throughout this book.

The CSIDS is designed to monitor for these types of attack and to notify the appropriate personnel in the event of such an attack. Logs are built that detail the suspicious packets. The CSIDS can also respond by denying service to the perpetrators of all three forms of attack.

Cisco has chosen to implement a packet-based detection method to determine when an attack is in progress. This method relies on comparing the data within each packet with a "signature" that indicates a possible attack. There are some differences between the signatures used within the Cisco IOS software used on routers and those found on the Cisco IDS equipment. One difference is the number of signatures: although the Cisco IOS has implemented 59 signatures and the PIX Firewall has implemented 57 signatures, the CSIDS has a much larger number of signatures. Additionally, CSIDS allows a skilled administrator to create new signatures. This allows the protection of the network to evolve as new threats emerge.

The CSIDS was formerly called NetRanger, and many of the existing URLs on the Cisco web site still refer to this product with the old name. Keep the old name in mind when searching the Cisco web site for specific information about the CSIDS.

Overview of the CSIDS Components

The CSIDS comprises three components: the Sensor, the Post Office Protocol, and the Director. Each has a unique function. This section provides an overview of the functions of each before the rest of the chapter goes on to delve into the specifics of each component.

CSIDS Sensor

The CSIDS Sensor is a high-performance hardware appliance used to detect intrusion attempts. In essence, this is a packet sniffer that analyzes all of the network traffic on a given network segment, comparing the packets to an attack signature database. When a packet with qualities matching a signature within the database is detected, the Sensor notifies the Director and logs alarm activities.

The Sensor can be configured to reset a TCP connection automatically, block an offending IP address, or log the session. The Sensor reassembles fragmented IP packets as necessary to determine the full threat posed by the packets.

CSIDS Post Office Protocol

The Post Office Protocol is responsible for delivering between the Sensors and the Directors. This protocol, using a UDP format on port 4500, is considered reliable because it requires an acknowledgement of all data sent and resends data as necessary.

The Post Office Protocol can be configured to send messages to up to 255 alternate Directors if the primary Director is unavailable. Directors are specified by IP address.

CSIDS Director

The Director can be considered the focal point of the CSIDS components, because this is where displays and logs about alarms are stored. The administrator uses the Director to manage and respond to alarms through a graphical user interface (GUI). The Director can also be configured to send e-mail or to execute a user script when an alarm is received.

The Director also allows for management and configuration of remote Sensors through the configuration management utility. This feature is especially useful in cases where a large corporation with multiple locations has chosen to centralize their security efforts.

Unit Identification

Both Directors and Sensors are identified uniquely. There are three parts to this identification, two of which are assigned by the administrator. The three parts are

- Host ID
- Organizational ID
- Application Identifier

Host ID

The Host ID is set to any number greater than zero. For example, one Sensor might be assigned number 1, a Director is assigned 2, and another Sensor is assigned 3.

Organizational ID

The Organizational ID is any number greater than zero. This is commonly used to group devices together according to region or function. For example, all Sensors and Directors in South America could be assigned 2000, while all Sensors and Directors within North America are assigned 3000. This makes it easier for the administrator of a large system to know where a device is located.

The Host and Organizational ID are combined by adding a period (.) between the Host and Organizational ID numbers. Examples of this are 3.2000 and 2.2000.

Alpha Identifiers

Associated with the Host and Organizational IDs are the Host Name and Organization Name, respectively. The names are joined together in the same manner as their numeric counterparts. These also allow for easier identification of devices. For example, Sensors might be labeled sensor1.southamerica and sensor2.southamerica, while Directors might be labeled director1.northamerica or director2.northamerica. Although there is no specific rule stating that any naming conventions should be used, labeling devices logically and consistently greatly eases both administration and training of new personnel.

Application Identifiers

The Application Identifier is a statistically unique number assigned by the software. This allows for a combination among the three parts of the Identifier that should always be unique. These identifiers are used to route all communications between devices.

The Sensor, the Post Office Protocol, and the Director work together to form the CSIDS. The next sections delve deeper into a discussion of the hardware associated with the CSIDS

Sensor, an explanation of the Post Office Protocol, and a discussion of the requirements for the CSIDS Director.

The CSIDS Sensor

The CSIDS Sensor comes in two basic models. The first model is a standalone rack-mountable version, and the second model is a Catalyst switch module, also called a *blade*, residing within the Catalyst 6000 series.

With the standalone rack-mountable version, there is a floppy disk provided for software upgrades and password recovery. The front cover is also lockable.

The standalone module number is based on the type of network interface used for monitoring. The CSIDS Sensor can be used on Ethernet, Fast Ethernet, Single or Dual FDDI, and Token Ring. There are a number of connections available on the back of the Sensor.

There are connections on the back for power, in addition to a COM port, and a monitor and a keyboard, which are used for initial configuration. Connecting a cable to the COM port of a computer is done in the same manner as with a router that uses the COM port.

Notice that there are two network interface ports on the rear of the Sensor. The built-in horizontal network port, called the *Command NIC*, is used for communications with routers and the Director. The vertically mounted *Monitoring NIC* port is used to monitor the network segment. Although a standard Ethernet connection could be used to monitor a network with a number of Fast Ethernet connections, such a configuration could easily cause the Ethernet link to become overused because of the large amount of traffic that is typically traversing such a network. Both NICs must be connected for the Sensor to operate properly.

When connecting the Monitoring NIC to a switch, ensure that SPAN monitoring is enabled for that port within the switch. Because a switch, by default, forwards packets only to the appropriate ports, failing to enable port monitoring on the switch will result in the Sensor being unable to see attacks that are not directed toward the Sensor itself. In the event that multiple VLANs are in use, the Sensor can monitor more than one VLAN, if the switch is properly configured with port monitoring on the desired VLANs through the Monitor NIC port.

The second form of the CSIDS Sensor is available in the form of a blade module for the Catalyst line of switches. This version of the Sensor becomes an integral part of the switch.

The advantage of using this form of the Sensor is that all data destined for the Sensor travels over the backplane of the switch. Assume for a moment that the network you wish to monitor uses a Cisco Catalyst 6509 with four sets of 48-port Fast Ethernet modules. There is very real possibility that the amount of data traveling through this switch could exceed the capacity of the single Fast Ethernet connection of Monitoring NIC on a standalone version. Having this data travel through the backplane of the switch on the blade version means that the maximum amount of data inspected is not limited by a Fast Ethernet connection (100 Mbps). The limitation while using the blade version comes from the processing speed of the Sensor itself, instead of the Ethernet connection. The configuration of the Sensor is virtually the same, whether the standalone or the blade version is used. Because a larger number of the standalone versions are used, the remainder of this section will focus on this form of the Sensor.

CSIDS Sensor Deployment

The CSIDS Sensor can be deployed in a number of ways. Because all networks vary, there can be no single method of deployment that fulfills the needs of all networks. This section will show the more common methods available and discuss the benefits and deficits of each.

Some items to consider while planning a Sensor deployment include the size and complexity of the network, the amounts and types of data traveling over the segment, and the connections between this network and other trusted and untrusted networks. Decisions also need to be made to determine which parts of the network should be monitored. If the sensor is placed on the outside of a firewall, that Sensor can be used to monitor attacks directed against the firewall from the outside. However, the Sensor will not be able to watch for threats originating on the inside of the firewall and directed only to machines inside the firewall. Conversely, placing the Sensor inside the firewall will not allow the sensor to monitor any attacks originating from the Internet directed toward the firewall. As with most networking decisions, a balance must be found that suits the administrator's individual situation.

The following sections cover some practical ways to deploy the CSIDS Sensor.

Simple CSIDS Deployment

Figure 6-3 shows a simple deployment where the Sensor monitors the interior of the network. The Director is also located on the interior network. The switch must be configured to send port-monitoring data to the Monitoring NIC. Notice that the area monitored is limited by the PIX Firewall.

Figure 6-3   *CSIDS Sensor Monitoring the Local Network*

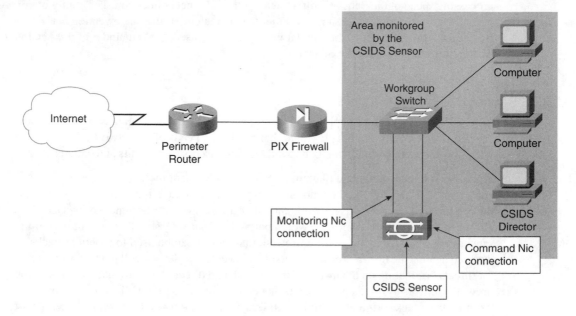

CSIDS Monitoring Beyond the Firewall

Figure 6-4 shows an example of how the Sensor could be deployed for purposes of monitoring the data transferred from the perimeter router to the firewall. In this model, the Command NIC is connected to inside the firewall, while the Monitoring NIC is connected to outside the firewall. The Command NIC sends information about possible attacks to the Director through the Command NIC. In this scenario, the administrator will be made aware of both when an attack on the firewall from the Internet occurs, and the form of the attack.

Figure 6-4   *CSIDS Sensor Monitoring Beyond the Firewall*

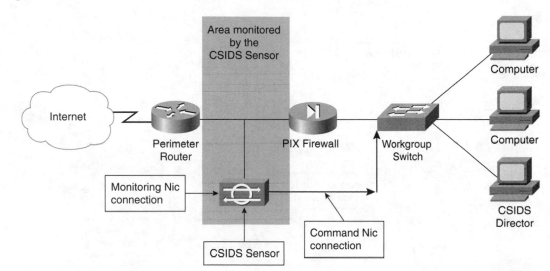

Because the PIX allows packets to travel from the inside to the outside interface by default, the Sensor is also able to communicate with the perimeter router. In the event that an attack is observed, the Sensor can be configured to add an access control list on the perimeter router to bypass the attack. Adding the access control list is referred to as *shunning*. For shunning to occur, Telnet services on the router must be enabled, the router must be added to the Sensor's management list, and an access control list must not be present on the interface in the same direction as the access list that will be applied by the CSIDS.

Monitoring Remote Sites

In some networks, there exists a need to monitor a network segment connected through a nonsecured medium. A remote site that has the capability of configuring a connection to the main office can use a Sensor on either the protected or the unprotected portion of the network. Figure 6-5 shows an example of a Sensor at a remote site that is configured to monitor the unprotected portion of the remote site's network. As in the case when a local site monitors the unprotected network, the Monitoring NIC is connected between the perimeter router and the PIX Firewall. The Command NIC is connected to the protected network with an IP address on that network.

Figure 6-5 *CSIDS Sensor Monitoring the Remote Network*

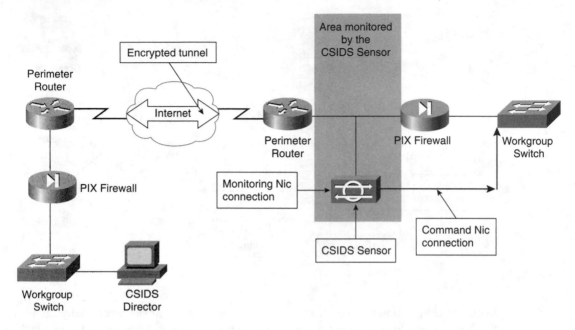

Notice that the remote site does not have a directly connected CSIDS Director. The requirement is that two-way UDP connectivity between the Command NIC and the Director should be maintained. As long as the firewalls on each side allow UDP connectivity, there are no requirements for the location of the Director.

In Figure 6-5, the connection from the remote site is over an encrypted tunnel. This is critical to the security of your network. Although there is no requirement by the Sensor or the Director that the path between the two is secure, it would be foolish to transfer data about the current vulnerabilities through the Internet. In the case that the connection to the remote site is through a more secure method such as dedicated Frame Relay, it might not be necessary to encrypt the connection. However, if the connection is not encrypted, any user with access to intermediate routers might be able to watch traffic traveling between the Sensor and the Director.

Noncontrolling Deployment

Another configuration is possible, although it is not recommended. It is pointed out to show how a common mistake can be avoided. Looking at Figure 6-6, notice that the Monitoring NIC is connected to the unprotected network, but the Command NIC is used to build a separate network to the Director. In this case, the Command NIC and the Director have no access to the perimeter router, because the Sensor does not route between the interfaces and only sends commands out through the Command NIC. Should an attack be discovered, there is no path from the Command NIC to the perimeter router that can be used to adjust the access control list on the perimeter router to block the attack. This scenario only allows for passive monitoring and logging of the network, while denying the functionality of responding to attacks in a real-time manner. Therefore, this configuration is not recommended.

Figure 6-6   *CSIDS Sensor Without Control Capability*

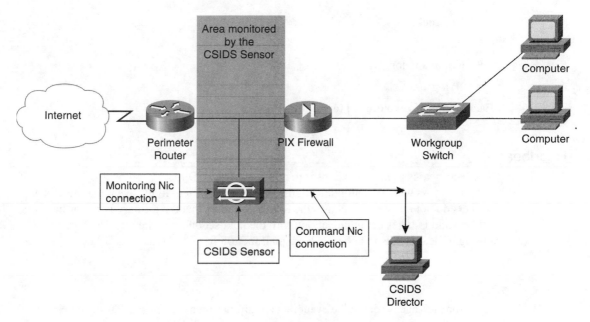

CSIDS Sensor Guidelines

So far, this section gave an overview of the CSIDS Sensor hardware and different common deployments. As with most other network configurations, a lot of the decisions on how to deploy something are individual to the needs of the particular network. There are, however, a few guidelines that should be remembered when deploying Sensors.

- The Sensor must be able to communicate with the Director through the Command NIC, using the UDP protocol on port 4500.

- The communications between the Sensor and the Director can provide hackers with data about the vulnerability of your network. Therefore, these communications should be treated as any other vital data.

- The Sensor only monitors a single segment at a time.

- The Catalyst IDS Sensor module accepts data at backplane speeds, bypassing the limitations of an Ethernet, Token Ring, or FDDI connection.

The CSIDS Post Office Protocol

The Post Office Protocol is used for communications between the Sensor and the Director. Both the Director and the Sensor can send a Post Office Protocol message. There are six types of messages that can be sent between the Sensor and the Director.

- Heartbeat
- Error
- Redirect
- Alarm
- Command log
- IP log

Each of these is explored in turn in the following sections.

Heartbeat

The heartbeat is used by the Sensor to poll the primary Director, and by a Director to poll the Sensor. As with all communications, a reply is expected. In the event that heartbeat packets do not receive a response, the Sensor assumes that the primary Director has gone off line and initiates communications with the next secondary Director. The Director, failing to hear a Sensor, believes that a malfunction has occurred.

Error

An error message is sent in the event that a malfunction has occurred. This can be because of a hardware issue, loss of connectivity on the monitoring NIC, or a problem within the operating system software.

Command

A command is used for configuration purposes. Commands can be used to change certain parameters, such as the level of alarms.

Alarm

An alarm is a message sent by the Sensor to the Director that an event of noticeable severity has been monitored. By default, there are five alarm levels, although the administrator can configure up to 255 levels.

Command Log

A command log is an entry made to record the commands issued between Sensors and Directors. All commands are recorded to the command log by default.

IP Log

An IP log message contains information concerning TCP sessions. This log is only written when a triggering event takes place. Once writing to an IP log initiates, the log continues to be written for a specified amount of time. Because IP is the only protocol supported at this time, there are no Internetwork Packet Exchange (IPX) or Systems Network Architecture (SNA) logs. These messages contain information such as the time, the source and destination IP addresses, and the associated ports.

The CSIDS Director

The CSIDS Director is a software package designed to operate in conjunction with the CSIDS Sensors. The main function of the Director is to manage the configuration of the Sensors.

Although it is possible to configure multiple directors to manage a given Sensor simultaneously, this should be avoided for two reasons. First, it is extremely easy for multiple Directors to give conflicting commands to a Sensor. Second, security is increased if only a single Director manages any Sensor at any given time. This, however, does not imply that it is wrong for more than one Director to be used to manage a Sensor on a routine basis. As long as only one Director is managing at any time, it is perfectly reasonable to have more than one Director capable of managing a Sensor. For example, the structure of a company might dictate that from 0800 through 1600 GMT time, Directors in the London office maintain Sensors. From 1600 through 2400 GMT, Directors in the Hong Kong office manage Sensors, and from 2400 through 0800, Directors in the San Francisco office manage Sensors. The CSIDS is perfectly capable of handling this scenario.

Director services are available in two forms: through the Cisco Secure Policy Manager and as a standalone server. Although the inner workings of these two forms of the Director vary, the basic available features are the same. The Cisco Secure Policy Manager is covered in Chapter 8, "Cisco Secure Policy Manager (CSPM)." The remainder of this section will deal with the standalone server version of the Director.

Configuration on the standalone version is accomplished through the CSIDS Configuration Management Utility, also called *nrConfigure*. This utility allows multiple configurations to be saved for each Sensor and downloaded to the Sensor when appropriate. One scenario where this can be advantageous is when the security requirements for a network change on a regular basis. For example, if a remote site should never have any network traffic over a holiday weekend, the administrator can download a very restrictive configuration that runs a script to page the administrator when any traffic traverses the network. Another benefit of the ability to maintain numerous configurations is that the administrators can test each of them to find the one that works best with their particular network.

Server-Based Director Hardware Requirements

The standalone CSIDS Director is designed to run on SPARC or HP processor platforms. As with most hardware requirements, the following should be considered the absolute minimum required to run the CSIDS Director software.

The minimum SPARC platform consists of the following:

- Solaris 2.51, 2.6, or 2.7 Operating System
- 50 MB CSIDS install partition
- 2 GB CSIDS log partition
- 110 MB HP OpenView partition
- 12 MB Java Runtime Partition
- 96 MB RAM
- HP OpenView 4.11, 5.01, or 6.0 to display the CSIDS GUI
- A Java-compatible Web browser for displaying the Network Security Database (NSDB)

The minimum HP-UX platform consists of the following:

- HP-UX 10.20
- 50 MB CSIDS install partition
- 2 GB CSIDS log partition
- 65 MB HP OpenView partition
- 10 MB Java Runtime Partition
- 96 MB RAM
- HP OpenView 4.11, 5.01, or 6.0 to display the CSIDS GUI
- A Java compatible Web browser for displaying the NSDB

Before attempting to install Director, several items should be checked for completeness. Among these items are

- HP OpenView completely installed and tested
- DNS configured and tested, if used
- UNIX host name configured and tested
- Web browser configured and tested
- IP address, subnet mask, and default gateway configured and tested
- All devices with concurrent times and time zones[1]

---

1. This is a critical item, because the times that activities occur will be recorded. All equipment, such as routers, the Director, and the Sensor, should have identical times. In cases where a network traverses multiple time zones, a single time zone, such as the GMT, should be chosen for all equipment. Using NTP to synchronize times on the equipment is recommended.

Managed Devices Requirements

The CSIDS is capable of changing access control lists on a router to shun an attack. There are only a few requirements to allow a device to be managed.

- Telnet must be allowed.
- A vty password must be set.
- An enable password must be set.

Director Deployment

One Director can be configured to manage multiple Sensors. The actual number of Sensors that can be successfully managed by a single Director is based on a number of factors, including the memory and CPU speed of the Director and the amount of data sent to the Director by the Sensors.

Directors can be configured in a hierarchical manner that allows messages to have propagation through the hierarchies. Using a hierarchical configuration allows personnel to monitor and respond to situations presented by locally placed Directors, while still allowing a centralized monitoring site to maintain an overview of the whole network. Alarms can be sent to the higher-level Directors through the locally administered Directors without broadcasting.

As shown in the example in Figure 6-7, the Director in Western Europe reports to the Director in Eastern Europe, which in turn reports to the Director in the Eastern United States. The Directors in South America report to Director in the Western United States, which in turn reports to the Director in the Eastern United States. The Director in Australia reports directly to the Director in the Eastern United States.

Figure 6-7 *CSIDS Director Hierarchy*

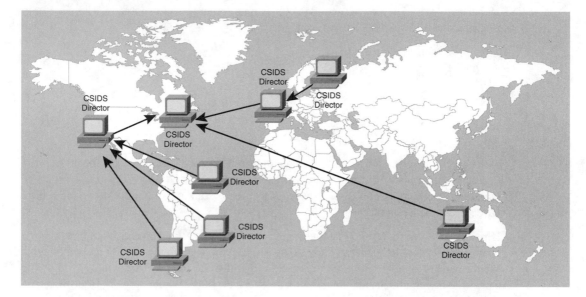

Signatures

A signature is a set of rules based on activity typically seen when an intrusion is attempted. This set of rules is matched to packets on the network. When a match is found, a unique response is generated. When a match occurs, a trigger is set that causes the Sensor to react by adjusting an access control list on a router, notifying the Director, or acting in another predefined manner. The CSIDS signatures are categorized according to the structure, implementation, and class of packets. A large number of signatures are included with the Sensor. The administrator can add to this list and change the characteristics of any signature.

Signature Structures

There are two types of signature structures: atomic and composite. A single packet triggers an atomic signature, while multiple packets trigger a composite signature.

For example, an IP packet with identical source and destination addresses might be considered an atomic signature. An intruder sweeping through port ranges would trigger a composite attack.

Signature Implementation

There are also two types of signature implementations: context and content. A content implementation is triggered by data contained within the packet payload. A context implementation is triggered by the data contained within the packet header.

For example, a packet containing data with the string "hack attack" would be a content implementation. An IP packet with a bad option can be considered a context implementation.

Signature Classes

There are four types of signature classes.

- **Reconnaissance Class**—A Reconnaissance Class triggers because of network activity that can be used to discover systems, services, and vulnerabilities on the network. Reconnaissance attacks include ping sweeps and port sweeps.

- **Access Class**—Access Class signatures trigger on activity that could lead to unauthorized system access, escalation of privileges, or data retrieval. Access Class attacks include phf (WWW), Back Orifice, and IP fragment attacks.

- **DoS Class**—A DoS Class signature is triggered when packets monitored could lead to the disabling of network equipment, systems, or services. DOS attacks include ping of death, half-open SYN attacks, and UDP bombs.

- **Information Class**—Information Class signatures trigger on packets that are normal within a network but still can be used maliciously. Information Class signatures are also triggered to enable the administrator to determine the validity and severity of an attack and to form a record for possible use in legal proceedings. Information Class signatures include TCP connection requests, UDP connections, and ICMP Echo Requests.

Signature Series

The CSIDS signatures are grouped in numbered series. There are seven series, each relating to signatures within the series level. The CSIDS signature series are shown in Table 6-1.

Table 6-1   *IP Signature Series*

Series Number	Type
1000	IP Signatures
2000	ICMP Signatures
3000	TCP Signatures
4000	UDP Signatures
6000	Miscellaneous Signatures
8000	String Match Signatures
10000	Policy Violations

Signature Severity Levels

Each signature has an associated severity level that indicates the probability that the signature is an actual attack. The default security levels for all signatures are preset, and the administrator can change the setting at any time. The five signature severity levels are shown in Table 6-2.

Table 6-2 *IP Signature Severity Levels*

Severity Level	Name	Description	Probability of Attack	Immediate Threat
1	Informational	Informational events are logged only on Sensors. Simply someone pinging a server can cause this.	Very low	No
2	Abnormal	An abnormal event is one that does not normally occur on a network. This could be caused by an unknown protocol.	Low	No
3	Marginal	The infrequent occurrence of the packets causing this trigger does not justify a higher severity level. The same packets in higher quantities could cause a higher severity level. An example could be an IP fragment attack.	Medium	Low
4	Serious	The signature indicates an attack of a suspicious nature. The administrator should investigate further. An example could be a TCP port sweep.	High	Medium
5	Critical	The attack signatures indicate that an attack of a severe nature is being launched. There is very little probability that the packets have a legitimate purpose. An example could be a ping of death attack.	Very high	High

Responding to Alarms

Now you have examined the hardware and software associated with the CSIDS. You have looked at signatures. This section also explores what happens when a packet on the monitored network matches a signature. This section walks through a theoretical attack on an e-mail server to illustrate how the CSIDS is capable of reacting to an attack.

Take a moment to review Figure 6-8. In this example, there is a Sensor monitoring the unprotected network between the perimeter router and the PIX Firewall. The Command NIC is connected to the local LAN, where the Director resides.

Figure 6-8   *CSIDS Sensor Notices an Attack*

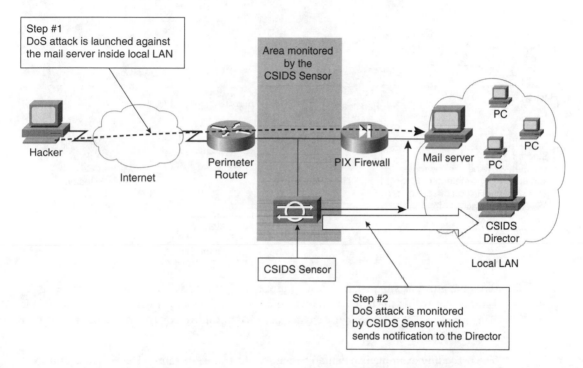

As shown in Figure 6-8, a hacker on the Internet has decided to attempt a DoS attack against the internal e-mail server through the use of half-open TCP connections. Although the PIX Firewall is fully capable of resisting such an attack, the Sensor still notices the attack the moment it has been launched. The FloodGuard algorithm on the PIX Firewall will not start to drop half-open connections until the defined threshold has been exceeded. The Sensor sends a message to the Director stating that an attack is under way. Entries are made in the log showing the packets received. This example uses the ability of the CSIDS to deny packets from the attacker through the adjustment of an access control list on the serial interface of the perimeter router.

The configuration of the signature definition for this type of attack specifies that a number of actions happen when this type of attack occurs. The first action is that e-mail is sent from the Director to the administrator stating that an attack is under way. The second action is that this type of attack notifies the administrator at the Director that a severe attack is under way. The third action is for the perimeter router's access control list on the serial interface to be changed by the Sensor to deny the IP address of the attacker. This is shown in Figure 6-9.

Figure 6-9   *CSIDS Responds to the Attack*

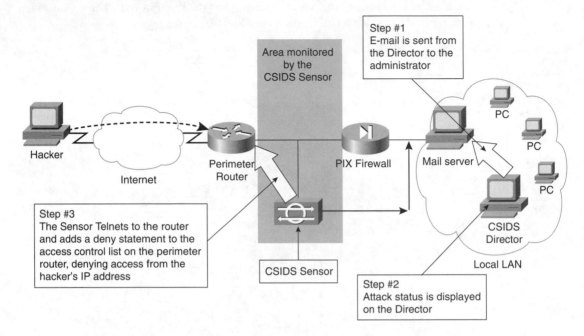

After the attack is stopped, the cleanup process begins. The PIX and the mail server automatically drop the half-open connections after a timeout period expires. Similarly, the Sensor removes the dynamically created access control list from the perimeter router after a specified amount of time.

The preceding example is meant to be purely illustrative in nature. Nearly all responses to signature detections, as well as the signatures themselves, are definable by the administrator. There is no requirement that any of the actions illustrated in the preceding example need to be taken. Instead of sending e-mail to the administrator, the signature definition could have easily had the Director run a script that defined actions to be taken. The administrator could have also chosen to allow all half-open connections from a particular host. The flexibility inherent within the CSIDS gives additional benefits to the administrator.

One benefit that the CSIDS has over other IDSs is because of this flexibility. Many IDSs do not allow the administrator to bypass certain types of apparent attacks. No two networks have the same characteristics regarding protocol distribution, number of broadcasts, and so on. Unless a detection system allows the administrator to completely adjust the parameters used to detect an attack, that system quickly becomes unusable in a number of networks. For example, the authors were once asked to install another manufacturer's IDS on a stockbroker's network. This network was unusual, because broadcasts were the main form of data transfer. Broadcasts were used so that all workstations received updates whenever any workstation requested a real-time quote. The IDS chosen by management was unable to recognize that the high number of broadcasts was not an attack on the system, and therefore, it was never successfully deployed. The CSIDS does not suffer from these shortcomings.

The CSIDS allows the administrator to ignore types of apparent attacks, ignore apparent attacks from individual or groups of hosts, and maintain multiple configurations that allow near-instantaneous changes to those signatures to which the Sensor will react. This flexibility allows the CSIDS to become a viable IDS for most networks.

Interpreting Logs

It is sometimes necessary to look at the actual log file to determine exactly what has occurred. This section explores how to interpret a log file.

The CSIDS stores four levels of logging to a comma-delimited file. The active log is stored in the /usr/nr/var directory with a file name of *YYYYMMDDHHMM*. By default, when the active log has reached 300 KB, or the elapsed time since the log creation has exceeded 240 minutes, the file is archived under the same name in the /usr/nr/nav/new directory.

The log file has a defined format and is easy to read. The following is a sample record from a log:

```
4,1034121,2001/04/08,14:04:01,11008,6,300,IN, OUT, 212,8543,51304,TOP/IP,
172.30.1.8,172.31.2.1,1015,25,0.0.0.0,hack attack,69576 ... AEBA0
```

The fields within the log file are described in Table 6-3.

Table 6-3   *CSIDS Record Format*

Value	Field Name	Description
4	Record Type	The record type can have one of 4 values: 2 is an error, 3 is a command, 4 is either an alarm or an event, 5 is an IP log.
1034121	Record Number	Record numbers start at 1,000,000 and increment by one with each record.
2001/04/08	Date	This is the date in YYYY/MM/DD format.
14:04:01	Time	This is the time in HH:MM:SS format.
11008	Application ID	This is the Application ID of the process that generated the log record.
6	Host ID	This is the Host ID of the Sensor that generated the log record.
300	Organizational ID	This is the Organizational ID of the Sensor that generated the log record.

Table 6-3   *CSIDS Record Format (Continued)*

Value	Field Name	Description
IN	Source	This is the source of the packet that triggered the alarm. The value can be either OUT (signifying that the source is outside of the monitored network) or IN (signifying that the source is within the monitored network).
OUT	Destination	This is the destination of the packet that triggered the alarm. The value can be either OUT (signifying that the destination is outside of the monitored network) or IN (signifying that the destination is within the monitored network).
212	Alarm Level	By default, there are 5 alarm levels. Here, the maximum of 255 levels is specified. This alarm is level 212.
8543	Signature ID	The signature ID is mapped to a signature name in the /usr/nr/etc/signatures files. Valid values range from 1000 through 10,000.
51304	SubSignature ID	The SubSignature ID is usually used on a string match signature, customizable by the administrator. If the value of this field is zero, there is no subsignature. Subsignatures start with the value 51,304. In this example record, this subsignature is associated with the string "hack attack."
TCP/IP	Protocol	This indicates that the packet was in TCP/IP format.
172.30.1.8	Source IP Address	This is the source IP address of the packet.
172.31.2.1	Destination IP Address	This is the destination IP address of the packet.
1015	Source Port	This is the source port of the packet.
25	Destination Port	This is the destination port of the packet.
0.0.0.0	External Data Source	This is the external IP address of the Sensor that detected the event. An IP address of 0.0.0.0 signifies that the Sensor that was specified by the Host and Organizational ID detected the event. A valid IP address is usually associated with a device, such as a router placing a syslog event because of an access list.
Hack attack	Event Detail	This is an optional field. In this example, the string "hack attack" was used to trigger the logging event.
69576 ... AEBA0	Context Data	This is an optional field. When populated, this field contains up to 512 bytes, showing the 256 bytes before and the 256 bytes after the string that triggered the event. This field allows the administrator to see most of the relevant portions of the packet.

Now that you have seen an overview of the major components of CSIDS, the next sections cover the Cisco IOS Firewall IDS and the Cisco PIX Firewall IDS.

Cisco IOS Firewall IDS

Intrusion detection has been available as part of the Cisco IOS Firewall from the 12.05(T) release. The IDS capabilities are only available on the midrange to high-end router platforms. These include the following platforms, with more scheduled for release in the near future:

- Cisco 1700
- Cisco 2600
- Cisco 3600
- Cisco 7100
- Cisco 7200

Once the router has the Cisco IOS Firewall IDS features installed and enabled, the router acts as an IDS sensor. The router passively monitors and analyzes all packet flow through the router and checks this data against the installed and configured IDS signatures. If suspect activity is detected, the router can be configured to

- **Send an alarm to a management platform**—In this instance, either a syslog server or the Cisco Secure IDS Director can be used to receive the alarm.
- **Drop the packet**—The packet is dropped from the router and not forwarded to its destination interface.
- **Reset the TCP connection**—The reset function will send a packet with the RST (Reset) flag set to both the source and destination. This will terminate the current session between the hosts.

The 59 default IDS signatures are available for use with the Cisco IOS Firewall IDS. These can be disabled on a signature-by-signature basis if the requirements do not fit the network design.

The Cisco IOS Firewall IDS features can improve on perimeter security by adding additional perimeter visibility of network intrusion attempts. Network-based IDS systems listen to traffic passing on the network segment, whereas a router will receive and process all inbound and outbound traffic to and from a network.

The Cisco IOS Firewall IDS complements an existing Cisco Secure IDS installation and can act as a perimeter-based sensor, reporting as the IDS Sensor does to the IDS Director.

One drawback of using the Cisco IOS Firewall IDS is that it can reduce the performance of your router due to the heavy workload in running the IDS software.

Cisco Secure PIX Firewall IDS

Intrusion detection on the Cisco Secure PIX Firewall became available with the 5.2(1) release of the PIX operating system. This is available on all current PIX platforms.

The configuration of IDS on the PIX is very limited compared with the configuration available on the Cisco Secure IDS and the Cisco IOS Firewall IDS. The PIX is always used as a network device to separate at least two networks and to provide adaptive security for the networks behind it. The IDS feature on the PIX Firewall enables administrators to enforce perimeter intrusion detection on a device that is already providing security services.

Unlike the Cisco IOS Firewall IDS, the PIX IDS can not send alarms to the Cisco Secure Policy Manager or the IDS Director, only to syslog.

A lot of Internet sites employ PIX Firewalls to protect the hosted network that exists behind the PIX. Including IDS with a PIX Firewall allows security administrators to gather intrusion data and automatically act on any suspected vulnerabilities. Until now, this was only available using a network-based IDS sensor connected to the protected VLANs within the hosted solution.

When suspect activity is identified, the Cisco PIX operates in a manner similar to the Cisco IOS Firewall IDS. It can either send an alarm, drop the connection, or reset the session. These are all explained in the "Cisco IOS Firewall IDS" section earlier in this chapter.

The PIX, like the Cisco IOS Firewall, supports the 59 default IDS signatures. These signatures can be seen in Table 6-4. Included in Table 6-4 is an indication of the type of signature: Info or Attack, Atomic or Compound. Atomic signatures that show as Atomic* are allocated memory for session states by CBAC.

Table 6-4   *The 59 Default IDS Signatures*

ID	Name	Trigger	Type
1000	IP options-Bad Option List	Triggered by receipt of an IP datagram with the list of IP options in the header incomplete or malformed.	Info, Atomic
1001	IP options-Record Packet Route	Triggered by receipt of an IP datagram with the Record Packet Route chosen.	Info, Atomic
1002	IP options-Timestamp	Triggered by receipt of an IP datagram where the Timestamp option is chosen.	Info, Atomic
1003	IP options-Provide s, c, h, tcc	Triggered by receipt of an IP datagram where the option list for the datagram includes option 2 (security options).	Info, Atomic
1004	IP options-Loose Source Route	Triggered by receipt of an IP datagram where the option list for the datagram includes option 3 (loose source route).	Info, Atomic

Table 6-4   *The 59 Default IDS Signatures (Continued)*

ID	Name	Trigger	Type
1005	IP options-SATNET ID	Triggered by receipt of an IP datagram where the option list for the datagram includes option 8 (SATNET stream identifier).	Info, Atomic
1006	IP options-Strict Source Route	Triggered by receipt of an IP datagram in which the IP option list for the datagram includes the strict source routing option.	Info, Atomic
1100	IP Fragment Attack	Triggered when any IP datagram is received with the more fragments flag set to 1 or if there is an offset indicated in the offset field.	Attack, Atomic
1101	Unknown IP Protocol	Triggered when an IP datagram is received with the protocol field set to 101 or greater. These protocol types are undefined or reserved and should not be used.	Attack, Atomic
1102	Impossible IP Packet	Triggered when an IP packet arrives with source equal to destination address. This signature will catch the so-called Land attack.	Attack, Atomic
2000	ICMP Echo Reply	Triggered when a IP datagram is received with the protocol field in the header set to 1 (ICMP) and the type field in the ICMP header set to 0 (Echo Reply).	Info, Atomic
2001	ICMP Host Unreachable	Triggered when an IP datagram is received with the protocol field in the header set to 1 (ICMP) and the type field in the ICMP header set to 3 (Host Unreachable).	Info, Atomic
2002	ICMP Source Quench	Triggered when an IP datagram is received with the protocol field in the header set to 1 (ICMP) and the type field in the ICMP header set to 4 (Source Quench).	Info, Atomic
2003	ICMP Redirect	Triggered when an IP datagram is received with the protocol field in the header set to 1 (ICMP) and the type field in the ICMP header set to 5 (Redirect).	Info, Atomic
2004	ICMP Echo Request	Triggered when an IP datagram is received with the protocol field in the header set to 1 (ICMP) and the type field in the ICMP header set to 8 (Echo Request).	Info, Atomic

Table 6-4   *The 59 Default IDS Signatures (Continued)*

ID	Name	Trigger	Type
2005	ICMP Time Exceeded for a Datagram	Triggered when an IP datagram is received with the protocol field in the header set to 1 (ICMP) and the type field in the ICMP header set to 11 (Time Exceeded for a Datagram).	Info, Atomic
2006	ICMP Parameter Problem on Datagram	Triggered when an IP datagram is received with the protocol field in the header set to 1 (ICMP) and the type field in the ICMP header set to 12 (Parameter Problem on Datagram).	Info, Atomic
2007	ICMP Timestamp Request	Triggered when an IP datagram is received with the protocol field in the header set to 1 (ICMP) and the type field in the ICMP header set to 13 (Timestamp Request).	Info, Atomic
2008	ICMP Timestamp Reply	Triggered when an IP datagram is received with the protocol field in the header set to 1 (ICMP) and the type field in the ICMP header set to 14 (Timestamp Reply).	Info, Atomic
2009	ICMP Information Request	Triggered when an IP datagram is received with the protocol field in the header set to 1 (ICMP) and the type field in the ICMP header set to 15 (Information Request).	Info, Atomic
2010	ICMP Information Reply	Triggered when an IP datagram is received with the protocol field in the header set to 1 (ICMP) and the type field in the ICMP header set to 16 (ICMP Information Reply).	Info, Atomic
2011	ICMP Address Mask Request	Triggered when an IP datagram is received with the protocol field in the header set to 1 (ICMP) and the type field in the ICMP header set to 17 (Address Mask Request).	Info, Atomic
2012	ICMP Address Mask Reply	Triggered when an IP datagram is received with the protocol field in the header set to 1 (ICMP) and the type field in the ICMP header set to 18 (Address Mask Reply).	Info, Atomic
2150	Fragmented ICMP Traffic	Triggered when an IP datagram is received with the protocol field in the header set to 1 (ICMP) and either the more fragments flag is set to 1 (ICMP) or there is an offset indicated in the offset field.	Attack, Atomic
2151	Large ICMP Traffic	Triggered when an IP datagram is received with the protocol field in the header set to 1 (ICMP) and the IP length is greater than 1024.	Attack, Atomic

Table 6-4   *The 59 Default IDS Signatures (Continued)*

ID	Name	Trigger	Type
2154	Ping of Death Attack	Triggered when an IP datagram is received with the protocol field in the header set to 1 (ICMP), the Last Fragment bit is set, and (IP offset x 8) + (IP data length) > 65,535 In other words, the IP offset (which represents the starting position of this fragment in the original packet and is in 8-byte units) plus the rest of the packet is greater than the maximum size for an IP packet.	Attack, Atomic
3040	TCP—no bits set in flags	Triggered when a TCP packet is received with no bits set in the flags field.	Attack, Atomic
3041	TCP—SYN and FIN bits set	Triggered when a TCP packet is received with both the SYN and FIN bits set in the flag field.	Attack, Atomic
3042	TCP—FIN bit with no ACK bit in flags	Triggered when a TCP packet is received with the FIN bit set but with no ACK bit set in the flags field.	Attack, Atomic
3050	Half-open SYN Attack/ SYN Flood	Triggered when multiple TCP sessions have been improperly initiated on any of several well-known service ports. Detection of this signature is currently limited to FTP, Telnet, HTTP, and e-mail servers (TCP ports 21, 23, 80, and 25, respectively).	Attack, Compound
3100	Smail Attack	Triggered by the very common smail attack against SMTP-compliant e-mail servers (frequently Sendmail).	Attack, Compound
3101	Sendmail Invalid Recipient	Triggered by any mail message with a pipe (|) symbol in the recipient field.	Attack, Compound
3102	Sendmail Invalid Sender	Triggered by any mail message with a pipe (|) symbol in the From: field.	Attack, Compound
3103	Sendmail Reconnaissance	Triggered when **expn** or **vrfy** commands are issued to the SMTP port.	Attack, Compound
3104	Archaic Sendmail Attacks	Triggered when **wiz** or **debug** commands are issued to the SMTP port.	Attack, Compound
3105	Sendmail Decode Alias	Triggered by any mail message with ": decode@" in the header.	Attack, Compound
3106	Mail Spam	Counts number of Rcpt to: lines in a single mail message and alarms after a user-definable maximum has been exceeded (default is 250).	Attack, Compound

Table 6-4 *The 59 Default IDS Signatures (Continued)*

ID	Name	Trigger	Type
3107	Majordomo Execute Attack	A bug in the Majordomo e-mail list program will allow remote users to execute arbitrary commands at the privilege level of the server. This triggers when a remote user issues a privileged level command.	Attack, Compound
3150	FTP Remote Command Execution	Triggered when someone tries to execute the **FTP SITE** command.	Attack, Compound
3151	FTP SYST Command Attempt	Triggered when someone tries to execute the **FTP SYST** command.	Info, Compound
3152	FTP CWD ~root	Triggered when someone tries to execute the **CWD ~root** command.	Attack, Compound
3153	FTP Improper Address Specified	Triggered if a port command is issued with an address that is not the same as the requesting host.	Attack, Atomic*
3154	FTP Improper Port Specified	Triggered if a port command is issued with a data port specified that is less than 1024 or greater than 65,535.	Attack, Atomic*
4050	UDP Bomb	Triggered when the UDP length specified is less than the IP length specified.	Attack, Atomic
4100	TFTP Passwd File	Triggered by an attempt to access the passwd file (typically /etc/passwd) via TFTP.	Attack, Compound
6100	RPC Port Registration	Triggered when attempts are made to register new RPC services on a target host.	Info, Atomic*
6101	RPC Port Unregistration	Triggered when attempts are made to unregister existing RPC services on a target host.	Info, Atomic*
6102	RPC Dump	Triggered when an RPC dump request is issued to a target host.	Info, Atomic*
6103	Proxied RPC Request	Triggered when a proxied RPC request is sent to the portmapper of a target host.	Attack, Atomic*
6150	ypserv Portmap Request	Triggered when a request is made to the portmapper for the YP server daemon (ypserv) port.	Info, Atomic*
6151	ypbind Portmap Request	Triggered when a request is made to the portmapper for the YP bind daemon (ypbind) port.	Info, Atomic*
6152	yppasswdd Portmap Request	Triggered when a request is made to the portmapper for the YP password daemon (yppasswdd) port.	Info, Atomic*

Table 6-4 *The 59 Default IDS Signatures (Continued)*

ID	Name	Trigger	Type
6153	ypupdated Portmap Request	Triggered when a request is made to the portmapper for the YP update daemon (ypupdated) port.	Info, Atomic*
6154	ypxfrd Portmap Request	Triggered when a request is made to the portmapper for the YP transfer daemon (ypxfrd) port.	Info, Atomic*
6155	mountd Portmap Request	Triggered when a request is made to the portmapper for the mount daemon (mountd) port.	Info, Atomic*
6175	rexd Portmap Request	Triggered when a request is made to the portmapper for the remote execution daemon (rexd) port.	Info, Atomic*
6180	rexd Attempt	Triggered when a call to the rexd program is made. The remote execution daemon is the server responsible for remote program execution. This may be indicative of an attempt to gain unauthorized access to system resources.	Info, Atomic*
6190	statd Buffer Overflow	Triggered when a large statd request is sent. This could be an attempt to overflow a buffer and gain access to system resources.	Attack, Atomic*
8000	FTP Retrieve Password File	SubSig ID: 2101 Triggered by string passwd issued during an FTP session. May indicate someone attempting to retrieve the password file from a machine in order to crack it and gain unauthorized access to system resources.	Attack, Atomic*

Cisco IDS Configuration

This section looks at the configuration tasks required to configure Cisco intrusion detection on the Cisco router and Cisco PIX Firewall. It does not cover the configuration of the Cisco Secure IDS (NetRanger) Sensor or Director, as these are beyond the scope of this book.

This section concentrates on intrusion detection from an Internet—and specifically, a hosted-solution—point of view. It starts by looking at the Cisco IOS Firewall IDS configuration that is located on a corporate router that provides Internet access to the organization. It then covers the Cisco Secure PIX Firewall IDS that is deployed to protect a corporate web site hosted at an ISP.

Cisco IOS Firewall IDS Configuration

Routers connect networks. The Internet connection point of nearly all companies is through some routing device. In this section, you will look at the configuration of the Cisco IOS Firewall IDS for a router that is acting as the Internet connection point for a large company. This company has other WAN links to other sites. All Internet-bound traffic is routed through the central site. The Internet connection is provided for Internet browsing and e-mail only. There are no Internet servers located at any corporate site. The router has been configured with Context-based Access Control (CBAC) to allow back through the firewall only what was originated from inside on the corporate network. Network Address Translation (NAT) has been used in an overload fashion. This is also known as Port Address Translation (PAT). Theoretically, from the outside, nothing on the inside should be visible.

Because all Internet traffic comes through this connection onto the corporate network, the company has decided to configure intrusion detection on this router to provide a further layer of security against any external threats that exist. Figure 6-10 shows this simple network.

Figure 6-10 *Corporate Internet Connection*

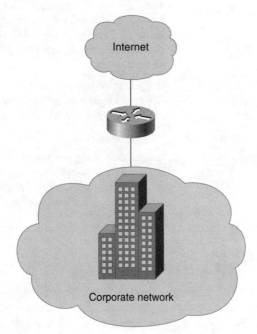

To configure intrusion detection on the Cisco IOS Firewall, you have to ensure that you are using the correct IOS level. You must be using IOS 12.0(5)T or later with the Cisco IOS Firewall included.

You are going to configure intrusion detection to use syslog logging and to protect the outside interface of the router.

The following configuration lines are all entered in global configuration mode:

```
ip audit notify log
ip audit name ids info action alarm
ip audit name ids attack action alarm drop reset
```

The first line configures the IDS to use syslog logging. With the Cisco IOS Firewall IDS, you have the option of using syslog or the Cisco Secure Intrusion Detection Director. The second and third lines specify the IDS profile called ids. This profile is set to alarm for informational messages and alarm, drop, and reset sessions for attack messages.

Once this IDS profile has been created, you have to apply it to an interface. Enter the following configuration line from the interface configuration mode for the interface to which you wish to apply the policy:

```
ip audit ids in
```

This command applies the IDS policy ids to the interface for inbound traffic. This is similar to the **ip access-group** command that applies access lists, either inbound or outbound, to interfaces.

A few **show** commands can be used on the router to look at the configuration of IDS.

The **show ip audit configuration** Command

The **show ip audit configuration** command displays the global configuration settings for IDS on the router:

```
Router#show ip audit configuration
Event notification through syslog is enabled
Event notification through Net Director is disabled
Default action(s) for info signatures is alarm
Default action(s) for attack signatures is alarm
Default threshold of recipients for spam signature is 250
PostOffice:HostID:0 OrgID:0 Msg dropped:0
          :Curr Event Buf Size:0  Configured:100
Post Office is not enabled - No connections are active
Audit Rule Configuration
 Audit name ids
    info actions alarm
    attack actions alarm drop reset
```

You can see from the command output that this router is using syslog logging and not the NetRanger (Cisco Secure) Director.

The **show ip audit interfaces** Command

The **show ip audit interfaces** command displays interface specific information about IDS for every interface that IDS is configured on:

```
Router#show ip audit interfaces
```

```
Interface Configuration
 Interface FastEthernet0/0
  Inbound IDS audit rule is ids
    info actions alarm
    attack actions alarm drop reset
  Outgoing IDS audit rule is not set
```

The output shows that the IDS profile ids is configured inbound on the Fast Ethernet 0/0 interface on the router.

The **show ip audit name** Command

This command displays the IDS information for the specific IDS profile:

```
Router#show ip audit name ids
Audit name ids
    info actions alarm
    attack actions alarm drop reset
```

The output shows the configuration of the IDS profile called ids that was previously configured for this example.

This concludes the simple configuration of the Cisco IOS Firewall IDS. As you can see, the configuration of IDS on the Cisco IOS Firewall is fairly straightforward. You have to ensure that the router is successfully logging to a syslog server. There are numerous syslog servers available for UNIX. For Windows platforms, there is an excellent syslog server available from www.ccstudy.com.

Cisco Secure PIX Firewall IDS Configuration

It is very common for hosted solutions that are located within an ISP to be behind a firewall. The firewall separates the hosted solution from the main ISP public network and provides NAT and stateful inspection of packets to protect the hosted network from various external attacks. This makes the firewall an ideal place to implement IDS.

IDS technologies operate by passively listening to traffic to ascertain whether the traffic is genuine or matches a known attack signature. This can be a problem in a shared network environment, because you do not want your IDS system to alert all of the time because of traffic destined for other networks. This can be true of a hosted solution from an ISP, because the public Ethernet connection that forms the outside interface of the PIX Firewall can be in the same broadcast domain as numerous other hosted networks. However, all ISPs should use switches to provide Ethernet connectivity. The switch ensures that only the required unicast traffic is delivered to each hosted network. The nature of the static NAT translations causes the outside switches to send unicast traffic for every host behind the firewall to the port where the outside interface of the firewall is physically connected. This removes potential false positives on the IDS from traffic that is directed toward other hosted networks. However, because the switch implements a single broadcast domain throughout the Layer 3 domain, you might still get false positives for broadcast-based attacks.

This section looks at a very simple hosted Internet solution and the commands that are required to install IDS on the firewall. Figure 6-11 displays this simple network.

Figure 6-11 *Simple Hosted Network*

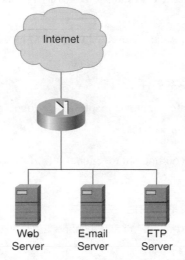

The configuration lines in this section configure IDS on the outside interface of the router. Remember that the outside interface is the Internet-facing interface. There is little use in this scenario to enable IDS on both the inside and outside interfaces.

You can see from the network diagram in Figure 6-11 that this is a simple model, where the hosted firewall's outside interface is connected to the Internet, and the inside interface provides access to the protected network. In this simple network, there is a Web server, an e-mail server, and an FTP server.

To enable IDS on the PIX Firewall, the software on the PIX must be release 5.2 or later.

IDS configuration on the PIX is carried out with one command that has numerous variables associated with it. This command is **ip audit**. The important point to remember is that the alarm action with both the info and attack signatures uses the currently configured syslog server. This means that syslog has to be configured and working on an inside interface. Syslog is enabled with the **logging** commands.

These commands are all entered in global configuration mode:

```
ip audit info action alarm
ip audit attack action alarm
ip audit name idsattack attack action alarm drop reset
ip audit name idsinfo info action alarm
ip audit interface outside idsinfo
ip audit interface outside idsattack
```

The first two lines are configured by default and apply to all interfaces. These alarm on info or attack signatures.

The third and fourth lines of the configuration specify an IDS policy with the name of idsattack and idsinfo. The fifth and sixth lines apply these named IDS policies to the outside interface.

A few **show** commands can be used on the PIX to look at the configuration of IDS.

The **show ip audit info** Command

The **show ip audit info** command displays the global info IDS policy on the firewall:

```
pixfirewall# show ip audit info
ip audit info action alarm
```

You can see from the output that the global info IDS policy is to alarm.

The **show ip audit attack** Command

The **show ip audit attack** command displays the global attack IDS policy on the firewall:

```
pixfirewall# show ip audit attack
ip audit attack action alarm
```

You can see from the output that the global attack IDS policy is to alarm.

The **show ip audit interface** Command

The **show ip audit interface** command displays the specific IDS policy that has been applied to an interface. From this example, the following is observed:

```
pixfirewall# show ip audit interface outside
ip audit interface outside idsinfo
ip audit interface outside idsattack
```

This shows that the named IDS policies idsinfo and idsattack have been applied to the outside interface of the PIX.

The **show ip audit name** Command

The **show ip audit name** command displays the IDS policy that has been specified in a named policy. From this example, you can observe that the IDS policy idsinfo is set just to alarm:

```
pixfirewall# show ip audit name idsinfo
ip audit name idsinfo info action alarm
```

The following shows that attack signatures are alarmed, dropped, and reset:

```
pixfirewall# show ip audit name idsattack
ip audit name idsattack attack action alarm drop reset
```

IDS Monitoring

Once intrusion detection has been configured, you can monitor the syslog information to identify any attempted security issues. The following log data are extracts from an actual Internet-facing PIX Firewall. You can see that the IDS on the PIX has intercepted quite a few items of suspicious activity:

```
%PIX-4-400027: IDS:3041 TCP SYN+FIN flags from 24.15.59.98 to 194.73.134.2
        on interface outside
%PIX-4-400027: IDS:3041 TCP SYN+FIN flags from 24.15.59.98 to 194.73.134.6
        on interface outside
%PIX-4-400027: IDS:3041 TCP SYN+FIN flags from 24.15.59.98 to 194.73.134.7
        on interface outside
%PIX-4-400027: IDS:3041 TCP SYN+FIN flags from 24.15.59.98 to 194.73.134.20
        on interface outside
%PIX-4-400027: IDS:3041 TCP SYN+FIN flags from 24.15.59.98 to 194.73.134.21
        on interface outside
%PIX-4-400027: IDS:3041 TCP SYN+FIN flags from 24.15.59.98 to 194.73.134.22
        on interface outside
%PIX-4-400027: IDS:3041 TCP SYN+FIN flags from 24.15.59.98 to 194.73.134.23
        on interface outside
%PIX-4-400027: IDS:3041 TCP SYN+FIN flags from 24.15.59.98 to 194.73.134.24
        on interface outside
%PIX-4-400027: IDS:3041 TCP SYN+FIN flags from 24.15.59.98 to 194.73.134.26
        on interface outside
%PIX-4-400027: IDS:3041 TCP SYN+FIN flags from 24.15.59.98 to 194.73.134.25
        on interface outside
%PIX-4-400027: IDS:3041 TCP SYN+FIN flags from 24.15.59.98 to 194.73.134.27
        on interface outside
%PIX-4-400027: IDS:3041 TCP SYN+FIN flags from 24.15.59.98 to 194.73.134.28
        on interface outside
%PIX-4-400027: IDS:3041 TCP SYN+FIN flags from 24.15.59.98 to 194.73.134.30
        on interface outside
%PIX-4-400027: IDS:3041 TCP SYN+FIN flags from 24.15.59.98 to 194.73.134.29
        on interface outside
%PIX-4-400027: IDS:3041 TCP SYN+FIN flags from 24.15.59.98 to 194.73.134.100
        on interface outside
```

The preceding messages indicate that the IP address 24.15.59.98 is attempting a reconnaissance sweep against the IP addresses on the 194.73.134.0 network. This is classified as an attack, and because of the policy that is in place, these sessions would be logged, dropped, and reset.

The following message could indicate that the IP address 137.39.5.35 is trying to overcome the packet-filtering security policy. This could indicate an attack:

```
%PIX-4-400011: IDS:2001 ICMP unreachable from 137.39.5.35 to 194.73.134.7
        on interface outside
```

The following message indicates that a successful ICMP echo reply (ping) was sent from the IP address 64.225.249.26. This is an informational message:

```
%PIX-4-400010: IDS:2000 ICMP echo reply from 64.225.249.26 to 194.73.134.2
        on interface outside
```

This concludes the simple configuration of the Cisco PIX IDS. As you can see, the configuration of IDS on the PIX is fairly straightforward. You have to ensure that the PIX is successfully logging to a syslog server. There are numerous syslog servers available for

UNIX. For Windows platforms, there is an excellent syslog server available from www.ccstudy.com.

Summary

This chapter provided an overview of intrusion detection. It started by providing an explanation of intrusion detection, its role in the total security solution, and the different forms that intrusion detection can assume within the network. The chapter then looked at the intrusion detection offerings available from Cisco Systems and provided a brief explanation of each of these and their associated features. It concluded by looking at some configuration examples for both the Cisco IOS Firewall IDS and the Cisco Secure PIX Firewall IDS.

Frequently Asked Questions

Question: What is intrusion detection?

Answer: Intrusion detection is the passive monitoring of the traffic flow on a network segment to detect any suspicious activity on the network. Once a problem is identified, an intrusion detection system can take action against the session to ensure that it is not maintained.

Question: I already have a firewall; why do I need intrusion detection as well?

Answer: A firewall is a device that can protect internal networks from external threats by providing address translation and stateful inspection of traffic flow. The firewall does not have the intelligence by default to know whether the packet flow through the firewall represents genuine traffic or an attempted attack that is hiding as a genuine service request. The inclusion of intrusion detection adds another layer of security and intelligence to ensure that the firewall only allows traffic through to the internal networks after screening.

Glossary

IDS (intrusion detection system)—Scans the network in real time to intercept attempted breaches of security.

ISP (Internet service provider)—A service provider that provides a connection to the public Internet.

NAT (Network Address Translation)—NAT is the translation of an IP address used within one network to a different IP address known within another network.

PIX (Private Internet Exchange)—The Cisco range of leading hardware-based firewalls.

This chapter contains the following sections:

- Cisco Secure Scanner Features
- Cisco Secure Scanner Installation
- Cisco Secure Scanner Configuration
- Summary
- Frequently Asked Questions
- Glossary
- URLs

CHAPTER 7

Cisco Secure Scanner

Chapter 3, "Overview of the Cisco Security Solution and the Cisco Secure Product Family," covered the Security Solution that has been devised by Cisco in order to provide total network security. This solution consists of five key elements:

- Identity
- Perimeter security
- Data privacy
- Security monitoring
- Policy management

This chapter delves deeper into the fourth key element of the Cisco Security Solution: security monitoring.

Security management, like network management, is a dynamic, ever-changing process. Once you have designed and implemented a security solution, it has to be measured. One way of measuring the integrity of your solution is with a network scanner, which will scan every live IP address on your network and check the results against well-known vulnerabilities. A full report is then created, and actions can be taken to remedy any shortcomings in the design or implementation. It's important to make the changes and then scan the network again to ensure that the changes have been effective and their implementation hasn't caused any further security vulnerabilities. The security vulnerability database for all leading network scanners is upgraded on a periodic basis, ensuring that every new vulnerability that is discovered is added to the database. When you run a network scan, you can be sure that you are scanning for the latest vulnerabilities.

Cisco Secure Scanner is a full, network-scanning utility that can be used for regular security-monitoring purposes.

This chapter takes a look at the Cisco Secure Scanner. The chapter starts by providing an explanation of the processes and theory behind network scanning, and it moves on to look at the Cisco Secure Scanner product and how it is used to carry out network scanning.

Cisco Secure Scanner Features

The Cisco Secure Scanner (formerly Cisco NetSonar) is a software application that offers a complete suite of network scanning tools designed to run on either Windows NT or Solaris.

Network scanning is the process in which a specific host is configured as a scanner and scans all or just configurable parts (depending on the scanner) of the network for known security threats. The design and operation of the scanner makes it a valuable asset to have in your quest for Internet security.

Cisco Secure Scanner follows a six-step process to identify any possible network vulnerabilities:

Step 1   Network mapping

Step 2   Data collection

Step 3   Data analysis

Step 4   Vulnerability confirmation

Step 5   Data presentation and navigation

Step 6   Reporting

Step 1: Network Mapping

Network mapping is the process that the Cisco Scanner uses to identify hosts. At this point, you have to provide a range of IP addresses that make up the network that you wish to scan. These addresses do not have to be your local network. They can be any remote IP address, as long as you have network layer access, that is, as long as you can run a successful network layer connectivity test such as ping.

Cisco Secure Scanner allows you to enter either single IP addresses or a complete range of IP addresses. You also have the option to exclude IP addresses or ranges to further simplify your scan.

Figure 7-1 shows you the network mapping configuration screen from the Cisco Secure Scanner.

You can see in Figure 7-1 that a session has been created for the IP address range 194.73.134.1 to 194.73.134.255. This is covered in the first configuration line. Note that the second and third configuration lines both have the **Excluded Address** checkbox selected. This means that the addresses specified thereafter are excluded from the address range. The second configuration line just excludes one address because **IP Address Begin** and **IP Address End** are the same. The third configuration line excludes the range of IP addresses 194.73.134.211 to 194.73.134.214. The addresses that will be included in the scan are shown in Table 7-1.

Figure 7-1   *Network Mapping Screen*

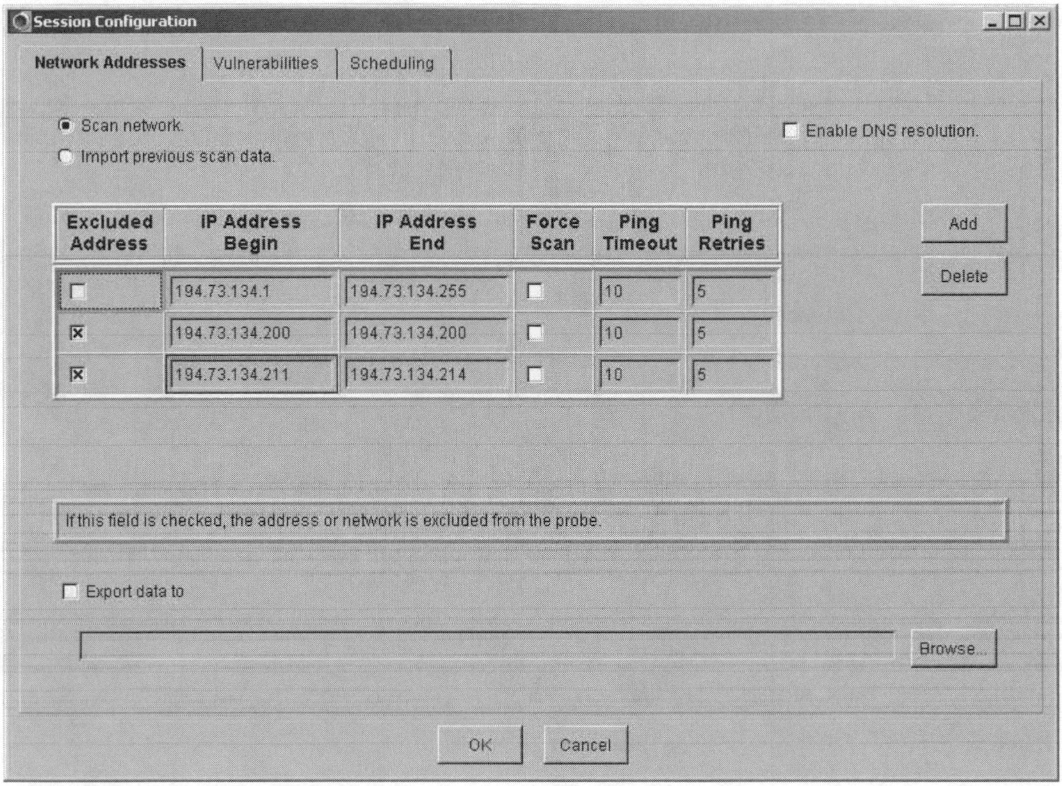

Table 7-1   *IP Addresses Included in the Scan*

IP Address Begin	IP Address End
194.73.134.1	194.73.134.199
194.73.134.201	194.73.134.210
194.73.134.215	194.73.134.255

Now there is a range of IP addresses that are going to make up the scan.

There are two ways of selecting how the network map is devised. The first and standard method is to use the network tool ping. The second and optional method is to force the scan.

You have created your range of IP addresses for the scan, but are you really sure that all of those IP addresses are valid hosts? The default resolution to this is for the scanner to test every IP address for basic network connectivity. The simplest way to do this, and the one the scanner employs, is simply to send an Internet Control Message Protocol (ICMP) Echo Request to the configured IP addresses. This is commonly known as a *ping*. If the scanner receives an ICMP Echo Reply, it assumes that the IP address is a valid host and adds it to the network map.

This process seems like a simple and constructive test for the scanner, preventing the waste of time and resources in scanning against a range of addresses that either do not exist or do not have powered-up network hosts configured to them.

However, this is not always the case. Many firewalls, especially those used to protect Internet services, are configured to deny all ICMP traffic to protected interfaces, those where security policies are defined to protect resources that are resident on those interfaces from external networks.

The simple Internet service displayed in Figure 7-2 shows this scenario.

Figure 7-2  *Simple Web Service*

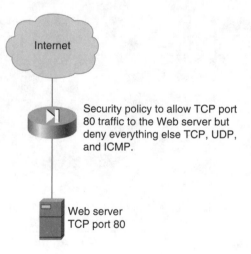

You can see in Figure 7-2 that the Internet firewall blocks all TCP, UDP, and ICMP traffic destined for the internal network. Only HTTP port 80 traffic is allowed through the firewall. In this instance, a standard scan against 194.73.134.100 would fail, because the scanner software would send an ICMP Echo Request packet to the IP address 194.73.134.100 and no ICMP Echo Reply would be received. The scanner software would presume that there is no host associated with the IP address 194.73.134.100 and simply move on to the next IP address.

Figure 7-3 slightly complicates Figure 7-2 by adding another interface to the firewall, the DMZ, and also an Internet mail server on the DMZ firewall interface.

Figure 7-3   *Expanded Simple Web Service*

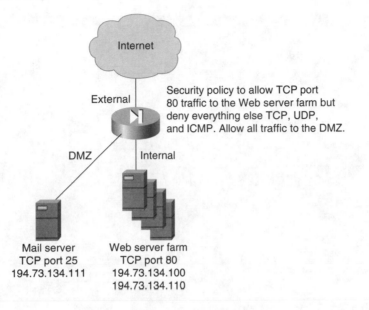

There are now two basic firewall rules in the security policy: to restrict all traffic except TCP port 80 to the internal interface, and to allow all traffic to the DMZ interface. These two distinct rules will alter the way the network map is created.

Cisco Secure Scanner has a feature where you can force a scan against an address. This is exactly the feature you need in this case because it circumvents the problem. When you force a scan, the IP address is probed without sending an ICMP echo.

Figure 7-4 shows the correct session configuration to scan the networks shown in Figure 7-3.

You can see that two ranges have been defined. The first range is for the Web server farm, 194.73.134.100 to 194.73.134.110. Note that the **Force Scan** checkbox is selected. This means that all of these hosts will be probed, regardless of whether they are active. The second range identifies the Internet mail server on 194.73.134.111. An ICMP Echo Request will be sent to this machine to ascertain whether or not the machine is running.

Cisco Secure Scanner is licensed based on the number of hosts available to any one network. The version used here is the 2500 host license that allows you to scan up to 2500 hosts in one session.

Figure 7-4 *Session Configuration*

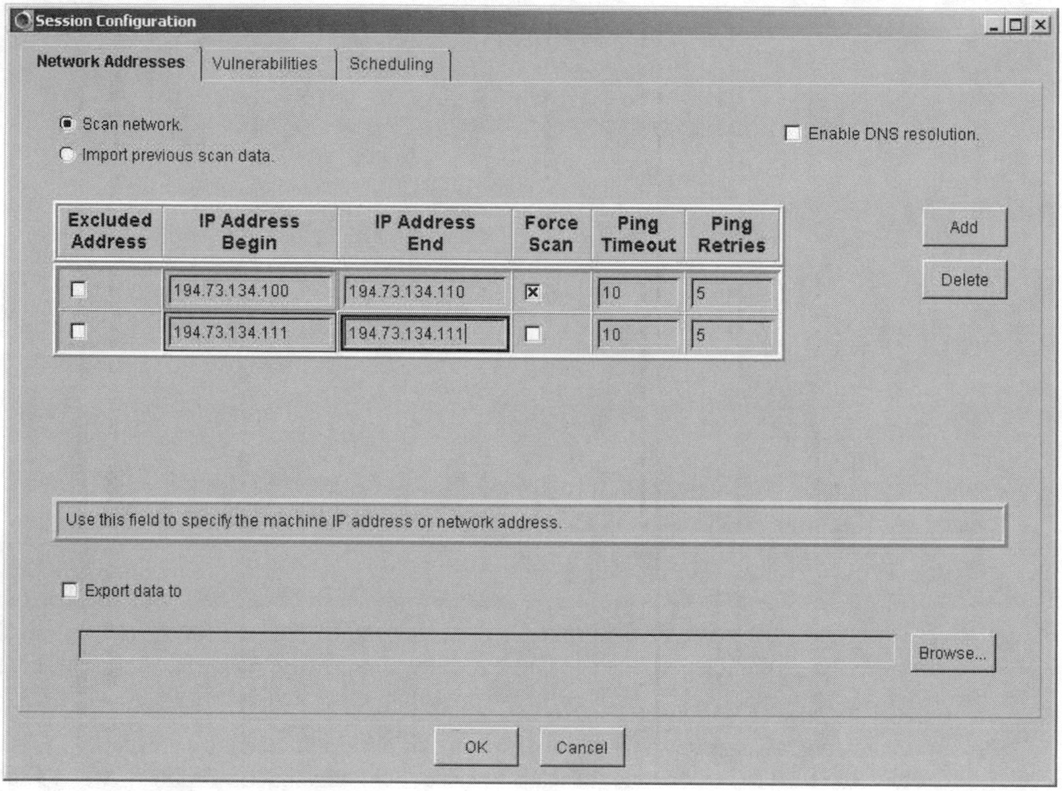

Step 2: Data Collection

Once the network mapping stage is completed, and the scanner has a valid range of IP addresses that have either been verified with a successful ICMP echo or set to be forced at the network mapping stage, the scanning software gathers data from these hosts.

Running a series of port scans against the valid hosts collects the data.

NOTE   A *port scan* can be defined as a way of identifying which services are running on a remote machine by testing connections to each port on the remote machine. Most network services have a well-known port, either TCP, UDP, or both, associated to them. These ports and associated services can be found in the Services text file located in the /etc directory on a UNIX box or in the C:\winnt\system32\drivers\etc folder on a Windows NT system.

The port scan will identify which services are running on the remote hosts. This information is added to the scanner's database for analysis.

Cisco Secure Scanner provides a configurable set of options for data collection. Figure 7-5 shows the data capture configuration screen.

Figure 7-5 *Data Capture Configuration*

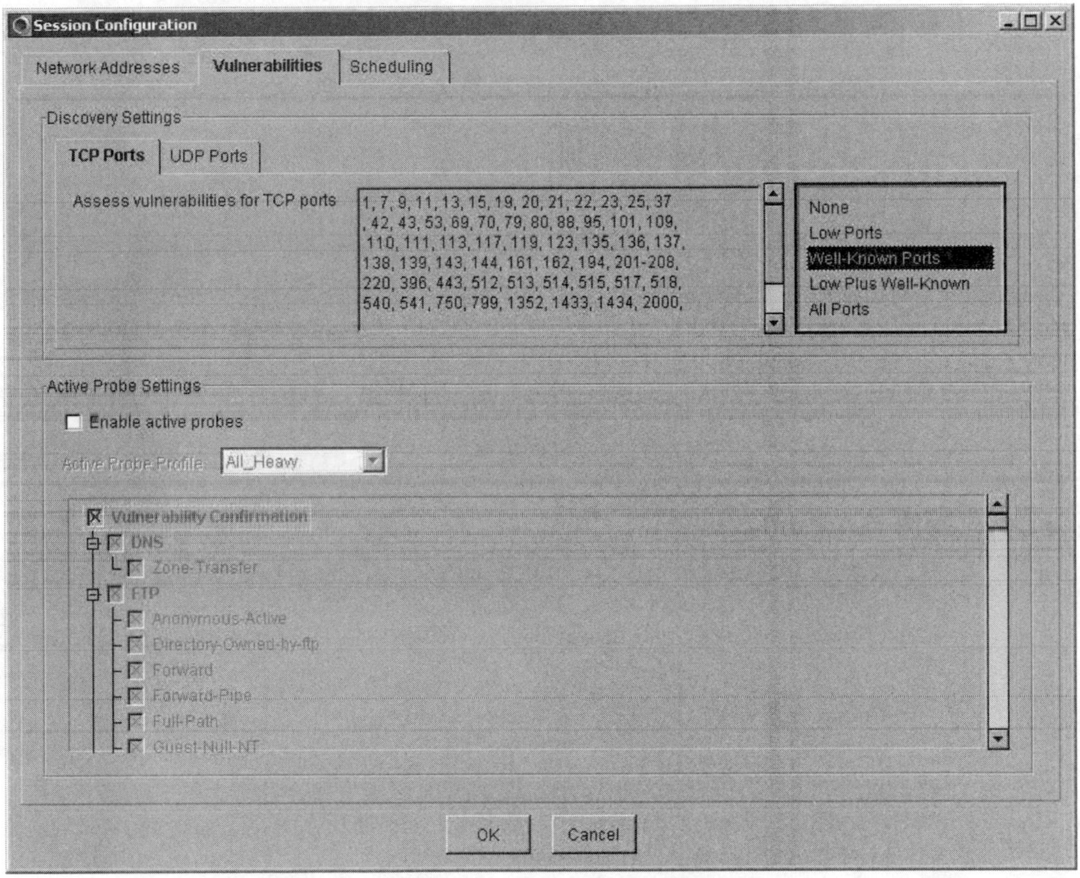

You can see in Figure 7-5 that there are five possible choices for the TCP data collection phase or port scan:

- **None**—This setting does not run a port scan for data collection, therefore, no data is recorded. The hosts are only checked against the scanner probes looking for well-known vulnerabilities.

- **Low Ports**—The ports 1 to 1024 are considered low ports, and most default network services operate here. For example, HTTP is TCP port 80, SMTP is TCP port 25, and Telnet is TCP port 23.

- **Well-Known Ports**—This setting selects ports that have well-known services associated to them. This includes all ports that can be found in the Services file.

- **Low Plus Well-Known Ports**—With this setting, all ports from 1 to 1024 are scanned, as well as well-known ports above 1024.

- **All Ports**—This scans all available ports from 1 to 65,535. This is a very time-consuming port scan, but it will guarantee that you scan the port you are looking for.

UDP is slightly more restrictive in what you can scan for, because UDP is classed as a connectionless service and therefore not as reliable as TCP. Even though UDP does have advantages over TCP, most network applications rely on the more robust TCP as their transport protocol.

The UDP options are:

- **None**—This setting does not run a port scan for data collection, therefore no data is recorded. The hosts are only checked against the scanner probes looking for well-known vulnerabilities.

- **Well-Known Ports**—This setting selects ports that have well-known services associated with them. This includes all ports that can be found in the Services file.

Once you have selected the required ports for both TCP and UDP, the port scan is ready to commence.

Step 3: Data Analysis

At this stage, the network map is complete and the valid hosts have been scanned for the network services running on them. This data has been collected and is stored in the internal scanner database. The Cisco Secure Scanner now analyzes this stored information for the following:

- **Network devices**—All network devices within the network map are identified. The software can identify routers, switches, firewalls, network servers, printers, desktops, and workstations.

- **Operating systems**—The scanner uses proven methods to identify the operating system that is running on the host.

- **Network services**—All network services running on the specific hosts are analyzed. All hosts, unless protected by a firewall, have network services running, as these services provide access to the host from the required clients.

- **Potential vulnerabilities**—Through passive analysis, Cisco Secure Scanner identifies potential vulnerabilities based on the data that has already been collected at the data collection stage. These passive vulnerabilities include:

  — Known security vulnerabilities in operating systems such as Windows NT and Linux

— Misconfigured network devices such as firewalls and routers

— Service-based vulnerabilities for public services such as File Transfer Protocol (FTP) and Remote Shell (RSH)

— Problems with the Sendmail UNIX application

— System misconfiguration

— Reconnaissance services, such as finger, that might be used by hackers

The analysis is carried out by comparing the data with the built-in rules base. This operates in a method similar to that of a virus detection application. The data is checked against the rules base, and any matches indicate a potential vulnerability. Once the vulnerabilities have been identified, the next step actively checks the hosts and confirms these vulnerabilities.

Step 4: Vulnerability Confirmation

Cisco Secure Scanner contains a very advanced vulnerability exploit engine that can be used to actively probe the network to confirm the presence of known vulnerabilities. These probes run against all hosts identified at the network mapping stage, as well as any other host where the decision has been made to carry out a forced scan.

Cisco Secure Scanner has nine built-in active probe profiles:

- **All Heavy**—The All Heavy profile selects all of the active probes for both UNIX and Windows machines.

- **All Light**—The All Light profile selects the active probes that are considered to be common known problems for both UNIX and Windows machines. This probe profile is a lot less resource- and time-intensive than the All Heavy profile.

- **All Severe**—The All Severe profile selects the active probes that are considered to be severe known problems for both UNIX and Windows machines. This probe profile is a lot less resource- and time-intensive than the All Heavy profile.

- **UNIX Heavy**—The UNIX Heavy profile selects all of the active probes for UNIX machines.

- **UNIX Light**—The UNIX Light profile selects the active probes that are considered to be common known problems for UNIX machines. This probe profile is a lot less resource- and time-intensive than the All Heavy profile.

- **UNIX Severe**—The UNIX Severe profile selects the active probes that are considered to be severe known problems for UNIX machines. This probe profile is a lot less resource- and time-intensive than the All Heavy profile.

- **Windows Heavy**—The Windows Heavy profile selects all of the active probes for Windows machines.

- **Windows Light**—The Windows Light profile selects the active probes that are considered to be common known problems for Windows machines. This probe profile is a lot less resource- and time-intensive than the All Heavy profile.

- **Windows Severe**—The Windows Severe profile selects the active probes that are considered to be severe known problems for Windows machines. This probe profile is a lot less resource- and time-intensive than the All Heavy profile.

Each of these profiles contains a preconfigured selection of the active probes.

In addition to the built-in probes, you can also create a customized probe by selecting an existing profile and then adding or removing individual probes.

NOTE   By default, the active probes are disabled. You have to enable the active probes and then choose your profile. The All Heavy profile is the default active probe profile.

Figure 7-6 shows the active probe configuration screen.

In Figure 7-6, you can see that active probes are enabled. This is indicated by the selection of the **Enable active probes** checkbox. Beneath this checkbox is the **Active Probe Profile** drop-down list. The figure provided is using the All Heavy profile.

NOTE   The nature of the active probes at the vulnerability confirmation stage makes them intrusive to the network on which the scan is run. This is important to understand, because active probes could raise alarms with any intrusion detection software that is configured on the network. Even though the probe is intrusive, no denial of service (DoS) type of probe that has destructive implications will be carried out.

After configuring the active probe profile, the scan is fully configured. Clicking the **OK** button as shown in Figure 7-6 will start the scan.

The scan will start by mapping the network, then it will collect and analyze the data. At this point, the data is ready for presentation and reporting.

Figure 7-6   *Active Probe Configuration*

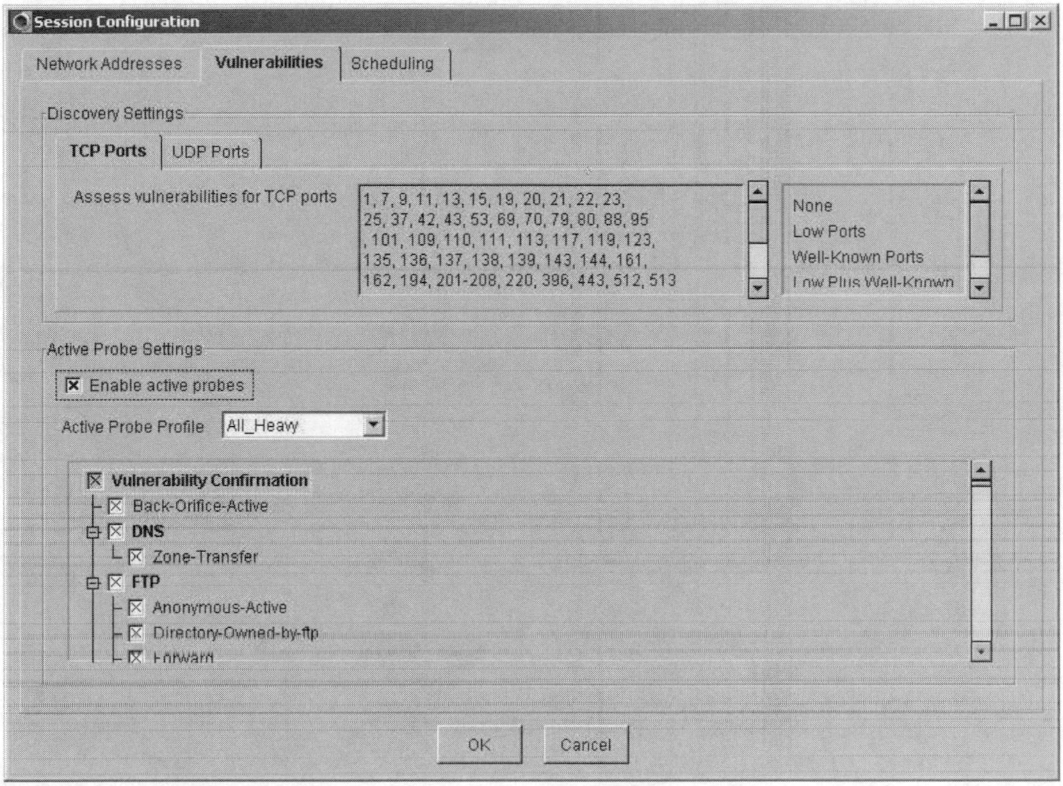

Step 5: Data Presentation and Navigation

By now, the data has been collected and analyzed. To make the scan worthwhile, you can view the results of the network scan.

Cisco Secure Scanner provides the most sophisticated reporting tools of any network scanner on the market. There are three presentation tools:

- Grid browser
- Charts
- Network Security Database (NSDB)

The following three sections look at each of these tools and provide samples of each.

Grid Browser

The grid browser is a spreadsheet that contains all of the data that has been collected and analyzed from the preceding four stages.

Figure 7-7 shows the grid browser.

Figure 7-7 *Grid Browser*

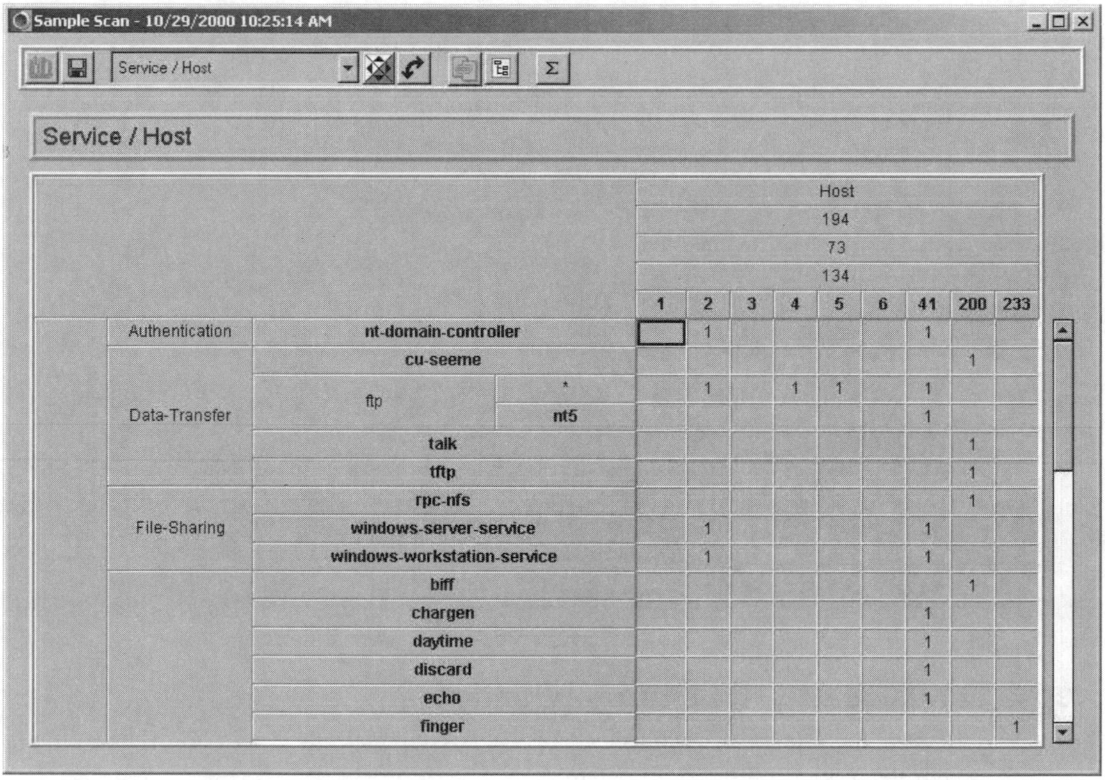

The grid browser in Figure 7-7 has been configured to display the Service/Host relationship. The identified services are shown down the left side (y-axis), and the identified hosts that make up the network map are on the top (x-axis). The presence of a **1** in the grid indicates that the specified service was found on the specified host.

From this example, you can see that the host 194.73.134.2 had the following services running:

- NT domain controller
- FTP
- Windows server service
- Windows workstation service

It is pretty easy to see that this machine is a Windows NT server running as a domain controller within a Windows NT domain.

Overall, there are 42 prebuilt grid configurations that you can select to view your data. There are numerous controls that can change the way the data is viewed within each grid configuration. Figure 7-8 shows a different grid configuration.

Figure 7-8   *An Alternate Grid Browser Configuration*

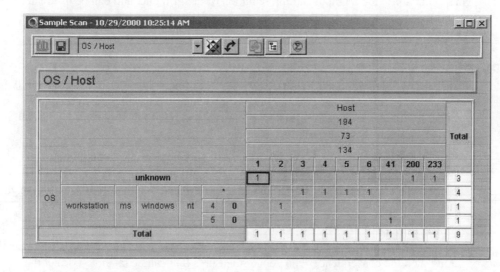

The example in Figure 7-8 shows the OS/Host relationship with the totals turned on. You can quickly see that there were three unknown operating systems, four Windows operating systems, one Windows NT 4.0 operating system, and one Windows NT 5 (Windows 2000) operating system, giving a total of nine hosts in the scan.

The grid data can be saved, creating an HTML report that is an exact replica of the grid that was viewed.

Charts

Besides viewing the data in the grid, you can also create charts from it. To do this, you first have to define the grid browser to display the data you want to chart. The Chart button on the toolbar becomes active when you select the data required for the chart from the grid browser. The following types of charts can be created:

- Area
- Line
- 3-D bar graph
- Pie chart

- 2.5-D column
- 3-D column
- 3-D horizontal row
- Stacked bar
- Stacked area

The charts provide a graphical representation of the grid data and can be used later at the reporting stage to add more clarity to printed and electronic reports.

Network Security Database (NSDB)

The NSDB is provided as a HTML-based resource that is installed when you install the Cisco Secure Scanner. The NSDB contains information regarding the known vulnerabilities, as well as other links to security resources on the Internet. Figure 7-9 shows the main screen of the NSDB.

Figure 7-9 shows the main NSDB index page. You can see that this main index page displays the vulnerability index. The Warning icon is the severity level, and the title is the name of the actual vulnerability. Clicking any of the listed vulnerabilities will give you further information on that vulnerability. Figure 7-10 shows the information received after clicking the Default Dangerous Accounts vulnerability.

You can see in this example that the NSDB provides you with a description of the exploit along with the consequences and countermeasures that can be taken to correct the vulnerability. The NSDB is an excellent resource and can be used to gain a good overview of the current vulnerabilities. It can also be used as a source of information, providing many links to security resources available on the Internet.

Step 6: Reporting

Cisco Secure Scanner has a built-in reporting wizard that can be used to create various reports based on the collected and analyzed data. These reports add real value to the collected data and provide you with a professional-looking report that can be used to explain the findings of the scan both technically and nontechnically.

Three main report types can be created:

- **Executive Summary**—The Executive Summary provides a brief executive-level report on the findings of the scan. The content is not very technical in nature and is geared toward senior nontechnical management.
- **Brief Technical Report**—The Brief Technical Report is a concise technical report without the Executive Summary and other explanatory sections. It presents a basic technical report of the findings and vulnerabilities, along with the required action to remedy the vulnerabilities.

Figure 7-9   *NSDB*

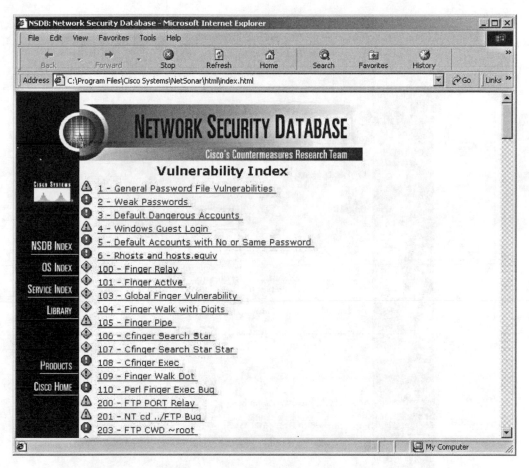

- **Full Technical Report**—The Full Technical Report contains the Executive Summary and other explanatory sections, as well as the full technical aspects regarding the discovered vulnerabilities. This can be a lengthy document if the findings are copious, but in the author's opinion, this is the most useful of the three reports.

Figure 7-11 shows the result of a Full Technical Report.

All of these reports can be customized using the wizard to add and remove content. Previously saved grid browsers and charts can also be incorporated within the report, further enhancing the quality of the report.

Figure 7-10 *NSDB Default Dangerous Accounts Vulnerability*

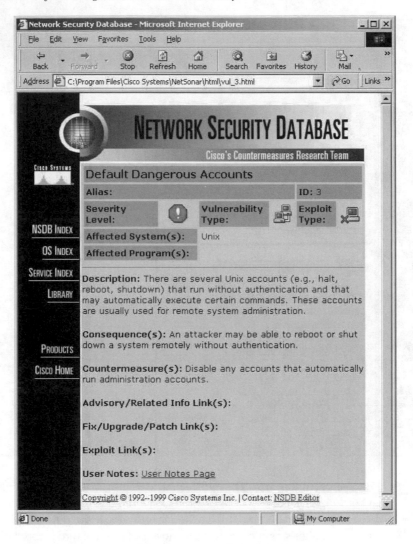

Figure 7-11 *Full Technical Report Showing Part of the Table of Contents*

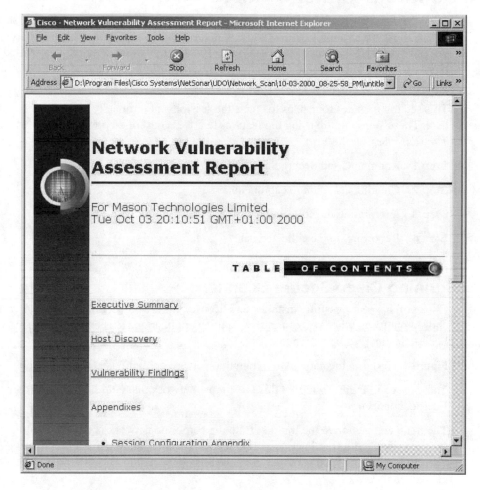

Cisco Secure Scanner Installation

Cisco Secure Scanner is available for both the Windows and Solaris platforms.

Cisco Secure Scanner is provided on a CD-ROM, which has to be installed to your host's hard disk for the application to function. Cisco Secure Scanner will not operate from the CD-ROM drive.

This chapter does not examine the full installation process. The process is fully documented on Cisco Connection Online (CCO) at www.cisco.com and also in the documentation provided with the Cisco Secure Scanner product.

Cisco Secure Scanner Configuration

Now that you have looked at the main features of the Cisco Secure Scanner, this section covers the configuration of the software with the goal of creating a session to check a sample network for security vulnerabilities. This configuration example is provided as a basic example, with steps you can emulate in your workplace to check your internal networks for security vulnerabilities.

This section includes four steps to create the session and ultimately report on the collected data. These steps require using the features that were described previously in this chapter. The steps are as follows:

Step 1 Running Cisco Secure Scanner

Step 2 Creating a session to capture data

Step 3 Interpreting the collected data

Step 4 Reporting on the collected data

Step 1: Running Cisco Secure Scanner

Once you have successfully installed and licensed the Cisco Secure Scanner for your chosen platform, you have to start the scanning application. This example uses the Cisco Secure Scanner V2.0 for Windows NT.

Figure 7-12 shows the network diagram that you are going to use for this exercise.

You can see in Figure 7-12 that this is a simple network that could represent a corporate Internet connection.

The main connection to the Internet from the corporate network is through an Internet-facing firewall with four interfaces. Interface 1 is connected to the Internet, interface 2 is connected to the internal network, interface 3 is connected to DMZ1, and interface 4 is connected to DMZ2.

Table 7-2 shows the simple security policy installed on the firewall.

Figure 7-12 *Sample Network Diagram*

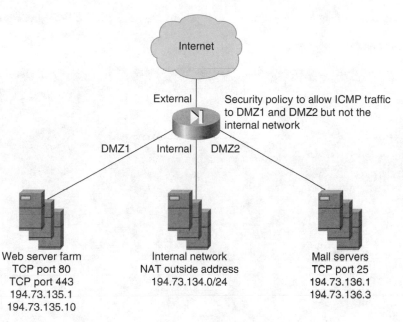

Table 7-2 *Simple Security Policy for the Example Network*

Source	Destination	Service	Permit/Deny
Any	Web servers	TCP Port 80	Permit
Any	Web servers	TCP Port 443	Permit
Any	Web servers	ICMP	Permit
Any	Mail servers	TCP Port 25	Permit
Any	Mail servers	ICMP	Permit
Any	Internal network	ICMP	Deny

Step 2: Creating a Session to Capture Data

The first thing that you need to do is create a session to capture the required data. To do this, click the **Create New Session** command button that is located in the top left corner of the Cisco Secure Scanner application window. Once the session configuration screen is displayed, you need to configure a session that will enable a scan of the DMZ1, DMZ2, and internal networks. You might ask why you are scanning the internal network. This is to confirm that the firewall is blocking access to inbound services on the internal network. You know that ICMP is not allowed to the internal network, so you will have to force a scan of these addresses.

For this exercise, the scanner will be run from the Internet.

Figure 7-13 shows the required configuration settings for the IP addresses in the session.

Figure 7-13 *Session Configuration Settings*

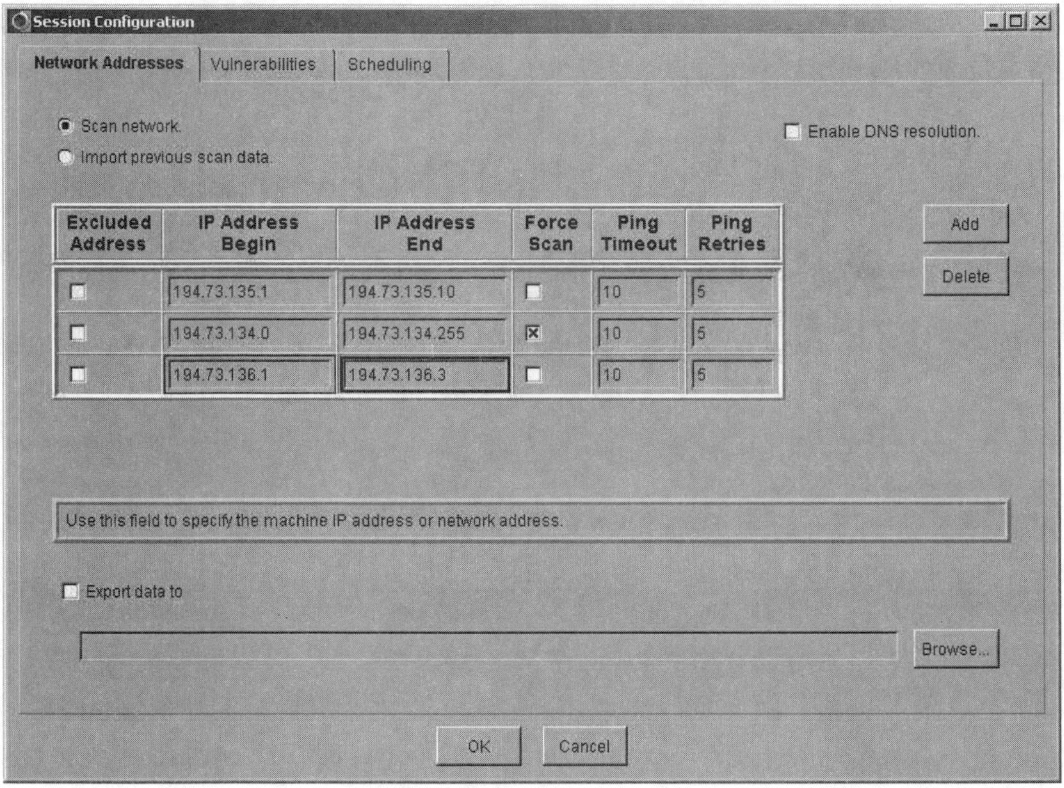

In Figure 7-13, you can see three configuration lines for the session. The first line configures the session to scan the Web servers on DMZ1. The second line configures the session to scan the internal network, and the third line configures the session to scan the mail servers on DMZ2. Note that the **Force Scan** checkbox is checked on the second configuration line. Because ICMP is not permitted through the firewall for the internal interface, forcing a scan is the only way to scan the hosts on the internal network. If you leave this blank, no hosts on the internal interface would be added to the network map because the scanning software would presume that the hosts are down.

The next step is to configure the ports for the scan and the active probes. Click the **Vulnerabilities** tab to display these options.

In this instance, you want to scan the well-known ports for both TCP and UDP. Do this by clicking the **Well-Known Ports** option for both TCP and UDP. You must then enable the active probes and select the **Windows_Heavy** profile, because you do not have any UNIX machines on the network. All of the active probes that correspond to known vulnerabilities on hosts running Windows as the operating system are then selected.

Figure 7-14 shows the finished port and probe configuration.

Figure 7-14 *Port and Probe Configuration Settings*

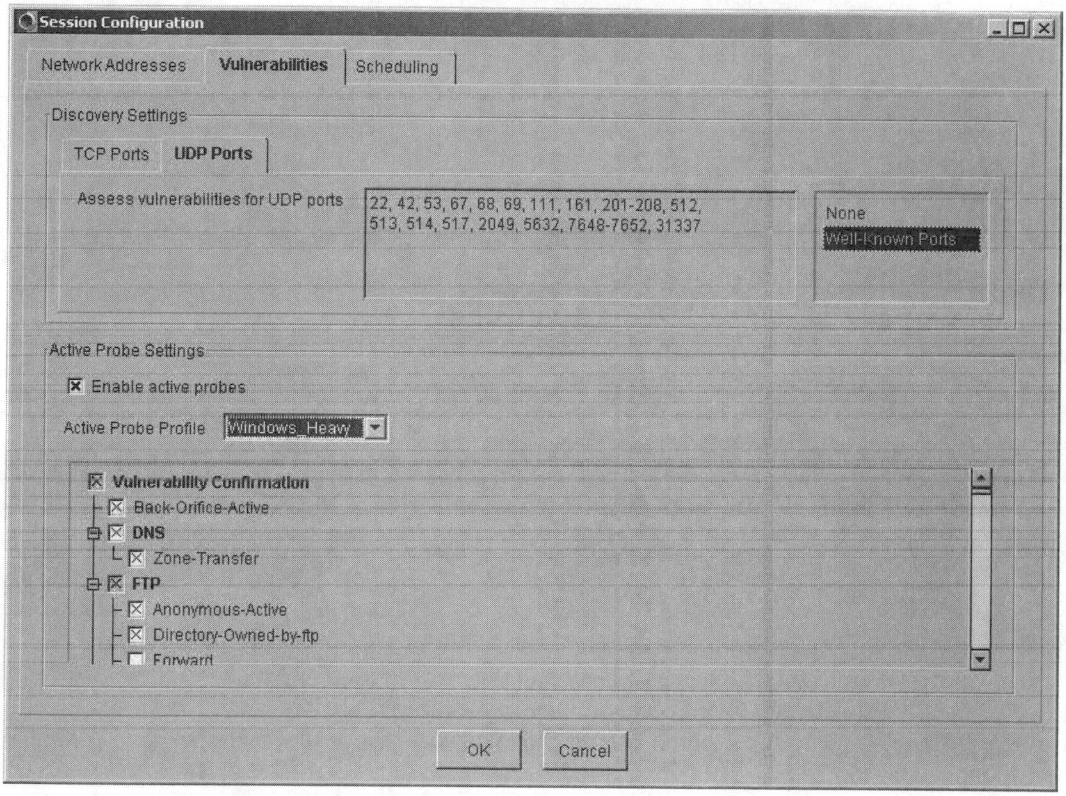

You can see the settings explained in the previous paragraph in Figure 7-14. **Well-Known Ports** and the **Windows Heavy** probe profile are selected.

The last tab on the session configuration screen is the **Scheduling** tab. Here you can set a schedule for the scan to run. The default is **Immediately**, but you have the option to choose a time of day and also the day and frequency of the scan. For this demonstration, you are going to configure the scan to run at 0700 every Monday. Figure 7-15 shows this configuration.

Figure 7-15 *Scheduling Settings*

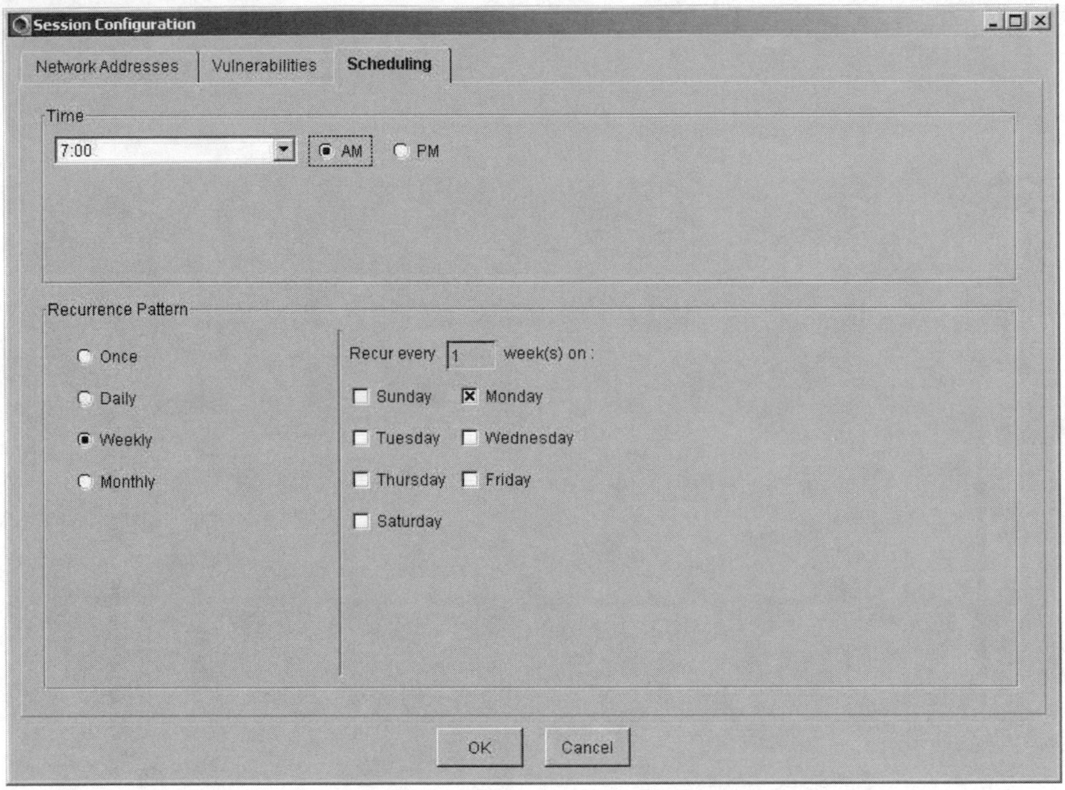

Figure 7-15 shows that the scan is set to run every week on a Monday at 0700. As long as the host with the Cisco Secure Scanner application installed is running the software at this time, the scan will occur. If not, the scan will occur the next time the software is run.

NOTE   It is possible to run Cisco Secure Scanner as a Windows NT service. This means that the scans would run even though the application is not loaded. Refer to the product manual for instructions on how to do this.

Clicking **OK** at this point will make the scan session ready for the next Monday morning at 0700. At that time, the scan will start, and you will see the scan status screen as shown in Figure 7-16.

Figure 7-16 *Scan Status Screen*

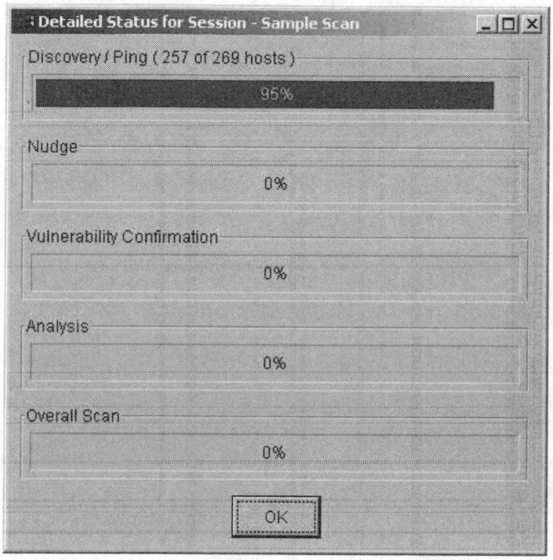

Step 3: Interpreting the Collected Data

After the scan has run, you will be presented with a result set item under the name of the session in the main Cisco Secure Scanner application window. This can be seen in Figure 7-17.

Figure 7-17 *Scanner Application Window*

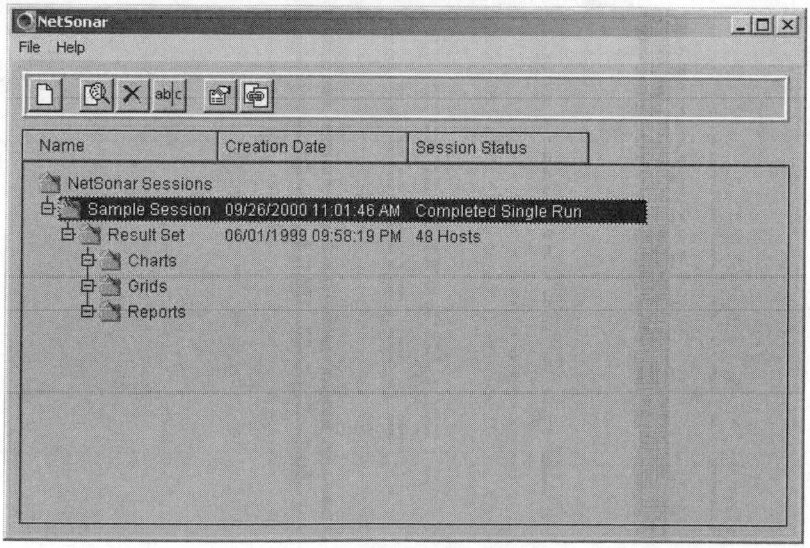

The session created is called Sample Session and can be seen along with the folders created by default: Charts, Grids, and Reports. Note that there is nothing listed under the Charts, Grids, or Reports folders. At this point, you have not created any objects that would normally be placed under these folders. You will now create a sample grid and chart, leaving the report to Step 4, "Reporting on the Collected Data," later in this chapter.

To create a grid and view it in a grid browser, right-click the result set and select **View Grid Data**. You are then presented with the grid browser. To configure the grid browser, refer to the configuration settings described under the "Cisco Secure Scanner Features" section at the beginning of this chapter. Once you have completed configuring your grid, save it by selecting the **Save** button on the command bar. After entering the name of the grid, it appears as an object below the Grid folder on the main configuration screen.

To create a chart, you first have to configure a grid to display the information you require on the chart. When you highlight this data, the Chart Wizard icon becomes active. Clicking this button enables the chart wizard. To configure the chart, refer to the configuration settings described under the "Cisco Secure Scanner Features" section earlier in this chapter. Once you have completed configuring your chart, save it by selecting the **Save** button on the command bar. After entering the name of the chart, it appears as an object below the Chart folder on the main configuration screen.

After you have completed these steps, you will have a main application window that looks similar to that in Figure 7-18.

Figure 7-18 *Scanner Application Window*

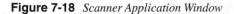

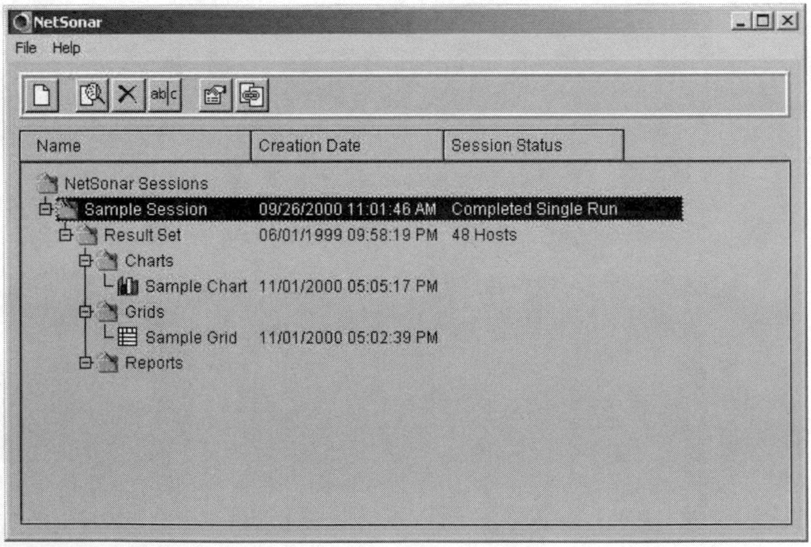

You can see in Figure 7-18 that along with the result set, you now have Sample Grid and Sample Chart objects under the corresponding folders.

The next step is to create the report.

Step 4: Reporting on the Collected Data

You now have run a successful port scan and probe of the intended hosts. The next requirement is to produce a Brief Technical Report to explain the findings of the scan. You should include the Sample Grid and Sample Chart that you produced in the previous section. To create a new report, you have to right-click the result set and select **Create a New Report**. From the Report Selection screen, choose the **Brief Technical Report** option. The main difference between the Brief and Full Technical Reports is the Executive Summary and the explanatory text. Because this report is of a technical nature and the scan is to be run every week, there is no need for the explanatory text or Executive Summary.

Be sure to include in the report the Sample Chart and Sample Grid that you previously created.

Once the report is created, you will have a Report object under the Report folder. To open the report, simply double-click the report title that is located within the Report folder. The report is HTML-based, so it will open in the default installed Internet browser.

Summary

This chapter provided an overview of the Cisco Secure Scanner. Network scanning is a very important part of the security policy for your organization; you may spend thousands of dollars on equipment and resources to protect your network. Network scanning provides an opportunity to test the effectiveness of these measures. Regular scanning of the network, especially after an updated NSDB containing new vulnerabilities is released, is important as an ongoing task to ensure that the network is secure from all threats.

The network scanner can be used not only in checking network security, but also in application testing to ensure that specific machines are listening for traffic on specific ports. This alternate use of the network scanner is one that the author has implemented numerous times.

Frequently Asked Questions

Question: I have heard the term *port scan* quite frequently. What exactly does it mean?

Answer: Port scanning is run by an application that is classified as a port scanner. Cisco Secure Scanner can be classified as a port scanner. A port scanner runs a series of network connectivity tests against a preconfigured range of IP addresses and ports. The result is called the port scan. The scan identifies what ports are open, that is, what network services are being run on each specific host.

Question: I cannot ping an internal Web server from the point where I will run the network scan. Can the Web server still be scanned?

Answer: Yes. You can set the scan to force specific addresses. This means that no network connectivity test, such as an ICMP echo, will be attempted. The object will automatically be added to the network map whether or not it is running and communicating on the network.

Glossary

DoS (denial of service)—A specific type of network attack that overloads some aspect of a server's network communication to force the server to deny access to legitimate traffic.

PIX (Private Internet Exchange)—The Cisco range of leading hardware-based firewalls.

VPN (Virtual Private Network)—A secure connection over an unsecured medium. The connection is secured by the use of tunneling encryption and protocols.

URLs

Cisco Secure Scanner:

www.cisco.com/go/netsonar/

This chapter contains the following sections:

- Cisco Secure Policy Manager Features
- Cisco Secure Policy Manager Installation
- Configuration Example
- Summary
- Frequently Asked Questions
- Glossary
- URLs

CHAPTER 8

Cisco Secure Policy Manager (CSPM)

As networks grow, so too does the administrative burden associated with the centralized control of the networking devices. One specific range of devices that requires stringent control is that group responsible for maintaining network integrity: the security devices. The security devices from Cisco include the Cisco Secure PIX Firewall and various Cisco routers running the Cisco IOS Firewall. By default, each of these security devices is a complete standalone entity that relies on editing the configuration with the command-line interface (CLI). As the network grows, a centralized, policy-based tool is required to keep control of network security, and a method of simplified administration and deployment becomes necessary.

Cisco provides the Cisco Secure Policy Manager (CSPM) to carry out such a function.

This chapter covers CSPM by first explaining exactly what CSPM is and what it strives to achieve. Installation of CSPM will be covered right through to the specific configuration requirements essential for obtaining the most out of the product.

CSPM Features

CSPM (formerly Cisco Security Manager) is a powerful security policy management application that is designed around the integration of Cisco Secure PIX Firewalls, Internet Protocol Security (IPSec) VPN-capable routers, routers running the Cisco IOS Firewall feature set, and Intrusion Detection System (IDS) sensors.

Currently, CSPM is available only on the Windows NT platform.

CSPM provides a tool that enables the security administrator to define, enforce, and audit security policies for distributed Cisco Secure PIX Firewalls, IPSec VPN-capable routers, and routers running the Cisco IOS Firewall feature set. The software enables the administrator to formulate complex security policies based on organizational needs. These policies are then converted to detailed configurations by the CSPM and distributed to the specific security devices in the network.

The main features of CSPM are as follows:

- **Cisco firewall management**—CSPM empowers the user to define complex security policies and then distribute these to several hundred PIX Firewalls or routers running the Cisco IOS Firewall. Full management capabilities are available for the firewalls.

- **Cisco VPN router management**—IPSec-based VPNs can be easily configured by using the simple graphical user interface (GUI). As with firewall management, this VPN configuration can be distributed to several hundred PIX Firewalls or routers running the Cisco IOS Firewall.

- **Security policy management**—The GUI enables the creation of network-wide security policies. These security policies can be managed from a single point and delivered to several hundred firewall devices without requiring extensive device knowledge and dependency on the CLI.

- **Intelligent network management**—The defined security policies are translated into the appropriate device commands to create the required device configuration. The device configuration is then securely distributed throughout the network, eliminating the need for device-by-device management.

- **Notification and reporting system**—CSPM provides a basic set of tools to monitor, alert, and report activity on the Cisco Secure devices. This provides the security administrator with both reporting information that can be used to ascertain the current state of the security policy and a notification system to report various conditions. Along with the built-in notification and reporting tools, the product also implements and integrates with leading third-party monitoring, billing, and reporting systems.

Figure 8-1 shows the main configuration screen of the CSPM.

The following devices and software revisions are supported by CSPM:

- Cisco Secure PIX Firewall
  - PIX OS 4.2.4, 4.2.5, 4.4.x, 5.1.x, 5.2.1
- Cisco router/firewall and Cisco VPN gateway
  - IOS 12.0(5)T, XE
  - IOS 12.0(7)T
  - IOS 12.1(1)T, E, XC
  - IOS 12.1(2), T, (2) T, E, XH, (3) T, X1
- Cisco Secure Intrusion Detection System sensor
  - 2.2.0.x
  - 2.2.1.x
  - 2.5.0

- Cisco Secure Intrusion Detection System line card

  — Catalyst 6000 2.5 IDSM

Figure 8-1   *CSPM*

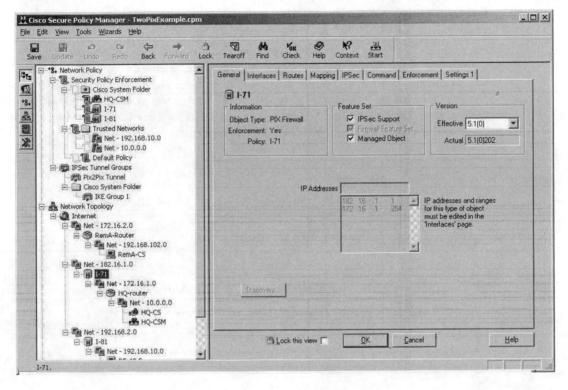

NOTE   A Cisco router/firewall is a Cisco router running the firewall feature set. A Cisco VPN gateway is a Cisco router running the IPSec VPN feature set. These feature sets are part of the Cisco IOS Firewall and Cisco Secure Integrated VPN Software solutions for Cisco routers.

CSPM Installation

This section covers the installation requirements for CSPM.

Before you install CSPM, you have to ensure that the installation system meets the hardware and software requirements. This section assumes that you are using version 2.2 of the CSPM. If you are using a different version, you should consult your documentation to ascertain the requirement differences.

Hardware Requirements

The target host for your CSPM system must meet the minimum hardware requirements to protect the integrity and functionality of the system that you install. However, you should always consider your network topology, the number of policy enforcement points you intend to manage, and your performance requirements for command distribution and monitoring when reviewing the minimum hardware requirements.

For example, the Policy Server is a multithreaded application that would benefit from multiple CPUs and available memory on a single host. Enhancing the Policy Administrator host would not necessarily optimize the GUI performance. The minimum hardware requirements may be sufficient for a standalone or client-server system, but they are not optimal for a distributed system. To ensure optimal performance, you should install CSPM on hosts that exceed the minimum hardware requirements.

Minimum Hardware Requirements

The minimum hardware requirements to run the CSPM are as follows:

- 200 MHz Pentium processor
- 96 MB of RAM
- 2 GB free hard drive space
- One or more properly configured network adapter cards
- 1024 by 768 video adapter card capable of at least 64 K color
- CD-ROM drive (preferably Autorun-enabled)
- Modem (optional for pager notifications)
- Mouse
- SVGA color monitor

Software Requirements

You can install the CSPM feature sets on any host that meets the minimum hardware requirements and that also runs Windows NT 4.0. To install version 2.2, you must be using Microsoft Windows NT 4.0 with Service Pack 6a installed. CSPM will not install on any other Service Pack built on Windows NT 4.0 or on a system running Microsoft Windows 2000.

The Policy Administrator feature set can also be installed on a host that runs Windows 95 or Windows 98.

Requisite Software

You cannot access the setup program unless the target host on which you are installing CSPM has the following requisite software properly installed:

- Service Pack 6a for Windows NT (to update files in the operating system)
- Microsoft Internet Explorer version 5 (for displaying system-generated reports)
- HTML Help 1.3 Update (for viewing online HTML-based help topics)

The Autostart utility automatically searches the target host for these requirements and lists the ones that you must install before proceeding with the setup program. You can install all three pieces of software from the Autostart panel.

Planning your Installation

Once you ascertain that you have met the hardware and software installation criteria, you can progress to planning the installation.

Before you can plan the installation, you have to fully understand three topics related to CSPM:

- Policy enforcement points
- Feature sets
- Installation options

Policy Enforcement Points

A *policy enforcement point* is defined as a networking device that can alter the traffic flow from one network to another.

Concerning the CSPM, a policy enforcement point can be any device that CSPM manages through the distribution of policies.

These policy enforcement points can be dedicated firewalls, such as the Cisco Secure PIX Firewall, router firewalls, or VPN gateways. Router firewalls are Cisco routers that are running the Cisco IOS Firewall, and VPN gateways are Cisco routers that are running the Cisco IOS Firewall with the IPSec VPN feature set.

Only specific versions of the Cisco Secure PIX Firewall and Cisco IOS Firewall will work with CSPM and in different ways. One restriction is with the PIX Firewall. All versions of the PIX software prior to 5.1(x) require the managed interface to be available on the inside interface. With version 5.1(x) and later, you can manage the PIX Firewall from any available interface on the PIX.

Table 8-1 shows the supported policy enforcement points and their interface dependencies.

Table 8-1 *Supported Policy Enforcement Points and Interface Dependencies*

Policy Enforcement Point	Supported Version	Managed Interface Dependency
Cisco Secure PIX Firewall	4.2(4)	Inside
	4.2(5)	Inside
	4.4(x)	Inside
	5.1(x)	None
	5.2(x)	None
Cisco Router Firewall	IOS 12.0(5)T	None
Cisco VPN gateway	IOS 12.0(5)XE	None
	IOS 12.0(7)T	None
	IOS 12.1(1)T, E, XC	None
	IOS 12.1(2), T, (2) T, E, XH, (3) T, X1	

The installation of the policy enforcement points is not included in the system. Each policy enforcement point must be configured to facilitate management from the CSPM. These configurations are called the *bootstrap settings*.

The bootstrap settings are very important for achieving communication between the policy server and the policy enforcement points. The bootstrap settings for each device are explained in detail in the section "Installation Procedures" later in this chapter.

Feature Sets

The CSPM system is composed of multiple subsystems. Each of these subsystems provides a specific functionality that makes up the whole CSPM product. A *feature set* is defined as a collection of these subsystems, which are offered at installation time as installable options. These also are related to the specific installation options that are discussed in Chapter 9, "Cisco Secure Access Control Server (ACS)." The options are dictated largely by the network topology and number and location of the policy enforcement points.

The five feature sets are as follows:

- Policy Administrator
- Policy Server
- Policy Monitor

- Policy Proxy
- Policy Proxy-Monitor

Policy Administrator

The Policy Administrator feature set is the primary GUI for policy definition, enforcement, and auditing for your CSPM system.

Policy Server

The Policy Server feature set contains the database subsystem. This subsystem is the main data store for all of the system configuration data and audit records. Besides the database subsystem, the reporting and generation subsystems are also within the Policy Server feature set.

The reporting subsystem is responsible for generating the on-demand and scheduled reports associated with CSPM.

The generation subsystem compiles the global policy into a collection of intermediate policies that are applied to the specific policy enforcement points.

The Policy Server feature set also includes the Policy Administrator, Policy Proxy, Policy Proxy-Monitor, and Policy Monitor feature sets.

NOTE   The Policy Server feature set always has to be the first feature set installed. The database key generated during this installation is required during installation of all other feature sets.

Policy Monitor

The Policy Monitor feature set contains the monitoring subsystem and a secondary database.

The monitoring subsystem is responsible for collecting all of the audit records from the policy enforcement points and processing this data to generate notification alerts appertaining to specific conditions.

The secondary database exchanges status and summary audit records with the primary database that is installed with the Policy Server feature set.

The Policy Administrator feature set is installed when you install the Policy Monitor feature set.

Policy Proxy

The Policy Proxy feature set contains the proxy subsystem and another secondary database.

The proxy subsystem maps and translates the intermediate policy into a device-specific rule set required by the managed policy enforcement points on your network.

The secondary database maintains a local copy of the intermediate policies and stores the system events that are generated by the proxy subsystem. This data is then synchronized with the Policy Server on the Policy Server host.

The Policy Administrator feature set is installed when you install the Policy Proxy feature set.

Policy Proxy-Monitor

The Policy Proxy-Monitor feature set basically combines the functionality of the proxy and monitoring subsystems. This allows you to have a distributed system with a reduced number of required hosts on which to run the feature sets.

The Policy Administrator feature set is installed when you install the Policy Proxy-Monitor feature set.

Installation Options

There are four ways of installing the CSPM. The method you choose largely depends on your network topology and the number of devices to be managed.

The four types of installation are:

- Standalone system
- Client-server system
- Distributed system
- Demo system

Standalone System

As you would expect, a standalone system installation is when the CSPM is installed on a single host. All of the CSPM functions are carried out on this single host.

A standalone installation should be used in a small office environment. This would normally be located on one site with no policy enforcement points located at the remote end of a WAN link. The centralized location of the installation enforces centralized management of the security policy.

Figure 8-2 shows a network topology where a standalone installation would suffice.

As you can see in Figure 8-2, this is a small office with a small number of policy enforcement points. This topology is suited to the standalone installation and is scalable to the client-server installation as the network grows.

Figure 8-2   *Sample Standalone Installation Network*

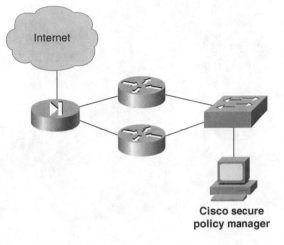

Client-Server System

The client-server installation is when you install the CSPM Policy Server feature set on one host and the Policy Administrator feature set on one or more different hosts in the network. The client-server architecture is followed in that the Policy Server is installed on a single host, the server, which can be administered from clients in various network locations.

A client-server installation is normally required for larger networks than those served by standalone systems. One key point is the management of the security policy. Standalone systems are necessary when only centralized management and administration is required. When management is decentralized and numerous separate entities require localized administration, it is necessary to scale to the client-server model. This model also fits into a multioffice topology, where multiple policy enforcement points are located throughout the entire network.

Figure 8-3 shows a network topology where a client-server installation is required.

You can see in the topology in Figure 8-3 that each site has its own policy enforcement point, and the remote offices each have their own policy administration host.

Distributed System

You should recall that the standalone system has all of the CSPM feature sets installed on one host, and the client-server system is theoretically the same, except that the Policy Administrator feature set can be installed on numerous hosts across the network.

Figure 8-3 *Sample Client-Server Installation Network*

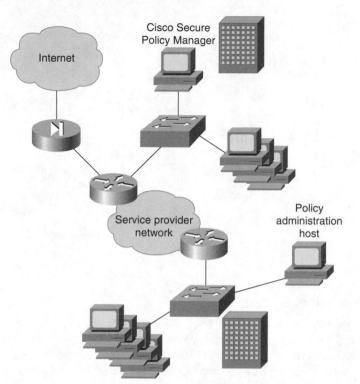

The distributed system expands the client-server model by allowing distribution of other CSPM feature sets to multiple hosts on the network.

With this model, you have to install the Policy Server feature set on a single host, which acts as the main policy server. The other features such as the Policy Proxy, Policy Proxy-Monitor, and Policy Monitor can all be installed on any number of additional hosts. This system distributes the components and allows these hosts to assume responsibility for monitoring and proxy functionality for a portion of the enterprise network.

Figure 8-4 shows a network topology where a distributed installation is required.

As you can see, the network in Figure 8-4 is spread over three main offices. Each office is classed as a separate administrative entity because of the internal and external protected links. You can see that each site is connected by the company intranet, and each site has its own external links. Internet access is provided through the company headquarters. This model gives every site its own Policy Administrator host, as well as a Policy Proxy-Monitor host that holds the secondary database. This model allows 24/7 management of security services throughout the corporate network from multiple locations. The distributed installation also provides better performance of the CSPM system by off-loading critical functions to different servers. In offices that contain several policy enforcement points, dedicated Policy Monitor and Policy Proxy hosts are deployed.

Figure 8-4   *Sample Distributed Installation Network*

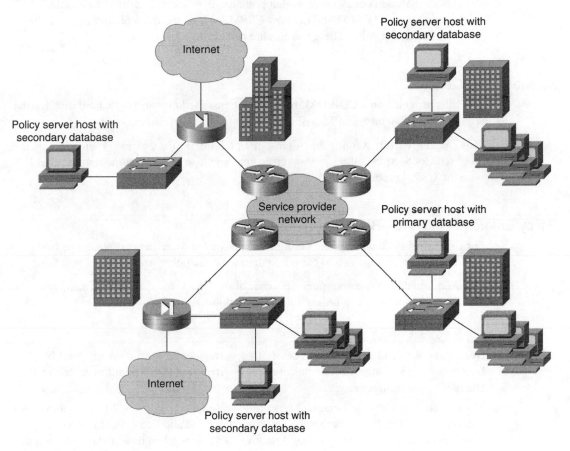

Demo System

In addition to installing CSPM in a live environment, you can install it in demo mode. This will only install it on a single host; the full feature set and the Policy Administrator feature are installed with various demonstration files. Demo mode's main purpose is to allow you to make a demo installation to explore the Policy Administrator interface and features without having to install a live system. This mode can be used for appraising the system or to train staff in the correct use of the CSPM's many features.

Installation Procedures

Now that you have seen the installation procedures and components, this section will concentrate on the actual software installation and policy enforcement point configuration. Remember that each policy enforcement point requires specific settings to enable communication with CSPM and to allow CSPM to fully and dynamically manage the policy enforcement point. These settings are called the bootstrap settings.

Software Installation

CSPM is provided on a CD-ROM that has to be installed to your host's hard disk for the application to function. CSPM will not operate from the CD drive.

This chapter will not examine the full installation process. The process is fully documented on Cisco Connection Online at www.cisco.com and also in the documentation provided with the CSPM product.

Policy Enforcement Point—Bootstrap Settings

For the CSPM to connect to and configure the policy enforcement points, some basic commands have to be added to the configuration of the policy enforcement points.

These commands enable communication and allow CSPM to take over the management of the device to control it as a policy enforcement point.

NOTE   Note that once you have enabled a device to become a policy enforcement point by bootstrapping, you must never connect to the device using the CLI and make manual changes to the configuration.

The devices must be either manually controlled or controlled by CSPM as a policy enforcement point. If you were to connect manually and add lines of configuration commands, the policy manager would remove these lines when it next synchronized the configuration.

There are different bootstrap settings required depending on whether the device is a PIX Firewall or a router with the Cisco IOS Firewall installed. Each is discussed separately in the following two sections.

Cisco Secure PIX Firewall Bootstrapping

You must connect to the PIX Firewall using a console cable to the console port and a terminal application. Once connected, follow these steps in order to configure the initial bootstrap settings:

Step 1   Enter global configuration mode from within privileged mode.

Step 2   Name each installed interface on the PIX Firewall. This is done by entering the following command:

```
nameif hardware_id if_name security_level
```

The *hardware_id* should reflect what type of hardware the interface is. For example, the first Ethernet interface is **ethernet0**, the second Ethernet interface is **ethernet1**, and so on. For Token Ring, use **token0** and increment the number for every interface.

The *if_name* relates to the naming and location of the interface:

— The interface installed in slot 0 must be named **outside** and the security level must be 0.

— The interface installed in slot 1 must be named **inside** and the security level must be 100.

— The interface installed in slot 2 must be named **DMZ-slot:2** and the security level must be an unused level between 1 and 99.

— The interface installed in slot 3 must be named **DMZ-slot:3** and the security level must be an unused level between 1 and 99.

The *security_level* is a value such as **security0** or **security100**. The outside interface must be **security0,** and the inside interface must be **security100**. For any other interfaces, the value must be between 1 and 99.

Step 3   Configure the network addresses for the inside and outside interfaces. This is achieved with the command

```
ip address int_name a.a.a.a m.m.m.m
```

int_name is either inside or outside, *a.a.a.a* is the IP address, and *m.m.m.m* is the subnet mask for that IP address. An example of this could be

```
ip address inside 192.168.0.1 255.255.255.0
```

This will assign the IP address of 192.168.0.1 to the inside interface.

Step 4 Specify the default gateway for the PIX Firewall. This is the next hop on the outside interface that all external bound traffic is passed to for onward delivery. This is achieved with the command

```
route outside 0 0 n.n.n.n 1
```

The address *n.n.n.n* is the IP address of the next hop router. For example the following command would set the default route on the outside interface to be 212.1.157.1:

```
route outside 0 0 212.1.157.1 1
```

Step 5 The next step is to configure Network Address Translation (NAT) on the firewall by entering two configuration commands, the **nat** and **global** commands.

Enter the following commands:

```
nat (inside) 1 0 0
global (outside) 1 a.a.a.a-b.b.b.b
```

The first command just starts NAT translation for process number 1 on the inside interface. The second command allocates global IP addresses to the same NAT process (1). The address *a.a.a.a* is the starting global IP address, and the address *b.b.b.b* is the last global IP address. For example:

```
nat (inside) 1 0 0
global (outside) 1 194.73.134.1-194.73.134.254
```

These commands would set up NAT for process 1 and allocate the public IP addresses 194.73.134.1 to 194.73.134.254 to be used for address translation.

Step 6 You now want the Policy Proxy to be able to distribute commands to the PIX over Telnet. To do this, you must allow Telnet connections to the Policy Proxy host on an internal network. The command to do this is

```
telnet a.a.a.a 255.255.255.255
```

The address *a.a.a.a* is the IP address of the Policy Proxy host and **255.255.255.255** is an example that specifies the Policy Proxy host.

NOTE Don't forget that in a single installation and some client-server installations, the Policy Proxy host may be the same as the Policy Server host.

Step 7 If the Policy Proxy host is not located on the same broadcast domain/subnet as the inside interface, you have to enter a static route to the Policy Proxy host's network. You do this with the **route** command in a similar fashion as entering a static route on a Cisco router by IOS. If the Policy Proxy is on the 192.168.2.0/24 network and the inside interface is addressed 192.168.1.1/24, you need the following command:

```
route inside 192.168.2.0 255.255.255.0 192.168.1.254 2
```

This presumes that the connected router between 192.168.1.0/24 and 192.168.2.0/24 is located at the IP address 192.168.1.254/24.

NOTE   If your PIX Firewall has more than two interfaces, you cannot specify a default inside route. A default inside route would be a route to 0.0.0.0 0.0.0.0.

Step 8   The final stage is to save your configuration to the flash memory of the PIX Firewall.

This is achieved with the following command:

```
write memory
```

This concludes the bootstrapping of the Cisco Secure PIX Firewall. The PIX Firewall is now ready to be managed by the CSPM.

Cisco IOS Firewall Bootstrapping

You must connect to the router running the Cisco IOS Firewall using a console cable to the console port and a terminal application. Once connected, follow these steps to configure the initial bootstrap settings.

Step 1   Enter global configuration mode from within privileged mode.

Step 2   Specify the static default gateway for the router. This is the next hop to which all external bound traffic is passed for onward delivery. Do this with the command

`ip route 0.0.0.0 0.0.0.0` *a.a.a.a*

The address *a.a.a.a* is the IP address of the next hop router. For example, the following command would set the default route for the router to be 212.1.157.1:

```
ip route 0.0.0.0 0.0.0.0 212.1.157.1
```

Step 3   If the Policy Proxy host is not located on the same broadcast domain/subnet as the inside interface, you have to enter a static route to the Policy Proxy host's network. You can do this with the **ip route** command.

If the Policy Proxy is on the 192.168.2.0/24 network and the router's local interface is 192.168.1.1/24, you need the following command:

```
ip route 192.168.2.0 255.255.255.0 192.168.1.254
```

This presumes that the connected router between 192.168.1.0/24 and 192.168.2.0/24 is located at the IP address 192.168.1.254/24.

Step 4   At this point, you are left with the decision of whether to configure NAT. If you do not want to configure NAT, skip to Step 9.

Step 5   The next step is to configure NAT on the router. This takes three steps. First, you must define a global pool of addresses. The next step is to create a standard access list to specify the inside/private addresses that you want to translate. Finally, you must apply the NAT pool to the inside interface on the router and specify the outside NAT interface.

Step 6   To configure the global pool of addresses, enter the following command:

```
ip nat pool pool_name first global address last global address netmask
subnet_mask
```

The *pool_name* is a name given to the NAT pool for applying to the required interface. The *first global address* and *last global address* explain themselves, as does the *subnet_mask*. An example of this command could be

```
ip nat pool nat1 194.73.134.10 194.73.134.20 netmask 255.255.255.0
```

The preceding command would define a global NAT pool called nat1. The pool would include the global addresses from 194.73.134.10 to 194.73.134.20.

Step 7   The next NAT step is to create the standard access list. This access list is used to specify exactly which internal hosts will have their addresses translated by the NAT process on the inside interface. As an example, to allow all hosts on the 192.168.1.0 network access to the translation process, enter the following command:

```
access-list 1 permit 192.168.1.0 255.255.255.0
```

Step 8   The final NAT step is to apply the created pool and access list to an inside interface. To apply the NAT pool and access list created in Step 6, the command would be

```
ip nat inside source list 1 pool nat1
```

The **1** relates to the access list and **nat1** relates to the previously created global NAT pool.

Then configure the outside interface to complete the NAT translation. This is configured by entering the command

```
ip nat outside
```

Step 9   Now, manually enter the IP addresses of all installed interfaces on your router. To do this, you must enter the interface configuration mode. For example:

```
Router(config)#
Router(config)#interface ethernet0
Router(config-if)#
```

You know that you are in interface configuration mode when you see the **Router(config-if)#** prompt. The command to set the IP address is simply

ip address *a.a.a.a m.m.m.m*

The address *a.a.a.a* is the IP address and *m.m.m.m* is the subnet mask.

Step 10   The final stage is to save your configuration to the flash memory of the router.

Do this with the following command:

```
write memory
```

This concludes the bootstrapping of the Cisco IOS Firewall-enabled router. The device is now ready to be managed by the CSPM.

Configuration Example

Now that you have seen an overview of the CSPM and the required basic installation requirements, this section will provide a simple configuration example. This example is based around a simple network with one Cisco Secure PIX Firewall and one Cisco Router running the Cisco IOS Firewall. The PIX is version 5.1(2) and the Cisco IOS Firewall is 12.0(7)T. Both of these are supported by the CSPM as policy enforcement points.

The network topology is shown in Figure 8-5.

You can see in the network in Figure 8-5 that there is one connection to the Internet by the Cisco Secure PIX Firewall. The clients reside on the 192.168.9.0 internal network, which is an RFC 1918-compliant private address. The external address and the outside PIX interface is on the 194.73.134.0/24 public network. The PIX has a default route set to 194.73.134.1 on the outside interface, which is provided by the Internet service provider and is out of your administrative control. Numerous other private network addresses exist between the client network and the Internet. All internal routing is already configured, so you need to be concerned only with the provision of the general Internet services (e-mail, Web, and DNS) through the PIX Firewall to the Internet.

Figure 8-5 *Configuration Example Network Topology*

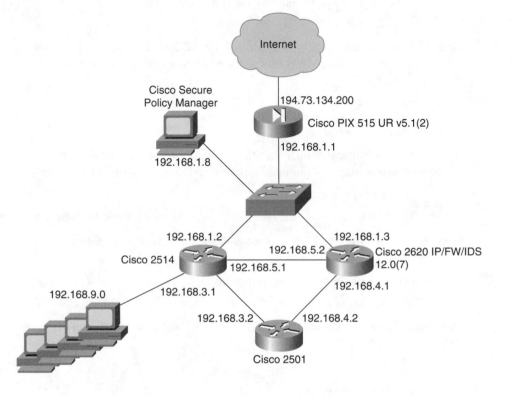

Configure the Network Topology

After a successful installation, the first thing to do is to configure the network topology. Figure 8-6 shows the basic screen that is presented before any configuration has commenced. This has no policy definitions and no defined objects.

As you can see in Figure 8-6, only the five branches exist in the left pane.

The first configuration procedure in any CSPM installation is to configure the network topology. A frequently asked question is, "What devices do I have to define in the network topology?" The answer contains two parts: There are network objects that you must define in order for the Policy Manager software to function, and there are network objects that you must define in order for the enforced policies to provide the level of security required. You may not have to define every network device as part of the network topology for the security policy to be enforced.

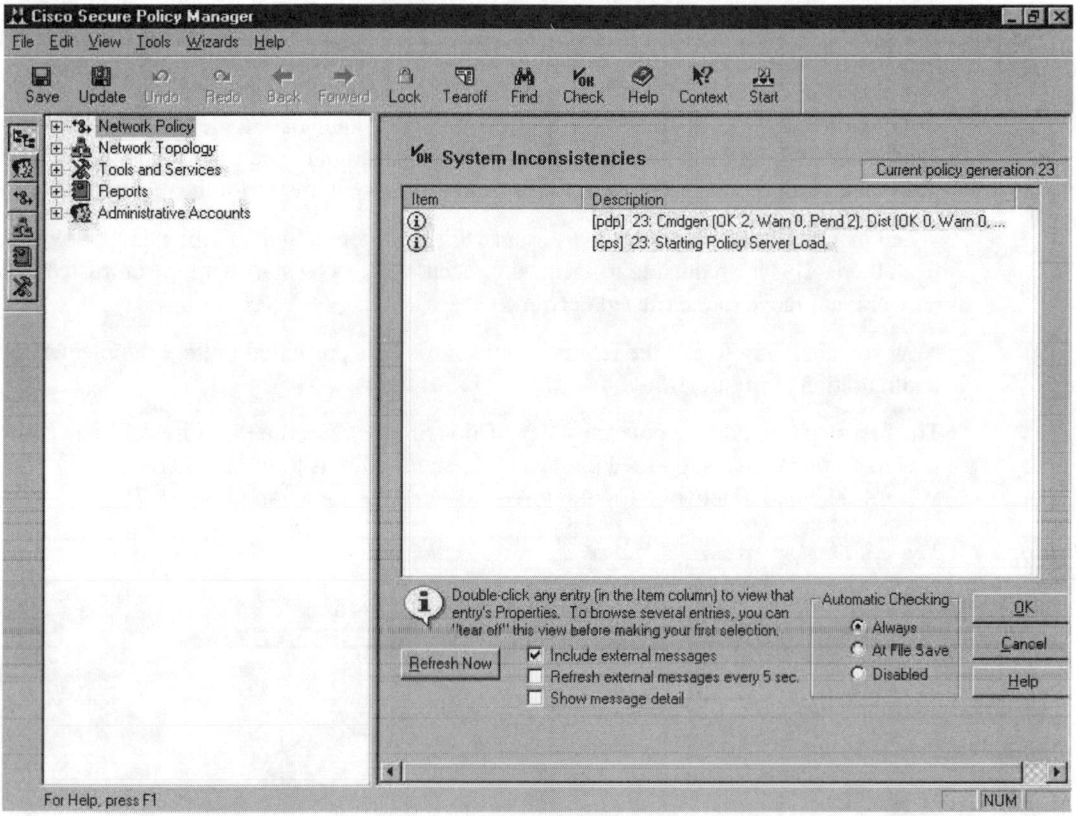

Figure 8-6   *Basic CSPM Configuration Screen*

The network objects required by the policy manager software are

- **Policy enforcement points**—All policy enforcement points, such as the managed PIX Firewalls and the Cisco Routers running the Cisco IOS Firewall, need to be defined in the network topology. CSPM will generate and deliver device-specific command sets to these policy enforcement points to implement the security policy.

- **The default gateway used by each policy enforcement point**—The policy enforcement point default gateway represents the downstream IP address to which a policy enforcement point delivers network packets for which it does not have a specific routing rule defined.

- **All hosts running CSPM components**—All hosts that are running CSPM components must be able to communicate with each other. CSPM looks after the configuration of this communication, but you must define these as objects in the network topology.

- **All networks where policy enforcement points or CSPM hosts reside**—Besides defining the policy enforcement points and CSPM hosts, you must define the networks that they reside on, if they have not already been defined.

In addition to these CSPM required network objects, you must remember to configure every network device, host, and network to which you wish to apply a security policy. In the example network topology in Figure 8-5, all clients reside on the 192.168.9.0/24 network. However, if no policy enforcement point or CSPM host resided on this network, the network would not be visible to CSPM and no hosts on the network would have access to the required basic Internet services. To enable access to hosts on this network, you would have to define either the individual hosts and the network or just the network as part of the network topology. Once this network is defined, you can apply a system policy to make it trusted for the required services.

When mapping your network, always start with the Internet and add the network objects from there. This is an outside-to-inside approach, where you start with the untrusted network and move to the trusted network.

Now you are going to add the required network objects presented in the example network configuration in Figure 8-5.

The first step is to add the outermost connection, in this case, the PIX Firewall. The easiest way to do this with a supported policy enforcement point is to use the network Topology Wizard. The initial network Topology Wizard screen is shown in Figure 8-7.

Figure 8-7   *Network Topology Wizard—Initial Screen*

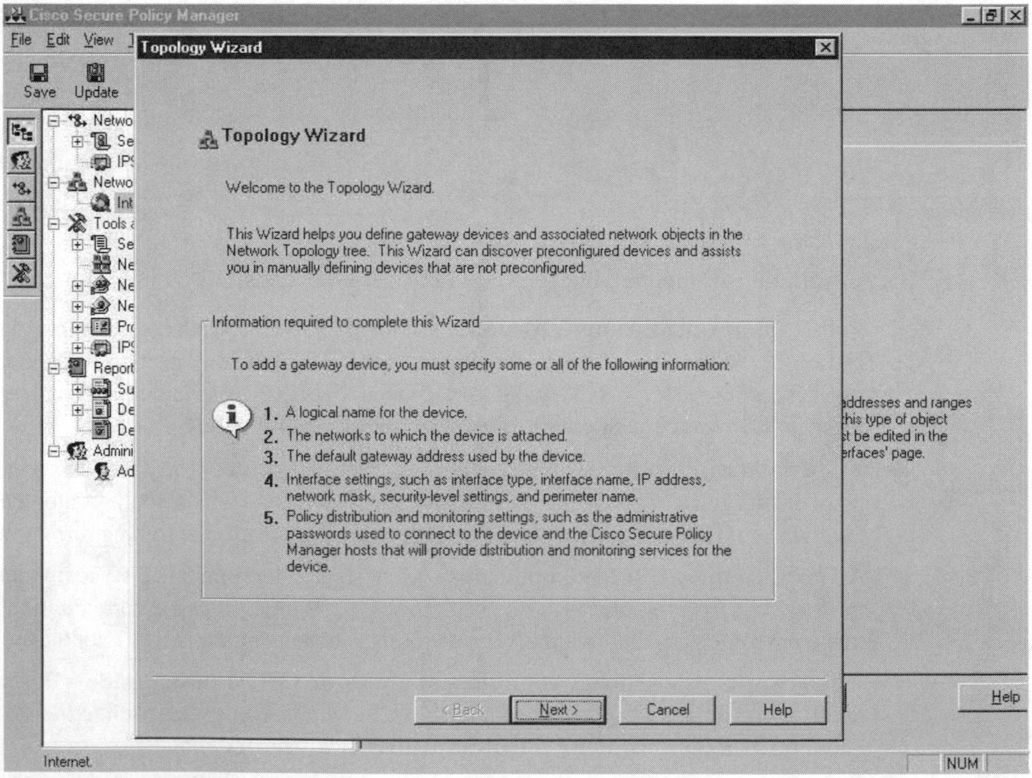

Select **Next,** and in the next screen, select the **PIX Firewall** object, as shown in Figure 8-8, and click **Next** once again to proceed to the next screen.

Figure 8-8   *Network Topology Wizard—Add A Gateway Screen*

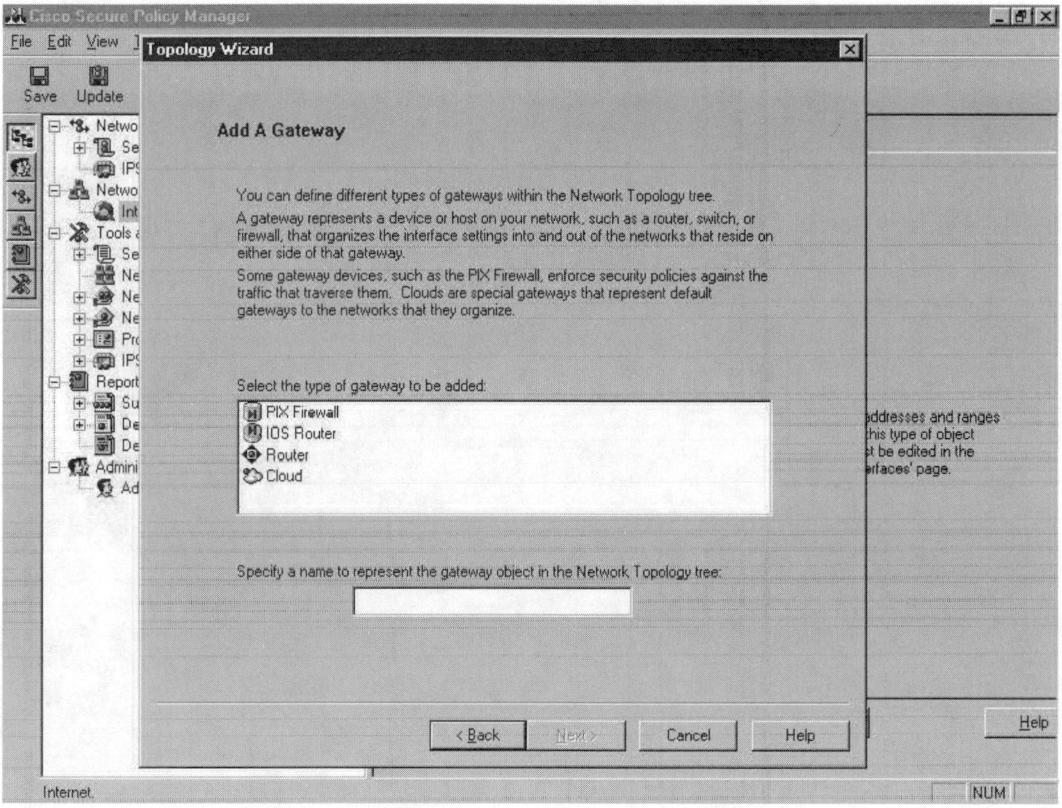

In this screen, shown in Figure 8-9, enter the default gateway address of the PIX. This is usually the direct ISP-provided connection to the Internet.

Figure 8-9 *Network Topology Wizard—Default Gateway Address Screen*

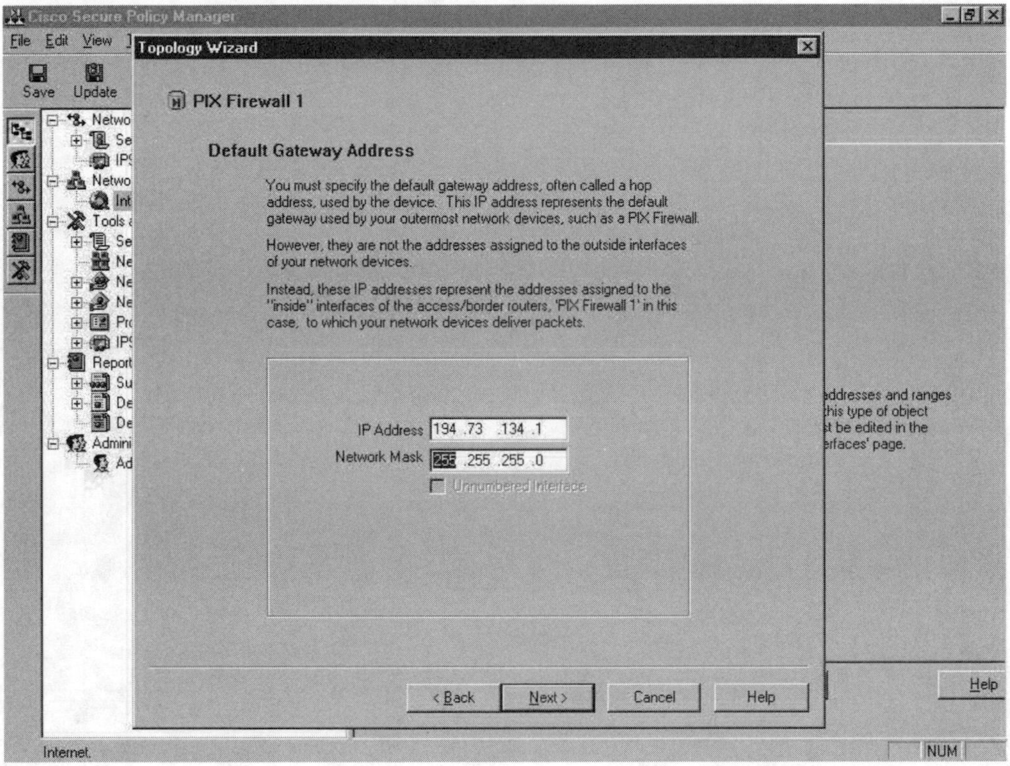

In the next screen, select to automatically discover the interfaces, as shown in Figure 8-10.

Figure 8-10 *Network Topology Wizard—Device Definition Option Screen*

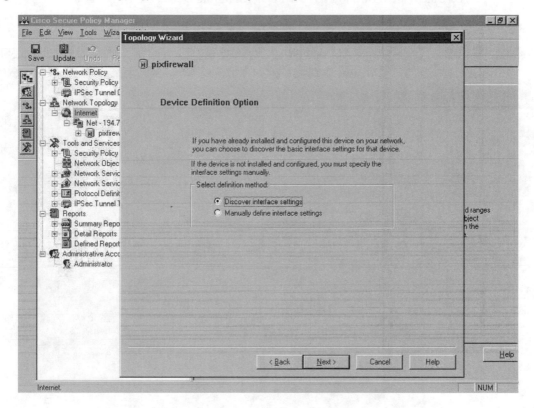

In the next screen, enter the IP address over which the CSPM host will configure the device, along with the enable password. The Policy Distribution Host should also be selected here. These steps are shown in Figure 8-11. When finished, click the **Discover** button.

Figure 8-11 *Network Topology Wizard—Device Connection and Policy Distribution Host Screen*

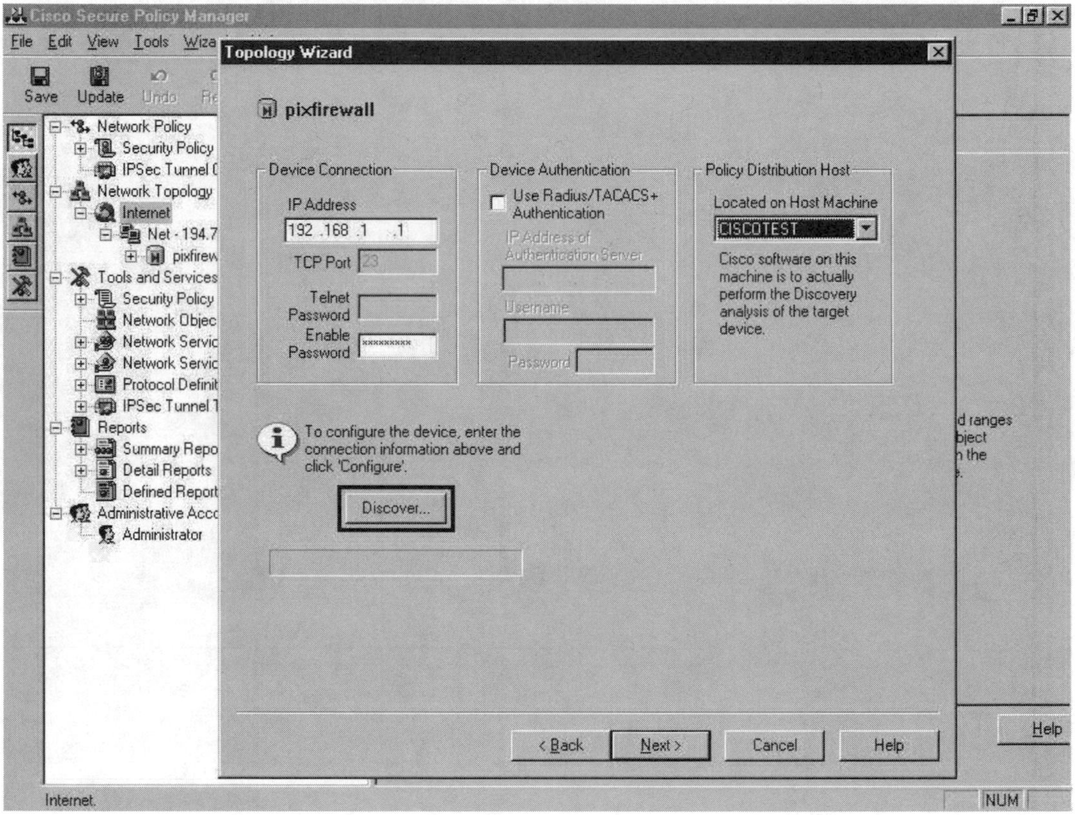

As you can see in Figure 8-12, the network Topology Wizard has identified the firewall and all of the interfaces within it.

Figure 8-12 *Network Topology Wizard—Settings Screen*

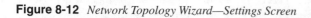

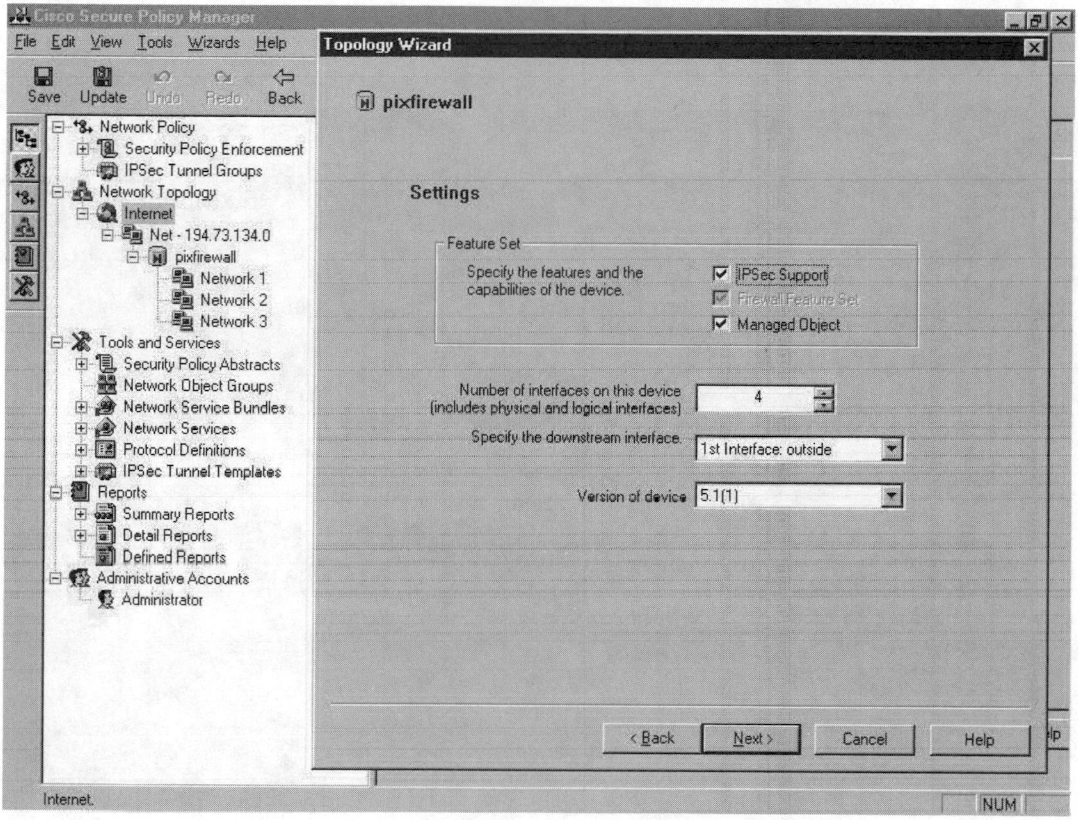

From the Topology Wizard screen shown in Figure 8-12, click **Next** until you reach the Distribution and Monitor Host Settings screen, as seen in Figure 8-13. Select the required host for both of these. Notice that the host is called CISCOTEST, but that there is a question mark by each name. You have yet to define the CSPM server as a network object.

Figure 8-13 *Network Topology Wizard—Distribution and Monitor Host Settings Screen*

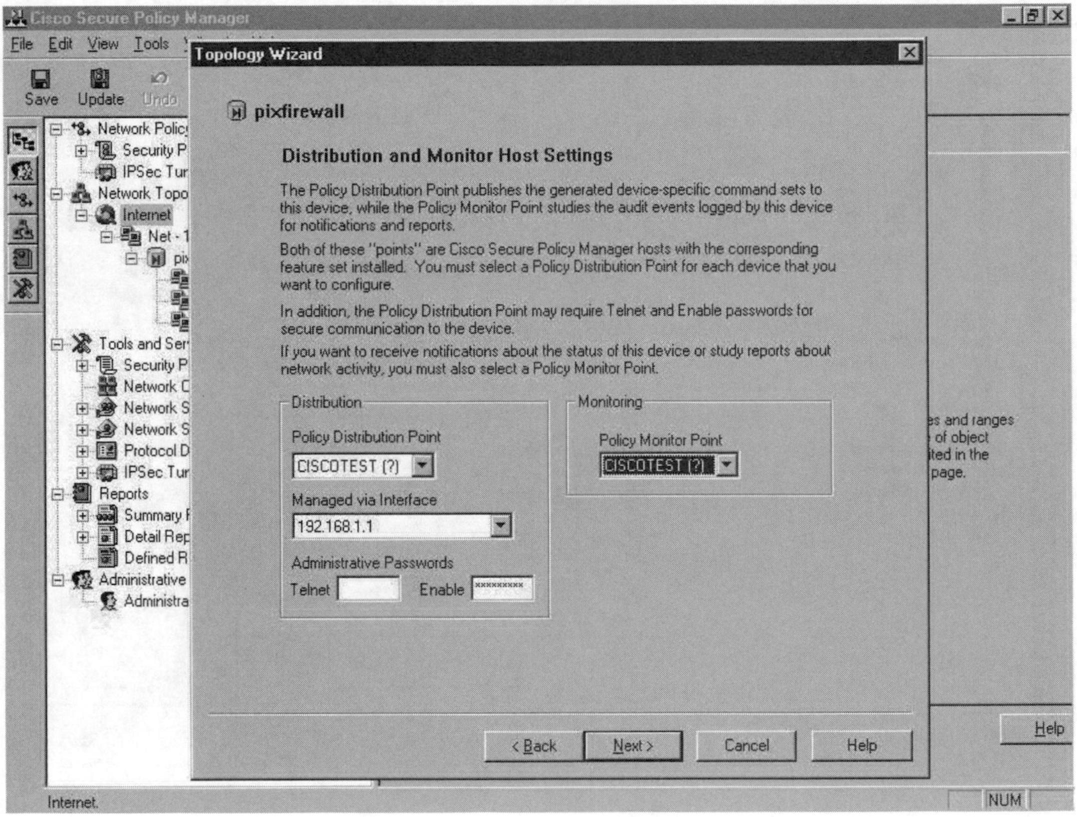

After configuration, you are ready to proceed. Figure 8-14 shows the screen that is presented. Click **Finish** to end the wizard.

Figure 8-14 *Network Topology Wizard—Final Screen*

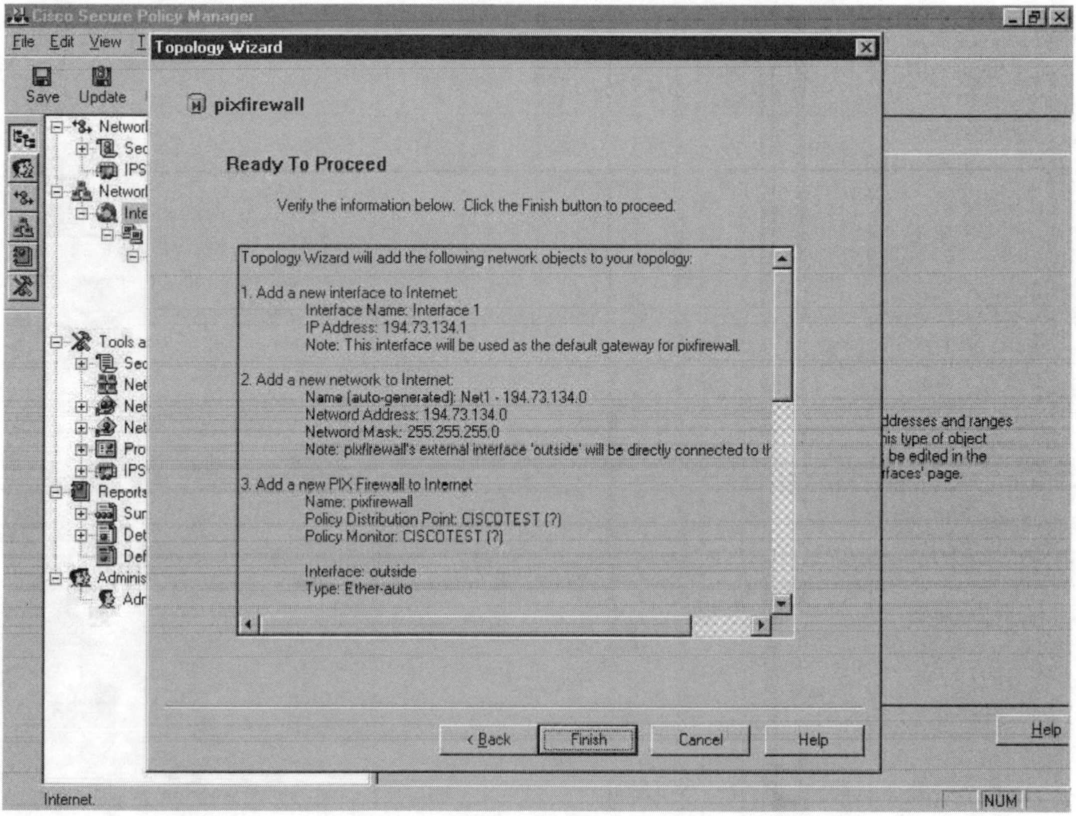

The PIX Firewall network object has been added to the left pane of the Policy Manager window, as shown in Figure 8-15.

Figure 8-15 *Policy Manager Window*

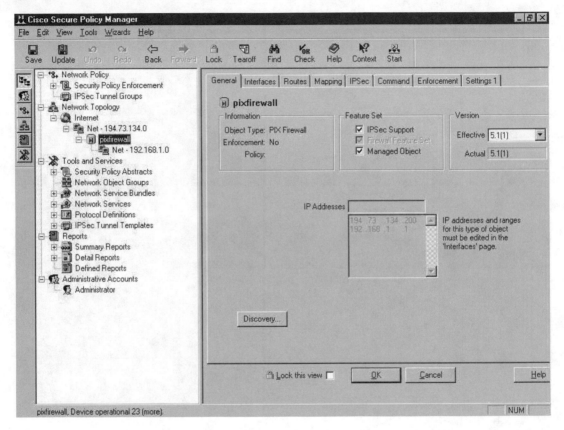

Figure 8-16 shows the **Interfaces** tab of the PIX Firewall network object. Note the correct network and IP addresses assigned to each interface. The PIX in question has four interfaces, and the two DMZ interfaces are disabled.

Figure 8-16 *PIX Firewall Interface Screen*

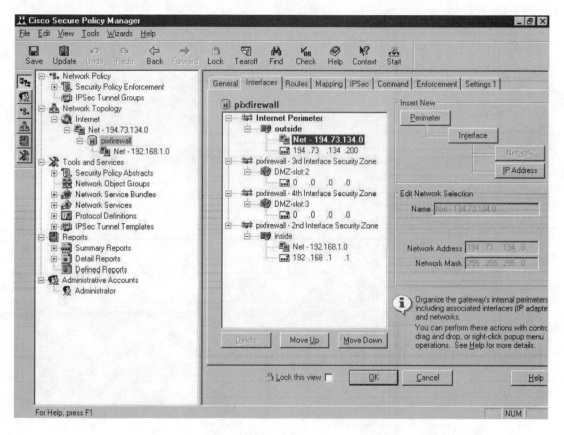

You will next have to manually configure NAT, which is configured on the **Mapping** tab of the PIX Firewall network object. Static translation is the same as the **static** command on the PIX, and address hiding is true NAT or Port Address Translation (PAT). Figure 8-17 shows the default empty **Mapping** tab screen.

Figure 8-17 *PIX Firewall Mapping Screen*

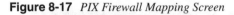

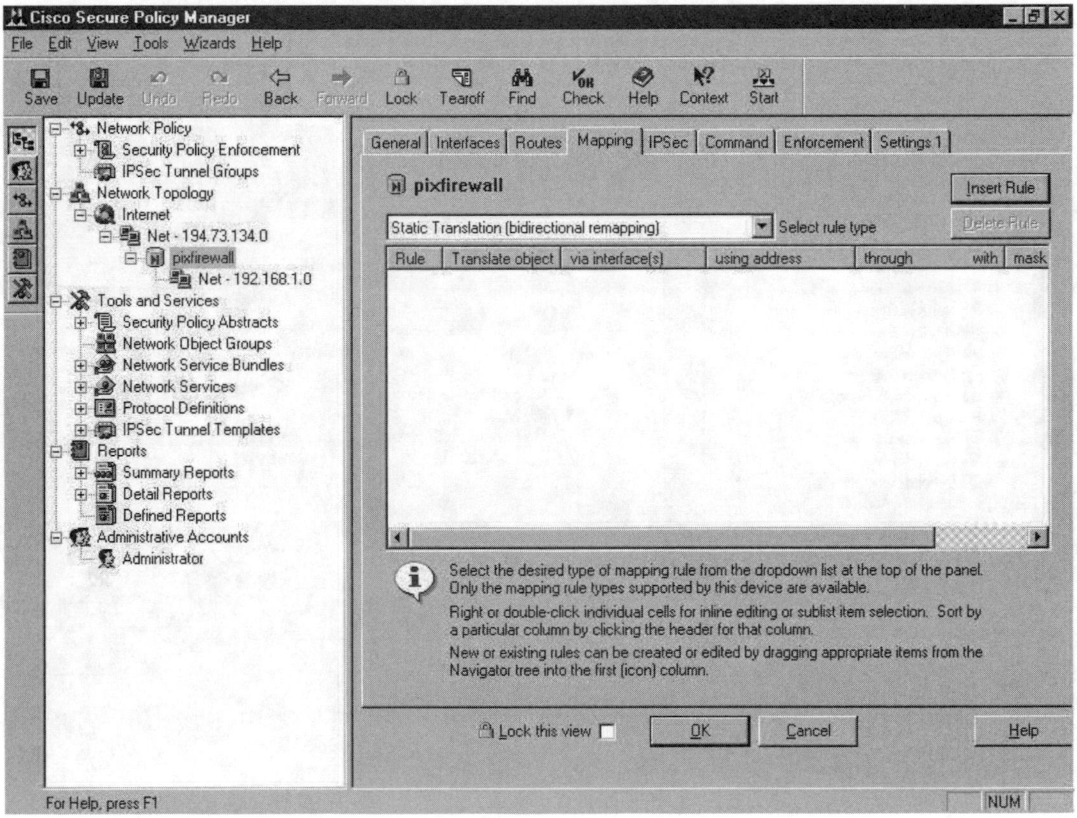

Figure 8-18 shows this screen after you add an address-hiding mapping rule. Here you are hiding the inside interface from the outside interface, using the address range of 194.73.134.205 to 194.73.134.208 with a subnet mask of 255.255.255.0.

Figure 8-18 *Completed PIX Firewall Mapping Screen*

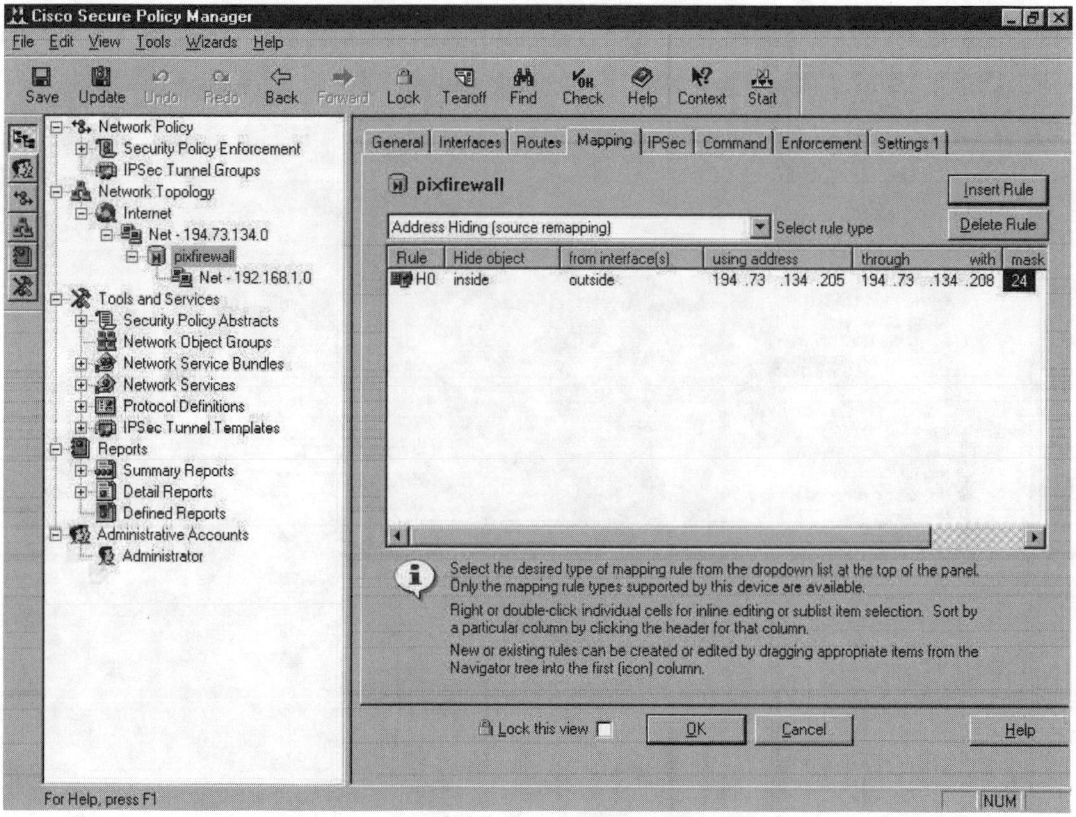

This completes the installation and initial configuration of the PIX Firewall. You are now going to enter the Cisco 2620 IOS router that is running the Cisco IOS Firewall. This device is going to be managed by CSPM; however, in this demonstration it has no real use. Configure the IOS router by using the network Topology Wizard as you did for the PIX Firewall. Figure 8-19 shows the result of adding the IOS router to the network topology.

Figure 8-19 *IOS Router as Part of the Network Topology*

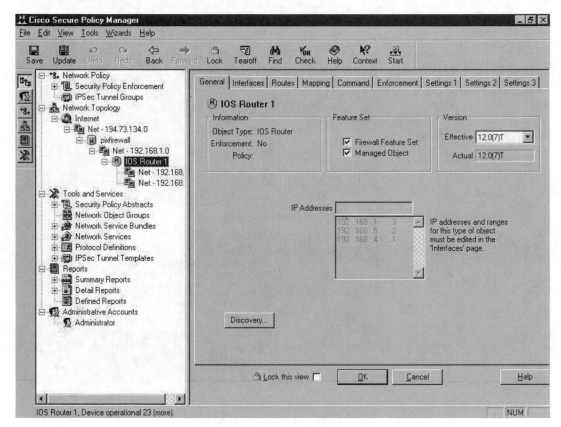

Next, add the CSPM server host to the network topology. This is pretty easy to do. Right-click the 192.168.1.0 network object and select **New** and then **Host**. Figure 8-20 shows this procedure.

Figure 8-20 *Insert the CSPM Host*

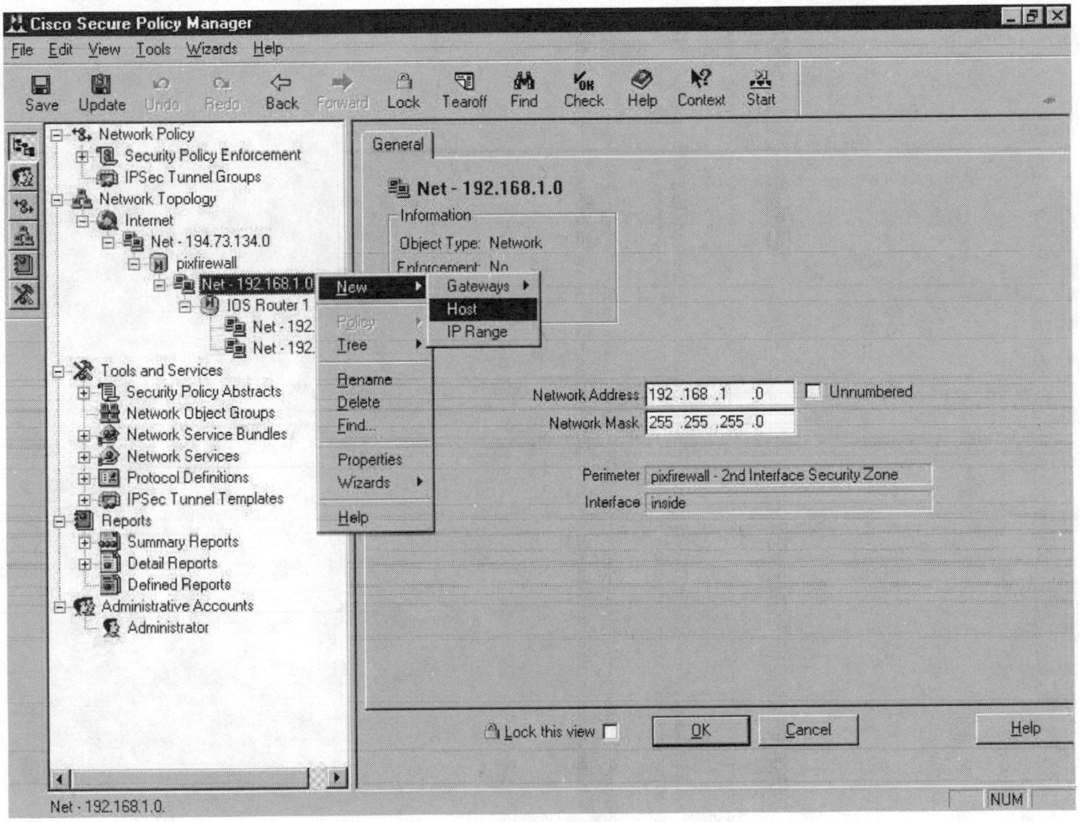

The CSPM administrator software is already aware of where it is running from, so the minute that you add the host to this network it presumes that this is the CSPM policy host. You are presented with a simple yes or no question. Clicking **Yes** will install this host as the CSPM server. This is shown in Figure 8-21.

Figure 8-21 *Configuring the CSPM Host*

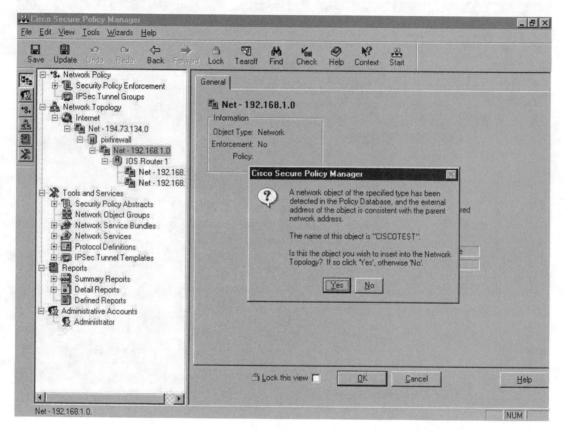

Figure 8-22 shows the CSPM server added to the network topology. The host is available in the left pane.

Figure 8-22 *Network Topology with the CSPM Host*

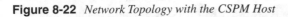

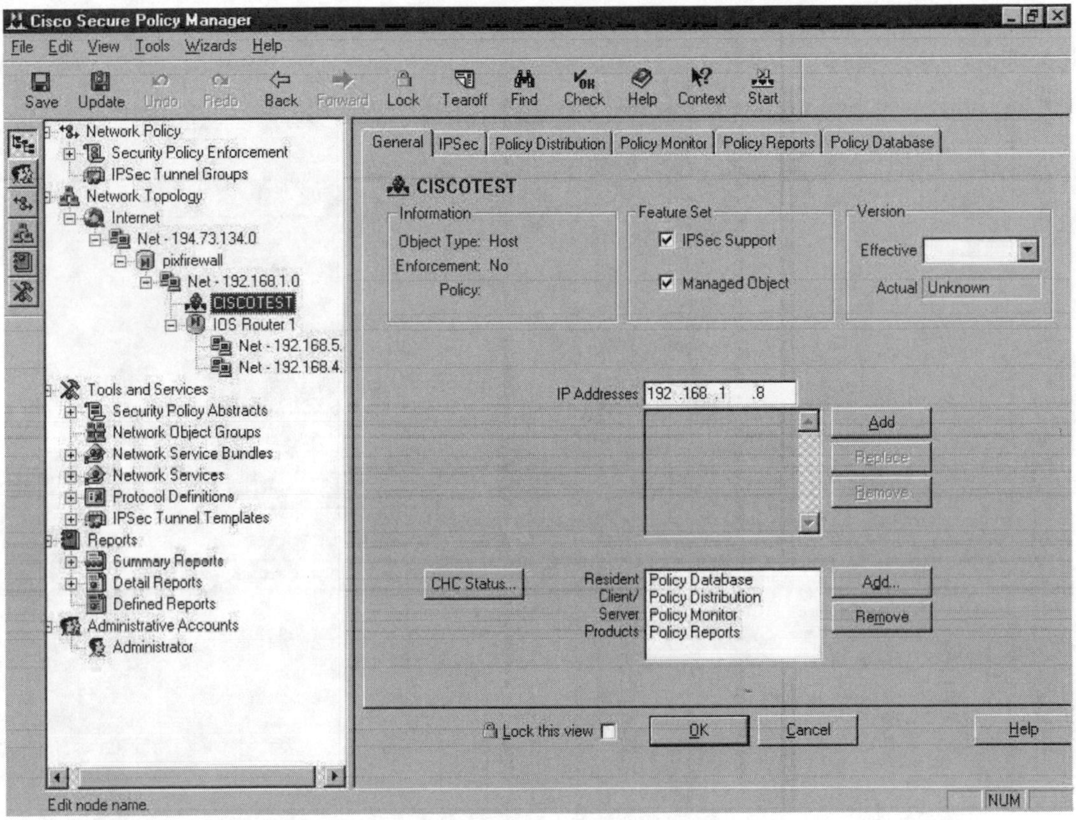

The final configuration step is to add the 2514 router and the 192.168.9.0 network. Remember, it is the 192.168.9.0 network where the clients reside, so this must be added to the network topology. This router has an interface in the 192.168.1.0 network, so right-click the 192.168.1.0 network and select **New**, **Gateway**, **Routers**, **IOS Router**. This is shown in Figure 8-23.

Figure 8-23 *Adding the 2514 IOS Router*

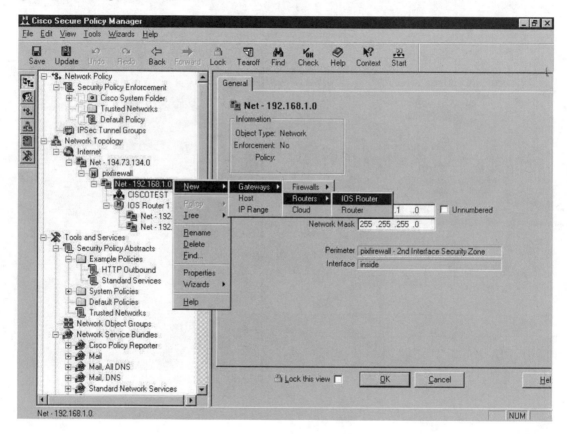

Because this is a manual installation, you are presented with blank configuration tabs, which you have to complete. Notice that there is no **Commands** tab, because this device is not managed by the CSPM. This is shown in Figure 8-24.

Figure 8-24 *IOS Router Configuration Screen*

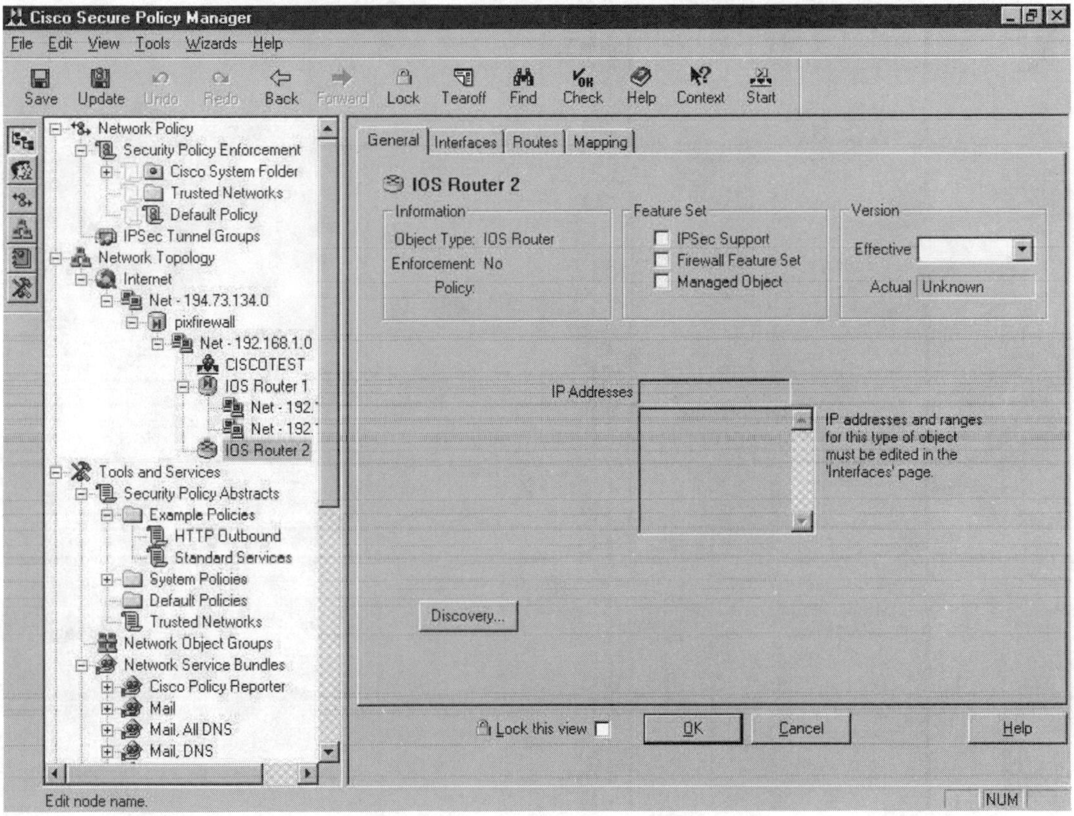

Click the **Interfaces** tab and configure the interfaces as addressed in the network topology diagram in Figure 8-5. The final result is shown in Figure 8-25.

Figure 8-25 *Completed Interface Configuration for the 2514*

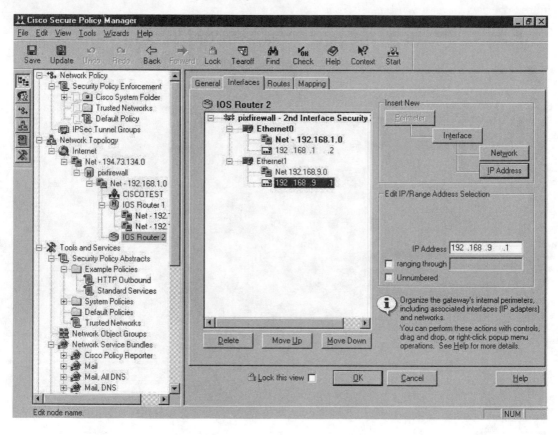

The added router and the complete network topology can be clearly seen in Figure 8-26.

Figure 8-26 *Completed Network Topology*

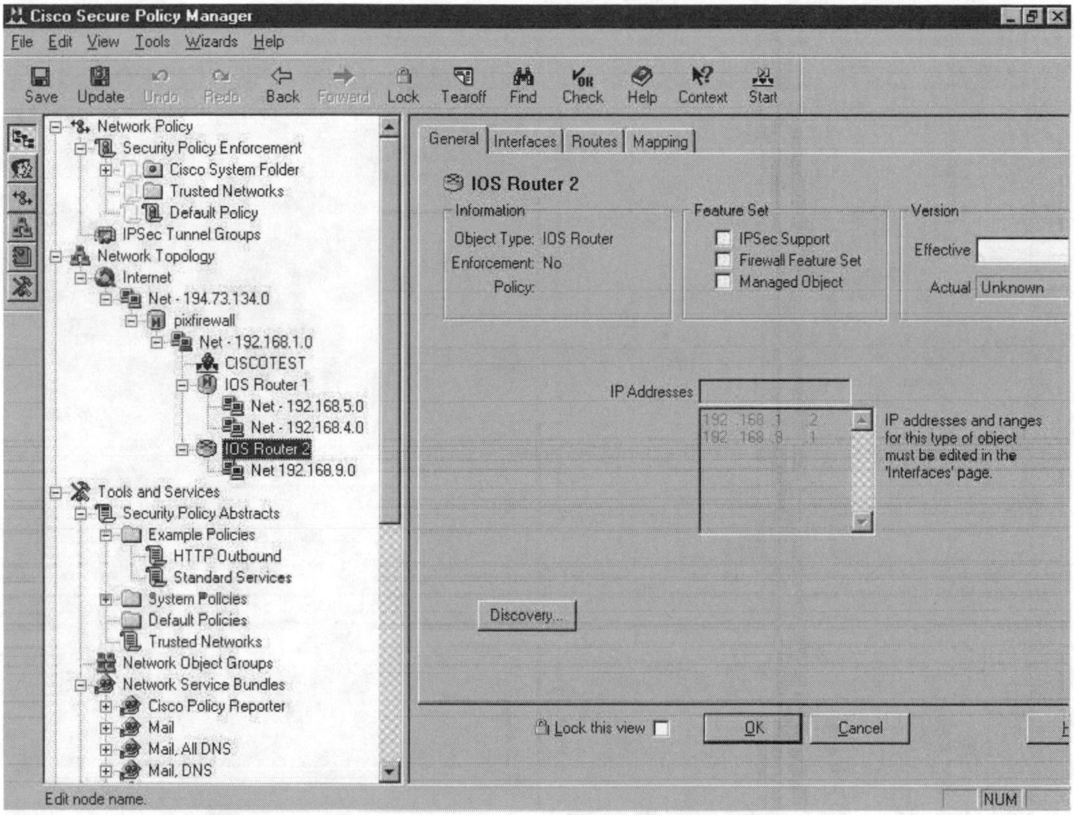

This completes the configuration of the network topology. Notice that the whole network has not been defined in the CSPM network topology. You have only defined the parts of the network that contain policy enforcement points and CSPM hosts.

The next step is to configure the security policy to enable your requirements to be implemented.

Configure the Security Policy

Once the network topology is configured, the next step is to configure the security policy. You are only concerned with the 192.168.9.0 network, so it is the only network or device for which you have to create a policy.

Start by dragging the 192.168.9.0 network object into the Security Policy Enforcement branch that is located at the top of the screen. Figure 8-27 shows this network object added to the branch.

Figure 8-27 *Security Policy Enforcement Branch*

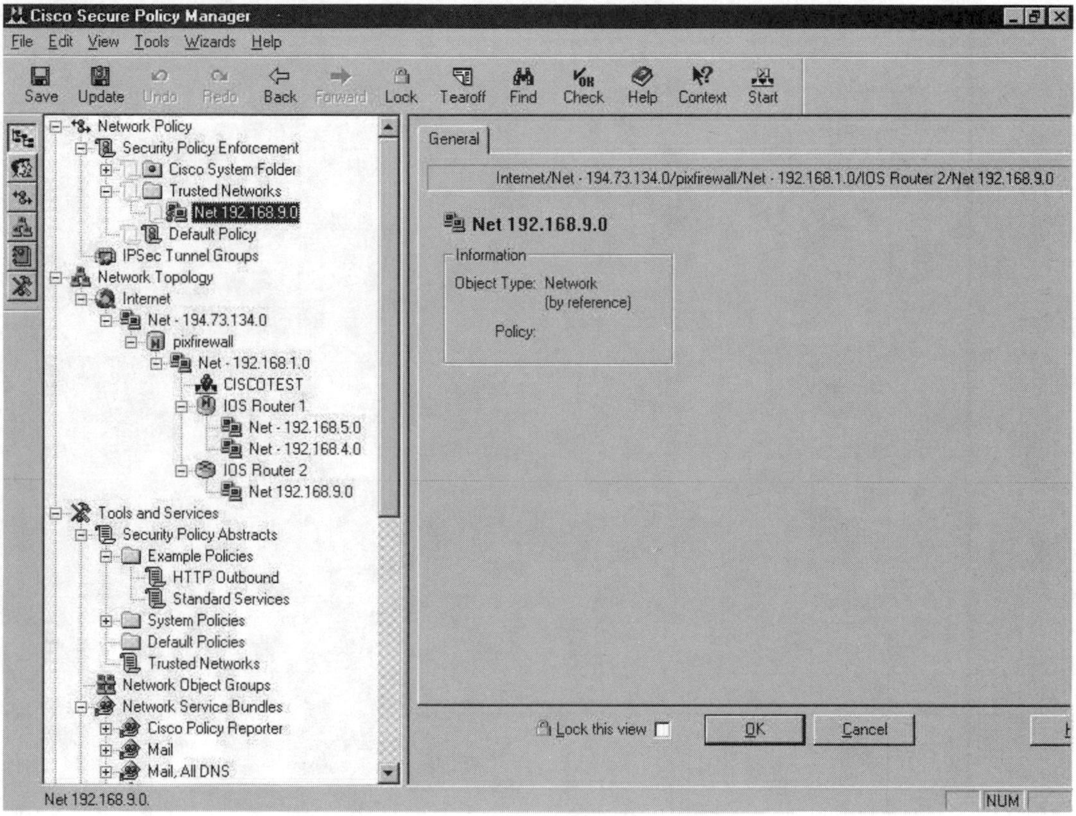

You can only assign policies to objects located within this branch. Right-click the object and select **Policy**, **New**, as shown in Figure 8-28.

Figure 8-28 *Creating a New Policy*

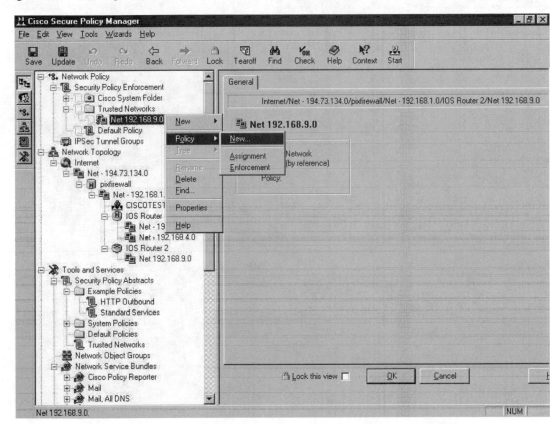

The blank policy with just the default If policy statement is displayed, as shown in Figure 8-29.

Figure 8-29 *The Default New Policy Screen*

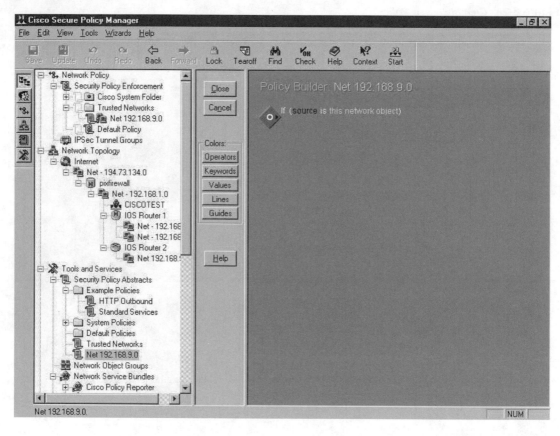

You need to build a policy that will allow the standard e-mail, Web, and DNS services to be passed to the Internet perimeter. Use the built-in policy tools to create a policy, as shown in Figure 8-30.

Figure 8-30 *Completed Policy Screen*

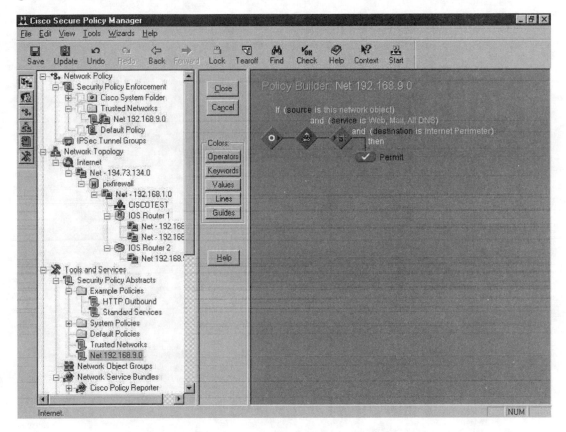

This policy will allow the 192.168.9.0 network access to the e-mail, Web, and DNS services through the Internet perimeter. This completes the creation of the system policy for the demonstration network.

Generate and Publish the Device-Specific Command Sets

After all of this configuration, you have to generate the device-specific command sets and publish them to the required managed policy enforcement points as configured in the Policy Manager software. The first step is to save and update the policy. This is shown in Figure 8-31.

Figure 8-31 *Saving and Updating the Policy*

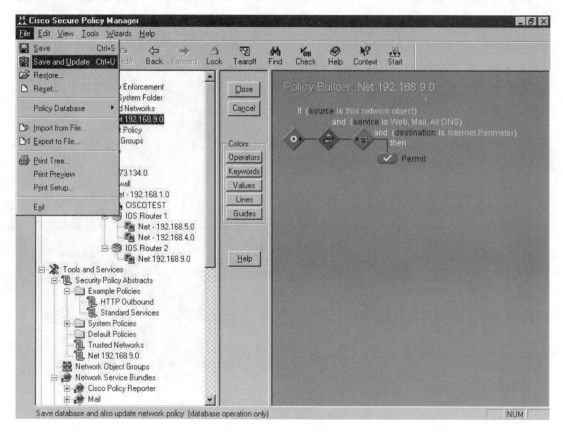

Saving and updating the policy generates the device-specific command sets that require distributing to the policy enforcement points. You can see in Figure 8-32 that the save and update operation completed successfully. If there are any inconsistencies with the distribution to the policy enforcement points, these would be displayed in Figure 8-32.

Figure 8-32 *System Inconsistencies After the Save and Update*

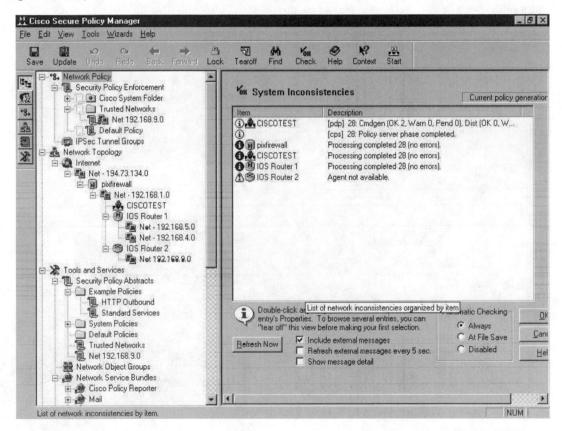

You are left with the task of deploying the device-specific command set to the appropriate devices. In this example, only the PIX Firewall command set will need updating. To do this, click the PIX Firewall object in the Network Topology section in the left pane. Select the **Command** tab, approve the command changes, and then click **Approve Now** in the bottom left corner to send the command changes to the device. Figure 8-33 shows this procedure.

Figure 8-33 *Deploying the Device-Specific Commands*

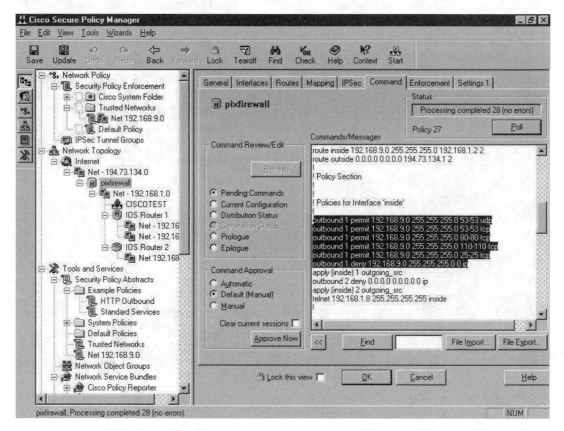

You can see the highlighted outbound commands that will allow the specified services. These were autogenerated after you created the security policy.

Summary

This chapter provided an overview of the CSPM, covering CSPM features, installation, and configuration. CSPM is a large product that is capable of much more than is described in this chapter; I could have written an entire book about CSPM. Refer to the CCO Web site for more detailed configuration and technical information about the CSPM product.

Frequently Asked Questions

Question: What devices do I have to define in the network topology?

Answer: This depends on what you are trying to achieve. As a basic rule of thumb, you need to define every device that you want to be administered by the CSPM. All policy enforcement points and CSPM hosts must be included.

Question: Can I use both CLI management and CSPM at the same time?

Answer: No. You can log in to the device with the CLI, but you must not commit any changes. CSPM will handle the configuration; any manual changes will interfere with the security policy configured and applied by the CSPM.

Glossary

AAA (authentication, authorization, accounting)—Often pronounced "triple a."

ACS (Access Control Server)—The Cisco Secure ACS is an integrated RADIUS and TACACS+ server for authentication, authorization, and accounting.

CCO (Cisco Connection Online)—The Cisco Systems home page on the Internet. Located at www.cisco.com.

CLI (command-line interface)—The UNIX-style command interface that is used to configure Cisco internetworking devices.

IDS (Intrusion Detection System)—Scans the network in real time to intercept attempted breaches of security.

ISP (Internet service provider)—A service provider that provides a connection to the public Internet.

IPSec (Internet Protocol Security)—A standards-based method of providing privacy, integrity, and authenticity to information transferred across IP networks.

NAS (network access server)—The connection point to the network for remote services, such as dial-in users over PPP.

NOS (network operating system)—The operating system of the network. This provides services to users such as file and print sharing. Common NOSs include Microsoft Windows NT and Novell NetWare.

PIX (Private Internet Exchange)—The Cisco range of leading hardware-based firewalls.

RADIUS (Remote Access Dial-In User Service)—A protocol used to authenticate users on a network.

TACACS+ (Terminal Access Controller Access Control System Plus)—A protocol used to authenticate users on a network. Also provides authorization and accounting facilities.

VPN (Virtual Private Network)—A secure connection over an unsecured medium. The connection is secured by the use of tunneling protocols and encryption.

URLs

Cisco Connection Online:

www.cisco.com

CSPM:

www.cisco.com/warp/public/cc/pd/sqsw/sqppmn/index.shtml

33This chapter contains the following sections:

- Cisco Secure Access Control Server (ACS) Features
- Overview of Authentication, Authorization, and Accounting (AAA)
- RADIUS and TACACS+
- Cisco Secure ACS Installation
- Cisco Secure ACS Configuration
- Network Access Server Configuration
- Configuration Example
- Summary
- Frequently Asked Questions
- Glossary
- Bibliography
- URLs

CHAPTER 9

Cisco Secure Access Control Server (ACS)

This chapter covers the Cisco Secure Access Control Server (ACS). As networks and network security have evolved, so too have the methods of controlling access to these networks and their associated resources. Ten years ago, it was deemed suitable to use a static username and password pair to gain access to resources on the corporate network. As time progressed, these methods became stronger from a security standpoint with the introduction of aging passwords and one-time passwords. Eventually, security professionals initiated the use of token cards and token servers to issue one-time passwords.

From an Internet security viewpoint, you can consider two distinct areas of concern:

* Access to the network by dial-up or other remote services
* Access to the internetworking devices at the perimeter or on the internal network

To manage these concerns, Cisco released the Cisco Secure Server, which was later renamed the Cisco Secure Access Control Server (ACS). This is a complete access control server that supports the industry-standard Remote Access Dial-In User Service (RADIUS) protocol in addition to the Cisco proprietary Terminal Access Controller Access Control System Plus (TACACS+) protocol.

Cisco Secure ACS Features

Cisco Secure ACS supports the industry-standard RADIUS protocol and the Cisco proprietary TACACS, XTACACS, and TACACS+ protocols.

Cisco Secure ACS helps to centralize access control and accounting for dial-in access servers and firewalls in addition to management of access to routers and switches. With Cisco Secure ACS, service providers can quickly administer accounts and globally change levels of service offerings for entire groups of users.

Cisco Secure ACS supports Cisco network access servers (NASs) such as the Cisco 2509, 2511, 3620, 3640, AS5200, and AS5300, the Cisco PIX Firewall, and any third-party device that can be configured with the TACACS+ or the RADIUS protocol. Cisco Secure ACS uses the TACACS+ or RADIUS protocols to provide authentication, authorization, and accounting (AAA) services to ensure a secure environment.

Cisco Secure ACS can authenticate users against any of the following user databases:

- Windows NT (only in the NT version)
- UNIX Databases (only in the UNIX version)
- Cisco Secure ACS
- Token-card servers, including:
  — AXENT
  — CRYPTOCard
  — SafeWord
  — RSA
- Novell Directory Services (NDS)
- Microsoft Commercial Internet System Lightweight Directory Access Protocol (MCIS LDAP)
- Microsoft Open DataBase Connectivity (ODBC)

The NAS directs all dial-in user access requests to Cisco Secure ACS for authentication and authorization of privileges. Using either the RADIUS or TACACS+ protocol, the NAS sends authentication requests to Cisco Secure ACS, which verifies the username and password. Cisco Secure ACS then returns a success or failure response to the NAS, which permits or denies user access. When the user has been authenticated, Cisco Secure ACS sends a set of authorization attributes to the NAS, and the accounting functions take effect.

Currently, two versions of Cisco Secure ACS are available. They are differentiated by platform, and there are no major differences in how they operate. The platforms available are Windows NT 4.0/2000 and Solaris. The tight integration of Cisco Secure ACS with the Windows NT operating system enables companies to leverage the working knowledge and investment already made in building a Windows NT network. Existing Windows NT domain accounts can be used to provide a single login to both the network resources and the Windows NT domain.

Overview of Authentication, Authorization, and Accounting (AAA)

You might be familiar with the term AAA (pronounced "triple a"). This is a security framework that stands for authentication, authorization, and accounting.

Basically, authentication is the actual permission to use the network, authorization is what you can do on the network, and accounting is what you did and how you did it. You have to be authenticated to be authorized or accounted.

Authentication

Authentication is the process of identification by the user to the ACS server. This can be carried out by a number of methods; the most frequently used is a username and password. The ACS server provides a means of authentication against various data sources, such as an Open DataBase Connectivity (ODBC) data source or the Windows NT domain. This way, you can authenticate against the existing Windows NT domain account to enforce a single login policy. Encryption can be also enabled depending on the authentication protocol and type, to further secure the login process.

You have to be authenticated by the ACS before you can perform any authorization or accounting function.

One good use of authentication is to provide a single login to all internetworking devices on the network. By enabling AAA on the Cisco devices, you can force your network administrative staff to use a single login for every device they manage. This eases the administrative burden of creating local accounts and synchronizing passwords across these devices. When a new device is installed, you have only to enable AAA authentication, and all existing users will be able to access the device right away.

Another point to consider is that local usernames and passwords are by default stored in clear-text form in the device configuration. Anybody snooping over your shoulder or obtaining configuration dumps either from paper or from direct access to the TFTP server will quickly be able to learn the usernames and passwords on the device. If these passwords are the same on other devices, you have an instantly recognizable problem. You can encrypt the local usernames and passwords by using the **service password-encryption** command. However, there are numerous applications that can easily crack these passwords, as the algorithm used is not very strong.

By implementing an AAA authentication service with the Cisco Secure ACS, you can ensure data integrity and security through advanced authentication methods and data encryption.

Combine this with the accounting features, and you have a very robust authentication method for internetworking devices.

Authorization

Once you have successfully authenticated against the selected ACS data source, you can be authorized for specific network resources.

Authorization is basically what a user can and cannot do on the network once he or she is authenticated.

Authorization works by using a created set of attributes that describe what the user can and cannot do on the network. These attributes are compared to the information contained within the AAA database on the Cisco Secure ACS server, and a determination of the user's actual restrictions is made and delivered to the local network access server where the user is connected. These attributes are normally called attribute-value (AV) pairs.

Accounting

Accounting is a method of collecting and reporting usage data so that it can be employed for purposes such as auditing or billing. Data that can be collected might include the start and stop times of connection, executed commands, number of packets, and number of bytes.

This service, once configured, reports usage statistics back to the ACS server. These statistics can be extracted to create detailed reports about the usage of the network.

One excellent and widely deployed use of accounting is in combination with AAA authentication for managing access to internetworking devices for network administrative staff. You have already seen how AAA authentication helps to centralize the account administration and improve security for staff who must log on to the command-line interface (CLI) of Cisco internetworking devices.

Accounting provides extra leverage and accountability on top of the authentication. Once authenticated, the Cisco Secure ACS server keeps a detailed log of exactly what the authenticated user is doing on the device. This includes all EXEC and configuration commands issued by the user. The log contains numerous data fields, including the username, the date and time, and the actual command that was entered by the user.

An example of the accounting log can be seen in Figure 9-1.

Figure 9-1   *Example of an Accounting ACS Report*

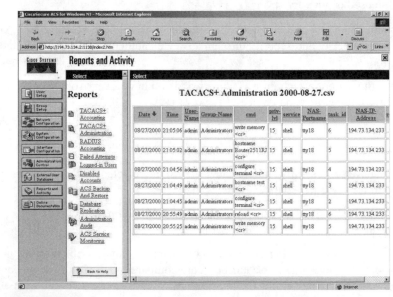

RADIUS and TACACS+

The Cisco Secure ACS supports two remote access protocols, the RADIUS protocol and the TACACS+ protocol. TACACS has three variations, all of which are supported by Cisco IOS:

- **TACACS**—TACACS is the original protocol that Cisco developed in response to RADIUS. It is incompatible with TACACS+ and has a lot of its own commands that are supported on Cisco IOS. It provides password checking, authentication, and basic accounting functions.

- **Extended TACACS (XTACACS)**—XTACACS is an extension to the original TACACS protocol. This adds functionality to the TACACS protocol by introducing features such as more complex authentication and accounting methods.

- **TACACS+**—TACACS+ is the most recent of the TACACS protocols. This protocol is not compatible with TACACS or XTACACS. It provides full AAA features through the Cisco IOS AAA commands and the use of a TACACS+ server, such as the Cisco Secure ACS.

All three of the above TACACS versions are supported by Cisco IOS, although Cisco Secure ACS only supports TACACS+.

RADIUS

The RADIUS protocol was developed by Livingston Enterprises and operates as a protocol to offer authentication and accounting services. Several large access server vendors have implemented RADIUS, and it has gained support among a wide customer base, including Internet service providers (ISPs). RADIUS is considered to be a standard and open-source protocol.

RADIUS is currently made up of the authentication service and the accounting service. Each of these two are documented separately and hold separate RFCs. The authentication service is explained in RFC 2058, and the accounting service is explained in RFC 2059.

RADIUS operates under the client/server model where a network access server operates as the RADIUS client and a centralized software-based server operates as the RADIUS server. The RADIUS client sends authentication requests to the RADIUS server. The RADIUS server acts upon this request to forward a reply to the RADIUS client. The RADIUS client then uses this reply to grant or deny access to the requesting host.

The RADIUS client can be any network access server that supports the RADIUS protocol. Cisco IOS from release 11.2 also supports RADIUS commands as part of its AAA model. This means that any Cisco router with IOS 11.2 or later can be used to authenticate inbound or outbound connections through RADIUS.

The RADIUS server component is a software application that is based around the RFC 2058 and RFC 2059 standards. Various vendors have released RADIUS servers, including Livingston and Merit. As previously discussed, Cisco Systems released the Cisco Secure ACS to act as a RADIUS server and to furnish the requests from RADIUS clients. The RADIUS server is usually a dedicated workstation or server with the required software installed.

RADIUS communicates using the User Datagram Protocol (UDP) as its transport protocol. All retransmissions and timeouts are handled by the RADIUS software on the client and server to provide the service not offered by the connectionless transport layer protocol.

TACACS+

The TACACS+ is the latest revision of the TACACS access control protocol. The first release of TACACS was improved on by Cisco Systems and named Extended TACACS (XTACACS). TACACS+ was then released and is the current version that is supported both by Cisco IOS and the Cisco Secure ACS. TACACS+ is a Cisco proprietary protocol and therefore is not classified as an industry standard. Other vendors' equipment generally will not support TACACS+; however, various companies are releasing TACACS+ server software to compete with the Cisco Secure ACS.

TACACS+ consists of three main services: the authentication service, the authorization service, and the accounting service. Each of these services is implemented independently of one another. This gives you the flexibility to combine other protocols with TACACS+.

TACACS+ operates under the client/server model where a network access server operates as the TACACS+ client and a centralized software-based server operates as the TACACS+ server. The TACACS+ client sends authentication requests to the TACACS+ server. The TACACS+ server acts upon this request to forward a reply to the TACACS+ client. The TACACS+ client then uses this reply to grant or deny access to the requesting host.

The TACACS+ client can be any network access server that supports the TACACS+ protocol. Cisco IOS from release 11.1 also supports TACACS+ commands as part of its AAA model. This means that any Cisco router with IOS 11.1 or later can be used to authenticate inbound or outbound connections through TACACS+.

The TACACS+ server component is a software application. Cisco Systems released the Cisco Secure ACS to act as a TACACS+ server and to furnish the requests from TACACS+ clients. The TACACS+ server is usually a dedicated workstation or server with the required software installed.

TACACS+ communicates using the Transmission Control Protocol (TCP) as its transport protocol. This connection-oriented protocol has the advantage of built-in error checking and retransmission functionality. The whole of the TCP packet, apart from the TACACS+ header, is encrypted to provide security on the local segment from eavesdropping.

Differences Between RADIUS and TACACS+

There are quite a few distinct differences between RADIUS and TACACS+. These differences can be vital in deciding which protocol to implement.

The main differences are shown in Table 9-1.

Table 9-1   *Differences Between RADIUS and TACACS+*

RADIUS	TACACS+
Uses UDP as the transport protocol	Uses TCP as the transport protocol
Encrypts only the password	Encrypts the entire body of the packet
Combines authentication and authorization	Uses the AAA architecture that separates authentication, authorization, and, accounting
RFC-based industry standard	Cisco proprietary
No support for ARA, NetBIOS, NASI, or X.25 connections	Multiprotocol support
No authorization	Authorization is supported as part of the AAA architecture
Does not allow the control of commands that can be executed at the router CLI	Allows control of commands that can be executed at the router CLI by either user or group

RADIUS uses UDP as its transport layer protocol, whereas TACACS+ uses TCP. There are several advantages of TCP over UDP but the main one is that TCP is considered a connection-oriented protocol and UDP is considered a connectionless-oriented protocol. This means that TCP has built-in mechanisms to protect against communication errors, and the protocol itself ensures delivery. With UDP, software at a higher layer has to be responsible for the safe delivery of the packets, which can add overhead to the integrity of the application.

When a user attempts authorization against a RADIUS client, the RADIUS client sends an access-request packet to the RADIUS server. This packet contains the user's login credentials such as the username and password pair. RADIUS only encrypts the password part of this packet and leaves the rest in clear text. This allows the sniffing of the username and could lead to a dictionary brute-force attack. TACACS+ encrypts the entire access-request packet and only leaves the TACACS header unencrypted for debugging purposes.

RADIUS combines both authentication and authorization services within the access-accept packet. With TACACS+, you can separate the authentication and authorization services because each of the AAA services is independent. For example, you could authenticate using another protocol such as Kerberos and still use TACACS+ for authorization. This cannot be done using only RADIUS services.

TACACS+ supports a wide range of access protocols. RADIUS does not support the following protocols that TACACS+ does support:

- AppleTalk Remote Access (ARA) Protocol
- NetBIOS Frame Protocol Control Protocol
- Novell Asynchronous Services Interface (NASI)
- X.25 Pad Connection

RADIUS does not allow you to control command access to the Cisco router CLI. With TACACS+, you can enable controls on a user or group level to specify exactly what commands a user or group can enter on a Cisco router with a supporting IOS version installed. This feature can be very useful for controlling the management of the internetworking devices within your organization. This can also be combined with AAA accounting to provide a robust, scalable solution to device management.

Cisco Secure ACS Installation

Now that you have seen a brief overview of the Cisco Secure ACS, the role it serves in the internetwork, and the two main authentication protocols, RADIUS and TACACS+, it is time to proceed on to the installation requirements for the actual Cisco Secure ACS server software.

Two versions of the Cisco Secure ACS are in operation: Cisco Secure ACS for Windows NT and Cisco Secure ACS for UNIX. This section covers the installation requirements for both of these versions.

Windows NT and Windows 2000 Installation

The main advantage of the Windows NT version of Cisco Secure ACS is the tight integration with the Windows NT domain database. This allows the users to log on using their existing Windows NT domain account to promote a single network login. The installation must be carried out on a Windows NT server (not a workstation), and the current supported version is version 4.0. For system requirements and service packs, see the release notes at:

www.cisco.com/univercd/cc/td/doc/product/access/acs_soft/csacs4nt/csnt26/index.htm

Windows NT System Requirements

Cisco Secure ACS is supported on Microsoft Windows NT 4.0 Server. To install Cisco Secure ACS on the Windows NT platform, the NT server must meet the following minimum requirements:

- Pentium processor running at 200 MHz or better

- Microsoft Windows NT Server 4.0 operating system, English language version
- 64 MB of RAM required, 128 MB recommended
- At least 150 MB of free disk space
- Minimum of 256 colors at resolution of 800 by 600 lines
- To have Cisco Secure ACS refer to the Grant Dial-in Permission to User feature, make sure this option is checked in the Windows NT User Manager for the applicable user accounts
- Make sure your NAS is running Cisco IOS Release 11.1 or higher (release 11.2 or higher for RADIUS) or you are using a third-party device that can be configured with TACACS+ or RADIUS
- Make sure dial-up clients can successfully dial in to your NAS
- Make sure the Windows NT server can ping the NAS
- One of the following browsers must be installed on the Windows NT server:
  - Microsoft Internet Explorer 3.02 or higher
  - Netscape Navigator 3.x or Communicator 4.x or higher
  - Java and JavaScript support must be enabled

Once these criteria have been met, you can install the Cisco Secure ACS software.

Windows NT Installation Process

Cisco Secure ACS is provided on a CD-ROM, which has to be installed to your server's hard disk for the application to function. Cisco Secure ACS will not operate from the CD drive.

This chapter does not examine the full installation process. This is fully documented on Cisco Connection Online at www.cisco.com/go/ciscosecure and also in the documentation provided with the Cisco Secure ACS product.

UNIX Installation

The UNIX version of Cisco Secure ACS is a robust application that provides AAA services against industry-standard databases such as SQL and Oracle. The UNIX version does not support authentication against a Windows NT domain.

UNIX System Requirements

The main requirement of the UNIX version is that it must run on Solaris.

The Cisco Secure ACS (and its optional backup server) requires the following hardware and software:

- UltraSPARC or compatible workstation
  - To support Cisco Secure ACS without the licensed Distributed Session Manager option:

    Ultra 1 with a processor speed of 167 MHz or faster; minimum 200 MHz if the Oracle or Sybase RDBMS is installed on the same system
  - To support Cisco Secure ACS with the licensed Distributed Session Manager option:

    Ultra 1 or faster; Ultra 10 or faster if the Oracle or Sybase RDBMS is installed on the same system
- Minimum 256 MB of swap space

  Minimum 512 MB of swap space if the Oracle or Sybase RDBMS is installed on the same system
- 128 MB of RAM

  256 MB of RAM if the Oracle or Sybase RDBMS is installed on the same system
- Minimum 256 MB of free disk space (if you are using the supplied SQLAnywhere database)

  Minimum 2 GB disk space if the Oracle or Sybase RDBMS is installed on the same system
- CD-ROM drive
- Solaris 2.6, or Solaris 2.5.1 with patches; more information on Solaris 2.5.1 with patches can be found on CCO at the following URL:

  www.cisco.com/univercd/cc/td/doc/product/access/acs_soft/cs_unx/instl23.htm#26679

UNIX Installation Process

Cisco Secure ACS is provided on a CD-ROM, which has to be installed to your server's hard disk for the application to function. Cisco Secure ACS will not operate from the CD drive.

This chapter does not examine the full installation process. This is fully documented on Cisco Connection Online at www.cisco.com/go/ciscosecure and also in the documentation provided with the Cisco Secure ACS product.

Cisco Secure ACS Configuration

This section covers the configuration of Cisco Secure ACS, including information on the client configuration and the server configuration. In this section, the client is a Cisco router running IOS 12 and supporting both RADIUS and TACACS+. The server is a Windows NT server that is authenticated against the Windows NT domain and also a remote ODBC data source. The section shows the configuration of RADIUS and TACACS+ for authentication and accounting both for EXEC and network connections.

This section starts by looking at the configuration options for the Cisco Secure ACS server. Nothing can be demonstrated with the ACS client until the ACS server is fully functional. Configuring an ACS client for authentication against a server that is not live can actually lock you out of the service. If you use this service to authenticate yourself for logging in to the router, you will not be able to log in. This section includes techniques to ensure that you can log in to the router at all times, even if the ACS server is offline for whatever reason.

As soon as you have successfully installed Cisco Secure ACS, you are ready to configure it.

Web-Based Configuration and the ACS Admin Site

Cisco Secure ACS is configured through a web-based application that is called *ACS Admin*. When you install Cisco Secure ACS, you also install a complete web server to which the ACS Admin site is bound. This web server only operates on port 2002, and it runs as a Windows NT service on the Windows NT version and as an application on the UNIX version. This service is called CSAdmin and can be stopped and started like any other Windows NT service.

An icon is created on the desktop and also on the Start menu for ACS Admin. Double-clicking this icon launches the ACS Admin web interface. If you are running the ACS Admin application from another machine, you have to enter the IP address of the machine followed by the port 2002. For example, if the ACS server was installed on 194.73.134.2, the URL would be http://194.73.134.2:2002. The colon indicates that the port number will follow. This connects to 194.73.134.2 on port 2002. Port 2002 is serviced by CSAdmin, therefore, the ACS Admin application is executed.

Figure 9-2 shows the ACS Admin configuration screen that you get when you log in.

Figure 9-2 *Cisco Secure ACS Admin Application*

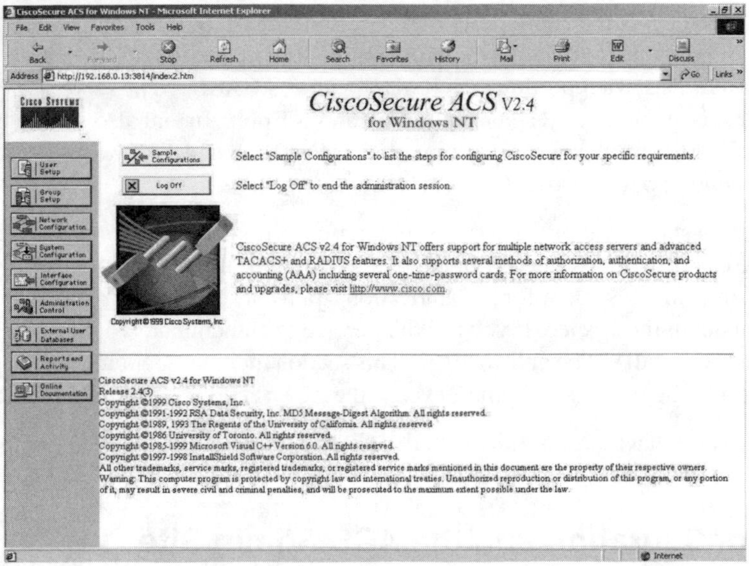

From here, you can see the main configuration options. These are represented as buttons down the left side of the screen.

These configuration options include:

- User Setup
- Group Setup
- Network Configuration
- System Configuration
- Interface Configuration
- Administration Control
- External User Databases
- Reports and Activity
- Online Documentation

Sample configurations also can be seen from here. The sample configurations give you numerous scenarios and the required configuration for both the ACS Server and ACS client.

The following sections look at each of the configuration options listed.

User and Group Setup

The User and Group Setup configuration options can both be reached from the main ACS Admin page.

The User Setup configuration option displays all users who have ever authenticated against the ACS server. For example, Figure 9-3 shows the details for the user chriswhite.

Figure 9-3 *User Setup Screen*

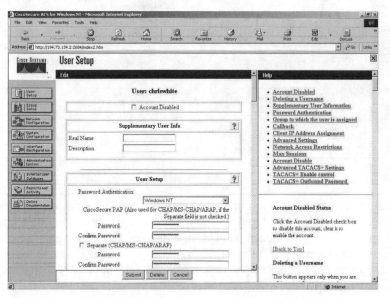

From this initial screen, you can see the user details for chriswhite. You can see that this user has been authenticated against the Windows NT database. This means that this user was first authenticated from an ACS client against the user's Windows NT username and password.

You can change a number of other settings here, such as the advanced settings and the advanced TACACS+ settings. The advanced TACACS+ settings can be seen in Figure 9-4.

Figure 9-4   *User Setup Screen—Advanced TACACS+ Settings*

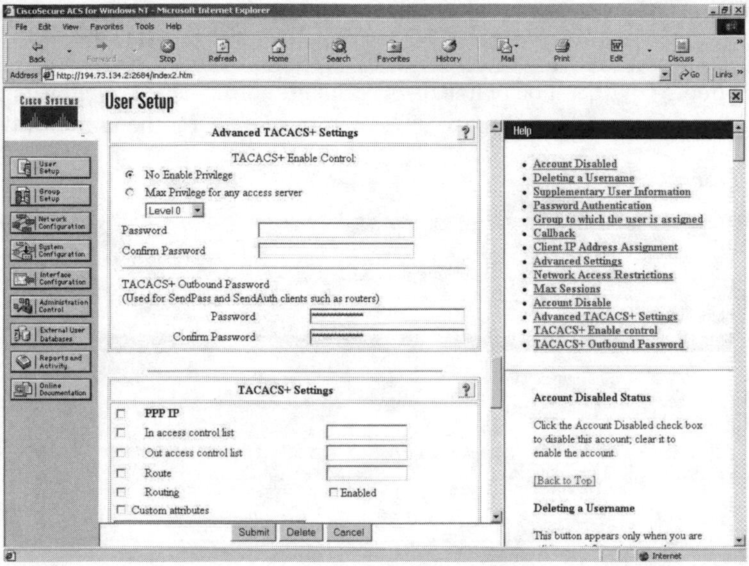

One other important point here is the group membership. Users can be members of groups and have the permissions and settings applied to the group instead of to each individual user. This eases the implementation of changes across groups of users. The groups can be either configured or mapped externally. As you can see in Figure 9-5, the user chriswhite is a member of groups that are mapped by an external authenticator. This means that the Windows NT groups that Chris is a member of are mapped to the Cisco Secure ACS groups. This is explained later in this chapter, in the section "External User Databases."

Figure 9-5   *User Setup Screen—Group Settings*

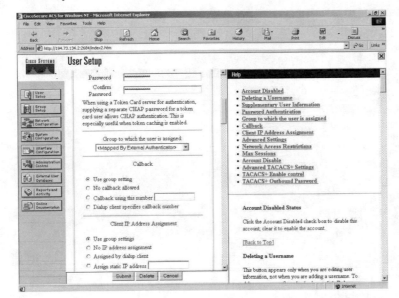

You can also add a new user from the User Setup screen. When you add a new user, by default you add it to the Cisco Secure internal database.

The Group Setup screen is similar to the User Setup screen, except that it deals with groups instead of users. From the main screen, you can view users in a group, edit settings, or rename the group. Figure 9-6 shows you the users in the default group.

Figure 9-6 *Group Setup Screen—Users in a Group*

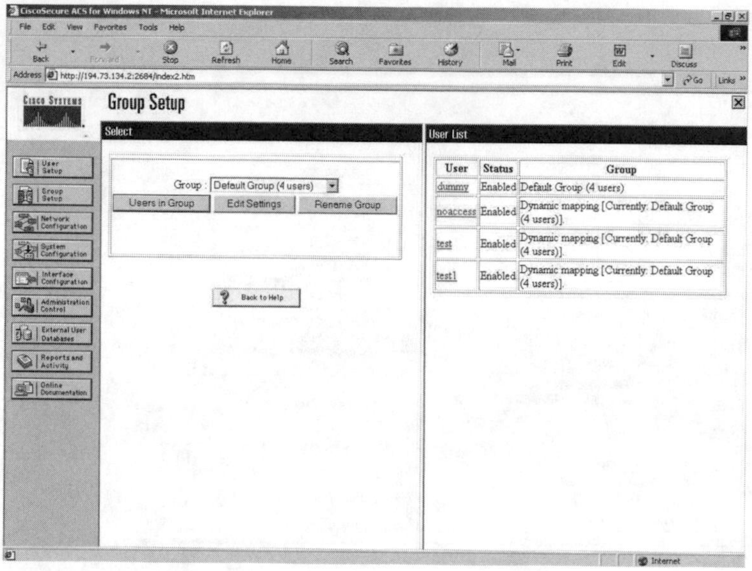

In the right pane of the window, you can see the four users who are members of the Default Group. Clicking the individual user will take you to the User Setup screen for that individual user.

Network Configuration

The Network Configuration screen is where you configure the network information for the ACS server.

From this screen, you enter the network access server information that will configure the ACS server to begin processing requests from that NAS. You can also add, remove, and edit AAA servers to the administrative console.

Figure 9-7 shows the standard screen displayed for Network Configuration.

Figure 9-7 *Network Configuration Screen*

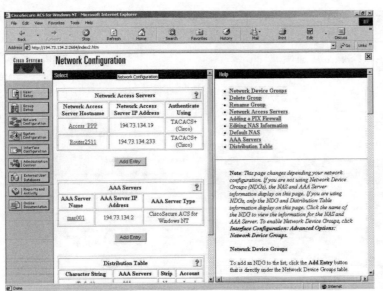

You can see from this screen that there are two network access servers and one AAA server. The two access servers are Access_PPP and Router2511. The AAA server is called mas001.

Clicking any of these items will take you to the individual configuration screen for that item.

To add a new NAS, click the **Add Entry** button below the Network Access Servers header. The following screen, shown in Figure 9-8, is the Add Access Server screen.

Figure 9-8   *Network Configuration Screen—Adding a New NAS*

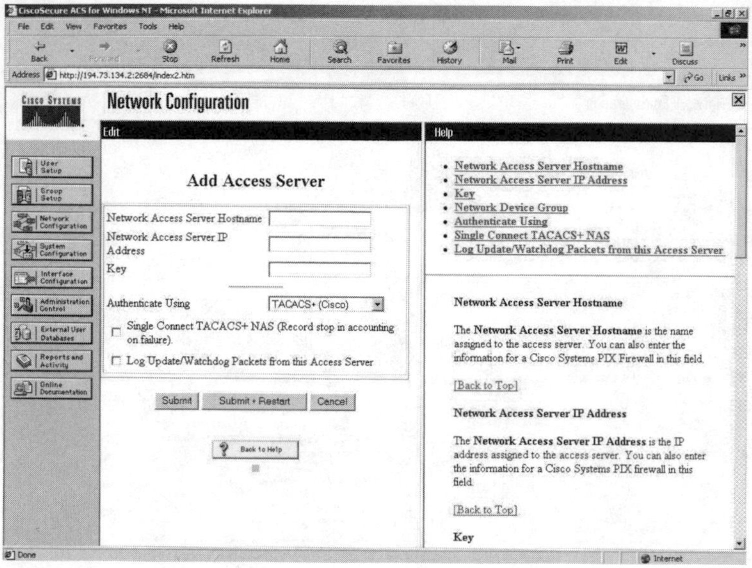

To add a new access server, you have to enter the network access server hostname, IP address, and key. The key is a shared security key that has to be the same on both the ACS server and the ACS client. You can then choose the authentication method. This obviously has to match the authentication type implemented on the ACS client or NAS. If you have configured TACACS+ on the NAS, select the default, TACACS+, on the ACS server. The other options are the different flavors of RADIUS. There is RADIUS (CISCO) for use with Cisco devices, RADIUS (IETF) for use with standards-based (RFC 2058 and RFC 2059) devices, RADIUS (ASCEND) for Ascend internetworking devices, and RADIUS (RedCreek) for Red Creek internetworking devices.

Clicking **Submit** configures the ACS server to start processing requests for AAA services for the newly configured network access server.

To add a new AAA server, click the **Add Entry** button below the AAA Servers header. The following screen, shown in Figure 9-9, is the Add AAA Server screen.

Figure 9-9   *Network Configuration Screen—Adding a New AAA Server*

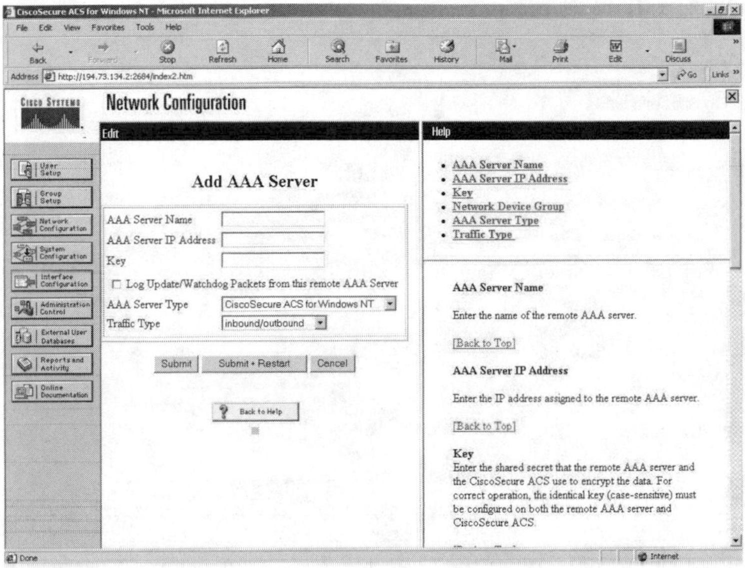

To add a new AAA server, you have to enter the AAA server name, IP address, and key. You then specify whether the server is a RADIUS, TACACS+, or Cisco Secure ACS server. Even though Cisco Secure ACS is both a RADIUS and TACACS+ server, it is important to select the Cisco Secure ACS option if the new AAA server is running the Cisco Secure ACS server software.

System Configuration

The next configuration option is the System Configuration. This option leads to seven other configuration options that are all related to the configuration of the Cisco Secure ACS system. These options are:

- Service Control
- Logging
- Password Validation
- Cisco Secure Database Replication
- ACS Backup
- ACS Restore
- ACS Service Management

The System Configuration screen can be seen in Figure 9-10.

Figure 9-10 *System Configuration Screen*

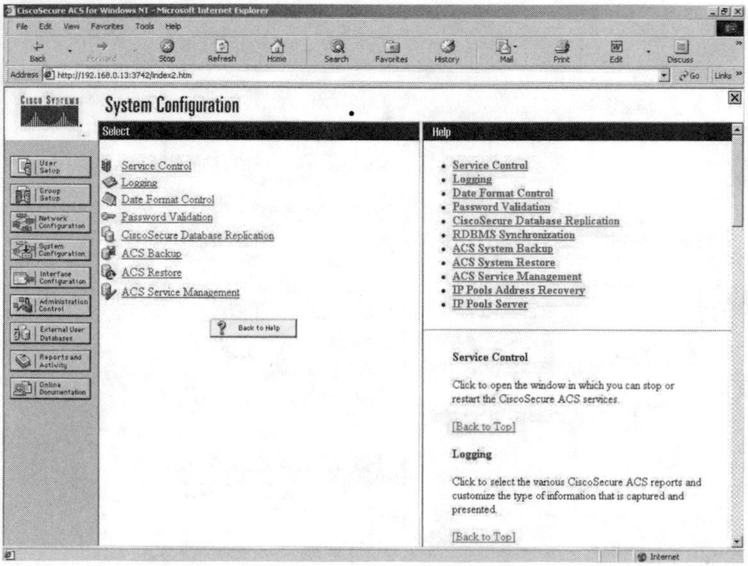

Service Control

The Service Control option reports information and lets you stop and start the Windows NT services that relate to the Cisco Secure ACS server.

Logging

The Logging option lets you configure what events and targets you wish to log. These logs are stored on the ACS server in comma separated value (.CSV) format.

Password Validation

The Password Validation option lets you force a minimum and maximum password length for the internal Cisco Secure ACS database. You can also specify further password options, such as deciding that the password and username cannot be the same.

Cisco Secure Database Replication

The Cisco Secure Database Replication option allows you to configure and schedule replication of the Cisco Secure ACS database to other installed Cisco Secure ACS servers. These servers have to be added under the Network Configuration option covered previously.

ACS Backup

The ACS Backup option allows you to back up the Cisco Secure ACS database, including the user, group, and configuration settings. This backup can be to a local or remote shared drive.

ACS Restore

The ACS Restore option performs a restore of the Cisco Secure ACS database, including the user, group, and configuration settings.

ACS Service Management

The ACS Service Management option allows you to specify system-monitoring and event-logging parameters. The system-monitoring option uses a dummy user to test authentication for a predetermined period. The event-logging option sets all events to be sent to the built-in Windows NT event log. These can also be configured to be e-mailed through an SMTP server to any valid e-mail account.

Interface Configuration

The Interface Configuration screen is where you can configure the Cisco Secure HTML interface. There are four further options within the interface configuration:

- User Data Configuration
- TACACS+ (Cisco IOS)
- RADIUS (Microsoft)
- RADIUS (Cisco VPN 3000)
- RADIUS (IETF)
- Advanced Options

Figure 9-11 shows these options on the Interface Configuration screen.

Figure 9-11 *Interface Configuration Screen*

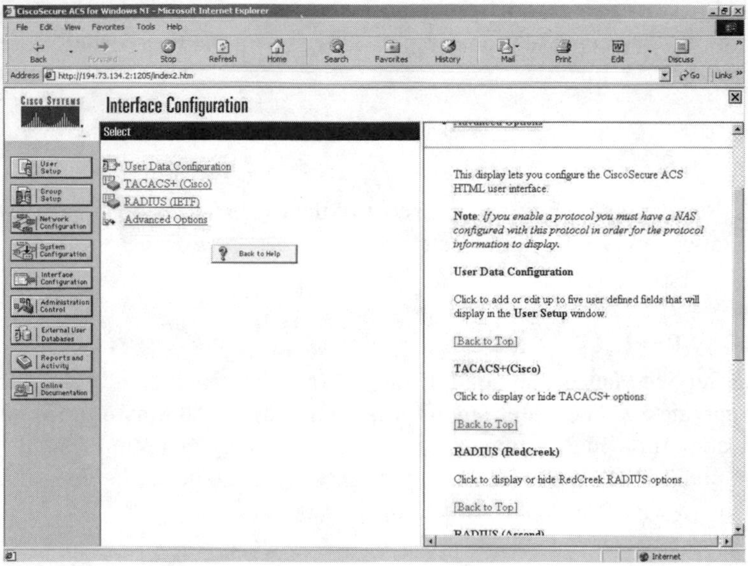

User Data Configuration

In the User Data Configuration screen, you can enter up to five user-defined fields that will be displayed in the User Setup configuration option.

TACACS+ (Cisco IOS)

The TACACS+ (Cisco) option allows you to change the TACACS+ services that you want to appear as configurable items in the User Setup and Group Setup screens.

RADIUS (Microsoft)

The RADIUS (Microsoft) option allows you to change the RADIUS services specific for Microsoft protocols that you want to appear as configurable items in the User Setup and Group Setup windows.

RADIUS (Cisco VPN 3000)

This option allows you to enable the RADIUS Vendor-Specific Attribute (VSA) number 26 for the Cisco VPN 3000 concentrator.

RADIUS (IETF)

The RADIUS (IETF) option allows you to change the RADIUS services that you want to appear as configurable items in the User Setup and Group Setup screens.

Advanced Options

The advanced options are a set of options that are only enabled as configurable if set here. These options are displayed in Figure 9-12.

Figure 9-12 *Interface Configuration Advanced Options Screen*

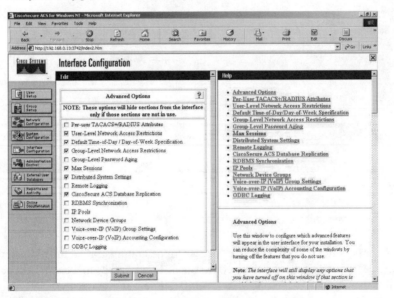

Administration Control

The Administration Control screen is where you can generate and configure users that are classified as administrators of the Cisco Secure ACS system. When you create these administrative users, you can also specify to which groups and functions they have access. This allows you to create tiered levels of administrators. There are three other options available from this configuration page:

- Access Policy
- Session Policy
- Audit Policy

Figure 9-13 shows the main Administration Control screen.

Figure 9-13 *Administration Control Screen*

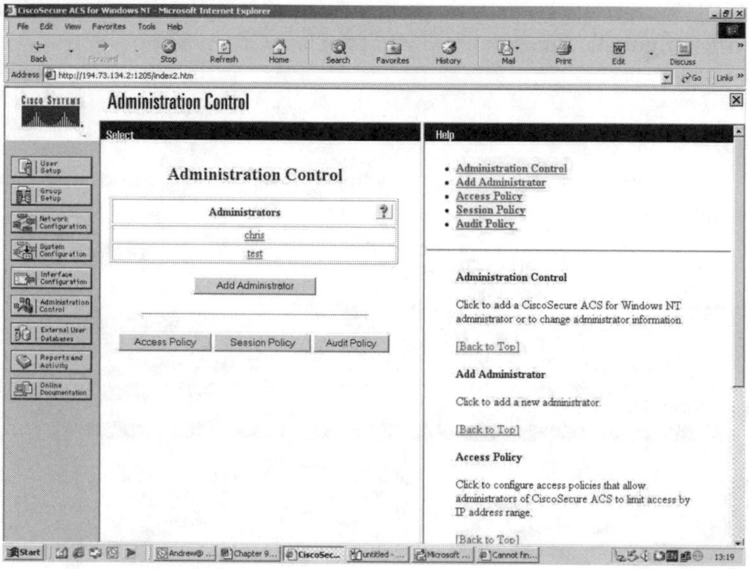

You can see from Figure 9-13 that this ACS server has two configured administrators, chris and test.

Access Policy

The Access Policy is used to restrict access to the administrative functions on the Cisco Secure ACS server. You can enter 10 ranges of IP addresses that can be either allowed or disallowed. The default setting is to let all IP addresses connect to the administrative console. This acts in a similar way to access lists on Cisco routers.

Session Policy

The Session Policy is concerned with the connected session. You can set the idle timeout for the session. This is set at 60 minutes by default, but it might be a good idea to lower this value to 10 minutes or even less. If somebody remains logged in and leaves the machine unattended, anybody with physical access to the machine can use the logged-in administrative rights on the ACS system. You can also set a login failure limit before the administrative account is locked out. This deters brute force and dictionary attacks. Another important setting here is the **Allow automatic local login** setting. By default, this is checked, which means that anybody with the sufficient privileges to log on locally to the server will be able to run the ACS Admin application without any further authentication. This is not very secure for obvious reasons, and it is a good idea to disable this and control access through administrative accounts for specific administrators.

Audit Policy

The Audit Policy sets the frequency of the audit log generation. The default setting is to create a new log for every day of the week. This can be changed to weekly, monthly, or when the log size reaches a specific value.

External User Databases

The External User Databases configuration screen is where you configure Cisco Secure ACS to authenticate users against external databases. You are presented with three options from the main page:

- Unknown User Policy
- Database Group Mappings
- Database Configuration

This screen is shown in Figure 9-14.

Figure 9-14 *External User Databases Screen*

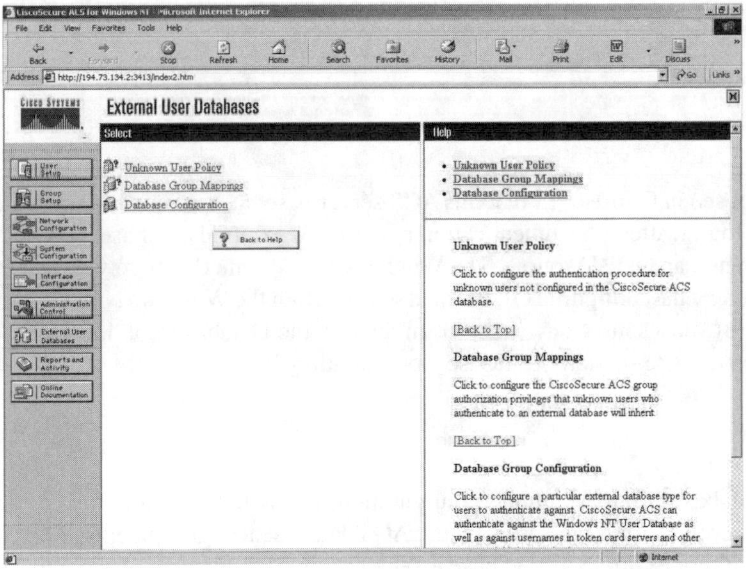

Unknown User Policy

The unknown user policy instructs the ACS server what to do if the user is not found in the built-in ACS database. This is a very important function if you wish to use a different authentication database than the built-in Cisco Secure ACS database.

The default setting is for the ACS to fail the authentication attempt. The only other setting is to use a configured external database. Figure 9-15 shows you the unknown user policy configuration screen.

Figure 9-15 *External User Databases Screen—Unknown User Policy Configuration*

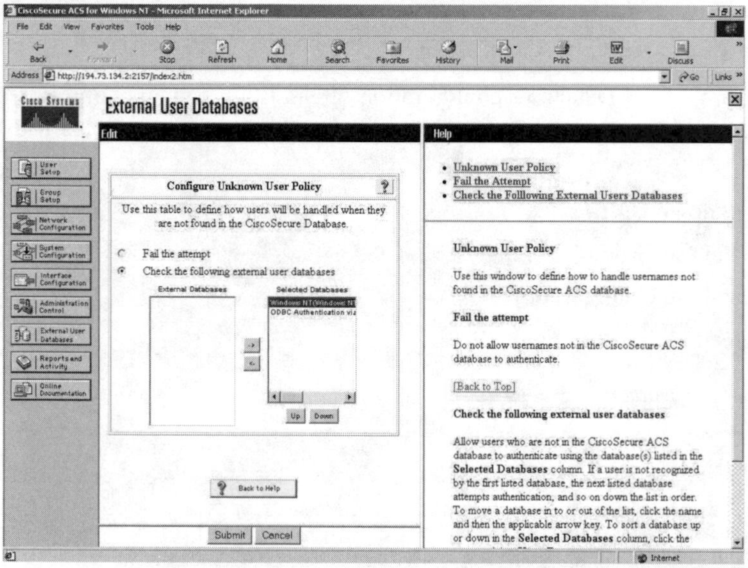

You can see in Figure 9-15 that this ACS server is set to try the internal ACS database, and failing that, it attempts authentication against two external databases, a Windows NT domain and an ODBC source. The Windows NT domain database will be checked first, followed by the configured ODBC data source. Both the Windows NT domain database and the ODBC data source have to be configured in the Database Configuration screen, which is covered in the section "Database Configuration."

Database Group Mappings

The Database Group Mappings configuration screen allows you to map a preconfigured built-in group within the Cisco Secure ACS database to a group configured on the external database. For example, if you have a Windows NT group called Accounts, you can also have a Cisco Secure ACS group called Accounts and create a mapping between these two groups. Then all members of the Windows group Accounts will be made members of the ACS group Accounts. This group can be configured from the Group Setup configuration screen that was explained earlier in the section "User and Group Setup."

Figure 9-16 shows some mappings between a Windows NT database and the Cisco Secure ACS database.

Figure 9-16 *External User Databases Screen—Database Group Mappings*

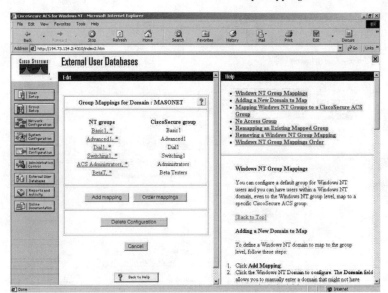

In Figure 9-16, you can clearly see the mappings in relation to the Windows NT database and the Cisco Secure ACS database.

Database Configuration

The External User Database Configuration screen is where you configure Cisco Secure ACS to use an external data source. Figure 9-17 shows the available options.

Figure 9-17 *External User Databases Screen—Database Configuration*

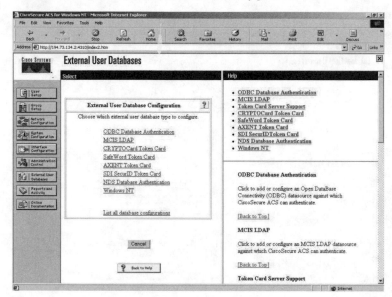

From the screen in Figure 9-17, you can see the external databases available from within Cisco Secure ACS. Each database has its own configuration settings associated with it.

Reports and Activity

The Reports and Activity configuration screen is where you can view the reports created by the Cisco Secure ACS server software. The prebuilt reports include:

- TACACS+ Accounting
- TACACS+ Administration
- RADIUS Accounting
- VoIP Accounting
- Passed Authentications
- Failed Attempts
- Logged-In Users
- Disabled Accounts
- ACS Backup and Restore
- RDBMS Synchronization
- Database Replication

- Administrative Audit
- ACS Service Monitoring

TACACS+ Accounting

The TACACS+ Accounting report provides information about the TACACS+ accounting. This report is gathered from information sent from TACACS+ clients that are configured to use TACACS+ for accounting. You can see a sample TACACS+ accounting report in Figure 9-18.

Figure 9-18   *Reports and Activity Screen—TACACS+ Accounting Report*

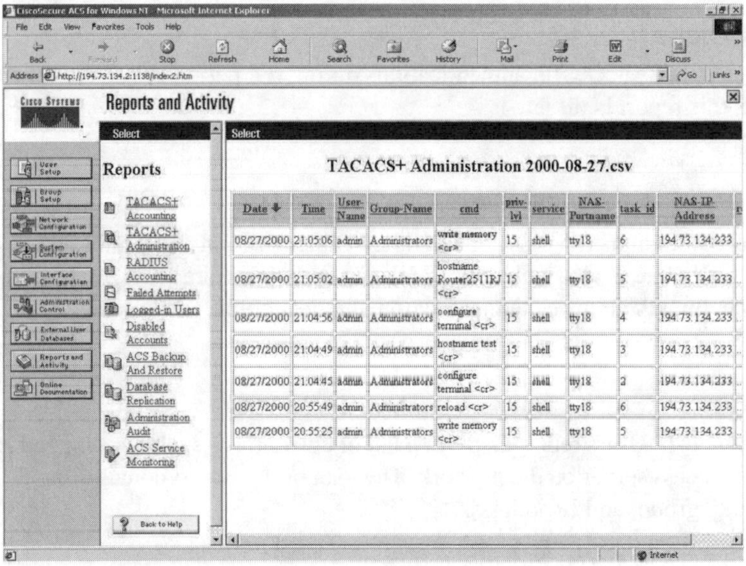

You can see in Figure 9-18 that commands have been executed at privilege level 15. The first command that was entered was **write memory**, and the last command entered was also **write memory**.

TACACS+ Administration

The TACACS+ Administration report contains details about the commands that were executed against the devices configured for TACACS+ accounting. This normally refers to Cisco routers that have been configured for TACACS+ accounting to track all commands entered against the router.

RADIUS Accounting

The RADIUS Accounting report provides information about the RADIUS accounting. This report is gathered from information sent from RADIUS clients that are configured to use RADIUS for accounting. This report is very similar to the TACACS+ accounting report.

VoIP Accounting

The VoIP Accounting report provides information about the VoIP RADIUS Accounting. This report is gathered from accounting information sent from RADIUS clients that are configured to use VoIP RADIUS for accounting.

Passed Authentications

This report lists successful authentications during the period covered by the report. By default, this report is disabled.

Failed Attempts

The Failed Attempts report is a list of failed authentication and authorization attempts. The reason for failure is also included, which can include expired accounts, disabled accounts, and exceeding the allowed authentication attempts count.

Logged-In Users

The Logged-In Users report displays a list of current users who are logged in to each network access server on the network. The data in the report contains the date, time, username, group, and IP address.

Disabled Accounts

The Disabled Accounts report is a list of accounts that have been disabled. These accounts might have been disabled manually or automatically by date expiration on the account. No .CSV file is created for this report, and it is only visible from the ACS Admin application.

ACS Backup and Restore

The ACS Backup and Restore report provides information about the ACS backup and restore operations. The date, time, and location of each operation are recorded, along with the administrator's username that started the process.

RDBMS Synchronization

This report contains the times the RDBMS database was synchronized and the cause of the synchronization: manual or scheduled.

Database Replication

The Database Replication report contains the date and time that the ACS database was successfully replicated to the backup server. The cause of the replication, either manual or automatic, is also recorded.

Administrative Audit

The Administrative Audit report contains a list of the Cisco Secure ACS administrators who accessed the ACS system on the specified date. All actions that the administrator carried out are logged, along with the date and time of the action. This report is similar to the TACACS+ accounting feature on Cisco internetworking devices, where all administrator duties are monitored and logged.

ACS Service Monitoring

The ACS Service Monitoring report provides details about the monitored Cisco Secure ACS-related Windows NT services. This information can also be viewed in the Windows NT event log.

These reports are all stored in .CSV files and are stored in the \Program Files\Cisco Secure ACS v2.3\Logs directory on the ACS server. These raw .CSV files can be imported into leading database and spreadsheet applications for further analysis and recording over and above the reports generated by the Cisco Secure ACS server.

Online Documentation

As you would expect, the Online Documentation screen is a collection of the related documents for Cisco Secure ACS server. These documents include the full documents for every feature supported on Cisco Secure ACS, in addition to sample configurations and example commands that are required to be entered on the network access servers. Updated documentation can always be found at the Cisco Connection Online web site at www.cisco.com.

Network Access Server Configuration

The previous section covered the basic configuration tasks required for the Cisco Secure ACS server. The ACS server acts as the authentication server, regardless of whether you use RADIUS or TACACS+ as the authentication protocol. The other required configuration task relates to the authentication client; again this is regardless of whether you choose RADIUS or TACACS+ as the authentication protocol.

The title given to these clients is usually network access servers. The NAS is usually an internetworking device capable of terminating many inbound connections. These can be dial-based connections over the PSTN or ISDN (BRI and PRI) or fixed, WAN-interconnect-based connections between corporate sites. AAA services can also be used on internetwork devices to ease the administrative burden of user-account creation and to provide a mechanism for recording the privileged-level commands that are run on the devices.

The remainder of this section concentrates on configuring Cisco devices for AAA services to the Cisco Secure ACS server. The client is referred to as the NAS in this section.

AAA Configuration Overview

In this section, you will see how to configure AAA services for both TACACS+ and RADIUS. This section does not cover the older TACACS and XTACACS protocols; for configuration information about TACACS and XTACACS, refer to the IOS Network Security documentation on CCO for the relevant release of the IOS software you are using.

Before you start configuring the specific AAA services, some basic configuration commands are required to initialize AAA on the NAS and to provide the type and location of the authentication server.

By default, the NAS will not be configured for TACACS+ and RADIUS configuration, because it will be in the default TACACS and XTACACS state. The first command you always enter when you configure RADIUS or TACACS+ is

```
aaa new-model
```

This command enables the configuration of TACACS+ and RADIUS and disables access to many of the old TACACS and XTACACS commands.

The next step is to configure the NAS with the required information of the TACACS+ and RADIUS servers. To enable TACACS+, the following two commands are required:

```
tacacs-server host ip address
tacacs-server key key
```

The first command configures the location of the TACACS+ server. The IP address has to be the IP address of the TACACS+ server. The second command sets the shared key for the TACACS+ connection. This shared key has to be the same on both the TACACS+ client and the TACACS+ server. This key is used in the encryption of the entire packet between the client and the server.

To enable RADIUS, the following two commands are required:

```
radius-server host ip address
radius-server key key
```

The first command configures the location of the RADIUS server. The IP address has to be the IP address of the RADIUS server. The second command sets the shared key for the RADIUS connection. This shared key has to be the same on both the RADIUS client and the RADIUS server. This key is used in the encryption of the password within the packet between the client and the server.

The following example enables AAA services, sets the TACACS+ server to 192.168.0.1, and sets the shared key to myKey:

```
NAS(config)aaa new-model
NAS(config)#tacacs-server host 192.168.0.1
NAS(config)#tacacs-server key myKey
```

This is the basic configuration required to activate both RADIUS and TACACS+. There are other commands that can be used; details about these can be found in the IOS Security Documentation online within CCO.

The remainder of this section looks at the specific AAA services and how to configure them.

Authentication Configuration

Authentication is required before both authorization and accounting can function. If the user is not authenticated, the user cannot be authorized or accounted. You can, however, just configure authentication and not authorization or accounting. Authentication performs adequately by itself and is not dependent on any other AAA service.

The first step in configuring authentication is to create a method list. The method list describes the authentication methods to be queried, in sequence, to authenticate the user. Method lists allow you to specify more than one source of authentication. This is useful in case one authentication source is not responding. For example, you could use TACACS+ first, then the local user database on the router.

The syntax for specifying an authentication method list on the access server is:

```
aaa authentication service {default | list-name}
    method1 [method2] [method3] [method4]
```

Method 2 through Method 4 are optional and are just used to select another authentication method.

NOTE   Even though you can specify multiple authentication methods, the NAS only tries the next method if no response is received from the previous method. If authentication fails at any point, the authentication process stops and the user is denied.

For authentication, there are five specified values for *service*:

- **arap**—Configures authentication for AppleTalk Remote Access users
- **nasi**—Configures authentication for NetWare Asynchronous Services Interface users
- **enable**—Configures authentication for enable mode access to the device
- **login**—Configures authentication for character mode connections to the device
- **ppp**—Configures authentication for PPP connections to the device

You can have up to four authentication methods per method list. The method list uses the first configured method and only moves on to the next method if no response is received. There are 11 authentication methods in total. Again, this section concentrates on RADIUS and TACACS+. The 11 methods are:

- **enable**—Uses the enable password for authentication
- **line**—Uses the line password for authentication
- **local**—Uses the local database for authentication
- **none**—Uses no authentication
- **tacacs+**—Uses a TACACS+ server for authentication
- **radius**—Uses a RADIUS server for authentication
- **krb5**—Uses Kerberos 5 for authentication
- **krb5-telnet**—Uses Kerberos 5 for Telnet authentication
- **auth-guest**—Guest logins are allowed only if the user has already logged in to EXEC
- **guest**—Guest logins are allowed
- **if-needed**—Do not authenticate the user if the user has already been authenticated by other means

There are 5 services and 11 authentication methods. Not all authentication methods are permitted for every service. Table 9-2 shows the available services and the corresponding authentication methods.

Table 9-2 *Authentication Methods*

Method	arap	nasi	enable	login	ppp
enable	No	Yes	Yes	Yes	No
line	Yes	Yes	Yes	Yes	No
local	Yes	Yes	No	Yes	Yes
none	No	Yes	Yes	Yes	Yes
tacacs+	Yes	Yes	Yes	Yes	Yes
radius	Yes	No	Yes	Yes	Yes
krb5	No	No	No	Yes	Yes

Table 9-2   *Authentication Methods (Continued)*

krb5-telnet	No	No	No	Yes	No
auth-guest	Yes	No	No	No	No
guest	Yes	No	No	No	No
if-needed	No	No	No	No	Yes

One important point to remember is the method list name. This can be any string value other than **default**. The list name of **default** is reserved and has the effect of applying the authentication method list to all interfaces for all valid connections without any further configuration. This might be what you want and is then an ideal solution, but there are many times when, for instance, you only want to use AAA for VTY authentication and not PPP authentication. The following line of configuration sets up a default method list:

```
NAS(config)#aaa authentication login default tacacs+ local
```

The preceding command enables login authentication for all interfaces against TACACS+ and, failing that, the local database stored on the device. If you decide that you want to specify a name for the method list, you have to apply it to the interfaces.

For example, the following configuration creates a method list called "execaccess":

```
NAS(config)#aaa authentication login execaccess radius local
```

The preceding method list authenticates against RADIUS, and if no response is received from the RADIUS server, the local database stored on the device is checked. This method list is to provide login authentication against the VTY lines on the device. The following command from line configuration mode is required:

```
NAS(config-line)#login authentication execaccess
```

This command applies the method list execaccess to the VTY lines.

More examples for authentication will be given at the end of this chapter. Also, there are numerous prebuilt configurations for AAA available at CCO.

Authorization Configuration

Once the user has been authenticated, you can apply authorization to that user. As with authentication, the first configuration step is to create a method list. The syntax is very similar, and the theory behind the method list is exactly the same as that for authentication. One difference is that you are not required to give the method list a name.

The syntax for specifying an authorization method list on the access server is:

```
aaa authorization service [default | list-name]
    method1 [method2] [method3] [method4]
```

Method 2 through Method 4 are optional and are just used to select another authorization method.

NOTE	Even though you can specify multiple authorization methods, the NAS only tries the next method if no response is received from the previous method.

For authorization, there are five specified services:

- **network**—Authorization is checked for all network connections. This includes connections over PPP, SLIP, and ARAP.

- **exec**—This relates to whether the user can run an EXEC shell on the NAS.

- **commands**—All commands entered are checked to ensure that the user has authorization to use them. You have to specify the command enable level (1–15) after the command service type.

- **config-commands**—All configuration commands entered are checked to ensure that the user has authorization to use them.

- **reverse-access**—Authorization for reverse Telnet sessions.

As with authentication, you also have to specify methods in the method list. Up to four of these can be specified, and they are contacted in order. For authorization, there are four methods to carry out authorization:

- **tacacs+**—The NAS contacts a TACACS+ server, and the TACACS+ database is checked for matching attribute value pairs.

- **radius**—The NAS contacts a RADIUS server, and the RADIUS database is checked to ascertain whether the user has the appropriate permissions.

- **if-authenticated**—This allows users to be authorized as long as they have been authenticated.

- **local**—The NAS consults the local database. Only very limited functions are supported.

So, to apply authorization against TACACS+ for all commands at exec level 4, the command is:

```
NAS(config)#aaa authorization commands 4 default tacacs+
```

The command to apply authorization to network connections if already authenticated is:

```
NAS(config)#aaa authorization network default if-authenticated
```

To add to this command, you could specify that all authenticated users should be authorized, and if they are not, they would be checked against RADIUS. This would be achieved by the following command:

```
NAS(config)#aaa authorization network default if-authenticated radius
```

By adding **radius** to the end of this command, you are telling the NAS to see if the user is authenticated and, if not, to contact the RADIUS server.

More examples for authorization will be given at the end of this chapter. Also, there are numerous prebuilt configurations for AAA available at CCO.

Accounting Configuration

Accounting is the third AAA service. Accounting is configured in a similar way to both authentication and authorization. Method lists are created for accounting as they are for authentication and authorization. However, the method list for accounting takes on a different form than for authentication and authorization.

The syntax for specifying an accounting method list on the access server is:

```
aaa accounting event type {default | list-name} {start-stop | wait-start
| stop-only | none} method1 [method2]
```

Method 2 is optional and is just used to select another accounting method.

NOTE   There are only two method types supported by accounting. These are RADIUS and TACACS+. Therefore, only two methods can be specified.

For accounting, there are nine specified *event types*:

- **commands**—Applies accounting for all EXEC mode commands
- **connection**—Applies accounting to all outbound connections from the NAS
- **exec**—Applies accounting for EXEC shells
- **nested**—Applies accounting to PPP sessions started from the EXEC process
- **network**—Applies accounting to network-based services such as PPP, SLIP, and ARAP
- **send**—Sends records to the accounting server
- **suppress**—Allows you to suppress the sending of accounting information for specific usernames
- **system**—Applies accounting to system events
- **update**—Enables accounting for update records

After you have specified the event type, you have to tell the NAS when to send the accounting records to the accounting server. There are four options:

- **start-stop**—As soon as the session begins, an accounting start record is sent to the accounting server. The NAS does not wait until the acknowledgement is received from the accounting server that the session has started. When the session stops, the stop record is sent to the accounting server along with the session statistics.

- **wait-start**—The start accounting record is not sent until an acknowledgement is received from the server that the session has started. When the session ends, the stop record is sent along with the session statistics.

- **stop-only**—The NAS only sends the stop accounting record and the session statistics. No start record is sent.

- **none**—All accounting activities are stopped. This is usually applied to an interface.

The only two methods available are **radius** and **tacacs+**. As an example, if you wanted to enable accounting for all network connections, including the start and stop records, accounted to the TACACS+ server, the command would be:

```
aaa accounting network default start-stop tacacs+
```

This sets up the default method list for network accounting to the TACACS+ server.

Now that you have reviewed the three AAA services, the next section covers some sample configurations that can be used in your place of work.

Also, there are numerous prebuilt configurations for AAA available at CCO.

Configuration Example

This section looks at some sample configurations of the NAS (client) and the ACS (server). Included are examples of authentication, authorization and accounting—all three of the AAA services. These examples are based on a simple case study.

Scenario

You are the security administrator responsible for ensuring that the corporate security policy is enforced throughout the company. You recently installed two new services, a direct Internet connection and remote dial-in access for senior management so that they can dial into the office at night and on weekends. You are concerned about the threats these new connections pose to the security of the internal network. No other third-party links have ever existed, so this is the first external penetration of the network.

Technical Aspects

The network diagram is shown in Figure 9-19.

Figure 9-19 *Example Network Diagram*

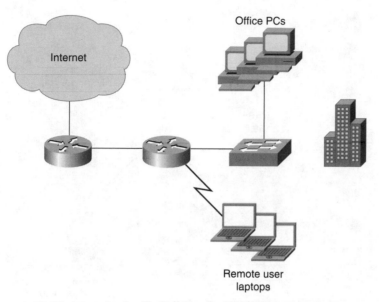

Office PCs

Internet

Remote user
laptops

You can see in Figure 9-19 that the network simply consists of a switched LAN, an internal router, and an Internet-connected router all located at one office. The internal router has eight asynchronous serial ports that provide remote access to the remote users over modems and PPP. An RFC 1918-compliant private address is used internally with NAT providing the public address over the leased-line 128-kbps Internet connection. Windows NT is currently used on the network as the network operating system (NOS).

Potential Risks

As the security administrator, your concerns are with the authentication of the remote access users and also with the authentication of administrators to the Cisco internetworking devices for command-line editing and monitoring.

Configuration

The first service to implement is authentication. For any of this to work, there must be an authentication server located on the network. You decide to install the Cisco Secure ACS on your network as shown in Figure 9-20. You give the ACS server an IP address of 192.168.0.10/24. You give the NAS an IP address of 192.168.0.9/24.

Figure 9-20   *Example Network Diagram with the AAA server*

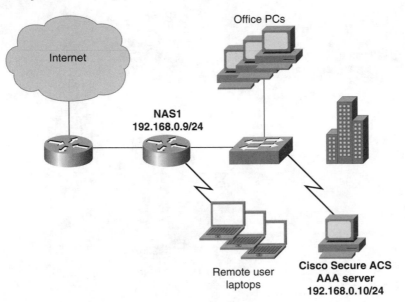

All users currently have a Windows NT user account, so you decide to use the Windows NT domain database instead of the built-in Cisco Secure ACS database. You also decide not to use any group mappings, but to allow and disallow remote access by the Grant Dial-In Permission, which is already available within the Windows NT user profile from the User Manager for Domains application.

ACS Server Configuration

Before you can configure anything on the network access server, you must configure the ACS server to communicate with the NAS and to authenticate against the Windows NT domain database. This is explained in the following steps:

Step 1   You have to configure the ACS server to accept AAA requests from the NAS. To do this, you have to go to the Network Configuration screen and click **Add Entry** for the network access servers. Figure 9-21 shows you the resulting screen.

Figure 9-21 *Network Configuration Screen*

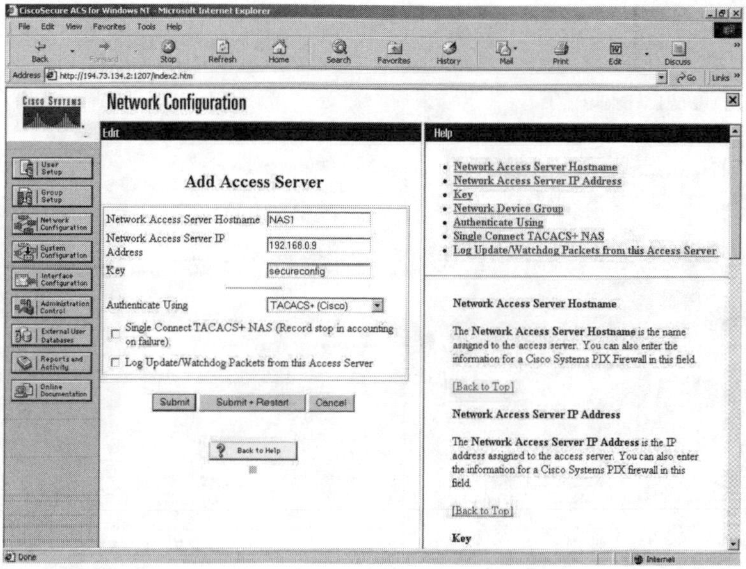

You can see in Figure 9-21 that the IP address, name, and key have been entered. The key entered is "secureconfig." This also has to be entered on the NAS. TACACS+ has been selected as the method of authentication. You should now click the **Submit+Restart** button to submit the addition and restart the AAA services on the Windows NT server.

Step 2 The next step is to enable authentication against the Windows NT domain database. This is a two-step process. The first step is to tell the ACS server to use NT. The second step is to set the unknown user policy to use the NT server for authentication. Both of these are done from within the External User Databases configuration screen. Click the **External User Databases** configuration icon, then click the **Database Configuration** link. Select **Windows NT** and check the box to allow access by the Grant Dial-in Permission. This is shown in Figure 9-22.

Figure 9-22 *External User Databases*

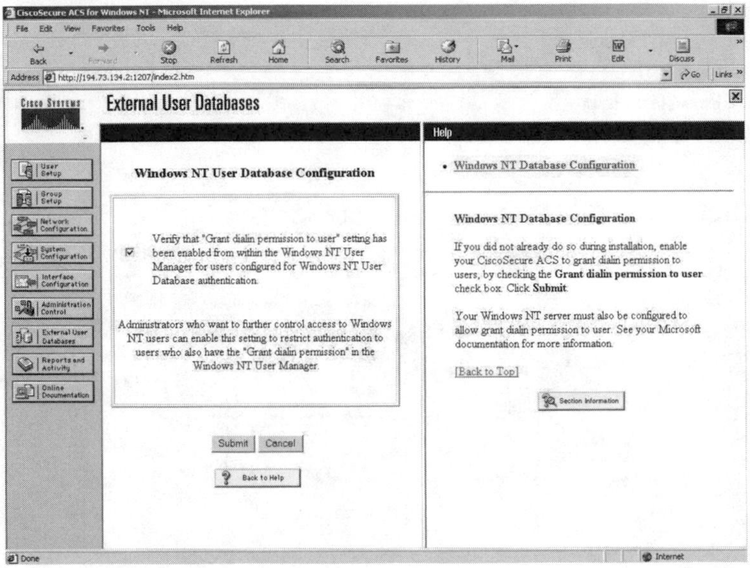

Return to the External User Databases configuration screen and select the **Unknown User Policy** link. You will now be presented with the screen shown in Figure 9-23.

Figure 9-23 *Unknown User Policy*

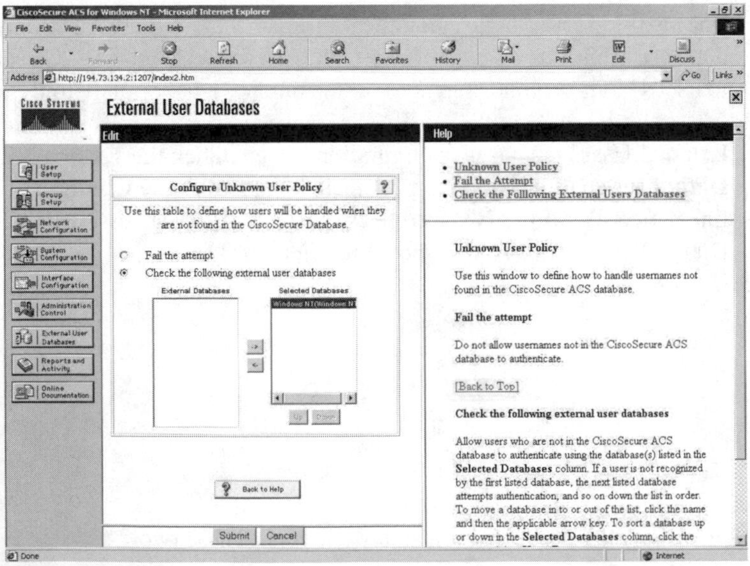

You can see in Figure 9-23 that you should select the second option button, which says *not* to fail the authentication attempt but to authenticate against the Windows NT data source.

This is all that is required to perform simple AAA services.

NAS Configuration

As with the ACS server, certain configuration tasks have to be carried out on the NAS just to initiate communication with the ACS server. You are using TACACS+ for this example. The following commands have to be entered on the NAS:

```
NAS1(Config)#aaa new-model
NAS1(Config)#tacacs-server host 192.168.0.10
NAS1(Config)#tacacs-server key secureconfig
```

These commands enable the new model for AAA on the NAS. The TACACS+ server is identified as IP address 192.168.0.10, and the shared key is set as "secureconfig." This matches the value entered into the ACS server and enables all traffic between the NAS and the ACS to be encrypted. The NAS is now configured to allow further AAA configuration.

Authentication Configuration

You are going to start the AAA services by configuring authentication on the NAS. You require authentication for both EXEC logins and PPP network connections. The easy way to achieve this is to create a method list named "default" for both login and PPP access. This is then applied to all lines and interfaces on the NAS. The following commands enable authentication:

```
NAS1(Config)#aaa authentication login default tacacs+ local
NAS1(Config)#aaa authentication ppp default tacacs+ local
```

These two commands both enable authentication for login and PPP access to the NAS. Notice that two methods are defined, TACACS+ and local. Authentication uses TACACS+ first, but if no response is received, it then uses the local user information on the NAS. It is useful always to include both in case the ACS server is ever unavailable. It is more for administrative access to the CLI than for PPP access. Create some administrative users on the NAS that can be used in an emergency to gain access to the CLI.

These two commands enable authentication for the NAS.

Authorization Configuration

With authentication configured, you now want to configure authorization to deny users access to the dial-in system between the hours of 22:00 and 06:00, and to ensure that each user can only have one active session at any one time. These two functions improve on the security of the system and are both configurable as authorization commands.

This process involves creating the changes on the Cisco Secure ACS server and a simple one-line configuration on the NAS.

On the ACS server, click the **Group Setup** configuration link. By default, all users are made members of the Default Users group. You want to apply these changes to every user, so choose to edit the settings for the default group. The first change is the time of day access for the users. Click the **Set As Default Access Times** checkbox and deny the times between 22:00 and 06:00. Figure 9-24 shows this completed task.

Figure 9-24 *Time of Day Settings*

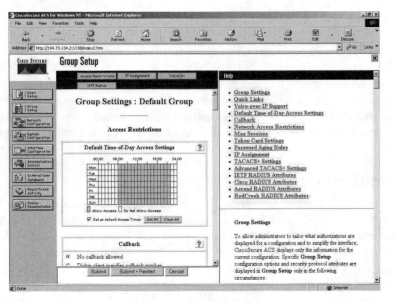

You can see in Figure 9-24 that during the times between 22:00 and 06:00, access is denied. You then need to scroll down this page to the Max Sessions section. Here you have two options. You can apply a max session figure to the entire group or to users of this group. You need to apply this to the users of this group and select the default, one connection. Figure 9-25 shows this configuration.

Figure 9-25 *Max User Connections*

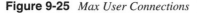

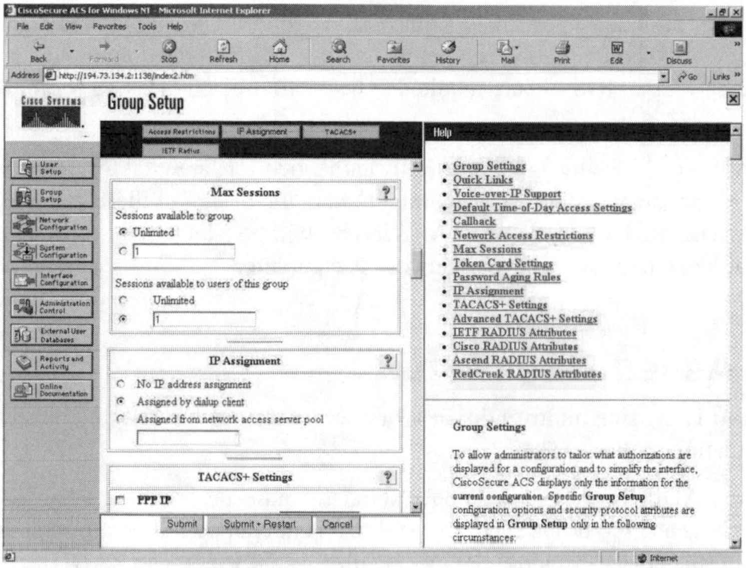

Now that you have configured the ACS server, you have to configure the NAS. To configure the NAS, enter this command:

```
NAS(Config)aaa authorization network default tacacs+
```

This command applies this method list to all lines and interfaces on the router. The network service type specifies that all network-based services such as PPP, SLIP, and ARAP will use the TACACS+ server for authorization.

Accounting Configuration

You wish to keep a record of all CLI access to the NAS to track administrator access of what commands are issued at EXEC level 15. No further configuration is required on the ACS server, and only one configuration line is required on the NAS to start this process:

```
NAS1(Config)#aaa accounting commands 15 default start-stop tacacs+
```

The preceding command sets up accounting for level 15 commands. The default method list is used, so it is applied to all lines and interfaces. Only one method is configured. TACACS+ and RADIUS are supported, but RADIUS is not configured on the ACS server, so it makes sense to use just TACACS+ for accounting.

This completes the simple case study configuration example. In it, you implemented authentication, authorization, and accounting both on the ACS server and the NAS.

Summary

This chapter provided an overview of the Cisco Secure ACS. You looked at the ACS server components and configuration requirements, in addition to the commands that are supported by Cisco IOS and are required to be configured on the NAS for the AAA process to work.

The services provided by AAA, especially authentication, are vital for the network security of your corporate network. It is important to plan the design of these services into your network. The late introduction of AAA services will be a lot harder to implement once the design and configuration for your network is complete.

Frequently Asked Questions

Question: I am using multivendor network access servers for dial-up connectivity. Which authentication protocol is best?

Answer: RADIUS is based on an open standard and is described in RFC 2058 and 2059. TACACS+ is a Cisco proprietary protocol that is not supported on all manufacturers' devices. If the devices support TACACS+, then use it. If not, use RADIUS.

Question: What are the main differences between RADIUS and TACACS+?

Answer: There are numerous differences between RADIUS and TACACS+. One main difference is that RADIUS is open source and TACACS+ is Cisco proprietary. TACACS+ generally has more features and is considered more secure.

Glossary

AAA (authentication, authorization, accounting)—Often pronounced "triple a."

ACS (Access Control Server)—The Cisco Secure ACS is an integrated RADIUS and TACACS+ server for authentication, authorization, and accounting.

CCO (Cisco Connection Online)—The Cisco Systems home page on the Internet. Located at www.cisco.com.

CLI (command-line interface)—The UNIX-style command interface that is used to configure Cisco internetworking devices.

NAS (network access server)—The connection point to the network for remote services such as dial-in users over PPP.

NOS (network operating system)—The operating system of the network. This provides users with services such as file and print sharing. Common NOSs include Microsoft Windows NT and Novell NetWare.

RADIUS (Remote Access Dial-In User Service)—A protocol used to authenticate users on a network.

TACACS+ (Terminal Access Controller Access Control System Plus)—A protocol used to authenticate users on a network. Also provides authorization and accounting facilities.

Bibliography

Designing Network Security by Merike Kaeo, Cisco Press 1999 (ISBN 1-57870-043-4)

URLs

Cisco Connection Online

www.cisco.com

Cisco Secure home page

www.cisco.com/warp/public/44/jump/secure.shtml

Security products and technologies

www.cisco.com/warp/public/cc/cisco/mkt/security/

Cisco Secure ACS

www.cisco.com/warp/public/cc/cisco/mkt/access/secure/

Sample Cisco Secure ACS and NAS configurations

www.cisco.com/univercd/cc/td/doc/product/access/acs_soft/csacs4nt/csnt23/csnt23ug/ch2.htm

Internet Security Situations

This chapter contains the following sections:

- Dial-In Security
- Dial-In User Authentication, Authorization, and Accounting (AAA)
- AAA Authentication Setup with TACACS+ and RADIUS
- AAA Authorization Setup
- AAA Accounting Setup
- Using All AAA Services Simultaneously
- Virtual Private Networks (VPNs)
- Summary

CHAPTER 10

Securing the Corporate Network

Sometimes security has more to do with politics and human resources issues than with networking. The security administrator is constantly pulled between needing to maintain a reasonable level of security and allowing users the flexibility to get their work done. The administrator is faced with balancing these two often-opposing needs. How can a balance be achieved? Security policies should be looked at in the same manner as clothing. Clothing should not be so tight that it restricts movement, but it still needs to cover that which should not be revealed to the public. A suit that is too restrictive will soon be left in the closet, along with a suit that is too big in the shoulders. Like a suit, the art of building a security system must balance between being too loose and too tight.

When thinking about securing the corporate network, keep in mind the three main ways someone can try to gain access to the corporate network:

- Through the Internet
- Through dial-in access
- Through Virtual Private Networks (VPNs)

Chapter 2, "Basic Cisco Router Security," and Chapter 5, "Cisco IOS Firewall," discussed methods of protecting your network from the Internet. Not covered in those chapters was how to protect your network from dial-in access and VPNs coming in through the Internet. The security needs of each of these access methods are discussed in this chapter.

Dial-In Security

The need to support dial-in users might prove to be the security administrator's largest challenge. This is especially true if users are allowed to dial in directly to their workstations or servers, bypassing all other security methods.

Dial-in access can be through either the plain old telephone service (POTS) or through an ISDN connection. Because ISDN connections are expensive, there are generally fewer individuals who have an ISDN connection at their desk. However, the price of telephone connections is so low that it is reasonable for individuals to have dedicated connections at their desktop. The remainder of this section deals with connections using the POTS.

Within some organizations, there are groups and individuals that insist that the normal security precautions need to be bypassed because of special circumstances. Sometimes those insisting on bypassing the security precautions are developers, sometimes they are managers, and sometimes they are network engineers. In most cases, the arguments as to why the security must be bypassed seem logical on the surface. For example, the argument can be made that direct access of the hardware is required for debugging purposes. Another common argument is that a connection must be made for testing purposes without interference or delays imposed by security methods. This scenario can be differentiated from one where there is a central device on the network for dial-in access (such as a Cisco access server or a single Windows NT RAS server) by the fact that there are multiple entries into the network. A company with multiple dial-in connections is shown in Figure 10-1.

Figure 10-1 *Multiple Dial-In Entry Point*

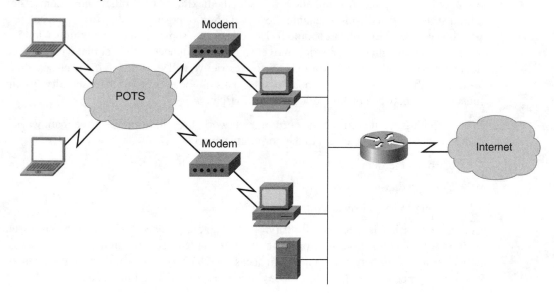

Once the network starts to become open to remote access without proper authorization, it can be very difficult for the administrator to regain control. Although it is much easier to maintain control than to regain control, it is still possible to move from an unsecured dial-in network to a fully secured dial-in network.

Assume for a moment that you are the newly hired administrator for a 600-host Windows NT network. You discover that there are approximately 50 users who connect a modem to their desktop PC and routinely call into the network through this connection for access to e-mail, network programs, and shared files. What, exactly, is the problem with this scenario? Several things can be improved in this scenario:

- If the phone lines can be eliminated through consolidation, recurring expenses in the form of unnecessary phone lines can be eliminated. Some phone systems require that modems use a dedicated line. In this case, a separate line must be purchased for use on each modem. Because all lines are not in use at exactly the same time, the company needs to purchase more lines than are ever used at one time. Building a modem pool allows the administrator to eliminate some of these lines. The authors of this book were faced with exactly this scenario and were able to remove a total of 24 dedicated lines by building a modem pool, saving the company a good deal of money over the first year.

- Allowing users to access their computers directly through an uncontrolled dial-up connection decentralizes security. It can become a nearly impossible task to ensure any semblance of security when individual users are setting up their own connections into the network. The user might set up the connection not to require a password or might make the password so obvious that it is useless. A single administrator would have an extremely difficult task of checking every single connection on a regular basis for configuration issues such as encryption and dial-back services.

- In this example, the company relies solely on the built-in security methods within the operating system of the desktop. Many operating systems were not built with security as a primary concern. Even those operating systems that claim to have strong security policies might be vulnerable, simply because they are well known. There are also usually no built-in methods within the operating system that allows the administrator to be notified if repeated attempts to break into the network occur.

- Unless the administrator has control over dial-in connections, the administrator is unable to limit the areas of the network that a dial-in user can access. Some companies might wish, for example, not to allow any confidential information to be accessed through a dial-in connection. With a large number of operating systems, a user dialing into a workstation has the same rights as that workstation. There might not be provisions made to differentiate the authority levels between a dial-in account and a local user. This means that there is no way to enforce the company's wish that sensitive information be available only through the local network.

For these reasons, the administrator is strongly urged to move toward a centralized dial-in point where appropriate controls can be used. The fact that all users enter at a single point simplifies all administrative efforts, including security. A diagram of a network using a single point of access through an access server and modem bank is shown in Figure 10-2.

Figure 10-2 *Single Dial-In Entry Point*

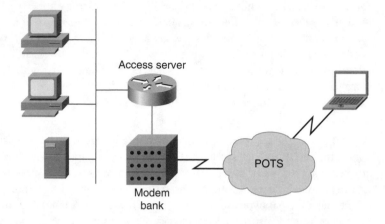

Dial-In User Authentication, Authorization, and Accounting (AAA)

This section deals with the authentication of users accessing dial-in services. Authentication can occur at either the user or the device level.

The most commonly used protocols for a dial-in connection are the Point-to-Point Protocol (PPP) and the Serial Line Internet Protocol (SLIP). Both of these protocols require a minimum of a 1200 baud connection.

Although using Password Authentication Protocol (PAP) or Challenge Handshake Authentication Protocol (CHAP) for authentication is a viable option in smaller environments, the administrative overhead involved might become unmanageable in a larger environment. This is because each user should have a separate entry. A single entry can be made for multiple users, but this practice violates a basic rule that passwords should not be shared. Imagine the overhead involved in setting up and maintaining 100 users, especially if you are trying to enforce a policy that requires changing of passwords every 60 days.

In addition to PAP and CHAP password authentication, TACACS+ or RADIUS authentication can also be used to perform AAA functions. Both of these build a database of users and passwords. Terminal Access Controller Access Control System Plus (TACACS+) and Remote Access Dial-In User Service (RADIUS) also have the added benefit of including authorization and accounting services.

NOTE	Some confusion within the industry surrounds the distinctions between the three areas of AAA: authentication, authorization, and accounting. This note is provided to clear up any residual uncertainty.

Authentication refers to the process of ensuring that the claimed identity of a device or end user is valid. An example is user Terry being authenticated through the use of a password.

Authorization refers to the act of allowing or disallowing access to certain areas of the network (programs, data, and so on) based on the user, system, or program. An example is user Terry being allowed to access payroll data as a member of the payroll department.

Accounting refers to tracking (and by implication, logging) the resources that are used by a given user or system. This allows a company to charge for the specific services used. An example is logging the time user Terry spends logged in through a dialed connection.

As an example, when Terry starts up the computer, there is a password prompt. If the password is the correct one, Terry is authenticated and can now use the computer.

Terry starts to open the payroll program, which resides on a network server. Before the program is opened, the authorization process occurs to ensure that Terry should have access to the program. If Terry is authorized to use the program, the process continues.

If Terry dials into the network, the accounting process would start recording facts about this access, such as the user and the date and time.

Now take a few minutes and explore a simple example configuration. In this example, AAA is enabled using the local security database, instead of either a TACACS+ or RADIUS server. This example will serve as a primer to the AAA methodology. The local database is stored within the router and does not require any outside entity to work properly. Look through this configuration and read the imbedded comment lines, which are preceded by a (!). The commands shown here will be more fully explained throughout the chapter.

```
aaa new-model
!Get ready to use AAA security

aaa authentication login default local
!By default, use the local database for authentication of logins

aaa authentication arap default local
!By default, use the local database for authentication of ARAP

aaa authentication ppp default local
!By default, use the local database for authentication on PPP

aaa authorization exec local
!Use the local database for authentication of EXEC commands

aaa authorization network local
!Use the local database for authentication of Network Services
```

```
!The aaa authorization command is fully explained later in this
!chapter in the section, "AAA Authorization Setup."
!For the moment, it is sufficient to know that this command
!authorized the user to do certain commands and run certain programs.

!Using the username command is what actually builds the local security database.
!In this example, three users are being added
!to the local database: amason, mnewcomb, and jkane.

username amason privilege exec level 7 password 7 Aeb98768
!Set Andrew Mason's exec privilege level at 7 and set Andrew Mason's password

username mnewcomb privilege exec level 6 password 7 010102238746
!Set Mark Newcomb's EXEC privilege level to 6 and set Mark Newcomb's password

username jkane privilege exec level 8 password 7 095E4F10140A1916
!Set John Kane's EXEC level to 8 and set John Kane's password


privilege exec level 6 slip
privilege exec level 7 ppp
privilege exec level 8 arap
!This associates the execution of SLIP, PPP, and ARAP with privilege levels.
!Because John Kane has a privilege level of 8, he can use ARAP, PPP, or SLIP.
!Andrew can use both ARAP and PPP because he has a privilege level of 7.
!Mark can only use SLIP because he has a privilege level of 6.
!The higher the privilege level, from 0-15, the more rights a user has.

interface Group-Async1
  ppp authentication chap default
!Use PPP authentication on this interface
  group-range 1 16
!
line console 0
  login authentication default
!Previously the default authentication method for
!logins was set to use the local database

line 1 16
  arap authentication default
!Previously the default authentication method for
!ARAP was set to use the local database
```

This configuration relies solely on the local security database to authenticate and authorize users. This is one of the simplest configurations available, but it should suffice to give you some exposure to the AAA model. The AAA model will continue to be explored throughout this chapter. The next section will deal with authentication using TACACS+ and RADIUS servers.

AAA Authentication Setup with TACACS+ and RADIUS

To authenticate large numbers of users, you need to have a database that stores the usernames and passwords. This is where either TACACS+ or RADIUS servers come into play.

On the router configuration, TACACS+ and RADIUS are not difficult to configure. They also allow for multiple forms of authentication, including:

- Digital certificates
- One-time passwords
- Changeable passwords
- Static passwords
- UNIX authentication using the /etc/password file
- NT database authentication

Three steps are required to make a router use AAA:

Step 1 Initial configuration

Step 2 Building a method list

Step 3 Linking the list to interfaces

Each of these will be discussed in turn.

Initial Configuration

You need to know a few new commands before using TACACS+ or RADIUS. These commands are used in global configuration mode. For TACACS+, the commands are as follows:

```
aaa new-model
tacacs-server host host-ip-address
tacacs-server key serverkey
```

The first command, **aaa new-model**, tells the router that you are using either TACACS+ or RADIUS for authentication. The next line tells the router the IP address of the TACACS+ server, where *host-ip-address* is the IP address of that server. The third line tells the router what password key is shared between the router and the server. Unlike passwords, which can be made to appear encrypted within configuration files, this password key always appears in plain text.

It is important that the key is used on both the router and within the configuration file on the server. This ensures that the key is encrypted before being sent to the server. Unless both the TACACS+ server and one of the Ethernet ports on the router are located on an extremely secure network, it is possible for someone to gather keys through the use of a packet analyzer. Therefore, the authors recommend that the key is always entered in both places. There is little sense in not encrypting the key after going through the effort of configuring TACACS+ or RADIUS authentication.

RADIUS authentication also relies on three initial commands. The first command, **aaa new-model**, is the same as on a TACACS+ system. The next two commands differ only in the replacement of **radius** for **tacacs**:

```
aaa new-model
radius-server host host-ip-address
radius-server key serverkey
```

Building a Method List

Now that the initial configuration of authentication is completed, you need to determine in what order the authentication methods will be accomplished. You have some flexibility in the order chosen. For example, you can make the router check the TACACS+ server first and then the local entry on the router, or check the local first and then the TACACS+ server.

A number of different authentication services also can be used. Table 10-1 contains a list of the available services and a description of each.

Table 10-1   *AAA Authentication Service Types*

Service	Description
arap	Uses AppleTalk Remote Access Protocol list
enable	Uses the enable mode list
login	Used for character mode connections
nasi	Uses NetWare Asynchronous Services Interface
ppp	Uses Point-to-Point Protocol

In addition to the service used, the order in which authentication is checked is also chosen. Up to four different authentication methods can be chosen. Multiple authentication methods are usually employed in case the authentication server is unreachable, but it can also be used to allow some individuals, such as the administrator, to completely bypass the server authentication process. Table 10-2 contains a list of valid authentication methods.

Table 10-2   *AAA Authentication Methods*

Method	Description
auth-guest	Allows a guest logon only if the user has already logged into the EXEC mode.
enable	Uses the enable password for authentication.
guest	Allows a guest logon.
if-needed	Authenticates only if the user has not already been authenticated.
krb5	Uses Kerberos 5 for authentication.
krb5-telnet	Uses Kerberos 5 for authentication on Telnet sessions. Note: This must be the first in the list.
line	Uses the line password for authentication.
local	Uses the local database for authentication.
none	No authentication is used.
radius	Uses RADIUS for authentication.
tacacs+	Uses TACACS+ for authentication.

Not all of the services can use all of the methods listed in Table 10-2. For example, the local method cannot use the enable service, and RADIUS cannot be used with NASI. A complete list of compatibilities can be found in Table 10-3.

Table 10-3   *Authentication Services and Methods Compatibility*

Method	arap	enable	login	nasi	ppp
auth-guest	Yes	No	No	No	No
enable	No	Yes	Yes	Yes	No
guest	Yes	No	No	No	No
if-needed	No	No	No	No	Yes
krb5	No	No	Yes	No	No
krb5-telnet	No	No	Yes	No	No
line	Yes	Yes	Yes	Yes	No
local	Yes	No	Yes	Yes	Yes
none	No	Yes	Yes	Yes	Yes
radius	Yes	Yes	Yes	No	Yes
tacacs+	Yes	Yes	Yes	Yes	Yes

The **aaa authentication** command is used to start authentication on the router. The general syntax of this command is

```
aaa authentication service-type {default | list-name}
    method1 [method2] [method3] [method4]
```

With this command, *service-type* is one of the services previously listed in Table 10-1, such as **arap**, **line**, **if-needed**, and so on. The next parameter is either the keyword **default** or a list name. The list name can be virtually any word except the word *default*, and it is used to name the following list of authentication methods. The parameters *method1*, *method2*, *method3,* and *method4* are used to specify the order in which authentication takes place. Use any of the methods listed in Table 10-2. At least one method must be used, with a maximum total of four methods specified.

There are three exceptions to the syntax described above. These exceptions are:

```
aaa authentication local-override
aaa authentication password-prompt text-string
aaa authentication username-prompt text-string
```

The **aaa authentication local-override** command is used on an individual interface to force the IOS to check the local database before attempting any other form of authentication. The **aaa authentication password-prompt** *text-string* command is used to change the text that is displayed when a user is prompted for a password. The parameter *text-string* is the text that is displayed. The **aaa authentication username-prompt** *text-string* changes the text that is displayed when a user is prompted for a username.

Now look at how these commands work. Assume that you want to make TACACS+ the default authentication method for PPP access. You would use the following command:

```
aaa authentication ppp default tacacs+
```

If you want to use TACACS+ as the default and also allow the local database to be used if the TACACS+ server does not respond, you would use the following command:

```
aaa authentication ppp branch-office-users tacacs+ login
```

Notice in this scenario that you have dropped the use of the word **default** and are now using **branch-office-users** instead. The parameter **branch-office-users** is an arbitrary name made up for this list. It is critical that the administrator understands that the local database is not used if any response is received from the TACACS+ server. In other words, the local database is only used if the TACACS+ server is not available. The local database is not consulted if the TACACS+ server rejects the request to log in.

To review, the following shows the new commands used in this configuration. For this example you will use TACACS+ to authenticate users logging into the router. If the TACACS+ server is not available, you will use the local database to authenticate. The set of global commands required follows:

```
aaa new-model
!Get ready to use AAA

tacacs-server host 172.30.1.50
!Set the server to look for the TACACS+ server at the IP address of 172.30.1.50

tacacs-server key mysecretkey
!Using the server key "mysecretkey" on both the router and
!within the configuration of the TACACS+ server forces
!encryption when the key is sent to the server

aaa authentication ppp branch-office-users tacacs+ login
!Set authentication for PPP to first use the TACACS+ server and
!then use the local database.
!The name of this list is "branch-office-users."
```

Now that the method list is built, you still need to link the list to an interface before authentication can take place.

Linking the List to Interfaces

Because the initial and method list configurations are done, you merely need to add the proper commands to the individual interfaces.

In this example, you are going to use AAA authentication on S2, which is connected to the branch office.

```
interface serial 2
!This interface is connected via ISDN to the branch office

ppp authentication chap
!You have set the PPP authentication to use CHAP
```

Although this configuration works to authenticate the users with CHAP, it might not be the best configuration for your purposes. Instead, you could use the TACACS+ server for the initial authentication. You would then use CHAP if the user is not already authenticated. To do this, you change the last interface configuration line to read:

```
ppp authentication chap if-needed branch-office-users
!You have set the PPP authentication to use CHAP if the user has
!not already been authenticated by the TACACS+ server.
```

This gives a little more protection. To refine this a little more, in the following configuration the router first expects a CHAP password. If the received password fails, the router then accepts another password attempt, this time expecting a PAP password. Because PAP sends the password itself in clear text, the administrator should ensure that the **chap** keyword is used before the **pap** keyword. This causes the first connection attempt password hash to be encrypted with a clear text password being sent only if the CHAP connection attempt fails. Using the **pap** keyword first would cause the first attempt to be accomplished with a clear-text password, which is a less secure method.

```
ppp authentication chap pap if-needed branch-office-users
!You have set the PPP authentication to use CHAP if the user has
!not already been authenticated by the TACACS+ server.
!If CHAP is not available, you use PAP.
```

Finally, because you only need to verify users from the remote office coming into the main branch, you can specify that only those calling in are authenticated. As the router is now configured, both incoming and outgoing users are authenticated. Adding the keyword **callin** to the previous command authenticates only incoming calls:

```
ppp authentication chap pap if-needed branch-office-users callin
!You have set the PPP authentication to use CHAP if the user has
!not already been authenticated by the TACACS+ server.
!If CHAP is not available, you use PAP.
!This only applies to connections initiated from the outside of this interface.
```

The final configuration looks like this:

```
aaa new-model
tacacs-server host 172.30.1.50
tacacs-server key mysecretkey
aaa authentication ppp branch-office-users tacacs+ login

interface serial 2
ppp authentication chap pap if-needed branch-office-users callin
```

Fine-Tuning the Configuration

You now have a configuration where the remote PPP user authenticates through the TACACS+ server. However, there is a configuration issue here that is sure to become a problem sometime in the future. You have not really secured how you log into the router for administrative purposes. You need to be extremely careful when authenticating users to the console. If you rely solely on a TACACS+ or RADIUS server, you will be unable to log onto the router if there are problems in communication between the two. Therefore, you need to enable another method of accessing the console.

This is very simple to do, but very important for troubleshooting purposes. First, set the default authentication for the login through the console and TTY to use TACACS+ or RADIUS. Then create a list that requires no authentication. Finally, associate this list with an interface. An example follows:

```
aaa authentication login default tacacs+
aaa authentication login administrative none

line con 0
login authentication administrative
```

The only security issue related to this configuration is that anyone who has physical access to the router can plug into the console and log in, bypassing the TACACS+ authentication. However, anyone with physical access to the router also has the ability to reset the router and bypass the current configuration anyway. As always, physical security is necessary on all equipment critical to your network.

AAA Authorization Setup

Whereas authentication is concerned with ensuring that the device or end user is who it claims to be, authorization is concerned with allowing and disallowing authenticated users access to certain areas and programs on the network.

The command for enabling authorization follows:

```
aaa authorization service-type {default | list-name}
     method1 [method2] [method3] [method4]
```

With this command, *service-type* must be one of the service types listed in Table 10-4.

Table 10-4 *AAA Authorization Service Types*

Service Type	Description
commands {*level*}	Checks authorization for any EXEC command at the optionally specified level
exec	Checks authorization to run an EXEC shell
network	Checks authorization for network activities
reverse-access	Checks authorization for reverse Telnet

The next parameter is either the key word **default** or a list name. The list name can be virtually any word except the word *default*, and it is used to name the following list of authorization methods. The parameters *method1*, *method2*, *method3*, and *method4* are used to specify the order in which authentication takes place. At least one method must be used, with a maximum total of four methods specified. The possible values for the method are shown in Table 10-5.

Table 10-5   *AAA Authorization Methods*

Method	Description
if-authenticated	If the user is already authenticated, the user is allowed to access the service.
krb5-instance	This uses the instance defined with the **kerberos instance map** command.
local	The local database is consulted.
radius	The RADIUS server's database is consulted to see if the user has the appropriate rights.
tacacs+	The TACACS+ server's database is consulted to see if the user has the appropriate rights.

NOTE   When AAA authorization is not enabled, all users are allowed full access. Once authentication is started, the default changes to allow no access.

This means that the administrator must create a user with full access rights configured before authorization is enabled. Failure to do so will immediately lock the administrators out of their own system the moment the **aaa authorization** command is entered.

The only way to recover from this is to reboot the router. If this is a production router, rebooting might be unacceptable. Be sure that at least one user always has full rights.

Configuring AAA authorization is very similar to AAA authentication. Look at the following configuration. This configuration checks the authorization for users of the S2 interface when accessing network service such as PPP:

```
aaa new-model
!Set up for AAA

tacacs-server host 172.30.1.50
!The TACACS+ server is at 172.30.1.50

tacacs-server key mysecretkey
!Use the encrypted keys

interface s2
aaa authorization network tacacs+
!Start authorization for network services
```

AAA Accounting Setup

Sometimes a corporation wishes to keep track of which resources individuals or groups use. Examples of this include when the IS department charges other departments for access, or one company provides internal support to another company. For whatever reason you choose, AAA accounting gives the ability to track usage, such as dial-in access; the ability to log the data gathered to a database; and the ability to produce reports on the data gathered.

Although accounting is generally considered a network management or financial management issue, it is looked at briefly here because it is so closely linked with security. One security issue that accounting can address is creating a list of users and the time of day they choose to dial into the system. If, for example, the administrator knows that a worker logs onto the system in the middle of the night, this information can be used to further investigate the purpose of the login.

Another reason to implement accounting is to create a list of changes occurring on the network, who made the changes, and the exact nature of the changes. Knowing this information helps in the troubleshooting process if the changes cause unexpected results.

AAA accounting is started with the **aaa accounting** command. Note that AAA accounting is currently supported only on TACACS+ and RADIUS servers. The full syntax of the **aaa accounting** command follows:

```
aaa accounting event-type {default | list-name}
    {start-stop | wait-start | stop-only | none} method1 [method2]
```

event-type can be one of the event types shown in Table 10-6.

Table 10-6   *AAA Accounting Event Types*

Event Type	Description
command {*level*}	Applies to all commands for the optionally specified level
connection	Applies to all outbound connections, including LAT, PAD, and so on
exec	Runs accounting for all user shell EXEC commands
network	Runs accounting for all network-related service requests such as PPP and ARAP
system	Runs accounting for system-related events that are not associated with users, for example, a **reload** command

As with AAA authentication, either the keyword **default** or a list name is used. Next, the trigger is entered. The trigger specifies what actions cause accounting records to be updated. The list of possible triggers and their meanings is shown in Table 10-7.

Table 10-7 *AAA Authentication Triggers*

Trigger	Description
none	Stops accounting on this interface.
start-stop	The accounting record is sent as soon as a session begins. This is in contrast to **wait-start**. Another accounting record (which includes the session statistics) is sent as soon as the session ends.
stop-only	A record is sent only when the session ends. This record includes the session statistics.
wait-start	The accounting record is sent when an acknowledgment is received from the server that a session has started. This is in contrast to **start-stop**. Another accounting record (which includes the session statistics) is sent as soon as the session ends.

The parameters *method1* and *method2* have only two possible values: **tacacs+** and **radius**. Using **tacacs+** uses a TACACS+ server, while **radius** uses a RADIUS server.

An example of using AAA accounting follows:

```
aaa new-model
!Set up for AAA

tacacs-server host 172.30.1.50
!The TACACS+ server is at 172.30.1.50

tacacs-server key mysecretkey
!Use the encrypted keys

aaa accounting exec start-stop tacacs+
!Start accounting whenever an exec command is issued
```

Using All AAA Services Simultaneously

It is possible, and sometimes desirable, to incorporate authentication, authorization, and accounting simultaneously on a router. This is actually easier than it sounds. The following is a configuration that combines all three parts of AAA using exactly the examples from the previous sections. All that is needed to run them at the same time is for the administrator to enter the appropriate configuration lines. Some commands, such as the **aaa new-model,** only needs to be entered once:

```
aaa new-model
!Set up for AAA

tacacs-server host 172.30.1.50
!The TACACS+ server is at 172.30.1.50
```

```
tacacs-server key mysecretkey
!Use the encrypted keys

aaa authentication login default tacacs+
!Set the default authentication to TACACS+

aaa authentication ppp branch-office-users tacacs+ login
!Sets authentication for PPP to first use TACACS+ if the server
!is available and then look at the local database

aaa authentication login administrative none
!Used to ensure the administrator has access

aaa accounting exec start-stop tacacs+
!Start accounting whenever an exec command is issued

interface serial 2
!Go to the interface

ppp authentication chap pap if-needed branch-office-users callin
!Enable authentication on the S2 interface

aaa authorization network tacacs+
!Start authorization for network services

line con 0
login authentication administrative
!Make sure the administrator can get into the console
```

Virtual Private Networks (VPNs)

The huge increase in the number of VPN clients and companies wanting to use VPNs requires administrators to understand the special security considerations necessary when dealing with VPNs. Because most VPNs are used over a connection to the Internet, any security gap has the potential to be exploited by hundreds of hackers.

VPNs are built by using tunneling protocols, which are protocols that are encapsulated within another protocol. Examples of tunneling protocols used in VPNs are General Routing Encapsulation (GRE), Layer 2 Tunneling Protocol (L2TP), Encapsulation Security Protocol (ESP), Cisco Encryption Technology (CET), and the Layer 2 Forwarding (L2F) protocols. This section covers some of the more commonly used tunneling protocols.

Although a tunneling protocol by itself does offer some protection, greater protection can be obtained by adding encryption within the tunnel. Because a tunnel can normally only be entered from one of the endpoints, some administrators consider them safe without encryption. Only encryption can truly protect data. The "man in the middle" form of attack can be used to inject a device in the middle of a tunnel. This is why a tunnel without encryption is not truly secure.

Because most tunnels can carry encrypted traffic, there is no reason other than router overhead not to also encrypt traffic running through the tunnel. If the performance of your routers is adversely affected by the combination of encryption and tunneling, the routers should be upgraded.

Before discussing how to set up an encrypted tunnel, this section includes a quick overview of some of the types of tunnels and encryption available on Cisco equipment.

L2F

The Layer 2 Forwarding (L2F) protocol is a Cisco proprietary protocol developed to allow Virtual Private Dial-up Network (VPDN) connections. While still supported for various other functions, L2F has largely been replaced by L2TP.

L2TP

Layer 2 Tunneling Protocol (L2TP) builds on the best features present in both the L2F and PPTP protocols. Supporting both IP and non-IP protocols, L2TP is used mainly for dial-up connections.

Generic Routing Encapsulation (GRE) Tunneling

Generic routing encapsulation (GRE) tunnels build a path through the public Internet while encapsulating traffic with new packet headers that ensure the delivery to a specified destination. GRE tunneling is also commonly used to transfer non-IP traffic over an IP network by encapsulating this non-IP traffic within IP.

Encryption

Cisco supports both IPSec and Cisco Encryption Technology (CET) data encryption within GRE tunnels.

IPSec is an open standard, supporting 56-bit, 128-bit, and 256-bit encryption algorithms. Supported on platforms such as Windows and UNIX, IPSec uses certificate authentication and Internet Key Exchange (IKE).

CET is a Cisco standard that supports 40-bit and 56-bit encryption algorithms. CET can be used only between two Cisco routers. Administrators need to be aware that with the exception of the acceleration card within the 7200 and 7500 series routers, CET will be discontinued with the next major release after IOS version 12.1.

If you are currently deploying CET, you should consider upgrading your configurations before you are forced to when installing a new IOS version. Cisco recommends that IPSec with IKE be used instead of CET for encryption within the tunnel.

See the article at this URL for more details about the CET end-of-life announcement: www.cisco.com/warp/public/cc/general/bulletin/security/1118_pp.htm

IPSec Configuration

The following configurations show how a main router and a branch router can be set up to accept a VPN connection using IPSec encryption. The new commands will be explored after the configurations. The following is the main office router configuration:

```
access-list 101 permit any any

crypto map branchoffice 10 ipsec-isakmp
match address 101
set transform-set mytransformset
set peer 172.30.2.2

interface Serial0
ip address 172.30.2.1
crypto map branchoffice
```

The following is the branch router configuration:

```
access-list 101 permit any any

crypto map branchoffice 10 ipsec-isakmp
match address 101
set transform-set mytransformset
set peer 172.30.2.1

interface Serial0
ip address 172.30.2.2
crypto map branchoffice
```

The **crypto map branchoffice 10 ipsec-isakmp** line defines a map name (**branchoffice**) and assigns a number (**10**) to that map name. Next, the line defines that you will use IKE to establish IPSec security associations for the traffic specified in the map statement.

The **match address** command specifies that extended access list 101 is used to determine what traffic is encrypted. A named access list can also be used.

The **set transform-set** command specifies the name **mytransformset**. This name is compared to the peer router. If the transform set on the peer router is the same, encryption and decryption takes place. If the names are different, no data transfer occurs.

The **set peer** command sets the IP address of the peer router. The peer router must also have the correct IP address configured.

Within the interface, there is the **crypto map** command that associates this interface with the globally defined mapping of **branchoffice**.

This was a very simple example. Next, look at an example that is closer to real life. Take extra time to read all of the imbedded comments within this configuration:

```
access-list 199 permit udp any eq 500 any eq 500
access-list 199 permit 50 any any
access-list 199 permit 51 any any
!These ports are necessary because IKE and IPSec use them

access-list 150 permit 50 any any
access-list 150 permit 51 any any
access-list 150 permit udp any eq 500 any eq 500
```

```
!Since you will have two access lists (one inbound and one outbound)
!on the serial interface, you will need to allow IKE
!and IPSec traffic for both of these interfaces.

access-list 101 permit tcp 172.30.1.0 0.0.0.255 172.20.3.0 0.0.0.255 eq 23
access-list 101 permit tcp 172.30.1.0 0.0.0.255 eq 23 172.20.3.0 0.0.0.255
!Why use another access list? You want to encrypt all
!data that uses port 23 (Telnet) either coming or going from the main branch.
!You will use the number 101 later to define what is encrypted.

crypto transform-set encryp-auth esp-des esp-sha-hmac
crypto transform-set auth-only ah-sha-hmac
!You define the IPSec protection types for use on each type of traffic

crypto map BranchOffice 10 ipsec-isakmp
match address 101
!Remember that you are watching for the number 101?
!This refers to access list number 101, which is used to determine
!what traffic should be encrypted

set transform-set mytransformset
set peer 172.30.2.1

interface Serial0
ip address 172.30.2.2
crypto map branchoffice
ip access-group 199 in
!You need to allow IKE and IPSec traffic through
ip access-group 150 out
!You need the traffic to flow both ways
```

Summary

This chapter discussed how dial-in users can be authenticated using the local database. As an example, the chapter included a basic AAA configuration. Next, the chapter took an in-depth look at the AAA authentication process using a TACACS+ server. Finally, the chapter explored how IPSec can be used to secure VPNs coming into the network through the Internet.

The next chapter, "Providing Secure Access to Internet Services," covers the requirements of securing the corporate network while still allowing access to Web servers.

This chapter contains the following sections:

- Internet Services
- Common Internet Security Threats
- Internet Service Security Example
- Web Servers
- File Transfer Protocol (FTP) Servers
- Internet e-Mail Servers (SMTP/POP3/IMAP4)
- Domain Name System (DNS) Servers
- Back-End Servers
- Summary
- Frequently Asked Questions
- Glossary

CHAPTER 11

Providing Secure Access to Internet Services

The Internet is growing at a phenomenal rate. It is estimated that several thousand web sites are added to the Internet on a daily basis. Never before has industry had such an aggressive medium for exploitation.

With this growth, it has become standard for the traditional retail store to gain a presence on the Internet. Initially, this presence was nothing more than a static Web page that acted purely as an online advertisement for the store. This progressed to becoming an online source that presented information about goods and services offered by the store. Pretty soon, e-commerce came along, and the store started actively trading on the Internet. The Internet has no geographical limits, so soon the retail store had a global market with unlimited potential at its disposal.

With this massive growth and dependence on the technology supporting it comes a new set of hazards. The advent of e-commerce brings with it unique risks, as financial data is being transferred over the Internet. This leads to a breed of cyber-criminals. These cyber-criminals are very intelligent network hackers who use tried and tested techniques to infiltrate corporate systems for their own financial gain or to cause a denial of service (DoS) to the corporate site, thus costing the corporation money in lost revenue.

This chapter covers common Internet services and the attacks that are launched on them. It starts by looking at some common security attacks that can be made over the Internet and concentrates on network intrusion and DoS attacks. Finally, the chapter moves on to look at each individual Internet service, consisting of Web servers, File Transfer Protocol (FTP) servers, Internet e-mail servers, and Domain Name System (DNS) servers.

The common threats to each service and preventive security strategies that can be applied to these services are identified in this chapter.

This chapter provides only an overview of Internet service threats and preventive measures. There are whole books that have been written on the subject, such as:

Web Security and Commerce. O'Reilly Nutshell, 1997.

E-Commerce Security: Weak Links, Best Defences. John Wiley and Sons, 1998.

Web Security: A Step-by-Step Reference Guide. Addison-Wesley, 1998.

Practical Unix and Internet Security. O'Reilly, 1996.

Internet Services

This chapter covers the common Internet services that most companies provide for public access. These services make up the Internet presence of the company. These services might interact with each other to provide the service to the public. This interaction itself might raise various security risks not associated with the devices on their own.

TCP/IP operates using what is called a *port* as a connection endpoint. The port is what TCP/IP uses to differentiate among the services within the TCP/IP protocol suite. All Internet services use ports; some use User Datagram Protocol (UDP), but most use TCP.

The following is a list of the common Internet services that most corporate businesses employ as part of their public Internet offering. These technologies can be used on intranets, extranets, and other private networks, as well as the public Internet:

- **Web servers**—Web servers provide access to the web sites of the business.

- **FTP servers**—FTP servers provide a source of downloadable files from the web site and also act as a medium for transferring files to and from the other servers.

- **Internet e-mail servers**—Internet e-mail servers are responsible for message delivery and routing of the corporate Internet-bound e-mails.

- **DNS servers**—DNS servers hold the domain and IP information for the corporate domain.

- **Back-end servers**—Back-end servers can fall into one of many categories. These include database servers, security authentication servers, and application servers. Back-end servers are not usually public-facing; that is, they do not usually have a publicly accessible IP address.

This chapter covers each individual service, gives a brief overview of the service, explains the specific threats posed to the individual service, and provides solutions to these threats. Solutions can be achieved by implementing products from the Cisco Secure product range.

Before covering the individual services, the chapter looks at aspects of Internet security in relation to the web site as a whole. To do this, the chapter includes a sample Internet service that is running under Mydomain.com. This Internet service includes Web servers, FTP servers, e-mail servers, DNS servers, and back-end servers.

You will see how to assess the security of the site in relation to the common attacks that are made on public Internet services. After looking at the threats, you will see how to outline how each of these affect each individual service.

The next section starts by looking at the common Internet security threats before going on to outline the sample Internet service.

Common Internet Security Threats

Throughout the short history of the Internet, attacks to the public servers of large corporations have been prevalent. These are usually for financial gain to the perpetrator, financial loss to the victim, or sense of personal achievement and increase in status to the perpetrator among the hacking community. These attacks can be categorized based on the type of attack. Most Internet attacks fall into one of these categories. However, just as the Internet evolves, new categories and new attacks evolve all of the time.

These attacks fall into two general categories. They are trying either to gain unauthorized access into the network or to deny service to the network. These two categories can intermingle such that a network intrusion could lead to the denial of service. Throughout this chapter, the following separate attacks are covered:

- Network intrusion
- Denial of service

Network Intrusion

Network intrusion is when unauthorized access is gained to a computer system or computer network. This can be achieved in many ways. The following are the two main types of network intrusion with which this book is concerned:

- Unauthorized access
- Eavesdropping

Unauthorized Access

Unauthorized access generally refers to the gaining of access to a network by using username and password pairs. These passwords can be obtained by the following methods:

- **Social engineering**—Social engineering is where the attacker gets someone of authority to release information, such as username and password pairs. A common social engineering attack could be someone telephoning a network user, pretending to be from the company's network help desk, and asking for the user's username and password. These attacks are very hard to overcome; the only real way is through staff training and fostering a secure office culture.

- **Dictionary attack**—A dictionary attack is a brute-force attack against a password system. The attacker runs a piece of dictionary software to try numerous passwords against the system. The attack gets its name from the fact that the method usually employs a *dictionary file*, which contains thousands of common and not-so-common words. Each of these words in turn is attempted in the authentication attempt.

Security policy should stipulate the maximum number of wrong passwords that can be entered before the account is locked. This feature is implemented in most mainstream network operating systems today. One way to overcome a majority of these attacks is to make all passwords a random set of alphanumeric characters with mixed case. For example, the password "dfgWJdHu75G4fo" would be a lot harder for a dictionary attack to break than the password "miamidolphins."

- **Exploitation of services**—In addition to password attacks, which encompass the previous two methods, there is the exploitation of the network services. For example, a bug with the UNIX sendmail service allowed a user to send a series of commands to the service that would gain the user administrative access to the host machine.

  Be sure to keep abreast of all the latest security vulnerabilities and ensure that all network services have the latest security patch.

Eavesdropping

Eavesdropping is where an attacker uses a network analyzer or sniffer to listen and decode the frames on the network medium. This type of attack is physically hard to achieve, because it has to be done either at the same location as the network or at the office of a service provider to that network. The traffic that the attacker can capture is limited by the location of the attacker. For example, if the sniff or trace is run on the corporate LAN, an attacker probably will not see WAN routing traffic because that traffic will not be local or contained to the LAN. A common use of sniffing is to obtain the username and password pairs of either users or network services.

Sniffing can also lead to session replay attacks and session hijacking:

- **Session replay attacks**—With most network analyzers available today, you can capture the data into a buffer. This buffer can then be replayed on the network. An attacker can capture a user logging into a system and running commands. By replaying the captured session, the attacker can recreate the initial user's actions and use it for personal benefit. The common method is for the attacker to change the source IP address of the capture so that the session initiates with another host. Even with encryption, session replays are very hard to spot and prevent.

- **Session hijacking**—Session hijacking is where the attacker inserts falsified IP data packets after the initial session has been established. This can alter the flow of the session and establish communication with a different network host than the one where the session was originally established.

Denial of Service (DoS)

The term *denial of service* has been heard quite a lot in the Internet community recently. This is partly because of frequent DoS attacks that have been carried out against leading e-commerce vendors, such as eBay.com and Amazon.com.

A DoS attack is the saturation of network resources targeted against a single host or range of hosts with the intent to stop that host from furnishing further network requests. This has the same effect as a server that is under too much strain and cannot deal with the concentration of requests for its services.

The problem with DoS attacks is that most of the attacks appear to be genuine requests for service. They just come in rather large numbers—large enough to make the server fall over.

Numerous DoS attacks exist, and new ones are found almost on a weekly basis. Web sites run by white hat hackers (hackers benevolently researching security issues) are being misused by black hat hackers (malevolent hackers) and script kiddies. This information is being misused in the form of DoS attacks against Internet hosts.

Attackers can run a DoS attack from anywhere. They target a public service, so they protect and hide their identity, and they can run the attack by a dial-up connection anywhere in the world.

Many DoS attacks are very simple to run, which has led to the increase in what are called *script kiddies*. A script kiddie is someone with limited knowledge who runs a prebuilt DoS script to attack an Internet host. The authors have even seen UNIX GUI-based applications that mimic numerous DoS attacks and make it extremely easy to use this technology against an unsuspecting host.

This section looks at some common and more famous DoS attacks. There are literally hundreds of these in existence now.

- **TCP SYN flooding attack**—The TCP SYN flood attack exploits the three-way handshake connection mechanism of TCP/IP. The attacker initiates a TCP session with the server by sending a TCP SYN packet to the server. The server responds to this initial packet with a TCP SYN/ACK response. The attacker's machine should then respond to this SYN/ACK by sending its own SYN/ACK back to the server. At this point, the session would be established. What happens in a TCP SYN attack is that the attacker's machine never responds to the TCP SYN/ACK sent by the server. This causes the server to wait for response and for the session to start. This is called a *half-open session*. Each of these half-open sessions uses resources on the server. The attacker floods the server with thousands of these session initiation packets, causing the server eventually to run out of resources, thus denying service to any other inbound connections.

- **Smurf attack**—A smurf attack is when an attacker sends an ICMP Echo Request to a network address rather than a specific host. The important point is that the attacker enters the IP address of the targeted server as the ICMP Echo Request source address.

This has the effect of every host on a network responding and sending an ICMP Echo Reply to the attacker-supplied source address of the ICMP Echo packet. This source address is the address of the server that the attacker wants to attack.

In this case, the attacker uses somebody else's resources and network to attack the victim. This attack works by simply consuming bandwidth to the victim. Once this bandwidth is consumed, all access to the server from other public hosts slowly grinds to a halt. The third party who is amplifying the attack is also affected because it consumes outbound bandwidth from the network.

Figure 11–1 depicts a smurf attack.

Figure 11-1 *Smurf Attack*

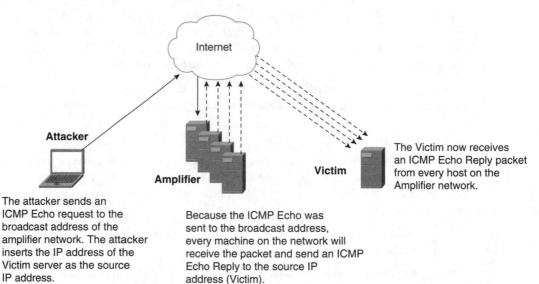

The attacker sends an ICMP Echo request to the broadcast address of the amplifier network. The attacker inserts the IP address of the Victim server as the source IP address.

Because the ICMP Echo was sent to the broadcast address, every machine on the network will receive the packet and send an ICMP Echo Reply to the source IP address (Victim).

The Victim now receives an ICMP Echo Reply packet from every host on the Amplifier network.

- **Ping of death**—The ping of death is a famous DoS attack that uses the ping ICMP Echo Request and Echo Reply to crash a remote system. It is classified as an elegant one-packet kill.

  This attack works by sending a large ICMP Echo Request packet that gets fragmented before sending. The receiving host, which is also the victim, reconstructs the fragmented packet. Because the packet size is above the maximum allowed packet size, it can cause system crashes, reboots, kernel dumps, and buffer overflows, thus rendering the system unusable.

  This attack, although still in existence, is well protected against with all recent operating systems.

- **Teardrop**—The teardrop attack is a classic DoS attack that normally causes memory problems on the server that is being attacked. Teardrop attacks use fragmentation and malformed packets to cause the victim host to miscalculate and perform illegal memory functions. These illegal memory functions can interact with other applications running on the server and result in crashing the server.

  Because this is a fragmentation attack, it can bypass some traditional intrusion detection systems (IDSs).

- **Land**—The land attack is where the attacker sends a spoofed packet to a server that has the same source IP address and port as the destination IP address and port. For example, if the server had an IP address of 192.168.0.1, both the source and destination IP addresses of the packet would be 192.168.0.1. The port is identified as being open by a network scan that the attacker runs before sending the packet. The result is that the server, if susceptible, will crash. This attack is also known as the LAND.c attack. The *.c* refers to the C script in which it is presented.

The preceding list represents only a small percentage of the network intrusions and DoS attacks that exist. White hat hackers who aim to educate security administrators about the new threats and vulnerabilities that emerge almost daily provide helpful web sites; among these sites are www.security-focus.com and www.rootshell.com. These sites should be examined frequently to keep network security up-to-date and as secure as possible.

Internet Service Security Example

This example presents the fictitious simple Internet service of Mydomain.com, a new dot-com startup selling CDs and videos online. Mydomain.com employs the full range of servers covered throughout this chapter, including Web servers, FTP servers, Internet e-mail servers, DNS servers, and back-end servers.

This example includes before and after designs. The before design uses a standard public-facing model, and the after design implements security elements based around a Cisco Secure PIX Firewall. The example identifies the common attacks that can be carried out and the way that the proposed secure solution will deal with these attacks.

The network is hosted at an Internet service provider (ISP) and is connected straight into a hosting switch. The ISP provides no upstream security for hosted solutions. Security is the responsibility of the individual clients. The network diagram can be seen at Figure 11-2.

Figure 11-2 *Mydomain.com Network Diagram*

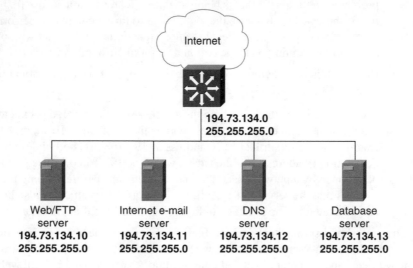

You can see in the network diagram in Figure 11-2 that the Mydomain.com solution consists of four servers. The Web and FTP services exist on the same server. Mydomain.com has been allocated 10 addresses in the 194.73.134.0/24 network that is registered to the ISP and is used for hosting solutions. The addresses allocated are 194.73.134.11/24 to 194.73.134.20/24.

This is a very common simple configuration for Web hosting from an ISP.

Initial Problems and Threats in the Internet Service Security Example

This solution is not ideal from a security point of view. As a general rule of thumb, the authors would never place an unprotected host on the public Internet. This solution places all four servers on the public Internet with public IP addresses. The IP address allocation is not within its own Layer 3 domain (VLAN/subnet); therefore, it is considered to be on the same broadcast domain as all of the other traffic within the 194.73.134.0/24 network. The following threats have been identified with this solution:

• **Network threats**—Because the servers are located on the public Internet, no security device is protecting the servers from a plethora of network threats. These threats include network intrusion attempts and DoS attacks. Without security devices protecting the solution, you are relying on the configuration of the actual server as the first and only line of defense.

- **Operating systems vulnerabilities**—Every operating system has known vulnerabilities. You have only to check the content of any security-focused web site to see the number of vulnerabilities that exist in every operating system. By placing these servers on the public Internet, you are making any security flaw in the operating system available for exploitation by potential hackers.

- **Application vulnerabilities**—Besides operating system vulnerabilities, there are application vulnerabilities. These vulnerabilities appertain to the applications running on the servers. Microsoft's Internet Information Server (IIS) is the standard Web server of choice for Windows NT and Windows 2000 servers. This application has numerous well-known vulnerabilities, and new patches are released frequently to protect against recently found vulnerabilities.

- **Server-to-server communication**—When the Web server communicates with the database server, this is classified as server-to-server communication. This traffic should never go across a public network. In the design in Figure 11-2, this traffic is going across the public network. Other machines that are not a part of the Mydomain.com network and within the same Layer 3 domain could easily capture this communication. This raises security issues.

- **Access to back-end servers**—Why make a server publicly accessible if only server-to-server communication is going to exist?

  Most back-end servers are not required to be accessed by outside hosts, because they might need only to communicate to other servers that are requesting their resources. The Mydomain.com service uses a Web server and a database server. The database server stores the stock details and is accessed by a Web page on the Web server. The public client is never required to access the server directly. In making it publicly accessible, you are also making every vulnerability on the server accessible.

Although there are obviously numerous threats to this solution, it is shocking to learn how many hosted solutions within the ISP environment are installed in this way. In security, there must always be a motive for attack. With low-risk and low-exposure sites, this motive might be so low as not to catch a hacker's attention.

Proposed Changes to the Internet Service Security Example

The most important change to implement in this solution is to place some sort of a firewall device in front of it. The term *firewall* can be defined as a device that simply protects internal networks from external threats. These devices normally carry out some sort of routing to route traffic from one interface to another and to perform packet or stateful inspection of traffic.

NOTE	Stateful inspection is a very important feature to have within a firewall. Early firewalls only implemented packet filtering. Stateful inspection and filtering maintain connection state information and allow policy decisions to be based on this state. Packet filtering just filters every packet, regardless of the existence of a current connection, session, or state.

Now see what happens if you decide to implement a Cisco Secure PIX Firewall to protect the solution. You only need two interfaces—one internal and one external. The proposed network diagram can be seen in Figure 11-3.

Figure 11-3 *Proposed Change to the Mydomain.com Network*

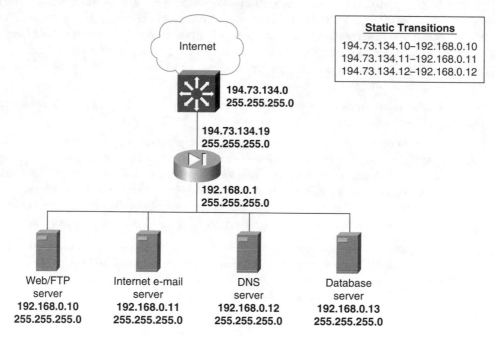

You can see from the network diagram in Figure 11-3 that there is now a Cisco Secure PIX Firewall between the hosted switch and the Mydomain.com network. This PIX Firewall also carries out Network Address Translation (NAT) for the Mydomain.com network. The use of NAT means that the Mydomain.com network can now use RFC 1918-compliant private addressing. In this case, Mydomain.com has opted for the 192.168.0.0/24 network. This address space is not routed on the public Internet and can protect the identity and addressing of the Mydomain.com network.

NAT is a method where public IP addresses get translated into private IP addresses for address-hiding purposes. You can create a private network behind a NAT device, such as a router or a firewall, and create static translations between these private addresses and public addresses. This hides the private addresses of the network from the public Internet and provides a method where the private servers can communicate with each other over the private addresses. There are two types of NAT. These are one-to-one NAT and one-to-many NAT. One-to-many NAT is also known as Port Address Translation (PAT).

Access to the specific servers from the public Internet is permitted through what are called *static translations*. The PIX Firewall maintains static translations between the public and private addresses. These are manually configured on the PIX Firewall—one per translation. Because the database server is only involved in communication with the Web server, there is no need to provide a static translation for this server.

The static translations for this solution are displayed in Table 11-1.

Table 11-1   *Static Translations*

Public IP Address	Private IP Address
194.73.134.10	192.168.0.10
194.73.134.11	192.168.0.11
194.73.134.12	192.168.0.12

In this case, a public client accessing www.mydomain.com receives the IP address of 194.73.134.10. The PIX Firewall intercepts this packet on the hosted switch, because the outside interface replies to Address Resolution Protocol (ARP) requests for its own interface and every other statically configured address. The PIX then redirects the packet to 192.168.0.10. This would be totally transparent to the public client.

You can further restrict access by configuring access lists on the PIX Firewall. On the PIX Firewall, these access lists are called *conduits*. You can allow specific traffic to specific servers and deny everything else. The PIX **conduit** command works in a similar way to the Router IOS **access-list** command. These conduits make up the basic firewall security policy for the solution. Table 11-2 shows the basic firewall security policy.

Table 11-2   *Sample Firewall Security Policy*

Source IP Address	Destination IP Address	Service	Permit/Deny
Any	194.73.134.10	WWW	Permit
Any	194.73.134.10	FTP	Permit
Any	194.73.134.11	SMTP	Permit
Any	194.73.134.11	POP3	Permit
Any	194.73.134.12	Domain	Permit
195.92.1.250	Any	Ping	Permit

This policy allows only specific services to specific hosts. One point to mention is the last line in the policy in Table 11-2. This line allows Internet Control Message Protocol (ICMP) ping access from the address 195.92.1.250 to any host within the Mydomain.com hosted network. The address 195.92.1.250 is the egress point from the Mydomain.com offices, which are in a different physical location than the hosted network. This is so that the network staff at the office can ping the solution for monitoring purposes.

The configuration of the PIX Firewall is as follows:

```
PIX Version 5.1(2)
nameif ethernet0 outside security0
nameif ethernet1 inside security100
enable password 8Ry2YjIyt7RRXU24 encrypted
passwd 2KFQnbNIdI.2KYOU encrypted
hostname pixfirewall
fixup protocol ftp 21
fixup protocol http 80
fixup protocol h323 1720
fixup protocol rsh 514
fixup protocol smtp 25
fixup protocol sqlnet 1521
names
pager lines 24
logging on
no logging timestamp
no logging standby
no logging console
no logging monitor
no logging buffered
no logging trap
no logging history
logging facility 20
logging queue 512
interface ethernet0 auto shutdown
interface ethernet1 auto
mtu outside 1500
mtu inside 1500
ip address outside 194.73.134.19 255.255.255.0
ip address inside 192.168.0.1 255.255.255.0
no failover
failover timeout 0:00:00
failover ip address outside 0.0.0.0
failover ip address inside 0.0.0.0
arp timeout 14400
static (inside,outside) 194.73.134.10 192.168.0.10 netmask 255.255.255.255 0 0
static (inside,outside) 194.73.134.11 192.168.0.11 netmask 255.255.255.255 0 0
static (inside,outside) 194.73.134.12 192.168.0.12 netmask 255.255.255.255 0 0
conduit permit tcp host 194.73.134.10 eq www any
conduit permit tcp host 194.73.134.10 eq ftp any
conduit permit tcp host 194.73.134.11 eq smtp any
conduit permit tcp host 194.73.134.11 eq pop3 any
conduit permit tcp host 194.73.134.12 eq domain any
conduit permit udp host 194.73.134.12 eq domain any
conduit permit icmp any host 195.92.1.250
timeout xlate 3:00:00 conn 1:00:00 half-closed 0:10:00 udp 0:02:00
timeout rpc 0:10:00 h323 0:05:00
timeout uauth 0:05:00 absolute
aaa-server TACACS+ protocol tacacs+
aaa-server RADIUS protocol radius
```

```
no snmp-server location
no snmp-server contact
snmp-server community public
no snmp-server enable traps
floodguard enable
isakmp identity hostname
telnet timeout 5
terminal width 80
Cryptochecksum:5884cc517ea6d0954099b857a8572c0c
```

If you are unsure about any of the configuration commands, refer to Chapter 4, "Cisco Secure PIX Firewall," or visit the Cisco Secure PIX web site at www.cisco.com/go/pix.

Revised Problems and Threats in the Internet Service Security Example

With the introduction of the firewall between the public Internet and the Mydomain.com network, most of the network threats have been addressed. The following is a revision of the original list from the section "Initial Problems and Threats in the Internet Service Security Example," now that the firewall has been added.

- **Network threats**—The servers are now located behind the firewall; therefore, they are not directly connected to the public Internet. Certain DoS attacks might still be possible, and the implementation of IDS technology will further protect the network. Ping access has been disallowed to all public addresses with the exception of the Mydomain.com offices. This is identified with the **conduit permit icmp any host 195.92.1.250** command. This means that Internet clients are not able to ping the machines to check for their existence. Attackers running port scans have to force the port scan to check the addresses because the firewall blocks all ICMP Echo Request packets.

- **Operating systems vulnerabilities**—The servers are not on the public Internet, and access has been restricted to the specific ports on the specific servers. This means that any port-specific operating system vulnerability should now be protected.

- **Application vulnerabilities**—Application vulnerabilities might still exist. This is because the application vulnerability might be related to the specific port that is allowed through the firewall. For example, Microsoft's IIS is a TCP port 80 service. There have been vulnerabilities in the past related to certain URLs causing crashes on the server. These URLs would come over the allowed TCP port 80. The only way to keep up with application vulnerabilities is to ensure that the applications are kept up-to-date with the latest service packs and fixes, which are available from the application vendors' web sites.

- **Server-to-server communication**—All server-to-server communication is now over the private 192.168.0.0/24 network. No broadcasts or multicasts are propagated by the firewall. This alleviates the security threat.

- **Access to back-end servers**—The back-end server is no longer publicly accessible. The back-end server does not have a static translation associated with it, so communication can only occur with the back-end server from the Mydomain.com network. This removes the security threat to the back-end servers.

In this example, you have seen a very basic Web installation, identified the security threats posed to this network, and implemented a proposed solution. It is very easy to reduce 95 percent of all threats from the Internet and very hard to protect against the remaining 5 percent. By simply implementing a firewall, you can reduce many risks associated with Internet security.

The remaining sections in this chapter cover the individual Internet services and the threats posed to these specific services.

Web Servers

The World Wide Web is the technology that is responsible for the massive growth of the Internet today.

The World Wide Web was born in 1990, when Tim Berners-Lee developed the first browser application and launched the internal World Wide Web within the European Laboratory for Particle Physics, or CERN, headquarters. At that time, the Web was only available to those who had access to the CERN system.

The next major point of mention is in 1993, when the National Center for Supercomputing Applications (NCSA) released the Mosaic browser. This gave users the ability to view graphics and text at the same time over the Web. In the same year, the *New York Times* announced the appearance of the World Wide Web, and the White House went online at www.whitehouse.gov.

The next seven years saw massive growth for the World Wide Web, with around 7000 new web sites being added daily. The largest growth sector of the Internet is still the World Wide Web.

The World Wide Web is made up of numerous Web servers that are located all over the world on a common network, the Internet. These servers all run the Hypertext Transfer Protocol (HTTP) service. HTTP is an application layer protocol that uses TCP as the transport protocol and maps to port 80. Besides HTTP, there is the Secure Hypertext Transfer Protocol (HTTPS). HTTPS uses client-to-server encryption to secure the normally clear text transmission of data between the HTTP client and the HTTP server.

Threats Posed to Web Servers

Web servers are the most common targets for attacks within a corporate web site. Web servers host the HTTP service and deliver the HTML pages to Internet clients browsing them. The very nature of this client/server relationship makes the Web server a target for abuse. The server is addressable on a specific IP address and a specific port.

The majority of DoS attacks are aimed at Web servers. The Web server is the main component that brings all of the other components together, and disruption of this server affects the overall Internet service.

Besides the DoS attacks, there are application-related vulnerabilities. The most common Web server application that is used on Windows NT is Microsoft's IIS, and the most common UNIX Web server is Apache. Both of these servers are under constant scrutiny from the Internet community, and vulnerabilities are found quite frequently.

Solutions to the Threats to Web Servers

In theory, the Internet service that runs on TCP port 80 is intrinsically secure and does not really require protection. However, it is the Web server itself and the network operating system that causes the security concerns. Any service other than the HTTP service running on the server increases the risk associated to the server. The best way to protect against this, as with most other services, is to deploy a firewall that is situated between the public Internet and the Web server. The Web server can then be on a private network, and Network Address Translation can provide the added security of hiding the real IP address of the Web server. The firewall should be further configured only to allow access to the Web server on the required ports. These are usually port 80 for general HTTP traffic and port 443 if the web site is using HTTPS and HTTP.

To protect against application vulnerabilities, it is important to ensure that the Web server applications are kept up with the latest service and security patches. These are provided on the vendors' web sites. Information about vulnerabilities can be obtained from white hat hacker web sites, such as www.rootshell.com, and various e-mail lists.

Configuration Recommendations for Web Servers

Using the Cisco Secure PIX Firewall, the following commands allow public Web traffic to the Web server with an internal address of 192.168.0.10/24 and provide static translation to the public address of 194.73.134.10/24. This is based on Figure 11-3:

```
static (inside,outside) 194.73.134.10 192.168.0.10 netmask 255.255.255.255 0 0
conduit permit tcp host 194.73.134.10 eq www any
```

File Transfer Protocol (FTP) Servers

The File Transfer Protocol (FTP) is an application layer protocol that provides file-sharing capabilities between hosts.

FTP was formally announced as part of the TCP/IP protocol suite in 1971. RFC 172 covers the design and implementation on FTP.

There are actually two ports associated with FTP: TCP 20 and 21. FTP creates a virtual connection over TCP port 21 for control information, and then it creates a separate TCP connection on port 20 for data transfers.

FTP is a very common application protocol that is used widely on the Internet to transfer files. Most public Web servers also provide some FTP functionality for public users to download files. For example, Cisco Systems has a corporate web site that is located at www.cisco.com. This serves the corporate web site. In addition, Cisco has an FTP server that can be accessed at ftp.cisco.com. This service is provided for downloading files from the Cisco web site. Registered users or users with support agreements can download IOS images and required software updates.

Many companies do not run their own Web servers in-house. They look to an ISP to provide Web space on a shared server or opt for a dedicated, colocated server. In doing this, they gain the benefit of the ISP's network and Internet connection. The ISP offers this as a service and usually provides fault-tolerant, secure access to the Internet services behind multitiered firewalls. In this situation, especially with shared Web space, most ISPs offer FTP services to their clients for uploading the required files to the Web server. Consequently, most web sites have an FTP service running that has direct access to the directory that contains the actual client web site HTML files.

FTP, by design, is a faster method of transferring files across the Internet than HTTP. Most sites offer either HTTP or FTP file download, but normally FTP download is the faster of the two.

Threats Posed to FTP Servers

The major concern with FTP is that the built-in authentication system uses a username and password pair that is transmitted in clear text to the FTP server. This causes obvious concerns when the remote FTP server is accessed across a public, untrusted network. If the FTP username and password are intercepted, the attacker has the same access to your files and directories as you have, leading to disastrous results.

As with any other server, FTP servers are susceptible to DoS attacks. These attacks can render the server unusable to the Internet public.

Solutions to the Threats to FTP Servers

FTP access for downloading files from a Web server is normally pretty safe and anonymous; access can be allowed for this purpose. The problems arise when you start to use FTP to upload files that make up the company web site or similar services. This access has to be protected against intrusion, because the files being uploaded make up the corporate web site and must be kept secure. A good idea in this instance is either to run the management FTP access on a different port or to use a different server completely for public FTP access.

A firewall should be placed between the FTP server and the public Internet. This firewall will protect against some network-based DoS attacks. It should be configured so that management FTP access is permitted from as few hosts as possible.

Configuration Recommendations for FTP Servers

Using the Cisco Secure PIX Firewall, the following commands allow public FTP traffic to the FTP server with an internal address of 192.168.0.10/24 and provide static translation to the public address of 194.73.134.10/24. This is based on Figure 11-3:

```
static (inside,outside) 194.73.134.10 192.168.0.10 netmask 255.255.255.255 0 0
conduit permit tcp host 194.73.134.10 eq ftp any
```

Although this configuration is sufficient for public FTP read access, it probably is not good enough for management FTP access—that is, FTP access to manage the configuration or files on the FTP server. This requires a change to the preceding configuration so that it is management FTP access only. There are two hosts at the Mydomain.com main office from which management FTP will be performed. The public addresses of these two hosts are 195.195.195.1 and 195.195.195.2. Observe the changes to the configuration:

```
static (inside, outside) 194.73.134.10 192.168.0.10 netmask 255.255.255.255 0 0
conduit permit tcp host 194.73.134.10 eq ftp host 195.195.195.1
conduit permit tcp host 194.73.134.10 eq ftp host 195.195.195.2
```

Note that now the hosts 195.195.195.1 and 195.195.195.2 are specifically allowed FTP access to the server 194.73.134.10. All public FTP access to this server will now be denied.

Internet e-Mail Servers (SMTP/POP3/IMAP4)

Besides the World Wide Web, the other major factor in the growth of the Internet has been electronic mail. e-mail allows users to send messages instantly to worldwide recipients without cost or delay. This has had a huge impact on business; almost every business worker has an e-mail address.

As computer networks grew in the early '90s, corporate e-mail became very common within companies. No longer did you have to print out memorandums and place them in the required physical mailboxes or pigeonholes. You could type a short memo and send it directly from your e-mail client to the intended recipients. The use of e-mail distribution lists allowed users to send one e-mail to multiple recipients, further improving the value of e-mail.

With the advent and growth of the Internet, more and more corporations connected their internal e-mail systems to the Internet and provided internal users with Internet e-mail addresses. This opened up the world for internal e-mail users, as they could now send a message to anyone who had a valid Internet address directly from their usual e-mail client installed on their workstation.

Internet e-mail systems use a combination of three application layer protocols that belong to the TCP/IP suite. These protocols are SMTP, POP3, and IMAP4, and they operate over TCP ports 25, 110, and 143 respectively.

- **Simple Mail Transfer Protocol (SMTP)**—SMTP is an application layer protocol that operates over TCP port 25. SMTP is defined in RFC 821 and was originally modeled on FTP. SMTP transfers e-mail messages between systems and provides notification regarding incoming e-mail.

- **Post Office Protocol version 3 (POP3)**—POP3 is an application layer protocol that operates over TCP port 110. POP3 is defined in RFC 1939 and is a protocol that allows workstations to access a mail drop dynamically on a server host. The typical use of POP3 is on the e-mail client, where the client retrieves messages that the e-mail server is holding for it.

- **Internet Message Access Protocol revision 4 (IMAP4)**—IMAP4 is an application layer protocol that operates over TCP port 143. IMAP4 is defined in RFC 2060 and is a protocol that allows an e-mail client to access and manipulate e-mail messages that are stored on a server.

  IMAP4 adds a lot more functionality compared with POP3 and is the latest e-mail protocol to be devised. With IMAP4, you can manipulate and control remote e-mail accounts similar to the way you can with local mailboxes in Microsoft Exchange or a similar corporate e-mail client.

E-mail will continue to add to the growth of the Internet. New media-rich improvements to e-mail are occurring all the time. These improvements further enhance the benefit of e-mail, both to corporate and to home users.

Threats Posed to Internet e-Mail Servers

Internet e-mail systems can be attacked to deny service, or they can be misused if they are incorrectly configured.

One common misuse of Internet e-mail systems is spam. Spam is unsolicited bulk e-mail; the people who send it are known as *spammers*. Spammers usually send bulk e-mails about get-rich-quick schemes or advertising pornographic web sites. Spam is enabled if the Web server is running as an *open relay*. Various Internet groups, such as the Open Relay Behavior-modification System (ORBS, www.orbs.org), have emerged to crack down on server administrators who are running open relays, either intentionally or unintentionally.

Spam results in the e-mail servers becoming heavily loaded while sending out e-mails to sometimes thousands of recipients; this increases the load on the server and utilizes bandwidth to the server.

Internet e-mail servers, as any other server, can be subject to the common DoS attacks. These attacks render the server unusable to the general public.

There are also application vulnerabilities relating to Internet e-mail servers. The common Microsoft Windows-based e-mail system is Microsoft Exchange, and the common UNIX-based e-mail system is Sendmail. Both of these applications have vulnerabilities associated with them. Recently, there has been a vulnerability with Microsoft IIS 4.0 where you could run a command such as **CMD.EXE** remotely over the Internet. A very simple **FORMAT C:** could then be carried out to format a drive on the server. Microsoft has recently fixed this with a service pack.

Solutions to the Threats to Internet e-Mail Servers

The provision of a firewall between the Internet e-mail server and the public network is the easiest way to reduce the threats to the Internet e-mail server. The firewall should be configured to restrict access to the specific ports used for e-mail communication—in this case, SMTP and POP3.

The operating system and e-mail application that are running on the server should both have the latest service and security patches. This ensures that any known vulnerabilities that exist within the operating system and application are protected.

The e-mail service should be configured to disallow spam. There are various documents on how to do this, based on the e-mail server that you are running. Further information can be found at www.orbs.org.

Configuration Recommendations for Internet e-Mail Servers

Using the Cisco Secure PIX Firewall, the following commands allow SMTP and POP3 traffic to the Internet e-mail server with an internal address of 192.168.0.11/24 and provide static translation to the public address of 194.73.134.11/24. This is based on Figure 11-3:

```
static (inside, outside) 194.73.134.11 192.168.0.11 netmask 255.255.255.255 0 0
conduit permit tcp host 194.73.134.11 eq smtp any
conduit permit tcp host 194.73.134.11 eq pop3 any
```

Domain Name System (DNS) Servers

The Domain Name System (DNS) is a distributed database of IP address-to-name translations.

When you type in a web site address or URL such as www.cisco.com, the first thing that happens is that this easy-to-use name gets converted into an IP address. The server is known on the network by its IP address, not by its name. It is easier for users to remember www.cisco.com than 192.168.10.12. This is the main reason that DNS was implemented, but there are other benefits of using a name-resolution service. One of these is *round-robin load balancing*, where one domain name can be translated to more than one IP address. For example, you could register www.mydomain.com to 192.168.0.1 and 192.168.0.2. Both of these could be Web servers serving the Mydomain.com web site. Users accessing www.mydomain.com from their Web browsers would get either of the Web servers in a round-robin fashion. This provides load balancing and a simple form of fault tolerance.

Another use of DNS is in e-mail. You can set what is called a *mail exchange* (MX) record for any particular domain. SMTP, when sending e-mail between e-mail servers, first does a DNS lookup for the destination domain. For example, if a user sends an e-mail to andrew@mydomain.com, the user's SMTP server tries to resolve the domain name mydomain.com and locate the MX record for that domain. The MX record points by IP address to a server or group of servers that serve Internet e-mail for the domain. The user's SMTP server then sends the message to the IP address represented by the mydomain.com MX record.

DNS is described in RFC 1035 and RFC 1706.

Threats Posed to DNS Servers

DNS operates over port 53, using both UDP and TCP as the transport layer protocol. Client name requests are carried out over UDP port 53, and domain zone transfers are carried out over TCP port 53. Zone transfers occur between the primary and secondary DNS servers. Updates are carried out on the primary server, and these changes get replicated down to the secondary servers.

The obvious threats that appertain to DNS servers are DoS attacks and network intrusion.

Internet clients require DNS servers to resolve the domain name to the IP address of the server they are trying to connect to. Attackers can either use a DoS attack against the server to deny access from other DNS servers and clients, or they can infiltrate the server and change the DNS information.

For example, www.mydomain.com could have a DNS entry of 194.73.134.10; an attacker could change this to 195.195.195.195, which points to a different web site, thus redirecting all traffic away from the Mydomain.com web site.

Because of the way DNS works and gets cached all over the Internet, the attack would have to be very prolonged—more than 48 hours at least—before any real effect would be noticed.

Solutions to the Threats to DNS Servers

The easiest way to protect a DNS server is to place it behind a firewall device and limit access to only TCP and UDP port 53. This allows the DNS service to function correctly and disallows any other access to the operating system or port advertising applications running on the server.

Configuration Recommendations for DNS Servers

Using the Cisco Secure PIX Firewall, the following commands allow DNS traffic to the DNS server with an internal address of 192.168.0.12/24 and provide static translation to the public address of 194.73.134.12/24. This is based on Figure 11-3:

```
static (inside, outside) 194.73.134.12 192.168.0.12 netmask 255.255.255.255 0 0
conduit permit tcp host 194.73.134.12 eq domain any
conduit permit udp host 194.73.134.12 eq domain any
```

Back-End Servers

A back-end server can be thought of as a server that is required for the Internet service to operate, but does not need to be public-facing or have a publicly accessible IP address. An example of this is a database server and is shown in Figure 11-3.

These servers have to be able to communicate with the public-facing servers to fulfill the requests sent to them.

In Figure 11-3, you can see that the Web server for Mydomain.com is serving Web files for www.mydomain.com. The Web server runs a stock lookup database that is linked to a back-end SQL database running on a server in the same Layer 3 domain as the Web server. NAT is used to statically translate the Web server's private IP address of 192.168.1.10 to the public IP address of 194.73.134.10. Therefore, Internet hosts access www.mydomain.com and DNS resolves this to 194.73.134.10. The Mydomain.com firewall handles this request and statically translates it inbound to 192.168.1.10. The SQL server has a private IP address of 192.168.1.20. There is no static translation for this server, so in theory, it cannot be accessed from the outside.

Back-end servers can be any combination of the following:

- Database servers
- E-commerce servers

- Content servers
- Application servers
- Authentication servers
- Communications servers

There are numerous other servers that could fall into the category of back-end servers.

Threats Posed to Back-End Servers

Back-end servers should not be accessible to the public Internet unless required. If a back-end server is connected to the public Internet, it opens up all of the vulnerabilities associated with the operating system and also with the application.

Solutions to the Threats to Back-End Servers

The easiest way to remove the threats associated with back-end servers is to place them on a private network behind a firewall and not to provide a static translation between the private address and public address.

If the back-end server does need to be publicly visible, it should be placed behind a firewall and access should only be allowed to the specific ports that are required. This restricts the risks associated with allowing the back-end server to be accessed over the Internet.

In addition, the latest service and security patches should be applied to the application to ensure that there are no backdoor vulnerabilities that can be exposed.

Summary

This chapter provided an overview of the common Internet services and the everyday threats these services are under when placed on the public Internet. The chapter looked at the main network intrusion methods and DoS attacks before presenting a basic example of a hosted network solution. This solution outlined the need for at least a firewall and NAT between the public Internet and the servers that make up the corporate Internet site. Finally, the chapter looked at each individual major Internet service, identified the threats, and outlined simple solutions to overcome these threats.

Frequently Asked Questions

Question: What exactly is a DoS attack?

Answer: DoS stands for denial of service. A DoS attack is a network-based attack on a server or group of servers that causes the server to deny service to other network requests.

This denial can be caused by an overload of the network with physical resources on the server.

Question: What is NAT?

Answer: NAT stands for Network Address Translation. It is a method where public IP addresses get translated into private IP addresses for address-hiding purposes. You can create a private network behind a NAT device, such as a router or a firewall, and create static translations between these private addresses and public addresses. This hides the private addresses of the network from the public Internet and provides a method where the private servers can communicate with each other over the private addresses. There are two types of NAT. These are one-to-one NAT and one-to-many NAT. One-to-many NAT is also known as Port Address Translation (PAT).

Glossary

IDS (Intrusion Detection System)—Scans the network in real time to intercept attempted breaches of security.

ISP (Internet service provider)—A service provider that provides a connection to the public Internet.

NAT (Network Address Translation)—NAT is the translation of an IP address used within one network to a different IP address known within another network.

PIX (Private Internet Exchange)—The Cisco range of leading hardware-based firewalls.

PART **IV**

Appendix

Cisco SAFE: A Security Blueprint for Enterprise Networks

This appendix was originally published as a white paper and is reproduced here by permission of the authors and Cisco Systems. The format of this appendix has been modified slightly so that it can conform to this book's design.

Authors of This Appendix

Sean Convery (CCIE #4232) and Bernie Trudel (CCIE #1884) are the authors of this appendix, which was originally published as a white paper. Sean is the lead architect for the reference implementation of this architecture at Cisco's headquarters in San Jose, California. Sean and Bernie are both members of the VPN and Security Architecture Technical Marketing team in Cisco's Enterprise Line of Business.

Abstract

The principal goal of SAFE, Cisco's secure blueprint for enterprise networks, is to provide the best practice information to interested parties on designing and implementing secure networks. SAFE serves as a guide to network designers considering the security requirements of their networks. SAFE takes a defense-in-depth approach to network security design. This type of design focuses on the expected threats and their methods of mitigation, rather than on "put the firewall here, put the intrusion detection system there" instructions. This strategy results in a layered approach to security, where the failure of one security system is not likely to lead to the compromise of network resources. SAFE is based on Cisco products and those of its partners.

This document begins with an overview of the architecture, then details the specific modules that make up the actual network design. The first three sections of each module describe the traffic flows, key devices, and expected threats with basic mitigation diagrams. Detailed technical analysis of the design follows, along with more detailed threat mitigation techniques and migration strategies. The section "Annex A: Validation Lab" details the validation lab for SAFE and includes configuration snapshots. The section "Annex B: Network Security Primer" is a primer on network security. Readers who are unfamiliar with basic network security concepts are encouraged to read this section before the rest of the document. "Annex C: Architecture Taxonomy" contains glossary definitions of the technical terms used in this document.

This document focuses heavily on threats encountered in enterprise environments. Network designers who understand these threats can better decide where and how to deploy mitigation technologies. Without a full understanding of the threats involved in network security, deployments tend to be incorrectly configured, are too focused on security devices, or lack threat response options. By taking the threat-mitigation approach, this document should provide network designers with information for making sound network security choices.

Audience

Though this document is technical in nature, it can be read at different levels of detail, depending on the reader. A network manager, for example, can read the introductory sections in each area to obtain a good overview of network security design strategies and considerations. A network engineer or designer can read this document in its entirety and gain design information and threat analysis details, which are supported by configuration snapshots for the devices involved.

Caveats

This document presumes that you already have a security policy in place. Cisco Systems does not recommend deploying security technologies without an associated policy. This document directly addresses the needs of large enterprise customers. Although most of the principles discussed here also apply directly to small and medium businesses and even to home offices, they do so on a different scale. A detailed analysis of these business types is outside the scope of this document. However, in order to address the issue of smaller-scale networks in a limited manner, the "Alternatives" and "Enterprise Options" sections outline devices that you can eliminate if you want to reduce the cost of the architecture.

Following the guidelines in this document does not guarantee a secure environment, or that you will prevent all intrusions. True absolute security can only be achieved by disconnecting a system from the network, encasing it in concrete, and putting it in the bottom floor of Fort Knox. Your data will be very safe, though inaccessible. However, you can achieve reasonable security by establishing a good security policy, following the guidelines in this document, staying up-to-date on the latest developments in the hacker and security communities, and maintaining and monitoring all systems with sound system-administration practices. This includes awareness of application security issues that are not comprehensively addressed in this paper.

Though virtual private networks (VPNs) are included in this architecture, they are not described in great detail. Information such as scaling details, resilience strategies, and other topics related to VPNs are not included. Like VPNs, identity strategies (including certificate authorities [CAs]) are not discussed at any level of detail in this paper. Similarly, CAs require a level of focus that this document could not provide and still adequately address all the other relevant areas of network security. Also, because most enterprise networks have yet to deploy fully functional CA environments, it is important to discuss how to deploy networks securely without them. Finally, certain advanced networked applications and technologies (such as content networking, caching, and server load balancing) are not included in this document. Although their use within SAFE is to be expected, this paper does not cover their specific security needs.

SAFE uses the products of Cisco Systems and its partners. However, this document does not specifically refer to products by name. Components are referred to by functional purpose, rather than model number or name. During the validation of SAFE, real products were configured in the exact network implementation described in this document. Specific configuration snapshots from the lab are included in Annex A.

Throughout this document, the term *hacker* denotes an individual who attempts to gain unauthorized access to network resources with malicious intent. Although the term *cracker* is generally regarded as the more accurate word for this type of individual, hacker is used here for readability.

Architecture Overview

This section covers an architectural overview of SAFE.

Design Fundamentals

SAFE emulates as closely as possible the functional requirements of today's enterprise networks. Implementation decisions vary depending on the network functionality required. However, the following design objectives, listed in order of priority, guide the decision-making process.

- Security and attack mitigation based on policy
- Security implementation throughout the infrastructure (not just on specialized security devices)
- Secure management and reporting
- Authentication and authorization of users and administrators to critical network resources
- Intrusion detection for critical resources and subnets
- Support for emerging networked applications

First and foremost, SAFE is a security architecture. It must prevent most attacks from successfully affecting valuable network resources. The attacks that succeed in penetrating the first line of defense or originate from inside the network must be accurately detected and quickly contained to minimize their effect on the rest of the network. However, while being secure, the network must continue to provide critical services that users expect. Proper network security and good network functionality can be provided at the same time. The SAFE architecture is not a revolutionary way of designing networks, but is merely a blueprint for making networks secure.

SAFE is also resilient and scalable. Resilience in networks includes physical redundancy to protect against a device failure, whether it is by misconfiguration, physical failure, or network attack. Although simpler designs are possible, particularly if a network's performance needs are not great, this document uses a complex design as an example because designing security in a complex environment is more involved than in simpler environments. Options to limit the complexity of the design are discussed throughout this document.

At many points in the network design process, you need to choose between using integrated functionality in a network device and using a specialized functional appliance. The integrated functionality is often attractive because you can implement it on existing equipment, or because the features can interoperate with the rest of the device to provide a better functional solution. Appliances are often used when the depth of functionality required is very advanced or when performance needs require using specialized hardware. Make your decisions based on the capacity and functionality of the appliance rather than the integration advantage of the device. For example, sometimes you can choose an integrated higher-capacity Cisco IOS router with IOS firewall software, as opposed to a smaller IOS router with a separate firewall. Throughout this architecture, both types of systems are used. Most critical security functions migrate to dedicated appliances because of the performance requirements of large enterprise networks.

Module Concept

Although most enterprise networks evolve with the growing IT requirements of the enterprise, the SAFE architecture uses a green-field modular approach. A modular approach has two main advantages. First, it allows the architecture to address the security relationship among the various functional blocks of the network. Second, it permits designers to evaluate and implement security on a module-by-module basis, instead of attempting the complete architecture in a single phase.

Figure A-1 illustrates the first layer of modularity in SAFE. Each block represents a functional area. The Internet service provider (ISP) module is not implemented by the enterprise, but it is included to the extent that specific security features should be requested of an ISP to mitigate against certain attacks.

Figure A-1 *Enterprise Composite Module*

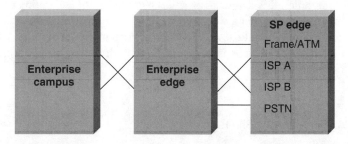

The second layer of modularity, which is illustrated in Figure A-2, represents a view of the modules within each functional area. These modules perform specific roles in the network and have specific security requirements, but their sizes are not meant to reflect their scale in a real network. For example, the building module, which represents the end-user devices, might include 80 percent of the network devices. The security design of each module is described separately but is validated as part of the complete enterprise design.

Figure A-2 *Enterprise SAFE Block Diagram*

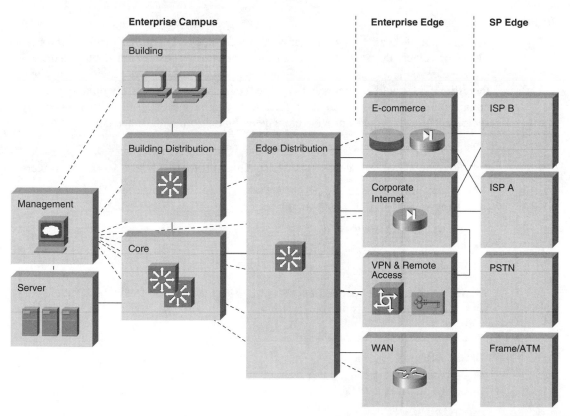

Although it is true that most existing enterprise networks cannot be easily dissected into clear-cut modules, this approach provides a guide for implementing different security functions throughout the network. The authors do not expect network engineers to design their networks to be identical to the SAFE implementation, but rather to use a combination of the modules described and integrate them into the existing network.

SAFE Axioms

This section covers the SAFE axioms:

- Routers Are Targets
- Switches Are Targets
- Hosts Are Targets
- Networks Are Targets
- Applications Are Targets
- Secure Management and Reporting

Routers Are Targets

Routers control access from every network to every network. They advertise networks and filter who can use them, and they are potentially a hacker's best friend. Router security is a critical element in any security deployment. By their nature, routers provide access, and therefore, you should secure them to reduce the likelihood that they are directly compromised. You can refer to other documents that have been written about router security. These documents provide more detail on the following subjects:

- Locking down Telnet access to a router
- Locking down Simple Network Management Protocol (SNMP) access to a router
- Controlling access to a router through the use of Terminal Access Controller Access Control System Plus (TACACS+)
- Turning off unneeded services
- Logging at appropriate levels
- Authentication of routing updates

The most current document on router security is available at the following URL: www.cisco.com/warp/customer/707/21.html.

Switches Are Targets

Like routers, switches (both Layer 2 and Layer 3) have their own set of security considerations. Unlike routers, not as much public information is available about the security risks in switches and what can be done to mitigate those risks. Most of the security techniques detailed in the preceding section, "Routers Are Targets," apply to switches. In addition, you should take the following precautions:

- Ports without any need to trunk should have any trunk settings set to off, as opposed to auto. This prevents a host from becoming a trunk port and receiving all traffic that would normally reside on a trunk port.

- Make sure that trunk ports use a virtual LAN (VLAN) number not used anywhere else in the switch. This prevents packets tagged with the same VLAN as the trunk port from reaching another VLAN without crossing a Layer 3 device. For more information, refer to the following URL: www.sans.org/newlook/resources/IDFAQ/vlan.htm.

- Set all unused ports on a switch to a VLAN that has no Layer 3 connectivity. Better yet, disable any port that is not needed. This prevents hackers from plugging into unused ports and communicating with the rest of the network.

- Avoid using VLANs as the sole method of securing access between two subnets. The capability for human error, combined with the understanding that VLANs and VLAN tagging protocols were not designed with security in mind, makes their use in sensitive environments inadvisable. When VLANs are needed in security deployments, be sure to pay close attention to the configurations and guidelines mentioned above.

Within an existing VLAN, private VLANs provide some added security to specific network applications. Private VLANs work by limiting which ports within a VLAN can communicate with other ports in the same VLAN. Isolated ports within a VLAN can communicate only with promiscuous ports. Community ports can communicate only with other members of the same community and promiscuous ports. Promiscuous ports can communicate with any port. This is an effective way to mitigate the effects of a single compromised host. Consider a standard public services segment with a Web, File Transfer Protocol (FTP), and Domain Name System (DNS) server. If the DNS server is compromised, a hacker can pursue the other two hosts without passing back through the firewall. If private VLANs are deployed, once one system is compromised, it cannot communicate with the other systems. The only targets a hacker can pursue are hosts on the other side of the firewall.

Hosts Are Targets

A host is the most likely target during an attack and presents some of the most difficult challenges from a security perspective. There are numerous hardware platforms, operating systems, and applications, all of which have updates, patches, and fixes available at different times. Because hosts provide the application services to other hosts that request them, they are extremely visible within the network. For example, many people have visited www.whitehouse.gov, which is a host, but few have attempted to access s2-0.whitehouseisp.net, which is a router. Because of this visibility, hosts are the most frequently attacked devices in any network intrusion attempt.

In part because of the security challenges mentioned above, hosts are also the most successfully compromised devices. For example, a given Web server on the Internet might run a hardware platform from one vendor, a network card from another, an operating system from still another vendor, and a Web server that is either open source or from yet another vendor. Additionally, the same Web server might run applications that are freely distributed over the Internet, and it might communicate with a database server that starts the variations all over again. That is not to say that the security vulnerabilities are specifically caused by the multisource nature of hosts, but rather that as the complexity of a system increases, so does the likelihood of a failure.

To secure hosts, pay careful attention to each of the components within the systems. Keep any systems up-to-date with the latest patches, fixes, and so forth. In particular, pay attention to how these patches affect the operation of other system components. Evaluate all updates on test systems before you implement them in a production environment. Failure to do so might result in the patch itself causing a denial of service (DoS).

Networks Are Targets

The worst attack is one that you cannot stop. When performed properly, distributed denial of service (DDoS) is just such an attack. As outlined in Annex B, DDoS works by causing tens or hundreds of machines to send spurious data simultaneously to an IP address. The goal of such an attack is generally not to shut down a particular host, but rather to make the entire network unresponsive. For example, consider an organization with a DS3 (45 Mbps) connection to the Internet that provides e-commerce services to its web site users. Such a site is very security conscious and has intrusion detection, firewalls, logging, and active monitoring. Unfortunately, all of these security devices do not help when a hacker launches a successful DDoS attack.

Consider 100 devices around the world, each with DS1 (1.5 Mbps) connections to the Internet. If these systems are told remotely to flood the serial interface of the e-commerce organization's Internet router, they can easily flood the DS3 with erroneous data. Even if each host is only able to generate 1 Mbps of traffic (lab tests indicate that a stock UNIX workstation can easily generate 50 Mbps with a popular DDoS tool), that amount is still more than twice the amount of traffic that the e-commerce site can handle. As a result, legitimate Web requests are lost, and the site appears to be down for most users. The local firewall drops all of the erroneous data, but by then, the damage is done. The traffic has crossed the WAN connection and filled up the link.

Only through cooperation with its ISP can this fictitious e-commerce company hope to thwart such an attack. An ISP can configure rate limiting on the outbound interface to the company's site. This rate limiting can drop most undesired traffic when it exceeds a prespecified amount of the available bandwidth. The key is to flag traffic correctly as undesired.

Common forms of DDoS attacks are ICMP floods, TCP SYN floods, or UDP floods. In an e-commerce environment, this type of traffic is fairly easy to categorize. Only when limiting a TCP SYN attack on port 80 (Hypertext Transfer Protocol [HTTP]) does an administrator run the risk of locking out legitimate users during an attack. Even then, it is better to lock out new legitimate users temporarily and retain routing and management connections than to have the router overrun and lose all connectivity.

More sophisticated attacks use port 80 traffic with the ACK bit set so that the traffic appears to be legitimate Web transactions. It is unlikely that an administrator could properly categorize such an attack, because acknowledged TCP communications are exactly the sort that you want to allow into your network.

One approach to limiting this sort of attack is to follow the guidelines outlined in RFC 1918 and RFC 2827. RFC 1918 specifies the networks that are reserved for private use and should never be seen across the public Internet. RFC 2827 filtering is discussed in the "IP Spoofing" section of Annex B. For inbound traffic on a router that is connected to the Internet, you could employ RFC 1918 and RFC 2827 filtering to prevent unauthorized traffic from reaching the corporate network. When implemented at the ISP, this filtering prevents DDoS attack packets that use these addresses as sources from traversing the WAN link, potentially saving bandwidth during the attack. Collectively, if ISPs worldwide were to implement the guidelines in RFC 2827, source address spoofing would be greatly diminished. Although this strategy does not directly prevent DDoS attacks, it does prevent such attacks from masking their source, which makes traceback to the attacking networks much easier.

Applications Are Targets

Applications are coded by human beings (mostly) and as such, are subject to numerous errors. These errors can be benign, for example, an error that causes your document to print incorrectly, or malignant, for example, an error that makes the credit card numbers on your database server available over anonymous FTP. It is the malignant problems, in addition to other more general security vulnerabilities, that intrusion detection systems (IDSs) aim to detect. Intrusion detection acts like an alarm system in the physical world. When an IDS detects something that it considers an attack, it can either take corrective action itself or notify a management system for actions by the administrator. Some systems are more or less equipped to respond and prevent such an attack. Host-based intrusion detection can work by intercepting OS and application calls on an individual host. It can also operate by after-the-fact analysis of local log files. The former approach allows better attack prevention, while the latter approach dictates a more passive attack-response role. Because of the specificity of its role, host-based IDS (HIDS) is often better at preventing specific attacks than network IDS (NIDS), which usually only issues an alert on discovery of an attack. However, the HIDS specificity causes a loss of perspective to the overall network. This is where NIDS excels. Cisco recommends a combination of the two systems—HIDS on critical hosts and NIDS looking over the whole network—for complete intrusion detection.

Once deployed, you must tune an IDS implementation to increase its effectiveness and remove *false positives*.

False positives are defined as alarms caused by legitimate traffic or activity. False negatives are attacks that the IDS system fails to see. Once the IDS is tuned, you can configure it more specifically to its threat mitigation role. As mentioned above, you should configure HIDS to stop most valid threats at the host level, because HIDS is well prepared to determine that certain activity is indeed a threat.

When deciding on mitigation roles for NIDS, there are two primary options.

The first option, and potentially the most damaging if improperly deployed, is to "shun" traffic by the addition of access-control filters on routers. When an NIDS detects an attack from a particular host over a particular protocol, it can block that host from coming into the network for a predetermined amount of time. Although on the surface, this might seem like a great aid to a security administrator, in reality it must be very carefully implemented, if at all. The first problem is spoofed addresses. If traffic that matches an attack is seen by the NIDS, and that particular alarm triggers a shun response, the NIDS will deploy the access list to the device. However, if the attack that caused the alarm used a spoofed address, the NIDS has now locked out an address that never initiated an attack. If the IP address that the hacker used happens to be the IP address of a major ISP's outbound HTTP proxy server, a huge number of users could be locked out. This by itself could be an interesting DoS threat in the hands of a creative hacker.

To mitigate the risks of shunning, you should generally use it only on TCP traffic, which is much more difficult to successfully spoof than UDP. Use it only in cases where the threat is real and the chance of the attack being a false positive is very low. However, in the interior of a network, many more options exist. With effectively deployed RFC 2827 filtering, spoofed traffic should be very limited. Also, because customers are not generally on the internal network, you can take a more restrictive stance against internally originated attack attempts. Another reason for this is that internal networks do not often have the same level of stateful filtering that edge connections possess. As such, IDS needs to be more heavily relied on than in the external environment.

The second option for NIDS threat mitigation is the use of TCP resets. As the name implies, TCP resets operate only on TCP traffic and terminate an active attack by sending TCP reset messages to the attacking and attacked host. Because TCP traffic is more difficult to spoof, you should consider using TCP resets more often than shunning.

From a performance standpoint, NIDS observes packets on the wire. If packets are sent faster than the NIDS can process them, there is no degradation to the network, because the NIDS does not sit directly in the flow of data. However, the NIDS will lose effectiveness and packets could be missed, causing both false negatives and false positives. Be sure to avoid exceeding the capabilities of IDS so that you can get its benefits. From a routing standpoint, IDS, like many state-aware engines, does not operate properly in an asymmetrically routed environment. Packets sent out from one set of routers and switches and returning through another will cause the IDS systems to see only half of the traffic, causing false positives and false negatives.

Secure Management and Reporting

"If you're going to log it, read it." It is such a simple proposition that almost everyone familiar with network security has said it at least once. Yet logging and reading information from more than 100 devices can prove to be a challenging proposition. Which logs are most important? How do I separate important messages from mere notifications? How do I ensure that logs are not tampered with in transit? How do I ensure my time stamps match each other when multiple devices report the same alarm? What information is needed if log data is required for a criminal investigation? How do I deal with the volume of messages that can be generated by a large network? You must address all of these questions when considering managing log files effectively. From a management standpoint, a different set of questions needs to be asked: How do I securely manage a device? How can I push content out to public servers and ensure that it is not tampered with in transit? How can I track changes on devices to troubleshoot when attacks or network failures occur?

From an architectural point of view, providing out-of-band (OOB) management of network systems is the best first step in any management and reporting strategy. OOB, as its name implies, refers to a network on which no production traffic resides. Devices should have a direct local connection to such a network where possible, and where impossible because of geographic or system-related issues, the device should connect by a private encrypted tunnel over the production network. Such a tunnel should be preconfigured to communicate only across the specific ports required for management and reporting. The tunnel should also be locked down so that only appropriate hosts can initiate and terminate tunnels. Be sure that the OOB network itself does not create security issues. See the "Management Module" section of this document for more details.

After implementing an OOB management network, dealing with logging and reporting becomes more straightforward. Most networking devices can send syslog data, which can be invaluable when troubleshooting network problems or security threats. Send this data to one or more syslog analysis hosts on the management network. Depending on the device involved, you can choose various logging levels to ensure that the correct amount of data is sent to the logging devices. You also need to flag device log data within the analysis software to permit granular viewing and reporting. For example, during an attack, the log data provided by Layer 2 switches might not be as interesting as the data provided by the IDS. Specialized applications, such as IDS, often use their own logging protocols to transmit alarm information. Usually this data should be logged to separate management hosts that are better equipped to deal with attack alarms. When combined, alarm data from many different sources can provide information about the overall health of the network. To ensure that log messages are time-synchronized to one another, clocks on hosts and network devices must be in sync. For devices that support it, Network Time Protocol (NTP) provides a way to ensure that accurate time is kept on all devices. When dealing with attacks, seconds matter because it is important to identify the order in which a specified attack took place.

From a management standpoint, which for the purposes of this document refers to any function performed on a device by an administrator other than logging and reporting, there are other issues and solutions. As with logging and reporting, the OOB network allows the transport of information to remain in a controlled environment where it is not subject to tampering. Still, when secure configuration is possible, such as through the use of Secure Socket Layer (SSL) or Secure Shell (SSH), it should be preferred. SNMP should be treated with the utmost care because the underlying protocol has its own set of security vulnerabilities. Consider providing read-only access to devices over SNMP and treat the SNMP community string with the same care that you might treat a root password on a critical UNIX host.

Configuration change management is another issue related to secure management. When a network is under attack, it is important to know the state of critical network devices and when the last known modifications took place. Creating a plan for change management should be a part of your comprehensive security policy, but at a minimum, you should record changes using authentication systems on the devices and archive configurations by FTP or Trivial File Transfer Protocol (TFTP).

Enterprise Module

The enterprise comprises two functional areas: the campus and the edge. These two areas are further divided into modules that define the various functions of each area in detail. Following the detailed discussion of the modules in the "Enterprise Campus" and "Enterprise Edge" sections, the "Enterprise Options" section of this document describes various options for the design.

Expected Threats

From a threat perspective, the enterprise network is like most networks connected to the Internet. There are internal users who need access out and external users who need access in. There are several common threats that can generate the initial compromise that a hacker needs to penetrate the network further with secondary exploits.

First is the threat from internal users. Though statistics vary on the percentage, it is an established fact that the majority of all attacks come from the internal network. Disgruntled employees, corporate spies, visiting guests, and inadvertently bumbling users are all potential sources of such attacks. When designing security, it is important to be aware of the potential for internal threats.

Second is the threat to the publicly addressable hosts that are connected to the Internet. These systems are likely to be attacked with application layer vulnerabilities and DoS attacks.

The final threat is that a hacker might try to determine your data phone numbers by using a *war-dialer* and try to gain access to the network. War-dialers are software or hardware that are designed to dial many phone numbers and determine the type of system on the other end of the connection. Personal systems with remote-control software installed by the user are the most vulnerable, because they typically are not very secure. Because these devices are behind the firewall, once hackers have access over the host they dialed into, they can impersonate users on the network.

For a complete discussion of threat details, refer to Annex B.

Enterprise Campus

Figure A-3 shows a detailed analysis of all of the modules contained within the enterprise campus.

Figure A-3 *Enterprise Campus Detail*

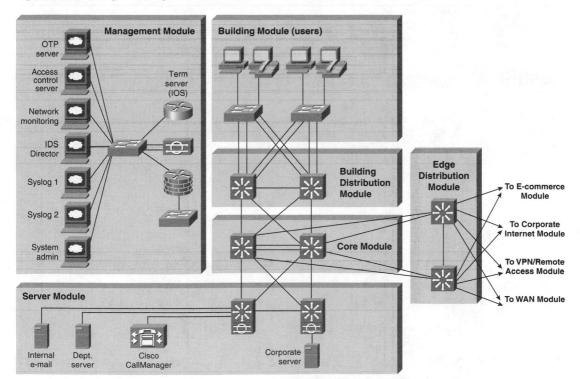

Management Module

The primary goal of the management module (see Figure A-4) is to facilitate the secure management of all devices and hosts within the enterprise SAFE architecture. Logging and reporting information flows from the devices to the management hosts, while content, configurations, and new software flow to the devices from the management hosts.

Figure A-4 *Management Traffic Flow*

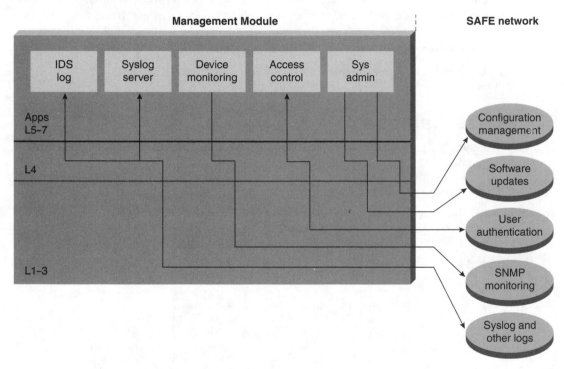

Key Devices

The key devices (see Figure A-5) are as follows:

- **SNMP management host**—Provides SNMP management for devices
- **NIDS host**—Provides alarm aggregation for all NIDS devices in the network
- **Syslog hosts**—Aggregates log information for firewall and NIDS hosts
- **Access control server**—Delivers one-time, two-factor authentication services to the network devices
- **One-time password (OTP) server**—Authorizes one-time password information relayed from the access control server

- **System admin host**—Provides configuration, software, and content changes on devices
- **NIDS appliance**—Provides Layer 4 to Layer 7 monitoring of key network segments in the module
- **Cisco IOS firewall**—Allows granular control for traffic flows between the management hosts and the managed devices
- **Layer 2 switch (with private VLAN support)**—Ensures data from managed devices can only cross directly to the IOS firewall

Figure A-5 *Management Module: Detail*

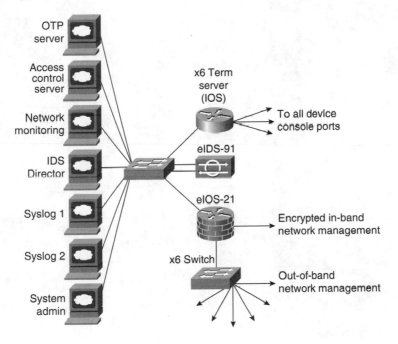

Threats Mitigated

The threats mitigated (see Figure A-6) are as follows:

- **Unauthorized access**—Filtering at the IOS firewall stops most unauthorized traffic in both directions.
- **Man-in-the-middle attacks**—Management data is crossing a private network, making man-in-the-middle attacks difficult.
- **Network reconnaissance**—Because all management traffic crosses this network, it does not cross the production network where it could be intercepted.

- **Password attacks**—The access control server allows for strong two-factor authentication at each device.

- **IP spoofing**—Spoofed traffic is stopped in both directions at the IOS firewall.

- **Packet sniffers**—A switched infrastructure limits the effectiveness of sniffing.

- **Trust exploitation**—Private VLANs prevent a compromised device from masquerading as a management host.

Figure A-6   *Attack Mitigation Roles for Management Module*

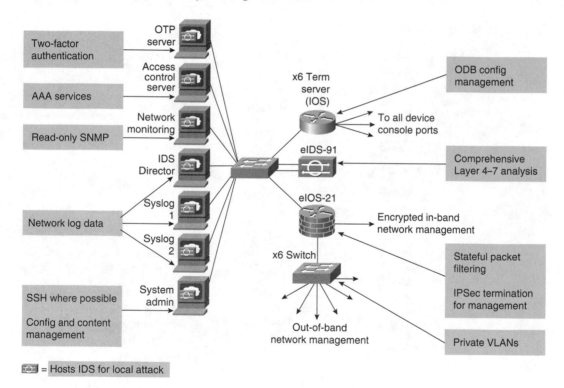

 = Hosts IDS for local attack

Design Guidelines

As can be seen in Figure A-6, the SAFE enterprise management network has two network segments that are separated by an IOS router, which acts as a firewall and a VPN termination device. The segment outside the firewall connects to all of the devices that require management. The segment inside the firewall contains the management hosts themselves and the IOS routers that act as terminal servers. The remaining interface connects to the production network, but only for IPSec-protected management traffic from predetermined hosts. This allows for management of a Cisco device that did not physically have enough interfaces to support the normal management connection. The IOS firewall is configured to allow syslog information into the management segment, in addition to Telnet, SSH, and SNMP if these are first initiated by the inside network.

Both management subnets operate under an address space that is completely separate from the rest of the production network. This ensures that the management network will not be advertised by any routing protocols. This also enables the production network devices to block any traffic from the management subnets that appear on the production network links.

The management module provides configuration management for nearly all devices in the network through the use of two primary technologies: Cisco IOS routers acting as terminal servers and a dedicated management network segment. The routers provide a reverse Telnet function to the console ports on the Cisco devices throughout the enterprise. More extensive management features (software changes, content updates, log and alarm aggregation, and SNMP management) are provided through the dedicated management network segment. The few other unmanaged devices and hosts are managed through IPSec tunnels that originate from the management router.

Because the management network has administrative access to nearly every area of the network, it can be a very attractive target to hackers. The management module has been built with several technologies designed to mitigate those risks. The first primary threat is a hacker attempting to gain access to the management network itself. This threat can only be mitigated through the effective deployment of security features in the remaining modules in the enterprise. All of the remaining threats assume that the primary line of defense has been breached. To mitigate the threat of a compromised device, access control is implemented at the firewall and at every other possible device to prevent exploitation of the management channel. A compromised device cannot even communicate with other hosts on the same subnet, because private VLANs on the management segment switches force all traffic from the managed devices directly to the IOS firewall where filtering takes place. Password sniffing reveals only useless information because of the OTP environment. HIDS and NIDS are also implemented on the management subnet and are configured in a very restrictive stance. Because the types of traffic on this network should be very limited, any signature match on this segment should be met with an immediate response.

SNMP management has its own set of security needs. Keeping SNMP traffic on the management segment allows it to traverse an isolated segment when pulling management information from devices. With SAFE, SNMP management only pulls information from devices, rather than being allowed to push changes. To ensure this, each device is configured with a read-only string.

Proper aggregation and analysis of the syslog information is critical to the proper management of a network. From a security perspective, syslog provides important information regarding security violations and configuration changes. Depending on the device in question, different levels of syslog information might be required. Having full logging with all messages sent might provide too much information for an individual or syslog analysis algorithm to sort. Logging for the sake of logging does not improve security.

For the SAFE validation lab, all configurations were done using standalone management applications and the command-line interface (CLI). Nothing in SAFE, however, precludes using policy management systems for configuration. Establishing this management module makes deployments of such technology completely viable. CLI and standalone management applications were chosen because the majority of current network deployments use this configuration method.

Alternatives

Complete OOB management is not always possible, because some devices might not support it or there might be geographic differences that dictate in-band management. When in-band management is required, more emphasis needs to be placed on securing the transport of the management protocols. This can be through the use of IPSec, SSH, SSL, or any other encrypted and authenticated transport that allows management information to traverse it. When management happens on the same interface that a device uses for user data, importance needs to be placed on passwords, community strings, cryptographic keys, and the access lists that control communications to the management services.

Future Near-Term Architecture Goals

The current reporting and alarming implementation is split across multiple hosts. Some hosts have intelligence for analyzing firewall and IDS data, while others are better suited to analyze router and switch data. In the future, all data will aggregate to the same set of redundant hosts so that event correlation between all of the devices can occur.

Core Module

The core module (see Figure A-7) in the SAFE architecture is nearly identical to the core module of any other network architecture. It merely routes and switches traffic as fast as possible from one network to another.

Figure A-7   *Core Module: Detail*

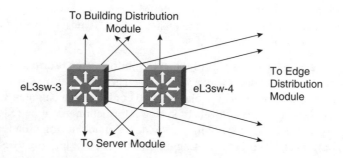

Key Devices

Layer 3 switches route and switch production network data from one module to another.

Threats Mitigated

Packet sniffers are the threats mitigated. A switched infrastructure limits the effectiveness of sniffing.

Design Guidelines

Standard implementation guidelines were followed in accordance with the core, distribution, and access layer deployments commonly seen in well-designed Cisco-based networks.

Though no unique requirements are defined by the SAFE architecture for the core of enterprise networks, the core switches follow the switch security axiom in the "Switches Are Targets" section to ensure that they are well protected against direct attacks.

Building Distribution Module

The goal of the building distribution module (see Figure A-8) is to provide distribution layer services to the building switches; these include routing, quality of service (QoS), and access control. Requests for data flow into these switches and onto the core, and responses follow the identical path in reverse.

Figure A-8   *Building Distribution Module: Detail*

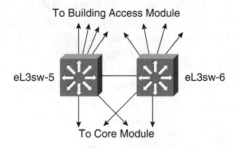

Key Devices

Layer 3 switches aggregate Layer 2 switches in the building module and provide advanced services.

Threats Mitigated

The threats mitigated (see Figure A-9) are as follows:

- **Unauthorized access**—Attacks against server module resources are limited by Layer 3 filtering of specific subnets.

- **IP spoofing**—RFC 2827 filtering stops most spoofing attempts.

- **Packet sniffers**—A switched infrastructure limits the effectiveness of sniffing.

Figure A-9 *Attack Mitigation Roles for Building Distribution Module*

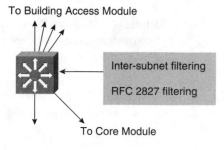

Design Guidelines

In addition to standard network design fundamentals, the optimizations described in the "Switches Are Targets" section were implemented to provide added security within the enterprise user community. Intrusion detection is not implemented at the building distribution module because it is implemented in the modules that contain the resources likely to be attacked for their content (server, remote access, Internet, and so forth). The building distribution module provides the first line of defense and prevention against internally originated attacks. It can mitigate the chance of a department accessing confidential information on another department's server through the use of access control. For example, a network that contains marketing and research and development (R&D) might segment off the R&D server to a specific VLAN and filter access to it, ensuring that only R&D staff have access to it. For performance reasons, it is important that this access control is implemented on a hardware platform that can deliver filtered traffic at near wire rates. This generally dictates the use of Layer 3 switching as opposed to more traditional dedicated routing devices. This same access control can also prevent local source-address spoofing by the use of RFC 2827 filtering. Finally, subnet isolation is used to route Voice over IP (VoIP) traffic to the call manager and any associated gateways. This prevents VoIP traffic from crossing the same segments that all other data traffic crosses, reducing the likelihood of sniffing voice communications and allowing a smoother implementation of QoS.

Alternatives

Depending on the size and performance requirements of the network, the distribution layer can be combined with the core layer to reduce the number of devices required in the environment.

Building Access Module

SAFE defines the building access module as the extensive network portion that contains end-user workstations, phones, and their associated Layer 2 access points. Its primary goal is to provide services to end users.

Key Devices

The key devices (see Figure A-10) are as follows:

- **Layer 2 switch**—Provides Layer 2 services to phones and user workstations
- **User workstation**—Provides data services to authorized users on the network
- **IP phone**—Provides IP telephony services to users on the network

Figure A-10 *Building Access Module: Detail*

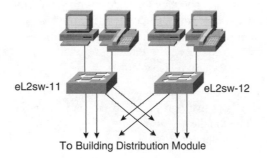

Threats Mitigated

The threats mitigated (see Figure A-11) are as follows:

- **Packet sniffers**—A switched infrastructure and default VLAN services limit the effectiveness of sniffing.
- **Virus and Trojan horse applications**—Host-based virus scanning prevents most viruses and many Trojan horses.

Figure A-11 *Attack Mitigation Roles for Building Access Module*

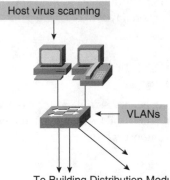

Design Guidelines

Because user devices are generally the largest single element of the network, implementing security in a concise and effective manner is challenging. From a security perspective, the building distribution module, rather than anything in the building module, provides most of the access control that is enforced at the end-user level. This is because the Layer 2 switch that the workstations and phones connect to has no capability for Layer 3 access control. In addition to the network security guidelines described in the switch security axiom, host-based virus scanning is implemented at the workstation level.

Server Module

The server module's primary goal is to provide application services to end users and devices. Traffic flow on the server module is inspected by onboard intrusion detection within the Layer 3 switches.

Key Devices

The key devices (see Figure A-12) are as follows:

- **Layer 3 switch**—Provides Layer 3 services to the servers and inspects data crossing the server module with NIDS

- **Call Manager**—Performs call-routing functions for IP telephony devices in the enterprise

- **Corporate and department servers**—Deliver file, print, and DNS services to workstations in the building module

- **E-mail server**—Provides Simple Mail Transfer Protocol (SMTP) and Post Office Protocol version 3 (POP3) services to internal users

Figure A-12 *Server Module: Detail*

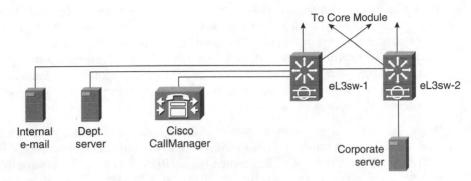

Threats Mitigated

The threats mitigated (see Figure A-13) are as follows:

- **Unauthorized access**—Mitigated through the use of host-based intrusion detection and access control.

- **Application layer attacks**—Operating systems, devices, and applications are kept up-to-date with the latest security fixes and are protected by HIDS.

- **IP spoofing**—RFC 2827 filtering prevents source address spoofing.

- **Packet sniffers**—A switched infrastructure limits the effectiveness of sniffing.

- **Trust exploitation**—Trust arrangements are very explicit; private VLANs prevent hosts on the same subnet from communicating unless necessary.

- **Port redirection**—HIDS prevents port redirection agents from being installed.

Figure A-13 *Attack Mitigation Roles for Server Module*

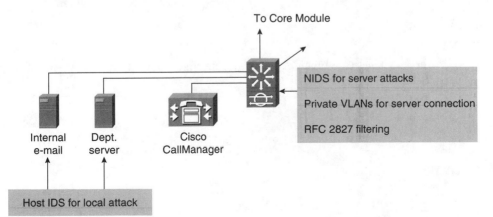

Design Guidelines

The server module is often overlooked from a security perspective. When examining the levels of access that most employees have to the servers to which they attach, the servers can often become the primary goal of internally originated attacks. Simply relying on effective passwords does not provide for a comprehensive attack mitigation strategy. Using HIDS and NIDS, private VLANs, access control, and good system administration practices (such as keeping systems up-to-date with the latest patches) provides a much more comprehensive response to attacks.

Because the NIDS is limited in the amount of traffic it can analyze, it is important to send only attack-sensitive traffic to it. This varies from network to network, but should include SMTP, Telnet, FTP, and WWW. The switch-based NIDS was chosen because of its ability to look only at interesting traffic across all VLANs as defined by the security policy. Once properly tuned, this IDS can be set up in a restrictive manner, because required traffic streams should be well known.

Alternatives

Like the building distribution module, the server module can be combined with the core module if performance needs do not dictate separation. For very sensitive high-performance server environments, the NIDS capability in the Layer 3 switch can be scaled by installing more than one NIDS blade and directing policy-matched traffic to specific blades.

Edge Distribution Module

The edge distribution module's goal is to aggregate the connectivity from the various elements at the edge. Traffic is filtered and routed from the edge modules and routed into the core.

Key Devices

Layer 3 switches (see Figure A-14) aggregate edge connectivity and provide advanced services.

Figure A-14 *Edge Distribution Module: Detail*

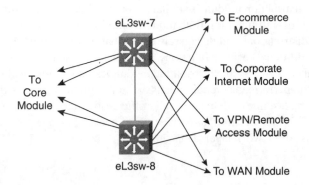

Threats Mitigated

The threats mitigated (see Figure A-15) are as follows:

- **Unauthorized access**—Filtering provides granular control over specific edge subnets and their ability to reach areas within the campus.

- **IP spoofing**—RFC 2827 filtering limits locally initiated spoof attacks.

- **Network reconnaissance**—Filtering limits nonessential traffic from entering the campus, limiting a hacker's ability to perform network reconnaissance.

- **Packet sniffers**—A switched infrastructure limits the effectiveness of sniffing.

Figure A-15 *Attack Mitigation Roles for Edge Distribution Module*

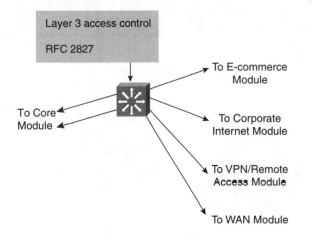

Design Guidelines

The edge distribution module is similar in some respects to the building distribution module in terms of overall function. Both modules employ access control to filter traffic, although the edge distribution module can rely somewhat on the entire edge functional area to perform additional security functions. Both modules use Layer 3 switching to achieve high performance, but the edge distribution module can add additional security functions because the performance requirements are not as great. The edge distribution module provides the last line of defense for all traffic destined to the campus module from the edge module. This includes mitigation of spoofed packets, erroneous routing updates, and provisions for network layer access control.

Alternatives

Like the server and building distribution modules, the edge distribution module can be combined with the core module if performance requirements are not as stringent as the SAFE reference implementation. NIDS is not present in this module, but it could be placed here through the use of IDS line cards in the Layer 3 switches. It would then reduce the need for NIDS appliances at the exit from the critical edge modules as they connect to the campus. However, performance reasons may dictate, as they did in SAFE's reference design, that dedicated intrusion detection be placed in the various edge modules, as opposed to using the edge distribution module.

Enterprise Edge

Figures A-16 and A-17 show a detailed analysis of all of the modules contained within the enterprise edge.

Figure A-16 *Enterprise Edge Detail—Part 1*

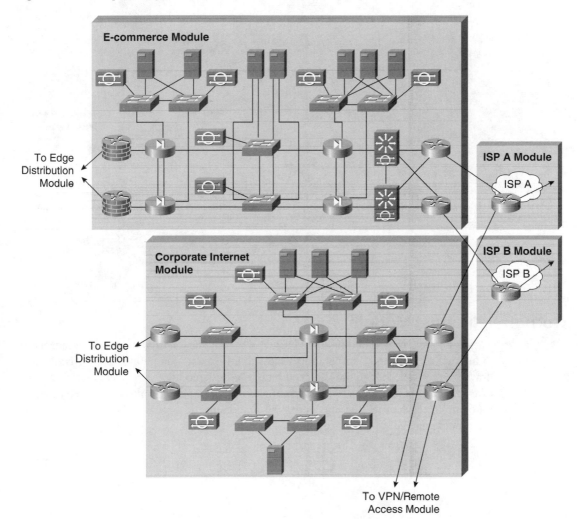

Figure A-17 *Enterprise Edge Detail—Part 2*

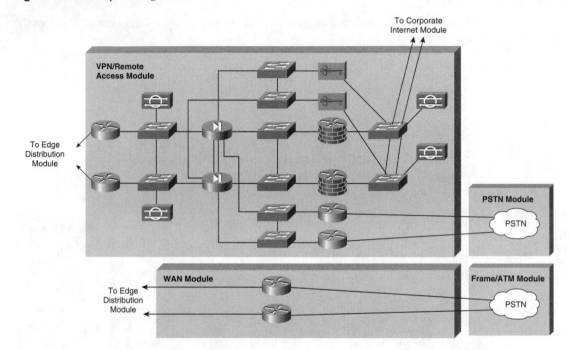

Corporate Internet Module

The corporate Internet module (see Figure A-18) provides internal users with connectivity to Internet services and Internet users access to information on public servers. Traffic also flows from this module to the VPN and remote-access module, where VPN termination takes place. This module is not designed to serve e-commerce applications. Refer to the "E-Commerce Module" section later in this document for more details on providing Internet commerce.

Figure A-18 *Corporate Internet Traffic Flow*

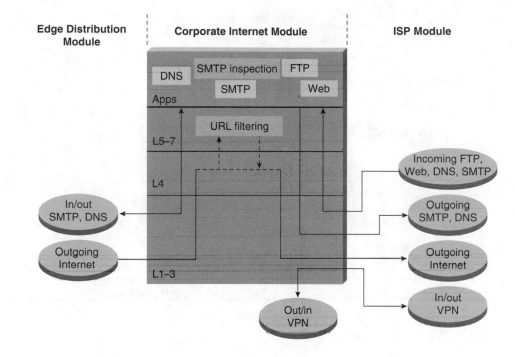

Key Devices

The key devices (see Figure A-19) are as follows:

- **SMTP server**—Acts as a relay between the Internet and the Internet mail servers; inspects content

- **DNS server**—Serves as authoritative external DNS server for the enterprise; relays internal requests to the Internet

- **FTP/HTTP server**—Provides public information about the organization

- **Firewall**—Provides network level protection of resources and stateful filtering of traffic

- **NIDS appliance**—Provides Layer 4 to Layer 7 monitoring of key network segments in the module

- **URL filtering server**—Filters unauthorized URL requests from the enterprise

Figure A-19 *Corporate Internet Module: Detail*

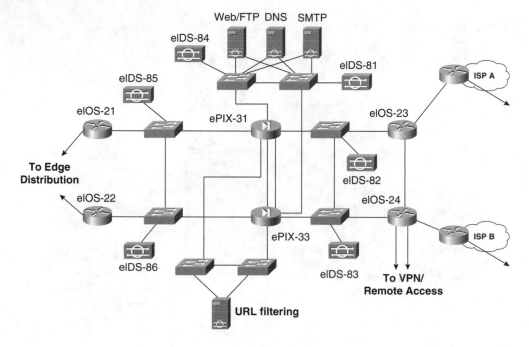

Threats Mitigated

The threats mitigated (see Figure A-20) are as follows:

- **Unauthorized access**—Mitigated through filtering at the ISP, edge router, and corporate firewall

- **Application layer attacks**—Mitigated through IDS at the host and network levels

- **Virus and Trojan horse**—Mitigated through e-mail content filtering and HIDS

- **Password attacks**—Limited services available to brute force; OS and IDS can detect the threat

- **DoS**—Committed access rate (CAR) at ISP edge and TCP setup controls at firewall

- **IP spoofing**—RFC 2827 and RFC 1918 filtering at ISP edge and enterprise edge router

- **Packet sniffers**—Switched infrastructure and HIDS limits exposure

- **Network reconnaissance**—IDS detects reconnaissance; protocols filtered to limit effectiveness

- **Trust exploitation**—Restrictive trust model and private VLANs limit trust-based attacks

- **Port redirection**—Restrictive filtering and HIDS limit attack

Figure A-20 *Attack Mitigation Roles for Corporate Internet Module*

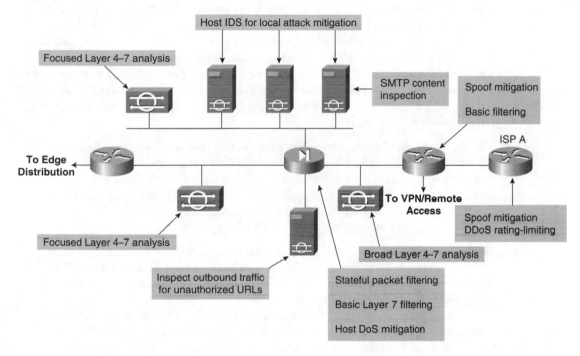

Design Guidelines

The heart of the module is a pair of resilient firewalls, which provide protection for the Internet public services and internal users. Stateful inspection examines traffic in all directions, ensuring only legitimate traffic crosses the firewall. Aside from the Layer 2 and Layer 3 resilience built into the module and the stateful failover capability of the firewall, all other design considerations center around security and attack mitigation.

Starting at the customer-edge router in the ISP, the egress out of the ISP rate limits nonessential traffic that exceeds prespecified thresholds to mitigate against DDoS or DoS attacks. Also at the egress of the ISP router, RFC 1918 and RFC 2827 filtering mitigate against source-address spoofing of local networks and private address ranges.

At the ingress of the first router on the enterprise network, basic filtering limits the traffic to the expected traffic (addresses and IP services), providing a coarse filter for the most basic attacks. RFC 1918 and RFC 2827 filtering is also provided here as a verification of the ISP's filtering. In addition, because of the enormous security threat that fragmented packets create, the router is configured to drop most fragmented packets that should not generally be seen for standard traffic types on the Internet. Any legitimate traffic lost because of this filtering is considered acceptable when compared to the risk of allowing such traffic. Finally, any IPSec traffic destined for the VPN and remote-access module is routed appropriately. Filtering on the interface that is connected to the VPN module is configured to allow only IPSec traffic to cross, and only when originated from and sent to authorized peers. With remote-access VPNs, you generally do not know the IP address of the system coming in, so filtering can be specific only to the head-end peers with which the remote users are communicating.

The NIDS appliance at the public side of the firewall monitors for attacks based on Layer 4 to Layer 7 analysis and comparisons against known signatures. Because the ISP and enterprise edge router filter certain address ranges and ports, the NIDS appliance can focus on some of the more complex attacks. Still, this NIDS should have alarms set to a lower level than appliances on the inside of the firewall, because alarms seen here do not represent actual breaches, but merely attempts.

The firewall provides connection state enforcement and detailed filtering for sessions initiated through it. Publicly addressable servers have some protection against TCP SYN floods through the use of half-open connection limits on the firewall. From a filtering standpoint, in addition to limiting traffic on the public services segment to relevant addresses and ports, filtering in the opposite direction also takes place. If an attack compromises one of the public servers (by circumventing the firewall, HIDS, and NIDS), that server should not be able to attack the network further. To mitigate against this type of attack, specific filtering prevents any unauthorized requests from being generated by the public servers to any other location. As an example, the Web server should be filtered so that it cannot originate requests of its own, but merely respond to requests from clients. This helps prevent a hacker from downloading additional utilities to the compromised box after the initial attack. It also helps stop unwanted sessions from being triggered by the hacker during the primary attack. An example of such an attack is one that generates an xterm from the Web server through the firewall to the hacker's machine. In addition, private VLANs prevent a compromised public server from attacking other servers on the same segment. This traffic is not even detected by the firewall, which is why private VLANs are critical.

Traffic on the content inspection segment is limited to URL filtering requests from the firewall to the URL filtering device. In addition, authenticated requests are allowed from the enterprise URL filtering device out to a master server for database updates. The URL filtering device inspects outbound traffic for unauthorized WWW requests. It communicates directly with the firewall and approves or rejects URL requests sent to its URL inspection engine by the firewall. Its decision is based on a policy managed by the enterprise using classification information of the WWW provided by a third-party service. URL inspection is preferred over standard access filtering because IP addresses often change for unauthorized web sites, and such filters can grow to be very large. HIDS software on this server protects against possible attacks that somehow circumvent the firewall.

The public services segment includes an NIDS appliance to detect attacks on ports that the firewall is configured to permit. These most often are application layer attacks against a specific service or password attacks against a protected service. You need to set this NIDS in a more restrictive stance than the NIDS on the outside of the firewall because signatures matched here have successfully passed through the firewall. Each of the servers have host intrusion detection software on them to monitor against any rogue activity at the OS level, in addition to activity in common server applications (HTTP, FTP, SMTP, and so forth). The DNS host should be locked down to respond only to desired commands and to eliminate any unnecessary responses that might assist hackers in network reconnaissance. This includes preventing zone transfers from anywhere but the internal DNS servers. The SMTP server includes mail-content inspection services to mitigate against virus and Trojan-type attacks generated against the internal network that are usually introduced through the mail system. The firewall itself filters SMTP messages at Layer 7 to allow only necessary commands to the mail server.

The NIDS appliance on the inside interface of the firewall provides a final analysis of attacks. Very few attacks should be detected on this segment, because only responses to initiated requests and a few select ports from the public services segment are allowed to the inside. Only sophisticated attacks should be seen on this segment, because they generally mean a system on the public services segment has been compromised and the hacker is attempting to leverage this foothold to attack the internal network. For example, if the public SMTP server is compromised, a hacker might try to attack the internal mail server over TCP port 25, which is permitted to allow mail transfer between the two hosts. If attacks are seen on this segment, the responses to those attacks should be more severe than those on other segments because they probably indicate that a compromise has already occurred. The use of TCP resets to thwart, for example, the SMTP attack mentioned above should be seriously considered.

Alternatives

There are several alternative designs for this module. For example, depending on your attitude toward attack awareness, the NIDS appliances might not be required in front of the firewall. In fact, without basic filtering on the access router, this type of monitoring is not recommended. With the appropriate basic filters, which exist in this design, the IDS outside the firewall can provide important alarm information that would otherwise be dropped by the firewall. Because the amount of alarms generated on this segment is probably large, alarms generated here should have a lower severity than alarms generated behind a firewall. Also, consider logging alarms from this segment to a separate management station to ensure that legitimate alarms from other segments get the appropriate attention. With the visibility that NIDS outside the firewall provides, evaluation of the attack types your organization is attracting can be better seen. In addition, evaluation of the effectiveness of ISP and enterprise edge filters can be performed.

Another possible alternative to the proposed design is the elimination of the router between the firewall and the edge distribution module. Though its functions can be integrated into the edge distribution module, the functional separation between modules would be lost, because the edge distribution switches would need to be aware of the entire topology of the corporate Internet module to ensure proper routing. In addition, this limits your ability to deploy this architecture in a modular fashion. If an enterprise's current core is Layer 2, for example, the routing provided in the corporate Internet module would be required.

Near-Term Architecture Goals

Developing Cisco firewall technology that can communicate directly with other content inspection devices is needed (for example, network-based virus scanning). Currently, URL filtering is the only supported content filtering function that is directly integrated with Cisco firewall technology. Nonintegrated products rely on users operating in a proxy mode that does not properly scale.

VPN and Remote-Access Module

As the name implies, the primary objective of the VPN and remote-access module (see Figure A-21) is threefold: terminate the VPN traffic from remote users, provide a hub for terminating VPN traffic from remote sites, and terminate traditional dial-in users. All of the traffic forwarded to the edge distribution is from remote corporate users that are authenticated in some fashion before being allowed through the firewall.

Figure A-21 *Remote-Access VPN Module Traffic Flow*

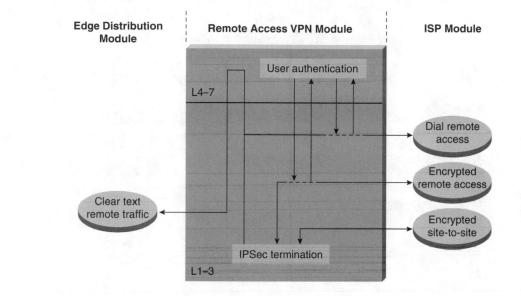

Key Devices

The key devices (see Figure A-22) are as follows:

- **VPN concentrator**—Authenticates individual remote users using Extended Authentication (Xauth) and terminate their IPSec tunnels

- **VPN router**—Authenticates trusted remote sites and provide connectivity using generic routing encapsulation (GRE) or IPSec tunnels

- **Dial-in server**—Authenticates individual remote users using TACACS+ and terminate their analog connections

- **Firewall**—Provides differentiated security for the three different types of remote access

- **NIDS appliance**—Provides Layer 4 to Layer 7 monitoring of key network segments in the module

Figure A-22 *Remote-Access VPN Module: Detail*

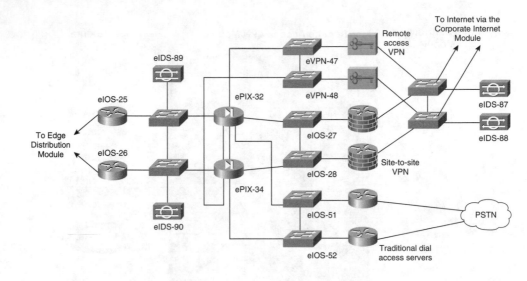

Threats Mitigated

The threats mitigated (see Figure A-23) are as follows:

- **Network topology discovery**—Only Internet Key Exchange (IKE) and Encapsulating Security Payload (ESP) are allowed into this segment from the Internet.

- **Password attack**—OTP authentication reduces the likelihood of a successful password attack.

- **Unauthorized access**—Firewall services after packet decryption prevent traffic on unauthorized ports.

- **Man-in-the-middle**—Mitigated through encrypted remote traffic.

- **Packet sniffers**—A switched infrastructure limits the effectiveness of sniffing.

Figure A-23 *Attack Mitigation Roles for Remote-Access VPN Module*

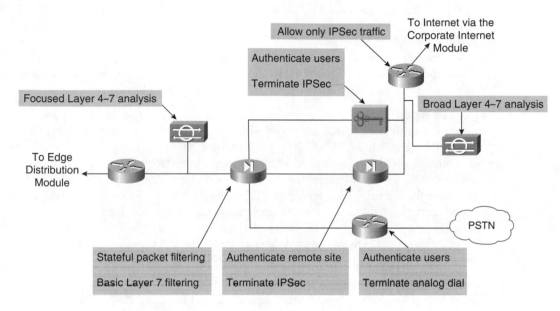

Design Guidelines

Resilience aside, the core requirement of this module is to have three separate external user services authenticate and terminate. Because the traffic comes from different sources outside of the enterprise network, the decision was made in the SAFE architecture to provide a separate interface on the firewall for each of these three services. The design consideration for each of these services are addressed below.

Remote-Access VPN

The VPN traffic is forwarded from the corporate Internet module access routers, where it is first filtered at the egress point to the specific IP addresses and protocols that are part of the VPN services. Today's remote-access VPNs can use several different tunneling and security protocols. Although IPSec is the tunneling protocol of choice, many organizations choose Point-to-Point Tunneling Protocol (PPTP) and Layer 2 Tunneling Protocol (L2TP) because they are natively supported by popular desktop operating systems. In SAFE, IPSec was chosen because the clients require minimal configuration and at the same time provide good security.

The remote-access VPN traffic is addressed to one specific public address using the IKE (UDP 500) protocol. Because the IKE connection is not completed until the correct authentication information is provided, this provides a level of deterrence for the potential hacker. As part of the extensions (draft RFCs) of IKE, XAUTH provides an additional user authentication mechanism before the remote user is assigned any IP parameters. The VPN concentrator is "connected" to the access control server on the management subnet by its management interface. Strong passwords are provided by the OTP server.

Once authenticated, the remote user is provided with access by receiving IP parameters using another extension of IKE, MODCFG. Besides an IP address and the location of name servers (DNS and WINS), MODCFG provides authorization services to control the access of the remote user. For example in SAFE, users are prevented from enabling split tunneling, thereby forcing the user to access the Internet via the corporate connection. The IPSec parameters that are being used are Triple DES (3DES) for encryption and SHA-HMAC for data integrity. The hardware encryption modules in the VPN concentrator allow scalable remote-access VPN services to be deployed to thousands of remote users. Following termination of the VPN tunnel, traffic is sent through a firewall to ensure that VPN users are appropriately filtered.

Secure management of this service is achieved by pushing all IPSec and security parameters to the remote users from the central site. Additionally, connections to all management functions are on a dedicated management interface.

Dial-In Access Users

The traditional dial-in users are terminated on one of the two access routers with built-in modems. Once the Layer 1 connection is established between the user and the server, three-way Challenge Handshake Authentication Protocol (CHAP) is used to authenticate the user. As in the remote-access VPN service, the authentication, authorization, and accounting (AAA) and OTP servers are used to authenticate and provide passwords. Once authenticated, the users are provided with IP addresses from an IP pool through Point-to-Point Protocol (PPP).

Site-to-Site VPN

The VPN traffic associated with site-to-site connections consists of GRE tunnels protected by an IPSec protocol in transport mode using ESP. As in the remote-access case, the traffic that is forwarded from the corporate Internet module can be limited to the specific destination addresses on the two VPN routers and the source addresses expected from the remote sites. The ESP protocol (IP 50) and the IKE protocol are the only two expected on this link.

GRE is used to provide a full-service routed link that will carry multiprotocol, routing protocol, and multicast traffic. Because routing protocols (Enhanced Interior Gateway Routing Protocol [EIGRP] is used between remote sites) can detect link failure, the GRE tunnel provides a resilience mechanism for the remote sites if they build two GRE connections, one to each of the central VPN routers.

As in remote-access VPN, 3DES and SHA-HMAC are used for IKE and IPSec parameters to provide the maximum security with little effect on performance. IPSec hardware accelerators are used in the VPN routers.

Rest of the Module

The traffic from the three services is aggregated by the firewall onto one private interface before being sent to the edge distribution module by a pair of routers. The firewall must be configured with the right type of constraining access control to allow only the appropriate traffic through to the inside interface of the firewall from each of the services. A pair of NIDS appliances are positioned at the public side of the module to detect any network reconnaissance activity targeted at the VPN termination devices. On this segment, only IPSec (IKE/ESP) traffic should be seen. Because the NIDS cannot see inside the IPSec packets, any alarm on this network indicates a failure or compromise of the surrounding devices. As such, these alarms should be set to high severity levels. A second pair of NIDS appliances are positioned after the firewall to detect any attacks that make it through the rest of the module. This NIDS device also has a restrictive policy in place. All users crossing this segment should be bound to or coming from a remote location, so any shunning or TCP resets will affect only those users.

Alternatives

In VPN and authentication technology, there are many alternatives available, depending on the requirements of the network. These alternatives are listed below for reference, but the details are not addressed in this document.

* Smart card or biometric authentication
* L2TP or PPTP remote-access VPN tunnels
* Certificate authorities (CAs)
* IKE keep-alive resilience mechanism
* Multiprotocol Label Switching (MPLS) VPNs

WAN Module

Rather than being all-inclusive of potential WAN designs, this module shows resilience and security for WAN termination. Using Frame Relay encapsulation, traffic is routed between remote sites and the central site.

Key Devices

The IOS router, using routing, access-control, and QoS mechanisms, is the key device (see Figure A-24).

Figure A-24 *WAN Module: Detail*

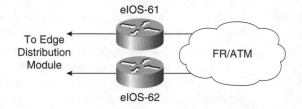

Threats Mitigated

The threats mitigated (see Figure A-25) are as follows:

- **IP spoofing**—Mitigated through Layer 3 filtering.
- **Unauthorized access**—Simple access control on the router can limit the types of protocols to which branches have access.

Figure A-25 *Attack Mitigation Roles for WAN Module*

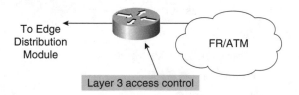

Design Guidelines

The resilience is provided by the dual connection from the service provider, through the routers, and to the edge distribution module. Security is provided by using IOS security features. Input access lists are used to block all unwanted traffic from the remote branch.

Alternatives

Some organizations that are very concerned about information privacy encrypt highly confidential traffic on their WAN links. Similar to site-to-site VPNs, you can use IPSec to achieve this information privacy.

E-Commerce Module

Because e-commerce is the primary objective of this module (see Figure A-26), the balance between access and security must be carefully weighed. Splitting the e-commerce transaction into three components allows the architecture to provide various levels of security without impeding access.

Figure A-26 *E-Commerce Traffic Flow*

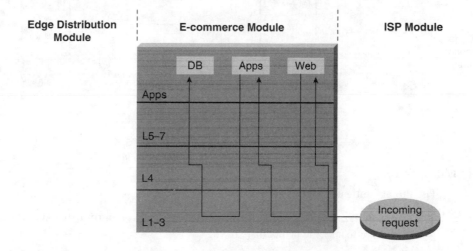

Key Devices

The key devices (see Figure A-27) are as follows:

- **Web server**—Acts as the primary user interface for the navigation of the e-commerce store

- **Application server**—Is the platform for the various applications required by the Web server

- **Database server**—Is the critical information that is the heart of the e-commerce business implementation

- **Firewall**—Governs communication between the various levels of security and trust in the system

- **NIDS appliance**—Provides monitoring of key network segments in the module
- **Layer 3 switch with IDS module**—Is the scalable e-commerce input device with integrated security monitoring

Figure A-27 *E-Commerce Module: Detail*

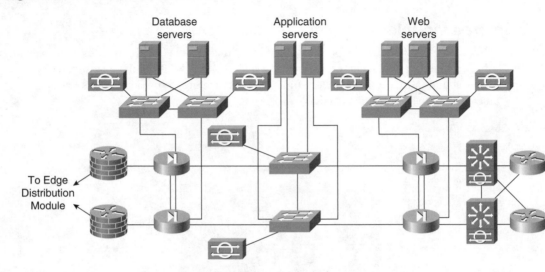

Threats Mitigated

The threats mitigated (see Figure A-28) are as follows:

- **Unauthorized access**—Stateful firewalls and access control lists (ACLs) limit exposure to specific protocols.
- **Application layer attacks**—Attacks are mitigated through the use of IDS.
- **DoS**—ISP filtering and rate limiting reduce DDoS or DoS potential.
- **IP spoofing**—RFC 2827 and RFC 1918 prevent locally originated spoofed packets and limit remote spoof attempts.
- **Packet sniffers**—A switched infrastructure and HIDS limit the effectiveness of sniffing.
- **Network reconnaissance**—Ports are limited to only what is necessary; ICMP is restricted.
- **Trust exploitation**—Firewalls ensure that communication flows only in the proper direction on the proper service.
- **Port redirection**—HIDS and firewall filtering limit exposure to these attacks.

Figure A-28 *Attack Mitigation Roles for E-Commerce Module*

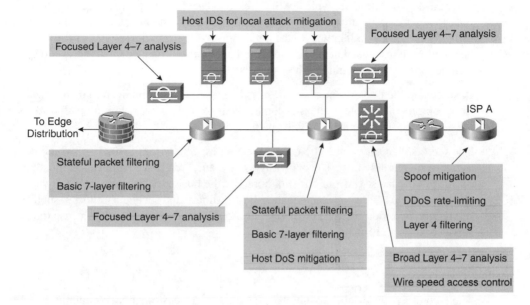

Design Implementation Description

The heart of the module is two pairs of resilient firewalls that provide protection for the three levels of servers: Web, application, and database. Some added protection is provided by the ISP edge routers at the ISP and the enterprise. The design is best understood by considering the traffic flow sequence and direction for a typical e-commerce transaction.

The e-commerce customer initiates an HTTP connection to the Web server after receiving the IP address from a DNS server hosted at the ISP network. The DNS is hosted on a different network to reduce the amount of protocols required by the e-commerce application. The first set of firewalls must be configured to allow this protocol through to that particular address. The return traffic for this connection is allowed back, but there is no need for any communication initiated by the Web server back out to the Internet. The firewall should block this path to limit the options of hackers if they get control of one of the Web servers.

As the user navigates the web site, certain link selections cause the Web server to initiate a request to the application server on the inside interface. This connection must be permitted by the first firewall, as well as the associated return traffic. As in the case with the Web server, there is no reason for the application server to initiate a connection to the Web server or even out to the Internet. Likewise, the user's entire session runs over HTTP and SSL with no ability to communicate directly with the application server or the database server.

At one point, the user might want to perform a transaction. The Web server should protect this transaction, and the SSL protocol will be required from the Internet to the Web server.

At the same time, the application server might want to query or pass information on to the database server. These are typically Structured Query Language (SQL) queries that are initiated by the application server to the database server, and not vice versa. These queries run through the second firewall to the database server. Depending on the specific applications in use, the database server might need to communicate with back-end systems located in the server module of the enterprise.

In summary, the firewalls must allow only three specific communication paths, each with its own protocol, and block all other communication, unless it is the return path packets that are associated with the three original paths.

The servers themselves must be fully protected, especially the Web server, which is a publicly addressable host. The operating system and Web server application must be patched to the latest versions and monitored by the host intrusion detection software. This should mitigate against most application layer primary and secondary attacks, such as port redirection and root kits. The other servers should have similar security in case the first server or firewall is compromised.

Beyond the Firewall

The e-commerce firewalls are initially protected by the customer edge router at the ISP. At the router egress point, toward the enterprise, the ISP can limit the traffic to the small number of protocols required for e-commerce with a destination address of the Web servers only. Routing protocol updates (generally Border Gateway Protocol [BGP]) are required by the edge routers, and all other traffic should be blocked. The ISP should implement rate limiting, as specified in the "SAFE Axioms" section, to mitigate DDoS or DoS attacks. In addition, filtering according to RFC 1918 and RFC 2827 should be implemented by the ISP.

On the enterprise premises, the initial router serves only as an interface to the ISP. The Layer 3 switch does all the network processing because it has features off-loaded to hardware processors. The Layer 3 switches participate in the full BGP routing decision to decide which ISP has the better route to the particular user. The Layer 3 switches also provide verification filtering in keeping with the ISP filtering described above; this provides overlapping security. The Layer 3 switches also provide built-in IDS monitoring. If the connection to the Internet exceeds the capacity of the IDS line card, you might need to look at inbound Web requests from the Internet on the IDS line card. Although this will miss some HTTP alarm signatures (approximately 10 percent), it is better than looking at the entire stream in both directions, where many misses would occur. The other NIDS appliances behind the various interfaces of the firewall monitor the segments for any attacks that might have penetrated the first line of defense. For example, if the Web server is out of date, hackers could compromise it over an application layer attack, assuming they were able to circumvent the HIDS. As in the corporate Internet module, the false positives must be removed so that all true attack detections are treated with the correct level of priority. In fact, because only certain types of traffic exist on certain segments, you can tune NIDS very tightly.

From an application standpoint, the communications paths between the various layers (web, apps, dbase) should be encrypted, transactional, and highly authenticated. For example, if the apps server was to get data from the database over some type of scripted interactive session (SSH, FTP, Telnet, and so forth), a hacker could leverage that interactive session to initiate an application layer attack. By employing secure communications, you can limit potential threats.

The Layer 2 switches that support the various firewall segments provide the ability to implement private VLANs, thereby implementing a trust model that matches the desired traffic communication on a particular segment and eliminates all others. For example, there is usually no reason for one Web server to communicate with another Web server.

The management of the entire module is done completely out of band, as in the rest of the architecture.

Alternatives

The principle alternative to this deployment is colocating the entire system at an ISP. Though the design remains the same, there are two primary differences. The first is that bandwidth is generally larger to the ISP and uses a LAN connection. Though not recommended, this potentially eliminates the need for the edge routers in the proposed design. The additional bandwidth also creates different requirements for DDoS or DoS mitigation. The second is the connection back to the enterprise, which needs to be managed in a different way. Alternatives include encryption and private lines. Using these technologies creates additional security considerations, depending on the location of the connections and their intended use.

There are several variations on the primary design for this module. Aside from listing the alternatives, further discussion is beyond the scope of this appendix.

- The use of additional firewalls is one alternative. Sample communications would be edge routing to firewall to Web server to firewall to applications server to firewall to database server. This allows each firewall to control communications for only one primary system.

- Load-balancing and caching technologies are not specifically discussed in this appendix, but they can be overlaid onto this architecture without major modifications. A future paper will address these needs.

- For very high security requirements, the use of multiple firewall types may be considered. Note that this creates additional management overhead in duplicating policy on disparate systems. The goal of these designs is to avoid a vulnerability in one firewall from circumventing the security of the entire system. These types of designs tend to be very firewall-centric and do not adequately take advantage of IDS and other security technologies to mitigate the risk of a single firewall vulnerability.

Enterprise Options

The design process is often a series of trade-offs. This short subsection of the document highlights some of the high-level options that a network designer could implement if faced with tighter budget constraints. Some of these trade-offs are done at the module level, while others are done at the component level.

One option is to collapse the distribution modules into the core module. This reduces the number of Layer 3 switches by 50 percent. The cost savings would be traded off against performance requirements in the core of the network and flexibility to implement all the distribution security filtering.

A second option is to merge the functionality of the VPN and remote-access module with the corporate Internet module. Their structure is very similar, with a pair of firewalls at the heart of the module surrounded by NIDS appliances. This may be possible without loss of functionality if the performance of the components matches the combined traffic requirements of the modules, and if the firewall has enough interfaces to accommodate the different services. Keep in mind that as functions are aggregated to single devices, the potential for human error increases. Some organizations go even further and include the e-commerce functions in the corporate Internet/VPN module. The authors feel that the risk of doing this far outweighs any cost savings unless the e-commerce needs are minimal. Separation of the e-commerce traffic from general Internet traffic allows the e-commerce bandwidth to be better optimized by allowing the ISP to place more restrictive filtering and rate-limiting technology to mitigate against DDoS attacks.

A third option is to eliminate some of the NIDS appliances. Depending on your operational threat response strategy, you might need fewer NIDS appliances. The number of appliances is also affected by the amount of HIDS deployed, because this might reduce the need for NIDS in certain locations. This is discussed, where appropriate, in the specific modules.

Clearly, network design is not an exact science. Choices must always be made depending on the specific requirements facing the designer. The authors are not proposing that any designer would implement this architecture verbatim, but are encouraging designers to make educated choices about network security grounded in this proven implementation.

Migration Strategies

SAFE is a guide for implementing security on the enterprise network. It is not meant to serve as a security policy for any enterprise networks, nor is it meant to serve as the all-encompassing design to provide full security for all existing networks. Rather, SAFE is a template that enables network designers to consider how they design and implement their enterprise networks to meet their security requirements.

Establishing a security policy should be the first activity in migrating the network to a secure infrastructure. Basic recommendations for a security policy can be found at the end of the document in Annex B. After the policy is established, the network designer should consider the security axioms described in the first section of this document and see how they provide more detail to map the policy on the existing network infrastructure.

There is enough flexibility in the architecture and detail of the design considerations to enable the SAFE architecture elements to be adapted to most enterprise networks. For example, in the VPN and remote-access module, the various flows of traffic from public networks are each given a separate pair of terminating devices and a separate interface on the firewall. The VPN traffic could be combined in one pair of devices, if the load requirements permitted it and the security policy was the same for both types of traffic. On another network, the traditional dial-in and remote-access VPN users might be allowed directly into the network because the security policy puts enough trust in the authentication mechanisms that permit the connection to the network in the first place.

SAFE allows the designer to address the security requirements of each network function almost independently of each other. Each module is generally self-contained and assumes that any interconnected module is only at a basic security level. This allows network designers to use a phased approach to securing the enterprise network. They can address securing the most critical network functions as determined by the policy without redesigning the entire network. The exception to this is the management module. During the initial SAFE implementation, the management module should be implemented in parallel with the first module. As the rest of the network is migrated, the management module can be connected to the remaining locations.

This first version of the SAFE architecture is meant to address the security implementation of a generic enterprise network. The authors know that there are many areas that need further detailed research, exploration, and improvement. Some of these areas include, but are not limited to, the following:

- In-depth security management analysis and implementation
- Specialized design information for smaller networks
- In-depth identity, directory services, AAA technologies, and CA analysis and implementation
- Scaled versions of VPN head-end and WAN design

Annex A: Validation Lab

A reference SAFE implementation exists to validate the functionality described in this document. This annex details the configurations of the specific devices within each module in addition to the overall guidelines for general device configuration. The following are configuration snapshots from the live devices in the lab. The authors do not recommend applying these configurations directly to a production network.

Overall Guidelines

The configurations presented here correspond in part to the "SAFE Axioms" section presented earlier in this document.

Routers

Here are the basic configuration options present on nearly all routers in the SAFE lab:

```
! turn off unnecessary services
!
no ip domain-lookup
no cdp run
no ip http server
no ip source-route
no service finger
no ip bootp server
no service udp-small-s
no service tcp-small-s
!
!turn on logging and snmp
!
service timestamp log datetime localtime
logging 192.168.253.56
logging 192.168.253.51
snmp-server community Txo~QbW3XM ro 98
!
!set passwords and access restrictions
!
service password-encryption
enable secret %Z<)| z9~zq
no enable password| z
no access-list 99
access-list 99 permit 192.168.253.0 0.0.0.255
access-list 99 deny any log
no access-list 98
access-list 98 permit host 192.168.253.51
access-list 98 deny any log
line vty 0 4
access-class 99 in
login
password 0 X)[^j+#T98
exec-timeout 2 0
line con 0
login
password 0 X)[^j+#T98
exec-timeout 2 0
line aux 0
transport input none
password 0 X)[^j+#T98
no exec
exit
banner motd #
        This is a private system operated for and by Cisco VSEC BU.
    Authorization from Cisco VSEC management is required to use this system.
            Use by unauthorized persons is prohibited.
```

```
#
!
!Turn on NTP
!
clock timezone PST -8
clock summer-time PST recurring
ntp authenticate
ntp authentication-key 1 md5 -UN&/6[oh6
ntp trusted-key 1
ntp access-group peer 96
ntp server 192.168.254.57 key 1
access-l 96 permit host 192.168.254.57
access-l 96 deny any log
!
!Turn on AAA
!
aaa new-model
aaa authentication login default tacacs+
aaa authentication login no_tacacs line
aaa authorization exec tacacs+
aaa authorization network tacacs+
aaa accounting network start-stop tacacs+
aaa accounting exec start-stop tacacs+
tacacs-server host 192.168.253.54 single
tacacs-server key SJj)j~t]6-
line con 0
login authentication no_tacacs
```

The following configuration snapshot defines the Open Shortest Path First (OSPF) authentication and filtering parameters for all OSPF routers within the network. Note the MD5 authentication and the distribute lists ensuring that the OOB network is not advertised.

```
interface Vlan13
 ip address 10.1.13.3 255.255.255.0
 ip ospf authentication message-digest
 ip ospf message-digest-key 1 md5 7 024D105641521F0A7E
 ip ospf priority 3
!
router ospf 1
 area 0 authentication message-digest
 network 10.1.0.0 0.0.255.255 area 0
 distribute-list 1 out
 distribute-list 1 in
!
access-list 1 deny 192.168.0.0 0.0.255.255
access-list 1 permit any
```

The following configuration snapshot defines the access control present on all of the OOB interfaces throughout the network. Keep in mind that this is in addition to the private VLANs that block access between managed host IP addresses.

```
interface FastEthernet1/0
 ip address 192.168.254.15 255.255.255.0
 ip access-group 101 in
 ip access-group 102 out
 no cdp enable
!
```

```
access-list 101 permit icmp any any
access-list 101 permit tcp 192.168.253.0 0.0.0.255 host 192.168.254.15 established
access-list 101 permit udp 192.168.253.0 0.0.0.255 host 192.168.254.15 gt 1023
access-list 101 permit tcp 192.168.253.0 0.0.0.255 host 192.168.254.15 eq telnet
access-list 101 permit udp host 192.168.253.51 host 192.168.254.15 eq snmp
access-list 101 permit udp host 192.168.253.53 host 192.168.254.15 eq tftp
access-list 101 permit udp host 192.168.254.57 host 192.168.254.15 eq ntp
access-list 101 deny ip any any log
access-list 102 deny ip any any log
```

Switches

Here is the base security configuration present on nearly all Cat OS switches in the SAFE lab. IOS switches use a configuration nearly identical to the router configuration.

```
!
!Turn on NTP
!
set timezone PST -8
set summertime PST
set summertime recurring
set ntp authentication enable
set ntp key 1 trusted md5 -UN&/6[oh6
set ntp server 192.168.254.57 key 1
set ntp client enable
!
! turn off un-needed services
!
set cdp disable
set ip http server disable
!
!turn on logging and snmp
!
set logging server 192.168.253.56
set logging server 192.168.253.51
set logging timestamp enable
set snmp community read-only Txo~QbW3XM
set ip permit enable snmp
set ip permit 192.168.253.51 snmp
!
!Turn on AAA
!
set tacacs server 192.168.253.54 primary
set tacacs key SJj)j~t]6-
set authentication login tacacs enable telnet
set authentication login local disable telnet
set authorization exec enable tacacs+ deny telnet
set accounting exec enable start-stop tacacs+
set accounting connect enable start-stop tacacs+
!
!set passwords and access restrictions
!
set banner motd <c>
           This is a private system operated for and by Cisco VSEC BU.
       Authorization from Cisco VSEC management is required to use this system.
                   Use by unauthorized persons is prohibited.
<c>
!console password is set by 'set password'
!enter old password followed by new password
!console password = X)[^j+#T98
!
```

```
!enable password is set by 'set enable'
!enter old password followed by new password
!enable password = %Z<)| z9~zq
!
!the following password configuration only works the first time
!
set password

X)[^j+#T98
X)[^j+#T98
set enable
cisco
%Z<)| z9~zq
%Z<)| z9~zq
!
!the above password configuration only works the first time
!
set logout 2
set ip permit enable telnet
set ip permit 192.168.253.0 255.255.255.0 telnet
```

Hosts

Hosts were patched with the latest fixes. HIDS was applied, as well. The HIDS application used in the lab is ClickNet's Entercept application. More information is available at www.clicknet.com.

Management Module

Refer to Figure A-5 for a detail of the management module.

Products Used

The products used are as follows:

- Cisco Catalyst 3500XL Layer 2 switches (all switching)
- Cisco 3640 IOS Router with Firewall Feature Set (eIOS-21)
- Cisco 2511 IOS Router (terminal servers)
- Cisco Secure Intrusion Detection System (CSIDS) sensor
- RSA SecureID OTP Server
- Cisco Secure Access Control Server
- Works 2000
- Cisco Secure Policy Manager
- netForensics syslog analysis tool
- ClickNet Entercept HIDS

EIOS-21

The following configuration sets the default IOS firewall parameters:

```
ip inspect audit-trail
ip inspect max-incomplete low 150
ip inspect max-incomplete high 250
ip inspect one-minute low 100
ip inspect one-minute high 200
ip inspect udp idle-time 20
ip inspect dns-timeout 3
ip inspect tcp idle-time 1800
ip inspect tcp finwait-time 3
ip inspect tcp synwait-time 15
ip inspect tcp max-incomplete host 40 block-time 0
ip inspect name mgmt_fw tcp timeout 300
ip inspect name mgmt_fw udp
ip inspect name mgmt_fw tftp
ip inspect name mgmt_fw http
ip inspect name mgmt_fw fragment maximum 256 timeout 1
ip audit notify log
ip audit po max-events 100
```

The following configuration sets up the encrypted in-band network management:

```
crypto isakmp policy 1
 encr 3des
 authentication pre-share
 group 2
crypto isakmp key A%Xr)7,_) address 172.16.224.24
crypto isakmp key A%Xr)7,_) address 172.16.224.23
!
crypto ipsec transform-set vpn_module_mgmt esp-3des esp-sha-hmac
!
crypto map mgmt1 100 ipsec-isakmp
 set peer 172.16.224.24
 set transform-set vpn_module_mgmt
 match address 111
crypto map mgmt1 200 ipsec-isakmp
 set peer 172.16.224.23
 set transform-set vpn_module_mgmt
 match address 110
access-list 110 permit ip 192.168.253.0 0.0.0.255 host 172.16.224.23
access-list 110 permit udp 192.168.254.0 0.0.0.255 host 172.16.224.23
access-list 111 permit ip 192.168.253.0 0.0.0.255 host 172.16.224.24
access-list 111 permit udp 192.168.254.0 0.0.0.255 host 172.16.224.24
```

The following configuration defines inbound access control from the managed host network. Port 45000 is for CSIDS and port 5000 is for ClickNet's HIDS.

```
access-list 114 permit icmp 192.168.254.0 0.0.0.255 192.168.253.0 0.0.0.255
     echo-reply
access-list 114 permit udp 192.168.254.0 0.0.0.255 host 192.168.253.56 eq syslog
access-list 114 permit udp 192.168.254.0 0.0.0.255 host 192.168.253.51 eq syslog
access-list 114 permit udp 192.168.254.0 0.0.0.255 host 192.168.253.50 eq 45000
access-list 114 permit tcp 192.168.254.0 0.0.0.255 host 192.168.253.50 eq 5000
access-list 114 permit udp 192.168.254.0 0.0.0.255 host 192.168.253.53 eq tftp
access-list 114 permit udp 192.168.254.0 0.0.0.255 host 192.168.254.57 eq ntp
access-list 114 permit tcp 192.168.254.0 0.0.0.255 host 192.168.253.54 eq tacacs
access-list 114 permit udp 192.168.254.0 0.0.0.255 host 192.168.253.54 eq 1645
access-list 114 permit udp 192.168.254.0 0.0.0.255 host 192.168.253.52 eq syslog
access-list 114 deny ip any any log
```

The following configuration defines inbound access control from the management host network:

```
access-list 113 permit icmp 192.168.253.0 0.0.0.255 192.168.254.0 0.0.0.255
access-list 113 permit icmp 192.168.253.0 0.0.0.255 host 192.168.253.57
access-list 113 permit tcp 192.168.253.0 0.0.0.255 host 192.168.253.57 eq telnet
access-list 113 permit tcp 192.168.253.0 0.0.0.255 192.168.254.0 0.0.0.255 eq
   telnet
access-list 113 permit tcp 192.168.253.0 0.0.0.255 192.168.254.0 0.0.0.255 eq 443
access-list 113 permit tcp 192.168.253.0 0.0.0.255 192.168.254.0 0.0.0.255 eq 22
access-list 113 permit udp host 192.168.253.50 192.168.254.0 0.0.0.255 eq 45000
access-list 113 permit tcp host 192.168.253.50 192.168.254.0 0.0.0.255 eq 5000
access-list 113 permit udp host 192.168.253.51 192.168.254.0 0.0.0.255 eq snmp
access-list 113 permit udp host 192.168.253.53 gt 1023 host 192.168.253.57 gt
   1023
access-list 113 permit udp 192.168.253.0 0.0.0.255 host 192.168.254.57 eq ntp
access-list 113 permit tcp host 192.168.253.54 eq tacacs host 192.168.253.57 gt
   1023
access-list 113 permit icmp 192.168.253.0 0.0.0.255 host 172.16.224.23
access-list 113 permit icmp 192.168.253.0 0.0.0.255 host 172.16.224.24
access-list 113 permit tcp 192.168.253.0 0.0.0.255 host 172.16.224.23 eq telnet
access-list 113 permit tcp 192.168.253.0 0.0.0.255 host 172.16.224.24 eq telnet
access-list 113 permit udp host 192.168.253.51 host 172.16.224.23 eq snmp
access-list 113 permit udp host 192.168.253.51 host 172.16.224.24 eq snmp
access-list 113 deny ip any any log
```

The following configuration defines inbound access control from the production network. This access allows only encrypted traffic, because that is the only communication allowed into the management module from the production network. The first four lines define access for the encrypted traffic. After decryption, traffic must again pass through the access list to be allowed into the management module.

```
access-list 112 permit esp host 172.16.224.23 host 10.1.20.57
access-list 112 permit esp host 172.16.224.24 host 10.1.20.57
access-list 112 permit udp host 172.16.224.24 host 10.1.20.57 eq isakmp
access-list 112 permit udp host 172.16.224.23 host 10.1.20.57 eq isakmp
access-list 112 permit udp host 172.16.224.24 host 192.168.253.56 eq syslog
access-list 112 permit udp host 172.16.224.23 host 192.168.253.56 eq syslog
access-list 112 permit udp host 172.16.224.24 host 192.168.253.51 eq syslog
access-list 112 permit udp host 172.16.224.23 host 192.168.253.51 eq syslog
access-list 112 permit udp host 172.16.224.24 host 192.168.253.53 eq tftp
access-list 112 permit udp host 172.16.224.23 host 192.168.253.53 eq tftp
access-list 112 permit udp host 172.16.224.24 host 192.168.253.57 eq ntp
access-list 112 permit udp host 172.16.224.23 host 192.168.253.57 eq ntp
access-list 112 permit tcp host 172.16.224.24 host 192.168.253.54 eq tacacs
access-list 112 permit tcp host 172.16.224.23 host 192.168.253.54 eq tacacs
access-list 112 permit icmp host 172.16.224.24 192.168.253.0 0.0.0.255 echo-reply
access-list 112 permit icmp host 172.16.224.23 192.168.253.0 0.0.0.255 echo-reply
access-list 112 deny ip any any log
```

Core Module

Refer to Figure A-7 for a detail of the core module.

Products Used

Cisco Catalyst 6500 Layer 3 switches are used.

Building Distribution Module

Refer to Figure A-8 for a detail of the building distribution module.

Products Used

Cisco Catalyst 6500 Layer 3 switches are used.

EL3SW-5

The following configuration snapshot defines the Layer 3 access control between subnets in this module. VLAN 5 defines the marketing subnet, VLAN 6 defines the R&D subnet, VLAN 7 defines the marketing IP phones, and VLAN 8 defines the R&D IP phones.

```
interface Vlan5
 ip address 10.1.5.5 255.255.255.0
 ip access-group 105 in
!
interface Vlan6
 ip address 10.1.6.5 255.255.255.0
 ip access-group 106 in
!
interface Vlan7
 ip address 10.1.7.5 255.255.255.0
 ip access-group 107 in
!
interface Vlan8
 ip address 10.1.8.5 255.255.255.0
 ip access-group 108 in
!
access-list 105 deny ip 10.1.5.0 0.0.0.255 10.1.6.0 0.0.0.255
access-list 105 deny ip 10.1.5.0 0.0.0.255 10.1.7.0 0.0.0.255
access-list 105 deny ip 10.1.5.0 0.0.0.255 10.1.8.0 0.0.0.255
access-list 105 deny ip 10.1.5.0 0.0.0.255 10.1.16.0 0.0.0.255
access-list 105 permit ip 10.1.5.0 0.0.0.255 any
access-list 105 deny ip any any log
access-list 106 deny ip 10.1.6.0 0.0.0.255 10.1.5.0 0.0.0.255
access-list 106 deny ip 10.1.6.0 0.0.0.255 10.1.7.0 0.0.0.255
access-list 106 deny ip 10.1.6.0 0.0.0.255 10.1.8.0 0.0.0.255
access-list 106 deny ip 10.1.6.0 0.0.0.255 10.1.15.0 0.0.0.255
access-list 106 deny ip 10.1.6.0 0.0.0.255 10.1.16.0 0.0.0.255
access-list 106 permit ip 10.1.6.0 0.0.0.255 any
access-list 106 deny ip any any log
access-list 107 permit ip 10.1.7.0 0.0.0.255 10.1.8.0 0.0.0.255
access-list 107 permit ip 10.1.7.0 0.0.0.255 10.1.16.0 0.0.0.255
access-list 107 permit ip 10.1.7.0 0.0.0.255 host 10.1.11.50
access-list 107 deny ip any any log
access-list 108 permit ip 10.1.8.0 0.0.0.255 10.1.7.0 0.0.0.255
access-list 108 permit ip 10.1.8.0 0.0.0.255 10.1.16.0 0.0.0.255
access-list 108 permit ip 10.1.8.0 0.0.0.255 host 10.1.11.50
access-list 108 deny ip any any log
```

Building Access Module

Refer to Figure A-10 for a detail of the building access module.

Products Used

The following products are used:

- Cisco Catalyst 4003 Layer 2 switches
- Cisco IP Phone

EL2SW-11 and 12

The following configuration snapshot shows some of the VLAN settings on the Layer 2 switches in this module. Notice that unneeded ports are disabled and set to a nonroutable VLAN. Also, trunking is turned off on all ports except those connecting to IP phones that use trunking for VLAN separation between phone and workstation.

```
set vlan 5 2/5,2/17
set vlan 6 2/6,2/18
set vlan 99 2/34
set vlan 999 2/1-3,2/7-16,2/19-33
set port disable 2/7-33
set trunk 2/1-34 off
set trunk 2/4 on dot1q 1,5-8
```

Server Module

Refer to Figure A-12 for a detail of the server module.

Products Used

The following products are used:

- Cisco Catalyst 6500 Layer 3 switches
- Cisco Catalyst 6500 Intrusion Detection Blade
- Cisco Call Manager
- ClickNet Entercept HIDS

EL3SW-1 and 2

The following configuration sets the private VLAN mappings for several of the ports within the same VLAN. This configuration prevents the internal e-mail server from communicating with the corporate server.

```
! CAT OS Config
!
#private vlans
set pvlan 11 437
set pvlan 11 437 3/3-4,3/14
set pvlan mapping 11 437 15/1
!
```

```
! MSFC Config
!
interface Vlan11
 ip address 10.1.11.1 255.255.255.0
 ip access-group 111 in
 no ip redirects
```

The following configuration sets the interface filtering on several of the interfaces in this module. This includes RFC 2827 filtering.

```
interface Vlan11
 ip address 10.1.11.1 255.255.255.0
 ip access-group 111 in
!
interface Vlan15
 ip address 10.1.15.1 255.255.255.0
 ip access-group 115 in
!
interface Vlan16
 ip address 10.1.16.1 255.255.255.0
 ip access-group 116 in
 ip access-group 126 out
!
access-list 111 permit ip 10.1.11.0 0.0.0.255 any
access-list 111 deny ip any any log
access-list 115 permit ip 10.1.15.0 0.0.0.255 any
access-list 115 deny ip any any log
access-list 116 permit ip 10.1.16.0 0.0.0.255 10.1.7.0 0.0.0.255
access-list 116 permit ip 10.1.16.0 0.0.0.255 10.1.8.0 0.0.0.255
access-list 116 permit ip 10.1.16.0 0.0.0.255 10.1.11.0 0.0.0.255
access-list 116 deny ip any any log
access-list 126 permit ip 10.1.7.0 0.0.0.255 10.1.16.0 0.0.0.255
access-list 126 permit ip 10.1.8.0 0.0.0.255 10.1.16.0 0.0.0.255
access-list 126 permit ip 10.1.11.0 0.0.0.255 10.1.16.0 0.0.0.255
```

The following configuration sets up the capture port for the Cat 6000 IDS module:

```
#module 4 : 2-port Intrusion Detection System
set module name 4
set module enable 4
set vlan 1 4/1
set vlan 99 4/2
set port name 4/1 Sniff-4
set port name 4/2 CandC-4
set trunk 4/1 nonegotiate dot1q 1-1005,1025-4094
set security acl capture-ports 4/1
```

Edge Distribution Module

Refer to Figure A-14 for a detail of the edge distribution module.

Products Used

Cisco Catalyst 6500 Layer 3 switches are used.

Corporate Internet Module

Refer to Figure A-19 for a detail of the corporate Internet module.

Products Used

The following products are used:

- Cisco Secure PIX Firewall
- Cisco Secure IDS Sensor
- Catalyst 3500 Layer 2 switches
- Cisco 7100 IOS router
- ClickNet Entercept HIDS
- Websense URL filtering server

EPIX-31 and 33

This configuration snapshot details the access control in place on the PIX Firewall. The name of the access list denotes the location in which the inbound ACL is placed. The name *in* is inbound, *out* is outbound, *pss* is the public services segment (DMZ), *url* is the content filtering segment, and *mgmt* is the OOB Interface.

```
access-list out deny ip any 192.168.254.0 255.255.255.0
access-list out deny ip any 192.168.253.0 255.255.255.0
access-list out permit icmp any any echo-reply
access-list out permit tcp any host 172.16.225.52 eq www
access-list out permit tcp any host 172.16.225.52 eq ftp
access-list out permit tcp any host 172.16.225.50 eq smtp
access-list out permit udp any host 172.16.225.51 eq domain
access-list out permit esp host 172.16.224.23 host 172.16.224.57
access-list out permit esp host 172.16.224.24 host 172.16.224.57
access-list out permit udp host 172.16.224.23 host 172.16.224.57 eq isakmp
access-list out permit udp host 172.16.224.24 host 172.16.224.57 eq isakmp
access-list in deny ip any 192.168.254.0 255.255.255.0
access-list in deny ip any 192.168.253.0 255.255.255.0
access-list in permit icmp any any echo
access-list in permit udp host 10.1.11.50 host 172.16.225.51 eq domain
access-list in permit tcp 10.0.0.0 255.0.0.0 host 172.16.225.52 eq www
access-list in permit tcp 10.0.0.0 255.0.0.0 host 10.1.103.50 eq 15871
access-list in permit tcp host 10.1.11.51 host 172.16.225.50 eq smtp
access-list in permit tcp host 10.1.11.51 host 172.16.225.50 eq 20389
access-list in permit tcp 10.0.0.0 255.0.0.0 host 172.16.225.52 eq ftp
access-list in deny ip any 172.16.225.0 255.255.255.0
access-list in permit ip 10.0.0.0 255.0.0.0 any
access-list in permit esp host 10.1.20.57 host 172.16.224.23
access-list in permit esp host 10.1.20.57 host 172.16.224.24
access-list in permit udp host 10.1.20.57 host 172.16.224.23 eq isakmp
access-list in permit udp host 10.1.20.57 host 172.16.224.24 eq isakmp
access-list pss deny ip any 192.168.254.0 255.255.255.0
access-list pss deny ip any 192.168.253.0 255.255.255.0
access-list pss permit tcp host 172.16.225.50 host 10.1.11.51 eq 20025
access-list pss permit tcp host 172.16.225.50 host 10.1.11.51 eq 20389
access-list pss deny ip 172.16.225.0 255.255.255.0 10.0.0.0 255.0.0.0
```

```
access-list pss permit tcp host 172.16.225.50 any eq smtp
access-list pss permit udp host 172.16.225.51 any eq domain
access-list url permit udp host 10.1.103.50 host 172.16.225.51 eq domain
access-list url permit ip any any
access-list mgmt permit icmp 192.168.253.0 255.255.255.0 any
```

EIOS-23 and 24

This configuration snapshot details the Hot Standby Router Protocol (HSRP) commands on many routers that use HSRP for high availability.

```
interface FastEthernet0/0
 ip address 172.16.226.23 255.255.255.0
 standby 2 timers 5 15
 standby 2 priority 110 preempt delay 2
 standby 2 authentication k&>9NG@6
 standby 2 ip 172.16.226.100
 standby 2 track ATM4/0 50
```

The following sets up the encrypted in-band network management link to the management module:

```
crypto isakmp policy 1
 encr 3des
 authentication pre-share
 group 2
crypto isakmp key A%Xr)7,_) address 172.16.224.57
!
crypto ipsec transform-set vpn_module_mgmt esp-3des esp-sha-hmac
!
crypto map mgmt1 100 ipsec-isakmp
 set peer 172.16.224.57
 set transform-set vpn_module_mgmt
 match address 103

access-list 103 permit ip host 172.16.224.23 192.168.253.0 0.0.0.255
access-list 103 permit udp host 172.16.224.23 192.168.254.0 0.0.0.255
```

The following ACL sits inbound from the enterprise network:

```
access-list 112 permit udp host 172.16.224.57 host 172.16.224.23 eq isakmp
access-list 112 permit esp host 172.16.224.57 host 172.16.224.23
access-list 112 permit tcp 192.168.253.0 0.0.0.255 host 172.16.224.23 established
access-list 112 permit udp 192.168.253.0 0.0.0.255 host 172.16.224.23 gt 1023
access-list 112 permit tcp 192.168.253.0 0.0.0.255 host 172.16.224.23 eq telnet
access-list 112 permit udp host 192.168.253.51 host 172.16.224.23 eq snmp
access-list 112 permit udp host 192.168.254.57 host 172.16.224.23 eq ntp
access-list 112 permit icmp any any
access-list 112 deny ip any host 172.16.224.23 log
access-list 112 deny ip any host 172.16.226.23 log
access-list 112 deny ip any host 172.16.145.23 log
access-list 112 permit ip 172.16.224.0 0.0.0.255 any
access-list 112 permit ip 172.16.225.0 0.0.0.255 any
```

The following ACL sits inbound from the ISP. Note that RFC 1918 filtering is not complete because these addresses are used as production addresses in the lab. Actual networks should implement full RFC 1918 filtering.

```
access-list 150 deny ip 10.0.0.0 0.255.255.255 any
access-list 150 deny ip 192.168.0.0 0.0.255.255 any
```

```
access-list 150 deny ip 172.16.224.0 0.0.7.255 any
access-list 150 permit ip any 172.16.224.0 0.0.7.255
access-list 150 permit ip any 172.16.145.0 0.0.0.255
access-list 150 permit esp any 172.16.226.0 0.0.0.255 fragments
access-list 150 deny ip any any fragments
access-list 150 deny ip any any log
```

The following filtering exists outbound to the remote-access and VPN module. Note that only IKE and ESP are permitted:

```
access-list 160 permit esp any host 172.16.226.27
access-list 160 permit esp any host 172.16.226.28
access-list 160 permit esp any host 172.16.226.48
access-list 160 permit udp any host 172.16.226.27 eq isakmp
access-list 160 permit udp any host 172.16.226.28 eq isakmp
access-list 160 permit udp any host 172.16.226.48 eq isakmp
access-list 160 deny ip any any log
```

Catalyst 3500XL Private VLANs

This configuration snapshot details the configuration for private VLANs on the public services segment:

```
interface FastEthernet0/1
 port protected
!
interface FastEthernet0/2
 port protected
```

VPN and Remote-Access Module

Refer to Figure A-22 for a detail of the VPN and remote-access module.

Products Used

The following products are used:

- Cisco Secure PIX Firewall
- Cisco Secure IDS Sensor
- Catalyst 3500 Layer 2 switches
- Cisco 7100 IOS router
- Cisco VPN 3060 Concentrator
- Cisco IOS Access Server
- ClickNet Entercept HIDS
- Websense URL Filtering Server

EPIX-32 and 34

This configuration snapshot details the access control in place on the PIX Firewall. The name of the access list denotes the location in which the inbound ACL is placed. The name *in* is inbound, *out* is the site-to-site VPN, *dun* is the Public Switched Telephone Network (PSTN) dial-up, *ra* is the remote-access VPN, and *mgmt* is the OOB interface.

```
access-list in deny ip any 192.168.253.0 255.255.255.0
access-list in deny ip any 192.168.254.0 255.255.255.0
access-list in permit icmp any any
access-list in permit tcp 10.0.0.0 255.0.0.0 10.0.0.0 255.0.0.0 eq smtp
access-list in permit tcp 10.0.0.0 255.0.0.0 10.0.0.0 255.0.0.0 eq pop3
access-list in permit tcp 10.0.0.0 255.0.0.0 10.0.0.0 255.0.0.0 eq www
access-list in permit tcp 10.0.0.0 255.0.0.0 10.0.0.0 255.0.0.0 eq ftp
access-list in permit udp 10.0.0.0 255.0.0.0 10.0.0.0 255.0.0.0 eq netbios-ns
access-list in permit udp 10.0.0.0 255.0.0.0 10.0.0.0 255.0.0.0 eq netbios-dgm
access-list in permit udp 10.0.0.0 255.0.0.0 10.0.0.0 255.0.0.0 eq domain
access-list out deny ip any 192.168.253.0 255.255.255.0
access-list out deny ip any 192.168.254.0 255.255.255.0
access-list out permit icmp any any
access-list out permit tcp 10.0.0.0 255.0.0.0 10.0.0.0 255.0.0.0 eq smtp
access-list out permit tcp 10.0.0.0 255.0.0.0 10.0.0.0 255.0.0.0 eq pop3
access-list out permit tcp 10.0.0.0 255.0.0.0 10.0.0.0 255.0.0.0 eq www
access-list out permit tcp 10.0.0.0 255.0.0.0 10.0.0.0 255.0.0.0 eq ftp
access-list out permit udp 10.0.0.0 255.0.0.0 10.0.0.0 255.0.0.0 eq netbios-ns
access-list out permit udp 10.0.0.0 255.0.0.0 10.0.0.0 255.0.0.0 eq netbios-dgm
access-list out permit udp 10.0.0.0 255.0.0.0 10.0.0.0 255.0.0.0 eq domain
access-list out permit tcp 10.0.0.0 255.0.0.0 172.16.255.0 255.255.255.0 eq www
access-list out permit tcp 10.0.0.0 255.0.0.0 172.16.255.0 255.255.255.0 eq ftp
access-list ra deny ip any 192.168.253.0 255.255.255.0
access-list ra deny ip any 192.168.254.0 255.255.255.0
access-list ra permit icmp any any
access-list ra permit tcp 10.1.198.0 255.255.254.0 10.0.0.0 255.0.0.0 eq smtp
access-list ra permit tcp 10.1.198.0 255.255.254.0 10.0.0.0 255.0.0.0 eq pop3
access-list ra permit tcp 10.1.198.0 255.255.254.0 10.0.0.0 255.0.0.0 eq www
access-list ra permit tcp 10.1.198.0 255.255.254.0 10.0.0.0 255.0.0.0 eq ftp
access-list ra permit udp 10.1.198.0 255.255.254.0 10.0.0.0 255.0.0.0 eq
    netbios-ns
access-list ra permit udp 10.1.198.0 255.255.254.0 10.0.0.0 255.0.0.0 eq
    netbios-dgm
access-list ra permit udp 10.1.198.0 255.255.254.0 10.0.0.0 255.0.0.0 eq domain
access-list ra deny ip 10.1.198.0 255.255.254.0 10.0.0.0 255.0.0.0
access-list ra permit tcp 10.1.198.0 255.255.254.0 172.16.225.0 255.255.255.0
    eq www
access-list ra permit tcp 10.1.198.0 255.255.254.0 172.16.225.0 255.255.255.0
    eq ftp
access-list ra deny ip 10.1.198.0 255.255.254.0 172.16.224.0 255.255.248.0
access-list ra permit ip 10.1.198.0 255.255.254.0 any
access-list dun deny ip any 192.168.253.0 255.255.255.0
access-list dun deny ip any 192.168.254.0 255.255.255.0
access-list dun permit icmp any any
access-list dun permit tcp 10.1.196.0 255.255.254.0 10.0.0.0 255.0.0.0 eq smtp
access-list dun permit tcp 10.1.196.0 255.255.254.0 10.0.0.0 255.0.0.0 eq pop3
access-list dun permit tcp 10.1.196.0 255.255.254.0 10.0.0.0 255.0.0.0 eq www
access-list dun permit tcp 10.1.196.0 255.255.254.0 10.0.0.0 255.0.0.0 eq ftp
access-list dun permit udp 10.1.196.0 255.255.254.0 10.0.0.0 255.0.0.0 eq
    netbios-ns
access-list dun permit udp 10.1.196.0 255.255.254.0 10.0.0.0 255.0.0.0 eq
    netbios-dgm
access-list dun permit udp 10.1.196.0 255.255.254.0 10.0.0.0 255.0.0.0 eq domain
access-list dun deny ip 10.1.196.0 255.255.254.0 10.0.0.0 255.0.0.0
```

```
access-list dun permit tcp 10.1.196.0 255.255.255.0 172.16.225.0 255.255.255.0
    eq www
access-list dun permit tcp 10.1.196.0 255.255.255.0 172.16.225.0 255.255.255.0
    eq ftp
access-list dun deny ip 10.1.196.0 255.255.254.0 172.16.224.0 255.255.248.0
access-list dun permit ip 10.1.196.0 255.255.254.0 any
access-list mgmt permit icmp 192.168.253.0 255.255.255.0 any
```

This configuration snapshot details the static NAT translations required to allow VPN traffic to pass back out the corporate internet module to the internet in the clear:

```
static (inside,ravpn) 128.0.0.0 128.0.0.0 netmask 128.0.0.0 0 0
static (inside,ravpn) 64.0.0.0 64.0.0.0 netmask 192.0.0.0 0 0
static (inside,ravpn) 32.0.0.0 32.0.0.0 netmask 224.0.0.0 0 0
static (inside,ravpn) 16.0.0.0 16.0.0.0 netmask 240.0.0.0 0 0
static (inside,ravpn) 8.0.0.0 8.0.0.0 netmask 248.0.0.0 0 0
static (inside,ravpn) 4.0.0.0 4.0.0.0 netmask 252.0.0.0 0 0
static (inside,ravpn) 2.0.0.0 2.0.0.0 netmask 254.0.0.0 0 0
static (inside,ravpn) 1.0.0.0 1.0.0.0 netmask 255.0.0.0 0 0
```

EIOS-27 and 28

This configuration snapshot details the crypto configuration for the site-to-site VPN:

```
!
! Basic Crypto Information
!
crypto isakmp policy 1
 encr 3des
 authentication pre-share
 group 2
crypto isakmp key 7Q!r$y$+xE address 172.16.132.2
crypto isakmp key 52TH^m&^qu address 172.16.131.2
!
!
crypto ipsec transform-set smbranch esp-3des esp-sha-hmac
 mode transport
!
crypto map secure1 100 ipsec-isakmp
 set peer 172.16.132.2
 set transform-set smbranch
 match address 105
crypto map secure1 300 ipsec-isakmp
 set peer 172.16.131.2
 set transform-set smbranch
 match address 107
!
!
! GRE Tunnel Information
!
interface Tunnel0
 ip address 10.1.249.27 255.255.255.0
 tunnel source 172.16.226.27
 tunnel destination 172.16.132.2
 crypto map secure1
!
```

```
interface Tunnel1
 ip address 10.1.247.27 255.255.255.0
 tunnel source 172.16.226.27
 tunnel destination 172.16.131.2
 crypto map secure1
!
!
! EIGRP Routing to keep links up
!
router eigrp 1
 redistribute static
 passive-interface FastEthernet0/1
 passive-interface FastEthernet4/0
 network 10.0.0.0
 distribute-list 2 out
 distribute-list 2 in
!
! Crypto ACLs
!
access-list 105 permit gre host 172.16.226.27 host 172.16.132.2
access-list 107 permit gre host 172.16.226.27 host 172.16.131.2
!
! Inbound ACLs from Internet
!
access-list 110 permit udp 172.16.0.0 0.0.255.255 host 172.16.226.27 eq isakmp
access-list 110 permit esp 172.16.0.0 0.0.255.255 host 172.16.226.27
access-list 110 permit gre 172.16.0.0 0.0.255.255 host 172.16.226.27
access-list 110 deny ip any any log
```

WAN Module

Refer to Figure A-24 for a detail of the VPN and remote-access module.

Products Used

A Cisco 3640 IOS Router is the product used.

EIOS-61

The following configuration details the access control on the routers in the WAN module:

```
!
! Inbound from the WAN
!
access-list 110 deny ip any 192.168.253.0 0.0.0.255 log
access-list 110 deny ip any 192.168.254.0 0.0.0.255 log
access-list 110 permit ospf any any
access-list 110 permit ip 10.2.0.0 0.0.255.255 10.1.0.0 0.0.255.255
access-list 110 permit ip 10.2.0.0 0.0.255.255 10.3.0.0 0.0.255.255
access-list 110 permit ip 10.2.0.0 0.0.255.255 10.4.0.0 0.0.255.255
access-list 110 permit ip 10.2.0.0 0.0.255.255 172.16.224.0 0.0.7.255
access-list 110 deny ip any any log
!
! Inbound from the Campus
!
access-list 111 deny ip any 192.168.253.0 0.0.0.255 log
```

```
access-list 111 deny ip any 192.168.254.0 0.0.0.255 log
access-list 111 permit ospf any any
access-list 111 permit ip 10.1.0.0 0.0.255.255 10.2.0.0 0.0.255.255
access-list 111 permit ip 10.3.0.0 0.0.255.255 10.2.0.0 0.0.255.255
access-list 111 permit ip 10.4.0.0 0.0.255.255 10.2.0.0 0.0.255.255
access-list 111 permit ip 172.16.224.0 0.0.7.255 10.2.0.0 0.0.255.255
access-list 111 deny ip any any log
```

Annex B: Network Security Primer

This annex is a network security primer.

The Need for Network Security

The Internet is changing the way we work, live, play, and learn. These changes are occurring both in the ways that we currently experience (e-commerce, real-time information access, e-learning, expanded communication options, and so forth) and in ways we have yet to experience. Imagine a day when your enterprise can make all of its telephone calls over the Internet for free. Or perhaps on a more personal note, consider logging on to a day-care provider's web site to check how your child is doing throughout the day. As a society, we are just beginning to unlock the potential of the Internet. But with the Internet's unparalleled growth comes unprecedented exposure of personal data, critical enterprise resources, government secrets, and so forth. Every day, hackers pose an increasing threat to these entities with several different types of attacks. These attacks, outlined in the next section, have become both more prolific and easier to implement. There are two primary reasons for this problem.

First is the ubiquity of the Internet. With millions of devices currently connected to the Internet and millions more on the way, a hacker's access to vulnerable devices continues to increase. The ubiquity of the Internet has also allowed hackers to share knowledge on a global scale. A simple Internet search on the words *hack, crack,* or *phreak* yields thousands of sites, many of which contain malicious code or the means with which to use that code.

Second is the pervasiveness of easy-to-use operating systems and development environments. This factor has reduced the overall ingenuity and knowledge required by hackers. A truly remarkable hacker can develop easy-to-use applications that can be distributed to the masses. Several hacker tools that are available in the public domain merely require an IP address or host name and a click of a mouse button to execute an attack.

Network Attack Taxonomy

Network attacks can be as varied as the systems that they attempt to penetrate. Some attacks are elaborately complex, while others are performed unknowingly by a well-intentioned device operator. It is important to understand some of the inherent limitations of the TCP/IP protocol when evaluating the types of attacks. When the Internet was formed, it linked various government entities and universities to one another with the express purpose of facilitating learning and research. The original architects of the Internet never anticipated the kind of widespread adoption that the Internet has achieved today. As a result, in the early days of the IP, security was not designed into the specification. For this reason, most IP implementations are inherently insecure. Only after many years and thousands of RFCs do we have the tools to begin to deploy IP securely. Because specific provisions for IP security were not designed from the onset, it is important to augment IP implementations with network security practices, services, and products to mitigate the inherent risks of the IP. The following is a brief discussion of the types of attacks commonly seen on IP networks and how these attacks can be mitigated.

Packet Sniffers

A *packet sniffer* is a software application that uses a network adapter card in promiscuous mode to capture all network packets that are sent across a particular collision domain. (*Promiscuous mode* is when the network adapter card sends all packets received on the physical network wire to an application for processing.) Sniffers are used legitimately in networks today to aid in troubleshooting and traffic analysis. However, because several network applications send data in clear text (Telnet, FTP, SMTP, POP3, and so forth), a packet sniffer can provide meaningful and often sensitive information, such as usernames and passwords.

One serious problem with acquiring usernames and passwords is that users often reuse their login names and passwords across multiple applications and systems. In fact, many users employ a single password for access to all accounts and applications. If an application is run in client/server mode and authentication information is sent across the network in clear text, it is likely that this same authentication information can be used to gain access to other corporate or external resources. Because hackers know and use human characteristics, such as using a single password for multiple accounts, in attack methods known collectively as *social engineering* attacks, they are often successful in gaining access to sensitive information. In a worst-case scenario, a hacker gains access to a system level user account, which the hacker uses to create a new account that can be used at any time as a back door to break into a network and its resources.

You can mitigate the threat of packet sniffers in several ways:

- **Authentication**—Using strong authentication is a first option for defense against packet sniffers. Strong authentication can be broadly defined as a method of authenticating users that cannot easily be circumvented. A common example of strong authentication is OTPs, which is a type of *two-factor authentication*. Two-factor authentication involves using something you have combined with something you know. Automated teller machines (ATMs) use two-factor authentication. A customer needs both an ATM card and a personal identification number (PIN) to make transactions. With OTP, you need a PIN and your token card to authenticate to a device or software application. A *token card* is a hardware or software device that generates new, seemingly random passwords at specified intervals (usually 60 seconds). A user combines that random password with a PIN to create a unique password that only works for one instance of authentication. If a hacker learns a password by using a packet sniffer, the information is useless because the password has already expired. Note that this mitigation technique is effective only against a sniffer implementation that is designed to grab passwords. Sniffers deployed to learn sensitive information (such as mail messages) will still be ineffective.

- **Switched infrastructure**—Another method to counter the use of packet sniffers in your environment is to deploy a switched infrastructure. For example, if an entire organization deploys switched Ethernet, hackers can only gain access to the traffic that flows on the specific port to which they connect. A switched infrastructure obviously does not eliminate the threat of packet sniffers, but it can greatly reduce their effectiveness.

- **Antisniffer tools**—A third method used against sniffers is to employ software and hardware designed to detect the use of sniffers on a network. Such software and hardware does not completely eliminate the threat, but like many network security tools, they are part of the overall system. These so-called antisniffers detect changes in the response time of hosts to determine whether the hosts are processing more traffic than their own. One such network security software tool, which is available from LOpht Heavy Industries, is called AntiSniff. For more information, refer to the URL www.l0pht.com/antisniff/.

- **Cryptography**—The most effective method for countering packet sniffers does not prevent or detect packet sniffers, but rather renders them irrelevant. If a communication channel is cryptographically secure, the only data that a packet sniffer will detect is cipher text (a seemingly random string of bits) and not the original message. Cisco's deployment of network level cryptography is based on IPSec, a standard method for networking devices to communicate privately using IP. Other cryptographic protocols for network management include SSH and SSL.

IP Spoofing

An IP spoofing attack occurs when a hacker inside or outside a network pretends to be a trusted computer. A hacker can do this in one of two ways. The hacker uses either an IP address that is within the range of trusted IP addresses for a network, or an authorized external IP address that is trusted and to which access is provided to specified resources on a network. IP spoofing attacks are often a launch point for other attacks. The classic example is to launch a DoS attack using spoofed source addresses to hide the hacker's identity.

Normally, an IP spoofing attack is limited to the injection of malicious data or commands into an existing stream of data that is passed between a client and server application or a peer-to-peer network connection. To enable bidirectional communication, the hacker must change all routing tables to point to the spoofed IP address. Another approach hackers sometimes take is simply not to worry about receiving any response from the applications. If a hacker tries to obtain a sensitive file from a system, application responses are unimportant.

However, if a hacker manages to change the routing tables to point to the spoofed IP address, the hacker can receive all of the network packets that are addressed to the spoofed address and reply just as any trusted user can.

The threat of IP spoofing can be reduced, but not eliminated, through the following measures.

- **Access control**—The most common method for preventing IP spoofing is to configure access control properly. To reduce the effectiveness of IP spoofing, configure access control to deny any traffic from the external network that has a source address that should reside on the internal network. Note that this only helps prevent spoofing attacks if the internal addresses are the only trusted addresses. If some external addresses are trusted, this method is not effective.

- **RFC 2827 filtering**—You can also prevent a network's users from spoofing other networks (and be a good Net citizen at the same time) by preventing any outbound traffic on your network that does not have a source address in your organization's own IP range. Your ISP can also implement this type of filtering, which is collectively referred to as RFC 2827 filtering. This filtering denies any traffic that does not have the source address that was expected on a particular interface. For example, if an ISP is providing a connection to the IP address 15.1.1.0/24, the ISP could filter traffic so that only traffic sourced from address 15.1.1.0/24 can enter the ISP router from that interface. Note that unless all ISPs implement this type of filtering, its effectiveness is significantly reduced. Also, the further you get from the devices you want to filter, the more difficult it becomes to do that filtering at a granular level. For example, performing RFC 2827 filtering at the access router to the Internet requires that you allow your entire major network number (that is, 10.0.0.0/8) to traverse the access router. If you perform filtering at the distribution layer, as in this architecture, you can achieve more specific filtering (that is, 10.1.5.0/24).

- **Additional authentication**—The most effective method for mitigating the threat of IP spoofing is the same as that for mitigating the threat of packet sniffers: namely, eliminating its effectiveness. IP spoofing can function correctly only when devices use IP address-based authentication. Therefore, if you use additional authentication methods, IP spoofing attacks are irrelevant. Cryptographic authentication is the best form of additional authentication, but when that is not possible, strong two-factor authentication using OTP can also be effective.

Denial of Service (DoS)

Certainly the most publicized form of attack, DoS is also among the most difficult to completely eliminate. Even among the hacker community, DoS attacks are regarded as trivial and considered bad form because they require so little effort to execute. Still, because of their ease of implementation and potentially significant damage, DoS attacks deserve special attention from security administrators. If you are interested in learning more about DoS attacks, researching the methods employed by some of the better-known attacks can be useful. These attacks include the following:

- TCP SYN flood
- Ping of death
- Tribe Flood Network (TFN) and Tribe Flood Network 2000 (TFN2K)
- Trinco
- Stacheldraht
- Trinity

Another excellent source on the topic of security is the Computer Emergency Response Team (CERT). It has published an excellent paper on dealing with DoS attacks, which you can find at the following URL: www.cert.org/tech_tips/denial_of_service.html.

DoS attacks are different from most other attacks because they are generally not targeted at gaining access to your network or the information on your network. These attacks focus on making a service unavailable for normal use, which is typically accomplished by exhausting some resource limitation on the network or within an operating system or application.

When involving specific network server applications, such as a Web server or an FTP server, these attacks can focus on acquiring and keeping open all the available connections supported by that server, effectively locking out valid users of the server or service. DoS attacks can also be implemented using common Internet protocols, such as TCP and ICMP. Most DoS attacks exploit a weakness in the overall architecture of the system being attacked, rather than a software bug or security hole. However, some attacks compromise the performance of your network by flooding the network with undesired and often useless network packets and by providing false information about the status of network resources. This type of attack is often the most difficult to prevent, as it requires coordination with your upstream network provider. If traffic meant to consume your available bandwidth is not stopped there, denying it at the point of entry into your network will do little good because your available bandwidth has already been consumed. When this type of attack is launched from many different systems at the same time, it is often referred to as a DDoS attack.

The threat of DoS attacks can be reduced through the following three methods:

- **Antispoof features**—Proper configuration of antispoof features on your routers and firewalls can reduce your risk. This includes RFC 2827 filtering, at the minimum. If hackers cannot mask their identities, they might not attack.

- **Anti-DoS features**—Proper configuration of anti-DoS features on routers and firewalls can help limit the effectiveness of an attack. These features often involve limits on the amount of half-open connections that a system allows at any given time.

- **Traffic rate limiting**—An organization can implement traffic rate limiting with your ISP. This type of filtering limits the amount of nonessential traffic that crosses network segments to a certain rate. A common example is to limit the amount of ICMP traffic allowed into a network, because this traffic is used only for diagnostic purposes. ICMP-based DDoS or DoS attacks are common.

Password Attacks

Hackers can implement password attacks using several different methods, including brute-force attacks, Trojan horse programs, IP spoofing, and packet sniffers. Although packet sniffers and IP spoofing can yield user accounts and passwords, password attacks usually refer to repeated attempts to identify a user account or password. These repeated attempts are called brute-force attacks.

Often, a brute-force attack is performed using a program that runs across the network and attempts to log into a shared resource, such as a server. When hackers successfully gain access to resources, they have the same rights as the users whose accounts have been compromised to gain access to those resources. If the compromised accounts have sufficient privileges, the hackers can create back doors for future access without concern for any status and password changes to the compromised user accounts.

Another problem exists when users have the same (possibly strong) password on every system to which they connect. Often, this includes personal systems, corporate systems, and systems on the Internet. Because that password is only as secure as the most weakly administered host that contains it, if that host is compromised, hackers have a whole range of hosts on which they can try the same password.

You can most easily eliminate password attacks by not relying on plain-text passwords in the first place. Using OTP or cryptographic authentication can virtually eliminate the threat of password attacks. Unfortunately, not all applications, hosts, and devices support these authentication methods. When standard passwords are used, it is important to choose a password that is difficult to guess. Passwords should be at least eight characters long and contain uppercase letters, lowercase letters, numbers, and special characters (#, %, $, and so forth). The best passwords are randomly generated, but these are very difficult to remember, often leading users to write their passwords down.

Several advances have been made relative to password maintenance—both for the user and the administrator. Software applications are now available that encrypt a list of passwords to be stored on a handheld computer. This allows the user to remember only one complex password and have the remaining passwords stored securely within the application. From the standpoint of the administrator, several methods exist to brute-force attack your own users' passwords. One such method involves a tool used by the hacker community called L0phtCrack. L0phtCrack brute-force attacks Windows NT passwords and can point out when a user has chosen a password that is very easy to guess. For more information, refer to the following URL: www.l0pht.com/l0phtcrack/.

Man-in-the-Middle Attacks

A man-in-the-middle attack requires that the hacker has access to network packets that come across a network. An example of such a situation could be someone who works for an ISP and has access to all network packets that are transferred between the employer's network and any other network. Such attacks are often implemented using network packet sniffers and routing and transport protocols. The possible uses of such attacks are theft of information, hijacking of an ongoing session to gain access to private network resources, traffic analysis to derive information about a network and its users, DoS, corruption of transmitted data, and introduction of new information into network sessions.

Man-in-the-middle attacks can be effectively mitigated only through the use of cryptography. If someone hijacks data in the middle of a cryptographically private session, all that the hacker will see is cipher text and not the original message. Note that if a hacker can learn information about the cryptographic session (such as the session key), man-in-the-middle attacks are still possible.

Application Layer Attacks

Application layer attacks can be implemented using several different methods. One of the most common methods is exploiting well-known weaknesses in software that is commonly found on servers, such as sendmail, HTTP, and FTP. By exploiting these weaknesses, hackers can gain access to a computer with the permissions of the account running the application, which is usually a privileged system level account. These application layer attacks are often widely publicized in an effort to allow administrators to rectify the problem with a patch. Unfortunately, many hackers also subscribe to these same mailing lists, which results in their learning about the attack at the same time (if they have not discovered it already).

The primary problem with application layer attacks is that they often use ports that are allowed through a firewall. For example, a hacker executing a known vulnerability against a Web server often uses TCP port 80 in the attack. Because the Web server serves pages to users, a firewall needs to allow access on that port. From a firewall's perspective, it is merely standard port 80 traffic.

Application layer attacks can never be completely eliminated. New vulnerabilities are always being discovered and publicized to the Internet community. The best way to reduce your risk is by practicing good system administration. The following are a few measures you can take to reduce your risks:

- Read OS and network log files or have them analyzed by log analysis applications.

- Subscribe to mailing lists that publicize vulnerabilities such as Bugtraq (www.securityfocus.com) and the CERT (www.cert.org).

- Keep your OS and applications current with the latest patches.

- In addition to proper system administration, using IDSs can aid in this effort. There are two complementary IDS technologies:

  — NIDS operates by watching all packets traversing a particular collision domain. When NIDS sees a packet or series of packets that match a known or suspect attack, it can flag an alarm or terminate the session.

  — HIDS operates by inserting agents into the host to be protected. It is then concerned only with attacks generated against that one host.

- IDSs operate by using *attack signatures*, which are the profile for a particular attack or kind of attack. They specify certain conditions that must be met before traffic is deemed to be an attack. In the physical world, IDS can be most closely compared to an alarm system or security camera. IDS's greatest limitation is the amount of false positive alarms a particular system generates. Tuning IDS to prevent such false alarms is critical to the proper operation of IDS in a network.

Network Reconnaissance

Network reconnaissance refers to the overall act of learning information about a target network by using publicly available information and applications. When hackers attempt to penetrate a particular network, they often need to learn as much information as possible about the network before launching attacks. This can take the form of DNS queries, ping sweeps, and port scans. DNS queries can reveal such information as who owns a particular domain and what addresses have been assigned to that domain. Ping sweeps of the addresses revealed by the DNS queries can present a picture of the live hosts in a particular environment. After such a list is generated, port-scanning tools can cycle through all well-known ports to provide a complete list of all services running on the hosts discovered by the ping sweep. Finally, the hackers can examine the characteristics of the applications that are running on the hosts. This can lead to specific information that is useful when the hacker attempts to compromise that service.

Network reconnaissance cannot be prevented entirely. If ICMP Echo and Echo Reply are turned off on edge routers, for example, ping sweeps can be stopped, but at the expense of network diagnostic data. However, port scans can easily be run without full ping sweeps; they simply take longer because they need to scan IP addresses that might not be live. IDS at the network and host levels can usually notify an administrator when a reconnaissance-gathering attack is under way. This allows the administrator to prepare better for the coming attack or to notify the ISP who is hosting the system that is launching the reconnaissance probe.

Trust Exploitation

Although not an attack in and of itself, trust exploitation refers to an attack where an individual takes advantage of a trust relationship within a network. The classic example is a perimeter network connection from a corporation. These network segments often house DNS, SMTP, and HTTP servers. Because they all reside on the same segment, a compromise of one system can lead to the compromise of other systems because they might trust other systems attached to their same network. Another example is a system on the outside of a firewall that has a trust relationship with a system on the inside of a firewall. When the outside system is compromised, it can leverage that trust relationship to attack the inside network.

You can mitigate trust-exploitation-based attacks through tight constraints on trust levels within a network. Systems on the outside of a firewall should never be absolutely trusted by systems on the inside of a firewall. Such trust should be limited to specific protocols and should be authenticated by something other than an IP address, where possible.

Port Redirection

Port redirection attacks are a type of trust exploitation attack that uses a compromised host to pass traffic that would otherwise be dropped through a firewall. Consider a firewall with three interfaces and a host on each interface. The host on the outside can reach the host on the public services segment (commonly referred to as a demilitarized zone [DMZ]), but not the host on the inside. The host on the public services segment can reach the host on both the outside and the inside. If hackers were able to compromise the public services segment host, they could install software to redirect traffic from the outside host directly to the inside host. Though neither communication violates the rules implemented in the firewall, the outside host has now achieved connectivity to the inside host through the port redirection process on the public services host. An example of an application that can provide this type of access is netcat. For more information, refer to the following URL: www.avian.org.

Port redirection can primarily be mitigated by the use of proper trust models (as mentioned earlier). Assuming a system is under attack, HIDS can help detect and prevent a hacker from installing such utilities on a host.

Unauthorized Access

Although not a specific type of attack, unauthorized access attacks refer to the majority of attacks executed in networks today. For hackers to brute-force attack a Telnet login, they must first get the Telnet prompt on a system. On connection to the Telnet port, a message might indicate "Authorization required to use this resource." If the hacker continues to attempt access, the actions become unauthorized. These kinds of attacks can be initiated both on the outside and inside of a network.

Mitigation techniques for unauthorized access attacks are very simple. They involve reducing or eliminating the ability of a hacker to gain access to a system using an unauthorized protocol. An example would be preventing hackers from having access to the Telnet port on a server that needs to provide Web services to the outside. If a hacker cannot reach that port, it is very difficult to attack it. The primary function of a firewall in a network is to prevent simple unauthorized access attacks.

Virus and Trojan Horse Applications

The primary vulnerabilities for end-user workstations are viruses and Trojan horse attacks. Viruses refer to malicious software that is attached to another program to execute a particular unwanted function on a user's workstation. An example of a virus is a program that is attached to command.com (the primary interpreter for Windows systems) that deletes certain files and infects any other versions of command.com that it can find. A Trojan horse is different only in that the entire application is written to look like something else, when in fact it is an attack tool. An example of a Trojan horse is a software application that runs a simple game on the user's workstation. While the user is occupied with the game, the Trojan horse mails a copy of itself to every user in the user's address book. Then other users get the game and play it, thus spreading the Trojan horse.

These kinds of applications can be contained through the effective use of antivirus software at the user level and potentially at the network level. Antivirus software can detect most viruses and many Trojan horse applications and prevent them from spreading in the network. Keeping up-to-date with the latest developments in these sorts of attacks can also lead to a more effective posture against them. As new virus or Trojan applications are released, enterprises need to keep up-to-date with the latest antivirus software and application versions.

What Is a Security Policy?

A security policy can be as simple as an acceptable use policy for network resources or can be several hundred pages in length and detail every element of connectivity and associated policies. Although somewhat narrow in scope, RFC 2196 suitably defines a security policy as follows:

"A security policy is a formal statement of the rules by which people who are given access to an organization's technology and information assets must abide."

This document does not attempt to go into detail on the development of a security policy. RFC 2196 has some good information available on the subject, and numerous locations on the Web have example policies and guidelines. The following Web pages may assist the interested reader:

- RFC 2196 Site Security Handbook

  www.ietf.org/rfc/rfc2196.txt

- A sample security policy for the University of Illinois

  www.aits.uillinois.edu/security/securestandards.html

- Design and Implementation of the Corporate Security Policy

  www.knowcisco.com/content/1578700434/ch06.shtml

The Need for a Security Policy

It is important to understand that network security is an evolutionary process. No one product can make an organization "secure." True network security comes from a combination of products and services, combined with a comprehensive security policy and a commitment to adhere to that policy from the top of the organization down. In fact, a properly implemented security policy without dedicated security hardware can be more effective at mitigating the threat to enterprise resources than a comprehensive security product implementation without an associated policy.

Annex C: Architecture Taxonomy

application server—Provides application services directly or indirectly for enterprise end users. Services can include work-flow, general office, and security applications.

firewall (stateful)—Stateful packet filtering device that maintains state tables for IP-based protocols. Traffic is only allowed to cross the firewall if it conforms to the access-control filters defined, or if it is part of an already established session in the state table.

host intrusion detection system (HIDS)—HIDS is a software application that monitors activity on an individual host. Monitoring techniques can include validating operating system and application calls, checking log files, file system information and network connections.

network intrusion detection system (NIDS)—Typically used in a nondisruptive manner, this device captures traffic on a LAN segment and tries to match the real-time traffic against known attack signatures. Signatures range from atomic (single packet and direction) signatures to composite (multipacket) signatures requiring state tables and Layer 7 application tracking.

IOS firewall—A stateful packet-filtering firewall running natively on Cisco IOS.

IOS router—A wide spectrum of flexible network devices that provide many routing and security services for all performance requirements. Most devices are modular and have a range of LAN and WAN physical interfaces.

Layer 2 switch—Provides bandwidth and VLAN services to network segments at the Ethernet level. Typically these devices offer 10/100 individual switched ports, gigabit Ethernet uplinks, VLAN trunking, and Layer 2 filtering features.

Layer 3 switch—Provides similar high throughput functions of a Layer 2 switch with added routing, QoS, and security features. These switches often have the capability of special function processors.

management server—Provides network management services for the operators of enterprise networks. Services can include general configuration management, monitoring of network security devices, and operation of the security functions.

SMTP content filtering server—An application typically running on an external SMTP server that monitors the content (including attachments) of incoming and outgoing mail. It decides whether that mail is authorized to be forwarded as is, altered and forwarded, or dropped.

URL filtering server—An application typically running on a standalone server that monitors URL requests forwarded to it by a network device and informs the network device whether the request should be forwarded on to the Internet. This allows an enterprise to implement a security policy dictating what categories of Internet sites are unauthorized.

VPN termination device—Terminates IPSec tunnels for either site-to-site or remote-access VPN connections. The device should provide additional services to offer the same network functionality as a classic WAN or dial-in connection.

workstation or user terminal—Any device on the network that is used directly by the end user. This includes PCs, IP phones, wireless devices, and so forth.

References

RFCs

RFC 2196 Site Security Handbook

www.ietf.org/rfc/rfc2196.txt

RFC 1918 Address Allocation for Private Internets

www.ietf.org/rfc/rfc1918.txt

RFC 2827 Network Ingress Filtering: Defeating Denial of Service Attacks which Employ IP Source Address Spoofing

www.ietf.org/rfc/rfc2827.txt

Miscellaneous References

Improving Security on Cisco Routers

www.cisco.com/warp/customer/707/21.html

VLAN Security Test Report

www.sans.org/newlook/resources/IDFAQ/vlan.htm

AntiSniff

www.l0pht.com/antisniff

L0phtCrack

www.l0pht.com/l0phtcrack

Denial of Service Attacks

www.cert.org/tech_tips/denial_of_service.html

Computer Emergency Response Team (CERT)

www.cert.org

Security Focus (Bugtraq)

www.securityfocus.com

Avian Research (netcat)

www.avian.org

University of Illinois Security Policy

www.aits.uillinois.edu/security/securestandards.html

Design and Implementation of the Corporate Security Policy

www.knowcisco.com/content/1578700434/ ch06.shtml

Partner Product References

ClickNet Entercept Host-Based IDS

www.clicknet.com

RSA SecureID OTP System

www.rsasecurity.com/products/securid

Content Technologies MIMESweeper E-mail Filtering System

www.contenttechnologies.com

Websense URL Filtering

www.websense.com/products/integrations/ciscopix.cfm

netForensics Syslog Analysis

www.netforensics.com

Acknowledgments

The authors of this appendix would like to thank publicly all of the individuals who contributed to the SAFE architecture and the writing of this document. Certainly, the successful completion of this architecture would not have been possible without the valuable input and review feedback from all of the Cisco employees both in corporate headquarters and in the field. In addition, many individuals contributed to the lab implementation and validation of the architecture. The core of this group included Roland Saville, Floyd Gerhardt, Majid Saee, Mark Doering, Charlie Stokes, Tom Hunter, Kevin McCormick, and Casey Smith. Thank you all for your special effort.

INDEX

Numerics

G

N

O

S

T

U

Cisco Interactive Mentor

The Cisco Interactive Mentor (CIM) product line is a series of e-learning solutions designed to provide entry-level networking professionals with the opportunity to gain practical, hands-on experience through self-paced instruction and network lab simulation exercises. This combination of computer-based training with lab exercises offers users a unique learning environment that eliminates the cost overhead necessary with the actual network devices, while offering the same degree of real-world experience. Current releases include the following:

Internetworking Basics
1-58720-034-1
$99.95
AVAILABLE JUNE 2001

LAN Switching
1-58720-021-X
$199.95
AVAILABLE NOW

IP Routing: Distance-Vector Protocols
1-58720-012-0
$149.95
AVAILABLE NOW

Access ISDN
1-58720-025-2
$199.95
AVAILABLE NOW

Expert Labs: IP Routing
1-58720-010-4
$149.95
AVAILABLE NOW

Voice Internetworking: Basic Voice over IP
1-58720-023-6
$149.95
AVAILABLE NOW

For an online demo of the CIM product line, go to www.ciscopress.com/cim today!

Cisco Career Certifications

Cisco CCNA Exam #640-507 Certification Guide
Wendell Odom

0-7357-0971-8 • AVAILABLE NOW

Although it's only the first step in Cisco Career Certification, the Cisco Certified Network Associate (CCNA) exam is a difficult test. Your first attempt at becoming Cisco certified requires plenty of study and confidence in your networking knowledge. When you're ready to test your skills, complete your knowledge of the exam topics, and prepare for exam day, you need the preparation tools found in *Cisco CCNA Exam #640-507 Certification Guide*.

CCDA Exam Certification Guide
Anthony Bruno

0-7357-0074-5 • AVAILABLE NOW

CCDA Exam Certification Guide is a comprehensive study tool for DCN Exam #640-441. Written by a CCIE and a CCDA, and reviewed by Cisco technical experts, CCDA Exam Certification Guide helps you understand and master the exam objectives. In this solid review on the design areas of the DCN exam, you learn to design a network that meets a customer's requirements for performance, security, capacity, and scalability.

Interconnecting Cisco Network Devices
Edited by Steve McQuerry

1-57870-111-2 • AVAILABLE NOW

Based on the Cisco course taught worldwide, Interconnecting Cisco Network Devices teaches you how to configure Cisco switches and routers in multiprotocol internetworks. ICND is the primary course recommended by Cisco Systems for CCNA #640-507 preparation. If you are pursuing CCNA certification, this book is an excellent starting point for your study.

Designing Cisco Networks
Edited by Diane Teare

1-57870-105-8 • AVAILABLE NOW

Based on the Cisco Systems instructor-led and self-study course available worldwide, *Designing Cisco Networks* teaches you how to become proficient in network design methodologies. Created for those seeking to attain CCDA certification, this book focuses on small- to medium-sized networks and provides a step-by-step process to follow when designing internetworks to ensure that all the important issues are considered, resulting in optimal network design.

Cisco Press   **ciscopress.com**

Cisco Press Solutions

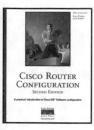

Cisco Router Configuration, Second Edition

Allan Leinwand and Bruce Pinsky

1-57870-241-0 • AVAILABLE NOW

Cisco Router Configuration, Second Edition, takes an example-oriented and chronological approach to helping you implement and administer your internetworking devices. Starting with the configuration of devices out of the box, this book moves to configuring the Cisco IOS for the three most popular networking protocols used today: Transmission Control Protocol/Internet Protocol (TCP/IP), AppleTalk, and Novell InterPacket eXchange (IPX). You also learn basic administrative and management configuration, including access control with TACACS+ and RADIUS, network management with SNMP, logging of messages, and time control with NTP. *Cisco Router Configuration*, Second Edition, is updated from the previous edition for many new features and configuration commands in Cisco IOS 12.1T. Updated in this edition are solutions for configuring Cisco IOS software for Gigabit Ethernet LANs, Digital Subscriber Line (DSL) networks, DHCP services and Secure Shell (SSH) access IOS devices.

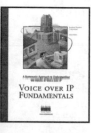

Voice over IP Fundamentals

Jonathan Davidson and Jim Peters

1-57870-168-6 • AVAILABLE NOW

This book provides you with a thorough introduction to the voice and data technology. You learn how the telephony infrastructure was built and how it works today. You also gain an understanding of the major concepts concerning voice and data networking, transmission of voice over data, and IP signaling protocols used to interwork with current telephony systems.

OpenCable Architecture

Michael Adams

1-57870-135-X • AVAILABLE NOW

This award-winning book explains key concepts in practical terms. It describes the digital headend, optical transport, distribution hub, hybrid-fiber coax, and set-top terminal equipment and how these components are interconnected. Whether you are a television, data communications, or telecommunications professional, or an interested layperson. *OpenCable Architecture* helps you understand the technical and business issues surrounding interactive television services. It provides you with an inside look at the combined efforts of the cable, data, and consumer electronics industries to develop those new services.

Cisco Press Solutions

Internet Routing Architectures, Second Edition
Sam Halabi and Danny McPherson
1-57870-233-x • Available Now

Internet Routing Architectures, Second Edition, explores the ins and outs of interdomain routing network designs with emphasis on BGP-4—the de facto interdomain routing protocol. The comprehensive resource provides you with real solutions for ISP connectivity issues. You learn how to integrate your network on the global Internet and discover how to build large-scale autonomous systems. You also learn to control expansion of interior routing protocols using BGP-4, design sound and stable networks, configure the required policies using Cisco IOS Software, and explore routing practices and rules on the Internet.

Integrating Voice and Data Networks
Scott Keagy
1-57870-196-1 • **AVAILABLE NOW**

Integrating Voice and Data Networks is both a conceptual reference and a practical how-to book that bridges the gap between existing telephony networks and the new world of packetized voice over data networks. Underlying technologies are explained in a context that gives a holistic understanding of voice/data integration. You then follow a complete process to design and implement a variety of network scenarios, leveraging author Scott Keagy's extensive experience with real voice/data networks. This book focuses on the implementation of Voice over Frame Relay, Voice over ATM, and Voice over IP using Cisco IOS voice gateways, including the Cisco MC3810, Cisco 2600/3600/7200/7500 series routers, and AS5300/AS5800 Access Servers.

MPLS and VPN Architectures
Ivan Pepelnjak and Jim Guichard
1-57870-002-1 • **AVAILABLE NOW**

This book provides an in-depth study of MPLS technology, including MPLS theory and configuration, network design issues, and case studies. The MPLS/VPN architecture and all its mechanisms are explained with configuration examples and suggested deployment guidelines. MPLS and VPNs provides the first in-depth discussion particular to Cisco's MPLS architecture. Multiprotocol Label Switching and Virtual Private Networks covers MPLS theory and configuration, network design issues, and case studies as well as one major MPLS application: MPLS-based VPNs. The MPLS/VPN architecture and all its mechanisms are explained with configuration examples, suggested design and deployment guidelines, and extensive case studies.

Cisco Press

ciscopress.com

Cisco Career Certifications

Building Cisco Remote Access Networks

Cisco Systems, Inc., Edited by Catherine Paquet

1-57870-091-4 • AVAILABLE NOW

Based on the Cisco Systems instructor-led course available worldwide, *Building Cisco Remote Access Networks* teaches you how to design, set up, configure, maintain, and scale a remote access network using Cisco products. In addition, *Building Cisco Remote Access Networks* provides chapter-ending questions to help you assess your understanding of key concepts and start you down the path for attaining your CCNP certification.

CCNP Remote Access Exam Certification Guide

Brian Morgan, CCIE #4865, and Craig Dennis

1-58720-003-1 • AVAILABLE NOW

CCNP Remote Access Exam Certification Guide is a comprehensive study tool for the Cisco Certified Network Professional Remote Access Exam #640-505. The exam evaluates your ability to build a remote access network to interconnect central sites to branch offices and home office/telecommuters, control access to the central site, as well as maximize bandwidth utilization over the remote links. This book provides you with concise reviews of all the major topics covered on the Remote Access Exam. You gain full mastery of all the concepts and technologies upon which you will be tested, including selecting the proper equipment, assembling and cabling WAN components, configuring asynchronous connections with modems, configuring PPP and controlling network access, using ISDN and DDR, establishing X.25 and Frame Relay connections, managing network performance, scaling IP addresses with NAT, and monitoring the access and use of the network with AAA. The book also includes a comprehensive testing engine on CD-ROM.

CCNP Switching Exam Certification Guide

David Hucaby, CCIE #4594, and Tim Boyles

1-58720-000-7 • AVAILABLE NOW

CCNP Switching Exam Certification Guide is a comprehensive study tool for the Cisco Certified Network Professional Switching Exam #640-504. The exam evaluates your ability to build campus networks using multilayer switching technologies and to manage campus network traffic. This book provides you with concise reviews of all the major topics covered on the Switching Exam. You gain full mastery of all the concepts and technologies upon which you will be tested, including switched Ethernet, trunking, multicasting, multilayer switching, VLANs, ATM, LANE, interVLAN routing, HSRP, network traffic control, and monitoring and troubleshooting techniques. This book also includes a comprehensive testing engine on CD-ROM.

Cisco Press

ciscopress.com

Cisco Career Certifications

CCNP Support Exam Certification Guide
Amir Ranjbar

0-7357-0995-5 • AVAILABLE NOW

Cisco Support Exam Certification Guide is a comprehensive study tool for the Cisco Certified Network Professional Support Exam #640-506. The exam evaluates your ability to diagnose, isolate, and correct network problems in a variety of environments. This book provides you with concise reviews of all the major topics covered on the Support Exam. You gain full mastery of all the concepts and technologies upon which you will be tested, including troubleshooting resources, tools, and methodology, understanding data-link layer troubleshooting, fast switching methods, and buffering technologies, network layer protocol troubleshooting, troubleshooting Catalyst 5000 switches, and troubleshooting WAN connections. This book also includes a comprehensive testing engine on CD-ROM.

CCNP Routing Exam Certification Guide
Clare Gough

1-58720-001-5 • AVAILABLE NOW

CCNP Routing Exam Certification Guide is a comprehensive study tool for the Cisco Certified Network Professional Routing Exam #640-503. The exam evaluates you ability to support and implement scalable routed internetworks for any size environment. This book provides you with concise reviews of all the major topic areas and objectives for the Routing exam. You gain full mastery of all the concepts and technologies upon which you will be tested, including principles of scalable internetworks, scalable routing protocols, managing traffic and access, and optimizing scalable internetworks. This book also includes a comprehensive testing engine on CD-ROM.

Cisco Internetwork Design
Cisco Systems, Inc., Edited by Matthew H. Birkner, CCIE

1-57870-171-6 • AVAILABLE NOW

Based on the Cisco Systems instructor-led course available worldwide, *Cisco Internetwork Design* teaches you how to plan and design a network using various internetworking technologies. Created for those seeking to attain CCDP certification, this book presents the fundamental, technical, and design issue associated with campus LANs; TCP/IP networks; IPX, AppleTalk, and Windows-based networks; WANs, and SNA networks.

Cisco Press   **ciscopress.com**

CCIE Professional Development

Routing TCP/IP, Volume I
Jeff Doyle, CCIE

1-57870-041-8 • AVAILABLE NOW

Routing TCP/IP, Volume I, takes the reader from a basic understanding of routers and routing protocols through a detailed examination of each of the IP interior routing protocols. Learn techniques for designing networks that maximize the efficiency of the protocol being used. Exercises and review questions provide core study for the CCIE Routing and Switching exam.

Routing TCP/IP, Volume II
Jeff Doyle, CCIE

1-57870-089-2 • AVAILABLE NOW

Routing TCP/IP, Volume II, presents a detailed examination of exterior routing protocols (EGP and BGP) and advanced IP routing issues, such as multicast routing, quality of service routing, IPv6, and router management. Readers learn IP design and management techniques for implementing routing protocols efficiently. Network planning, design, implementation, operation, and optimization are stressed in each chapter. Cisco-specific configurations for each routing protocol are examined in detail. Plentiful review questions and configuration and troubleshooting exercises make this an excellent self-study tool for CCIE exam preparation.

Inside Cisco IOS Software Architecture
Vijay Bollapragada, CCIE; Curtis Murphy, CCIE; and Russ White, CCIE

1-57870-181-3 • AVAILABLE NOW

Part of the Cisco CCIE Professional Development Series, *Inside Cisco IOS Software Architecture* offers crucial and hard-to-find information on Cisco's Internetwork Operating System (IOS) Software. This book begins with an overview of operating system concepts and the IOS software infrastructure, then delves into the intricate details of the design and operation of platform specific features, including the 1600, 2500, 4x00, 3600, 7200, 7500, and GSR Cisco Routers, and ends with an overview of IOS quality of service.

CISCO SYSTEMS

Cisco Press

ciscopress.com

Committed to being your long-term learning resource while you grow as a Cisco Networking Professional

Help Cisco Press **stay connected** to the issues and challenges you face on a daily basis by registering your product and filling out our brief survey. Complete and mail this form, or better yet ...

Register online and enter to win a FREE book!

Jump to **www.ciscopress.com/register** and register your product online. Each complete entry will be eligible for our monthly drawing to win a FREE book of the winner's choice from the Cisco Press library.

May we contact you via e-mail with information about **new releases, special promotions,** and **customer benefits?**

❒ Yes   ❒ No

E-mail address _____

Name _____

Address_____

City _____ State/Province _____

Country_____ Zip/Post code _____

Where did you buy this product?

❒ Bookstore   ❒ Computer store/Electronics store   ❒ Direct from Cisco Systems
❒ Online retailer   ❒ Direct from Cisco Press   ❒ Office supply store
❒ Mail order   ❒ Class/Seminar   ❒ Discount store
❒ Other_____

When did you buy this product? _____ Month _____ Year

What price did you pay for this product?

❒ Full retail price   ❒ Discounted price   ❒ Gift

Was this purchase reimbursed as a company expense?

❒ Yes   ❒ No

How did you learn about this product?

❒ Friend   ❒ Store personnel   ❒ In-store ad   ❒ cisco.com
❒ Cisco Press catalog   ❒ Postcard in the mail   ❒ Saw it on the shelf   ❒ ciscopress.com
❒ Other catalog   ❒ Magazine ad   ❒ Article or review
❒ School   ❒ Professional organization ❒ Used other products
❒ Other_____

What will this product be used for?

❒ Business use   ❒ School/Education
❒ Certification training   ❒ Professional development/Career growth
❒ Other_____

How many years have you been employed in a computer-related industry?

❒ less than 2 years   ❒ 2–5 years   ❒ more than 5 years

Have you purchased a Cisco Press product before?

❒ Yes   ❒ No

CISCO SYSTEMS

Cisco Press

ciscopress.com

How many computer technology books do you own?
- ❏ 1
- ❏ 2–7
- ❏ more than 7

Which best describes your job function? (check all that apply)
- ❏ Corporate Management
- ❏ Network Design
- ❏ Marketing/Sales
- ❏ Professor/Teacher
- ❏ Systems Engineering
- ❏ Network Support
- ❏ Consultant
- ❏ Other _____
- ❏ IS Management
- ❏ Webmaster
- ❏ Student
- ❏ Cisco Networking Academy Program Instuctor

Do you hold any computer certifications? (check all that apply)
- ❏ MCSE
- ❏ CCNP
- ❏ CCNA
- ❏ CCDP
- ❏ CCDA
- ❏ CCIE
- ❏ Other _____

Are you currently pursuing a certification? (check all that apply)
- ❏ MCSE
- ❏ CCNP
- ❏ CCNA
- ❏ CCDP
- ❏ CCDA
- ❏ CCIE
- ❏ Other _____

On what topics would you like to see more coverage?

_____

_____

Do you have any additional comments or suggestions?

_____

_____

Thank you for completing this survey and registration. Please fold here, seal, and mail to Cisco Press.

Cisco Secure Internet Solutions (1-58705-016-1)

Indianapolis, IN 46278-8046
P.O. Box #781046
Customer Registration—CP0500227
Cisco Press

ciscopress.com
Indianapolis, IN 46290
201 West 103rd Street
Cisco Press

BUSINESS REPLY MAIL

FIRST-CLASS MAIL   PERMIT NO. 25788   SAN FRANCISCO CA

POSTAGE WILL BE PAID BY ADDRESSEE

CISCO SYSTEMS / PACKET MAGAZINE
PO BOX 60939
SUNNYVALE CA 94088-9741

NO POSTAGE
NECESSARY
IF MAILED
IN THE
UNITED STATES

PACKET

Packet magazine serves as the premier publication linking customers to Cisco Systems, Inc. Delivering complete coverage of cutting-edge networking trends and innovations, *Packet* is a magazine for technical, hands-on users. It delivers industry-specific information for enterprise, service provider, and small and midsized business market segments. A toolchest for planners and decision makers, *Packet* contains a vast array of practical information, boasting sample configurations, real-life customer examples, and tips on getting the most from your Cisco Systems' investments. Simply put, *Packet* magazine is straight talk straight from the worldwide leader in networking for the Internet, Cisco Systems, Inc.

We hope you'll take advantage of this useful resource. I look forward to hearing from you!

Jennifer Biondi
Packet Circulation Manager
packet@cisco.com
www.cisco.com/go/packet

☐ **YES!** I'm requesting a **free** subscription to *Packet™* magazine.

☐   No. I'm not interested at this time.

☐ Mr.
☐ Ms.

First Name (Please Print) · Last Name

Title/Position (Required)

Company (Required)

Address

City · State/Province

Zip/Postal Code · Country

Telephone (Include country and area codes) · Fax

E-mail

Signature (Required) · Date

☐ I would like to receive additional information on Cisco's services and products by e-mail

1.0 Do you or your company:
A ☐ Use Cisco products   C ☐ Both
B ☐ Resell Cisco products D ☐ Neither

1. Your organization's relationship to Cisco Systems:
A ☐ Customer/End User   DI ☐ Non-Authorized Reseller   J ☐ Consultant
B ☐ Prospective Customer   E ☐ Integrator   K ☐ Other (specify):
C ☐ Cisco Reseller   G ☐ Cisco Training Partner
D ☐ Cisco Distributor   I ☐ Cisco OEM

2. How would you classify your business?
A ☐ Small/Medium-Sized   B ☐ Enterprise   C ☐ Service Provider

3. Your involvement in network equipment purchases:
A ☐ Recommend   B ☐ Approve   C ☐ Neither

4. Your personal involvement in networking:
A ☐ Entire enterprise at all sites   F ☐ Public network
B ☐ Departments or network segments at more than one site   D ☐ No involvement
C ☐ Single department or network segment   E ☐ Other (specify):

5. Your Industry:
A ☐ Aerospace   G ☐ a. Education (K–12)   K ☐ Health Care
B ☐ Agriculture/Mining/Construction ☐ b. Education (College/Univ.) L ☐ Telecommunications
C ☐ Banking/Finance   H ☐ Government—Federal   M ☐ Utilities/Transportati
D ☐ Chemical/Pharmaceutical   I ☐ Government—State   N ☐ Other (specify):
E ☐ Consultant   J ☐ Government—Local
F ☐ Computer/Systems/Electronics

PACKET